# CAN
# "IT"
# HAPPEN
# AGAIN?

HYMAN P. MINSKY

# CAN "IT" HAPPEN AGAIN?

## Essays on Instability and Finance

M. E. SHARPE, INC. ARMONK, NEW YORK

Copyright © 1982 by M. E. Sharpe, Inc.
80 Business Park Drive, Armonk, New York 10504

First paperback printing—1984.

**Library of Congress Cataloging in Publication Data**

Minsky, Hyman P.
  Can "It" happen again?

  Includes bibliographical references and index.
  1. Finance—United States—Addresses, essays, lectures.
2. United States—Economic conditions—1945-     —Addresses,
essays, lectures. 3. Business cycles—Addresses, essays, lectures.
4. Depressions—Addresses, essays, lectures. I. Title.
HG181.M555 1982     338.5′42     82-10789
ISBN 0-87332-213-4
ISBN 0-87332-305-X (pbk.)


Printed in the United States of America


BM (p) 10  9

# Contents

To Esther

# Preface

Fifty years ago, in the winter of 1932-33, the American financial and economic system came to a halt: the collapse was well nigh complete. Two generations of the public (and the politicians they elect) have been haunted by the spector of "It" (such a great collapse) happening again. We cannot understand the institutional structure of our economy, which was largely put into place during the first years of the Roosevelt era, without recognizing that a major aim of the reformers was to organize the financial and economic institutions so that "It" could not happen again.

The common themes running through these papers are to define "It," to determine whether "It" can happen again, and to understand why "It" has not as yet happened. The earliest of the papers that follow were published some twenty-five years ago; the most recent appeared in late 1980. They deal with questions of abstract theory, institutional evolution, and Federal Reserve Policy. In spite of the span of time and themes, these papers have in common an emphasis upon the need to integrate an understanding of the effects of evolving institutional structures into economic theory. A further common theme is that any economic theory which separates what economists are wont to call the real economy from the financial system can only mislead and bear false witness as to how our world works.

The big conclusion of these papers is that the processes which make for financial instability are an inescapable part of any decentralized capitalist economy——i.e., capitalism is inherently flawed ——but financial instability need not lead to a great depression; "It" need not happen. To use a slang phrase, the American economy "lucked out" when the end result of the New Deal and subsequent changes was a substantially larger government (relative to the size of the economy) than that which ruled in 1929, together with a structure of regulation of and intervention in financial practices which provides a spectrum of "lender of last resort" protections. However, as the system that was in place in 1946 evolved over the two successful decades that followed, "institutional" and "portfolio" experiments and innovations absorbed the liquidity protection that was a legacy of the reforms and war finance. As a result, ever greater and more frequent interventions became necessary to abort financial dislocations that threatened to trigger serious depressions. The evolution of financial relations led to intermittent "crises" that posed clear and present dangers of a serious depression. To date, interventions by the Federal Reserve and the other financial authorities along with the deficits of the Treasury have combined to contain and manage these crises; in the financial and economic structure that now rules, however, this leads to inflation. We now have an inflation-prone system in which conventional steps to contain inflation tend to trigger a debt deflation process, which unless it is aborted will lead to a deep depression.

It is now apparent that we need to construct a system of institutions and interventions that can contain the thrust to financial collapse and deep depressions without inducing chronic inflation. In this book I only offer hints as to what can be done; I feel more confident as a diagnostician than as a prescriber of remedies.

Over the years I have accumulated intellectual debts, some of which I can identify and therefore can acknowledge. As a student I was most influenced by Henry C. Simons, Oscar Lange, and Josef Schumpeter.

Soon after I joined the faculty of Washington University in St. Louis I became associated with the Mark Twain family of banks. Over the years this association, and particularly the insights garnered from Adam Aronson, John P. Dubinsky, and the late Edwin W. Hudspeth, has significantly improved my understanding of how our economy works.

When Bernard Shull was on the staff of the Board of Governors of the Federal Reserve System he was a source of insights and of support for my work.

I spent a sabbatical year (1969-70) in Cambridge, England. I owe an immense debt to Aubrey Silberston for facilitating my becoming a part of that community.

Over the years Maurice Townsend has encouraged me by reading and commenting on my work in progress and encouraging me to carry on. He has been a true friend and support.

Alice Lipowicz helped immeasurably during the reading and selecting of papers for this volume. Arnold Tovell of M. E. Sharpe, Inc. and Alfred Eichner of Rutgers University were most helpful. Bess Erlich and the staff of the Department of Economics at Washington University were always patient in dealing with my scrawls and scribblings.

Hyman P. Minsky

# Introduction

*Can "It"*
*Happen Again?*
*A Reprise*

The most significant economic event of the era since World War II is something that has not happened: there has not been a deep and long-lasting depression.

As measured by the record of history, to go more than thirty-five years without a severe and protracted depression is a striking success. Before World War II, serious depressions occurred regularly. The Great Depression of the 1930s was just a "bigger and better" example of the hard times that occurred so frequently. This postwar success indicates that something is right about the institutional structure and the policy interventions that were largely created by the reforms of the 1930s.

Can "It"—a Great Depression—happen again? And if "It" can happen, why didn't "It" occur in the years since World War II? These are questions that naturally follow from both the historical record and the comparative success of the past thirty-five years. To answer these questions it is necessary to have an economic theory which makes great depressions one of the possible states in which our type of capitalist economy can find itself. We need a theory which will enable us to identify which of the many differences between the economy of 1980 and that of 1930 are responsible for the success of the postwar era.

The Reagan administration has mounted a program to change markedly economic institutions and policies. These programs reflect some well-articulated conservative critiques of the interventionist capitalism that grew up during the New Deal and postwar administrations. These critiques, which come in various brands labeled monetarism, supply-side economics, and fiscal orthodoxy, are alike in that they claim to reflect the results of modern economic theory, usually called the neoclassical synthesis. The abstract foundation of the neoclassical synthesis reached its full development with the flowering of mathematical economics after World War II. (The underlying theory of the orthodox Keynesians, who served as economic advisers to prior administrations, is this same neoclassical synthesis.)

The major theorems of the neoclassical synthesis are that a system of decentralized markets, where units are motivated by self-interest, is capable of yielding a coherent result and, in some very special cases, the result can be characterized as efficient. These main conclusions are true, however, only if very strong assumptions are made. They have never been shown to hold for an economy with privately owned capital assets and complex, ever-evolving financial institutions and practices. Indeed, we live in an economy which is developing through time, whereas the basic theorems on which the conservative critique of intervention rests have been proven only for "models" which abstract from time.

Instability is an observed characteristic of our economy. For a theory to be useful as a guide to policy for the control of instability, the theory must show how instability is generated. The abstract model of the neoclassical synthesis cannot generate instability. When the neoclassical synthesis is constructed, capital assets, financing arrangements that center around banks and money creation, constraints imposed by liabilities, and the problems associated with knowledge about uncertain futures are all assumed away. For economists and policy-makers to do better we have to abandon the neoclassical synthesis. We have to examine economic processes that go forward in time, which means that investment, the ownership of capital assets, and the accompanying financial activity become the central concerns of the theorizing. Once this is done, then instability can be shown to be a normal result of the economic process. Once instability is understood as a theoretical possibility, then we are in a position to design appropriate interventions to constrain it.

## The economic sources of Reagan's victory

Reagan's political victory in 1980 took place because, after the mid-1960s, the performance of the economy deteriorated in terms of inflation, employment, and the rise in material well-being. A close examination of experience since World War II shows that the era quite naturally falls into two parts. The first part, which ran for almost twenty years (1948-1966), was an era of largely tranquil progress. This was followed by an era of increasing turbulence, which has continued until today.

The tranquil era was characterized by modest inflation rates (especially by the standard of the 1970s), low unemployment rates, and seemingly rapid economic growth. These years, which began once the immediate postwar adjustments were complete, may very well have been the most successful period in the history of the American economy. The New Deal era and World War II were years of large-scale resource creation. The postwar era began with a legacy of capital assets, a trained labor force, and in-place research organizations. Furthermore, households, businesses, and financial institutions were both richer and more liquid than they had been before. In addition, the memory of the Great Depression led households, businesses, and financial institutions to prize their liquidity. Because conservatism ruled in finance, the liquidity amassed during the war did not lead to a burst of spending and speculation once peace came. Furthermore, the federal government's budget was an active constraint on an inflationary expansion, for it would go into surplus whenever inflation seemed ready to accelerate.

Instead of an inflationary explosion at the war's end, there was a gradual and often tentative expansion of debt-financed spending by households and business firms. The newfound liquidity was gradually absorbed, and the regulations and standards that determined permissible contracts were gradually relaxed. Only as the successful performance of the economy attenuated the fear of another great depression did households, businesses, and financial institutions increase the ratios of debts to income and of debts to liquid assets so that these ratios rose to levels that had ruled prior to the Great Depression. As the financial system became more heavily weighted with layered private debts, the susceptibility of the financial structure to disturbances increased. With these disturbances, the economy moved to the turbulent regime that still rules.

The first serious break in the apparently tranquil progress was the credit crunch of 1966. Then, for the first time in the postwar era, the Federal Reserve intervened as a lender of last resort to refinance institutions—in this case banks—which were experiencing losses in an effort to meet liquidity requirements. The credit crunch was followed by a "growth" recession, but the expansion of the Vietnam war promptly led to a large federal deficit which facilitated a recovery from the growth recession.

The 1966 episode was characterized by four elements: (1) a disturbance in financial markets that led to lender-of-last-resort intervention by the monetary authorities; (2) a recession (a growth recession in 1966); (3) a sizable increase in the federal deficit; and (4) a recovery followed by an acceleration of inflation that set the stage for the next disturbance. The same four elements can be found in the turbulence of 1969-70, 1974-75, 1980, and 1981. The details of the lender-of-last-resort intervention differed in each case because the particular financial markets and institutions under the gun of illiquidity or insolvency differed. The recessions—aside from that of 1980—seem to have gotten progressively worse. The deficits, which became chronic after 1975, continued to rise in response to recessions.

Each of these financial disturbances occurred after a period of rapid expansion in short-term financing; indeed the precise timing was part of the reaction to efforts by the Federal Reserve to slow down the growth of such financing (because the rapid increase in short term-financing was associated with price increases). The "rationale" for the Federal Reserve's action was that inflation had to be fought. Each of the financial disturbances was followed by a recession, and during the recession unemployment increased and the rate of inflation declined.

The various crunches (financial disturbances), recessions, and recoveries in the years since 1966 delineate what are commonly referred to as business "cycles." Over these cycles the minimum rate of unemployment increased monotonically. There was a clear trend of worsening inflation and unemployment: The maximum rate of inflation and the minimum rate of unemployment were higher between 1966 and 1969 than before 1966, higher between 1970 and 1974 than before 1969, and higher between 1975 and 1979 than before 1974. Furthermore, over this period there was a similiar upward trend in interest rates, fluctuations of the dollar on the foreign exchanges, and a significant decline in the growth of consumption. In spite of this turbulence, the economy remained successful in that there was no serious depression. The failure was with respect to price-level stability, unemployment rates, and the perceived "improvement" in the material standard of living. These were the failures that opened the way for the Reagan rejection of the ruling system of institutions and interventions.

### The roots of instability

The policy challenge is to recapture the tranquil progress of the first part of the postwar period without going through a serious depression. To design such a policy we need to understand why the many-faceted success of the years between 1948 and 1966 gave way to the combination of continuing success in avoiding depression and the progressive failures in so many other dimensions of economic life.

In "Central Banking and Money Market Changes" (pp. 162 to 177 below, published in 1957), I argued that over an extended period of prosperity ". . . velocity-increasing and liquidity-decreasing money-market innovations will take place. As a result, the decrease in liquidity is compounded. In time, these compounded changes will result in an inherently unstable money market so that a slight reversal of prosperity can trigger a financial crisis" (p. 173). Even then it was understood that a crisis-prone financial structure did not make a deep depression inevitable, for "the central bank's function is to act as a lender of last resort and therefore to limit the losses due to the financial crisis which follows from the instability induced by the innovations during the boom. A combination of rapid central bank action to stabilize financial markets and rapid fiscal policy action to increase community liquidity will minimize the repercussion of the crisis upon consumption and investment expenditures. Thus a deep depression can be avoided. The function of central banks therefore is not to stabilize the economy so much as to act as a lender of last resort" (pp. 175-176).

In a later work, "Can 'It' Happen Again?" (pp. 3 to 13 below) I argued that cumulative changes in financial relations were taking place so that the susceptibility of the economy to a financial crisis was increasing, but that as of the date of the paper (1963), the changes had not gone far enough for a full-blown debt deflation to take place. In 1966 the first "credit crunch" occurred.

The Federal Reserve promptly intervened as a lender of last resort to refinance banks that were faced with portfolio losses. The escalation of the war in Vietnam in the mid-1960s meant that fiscal policy was necessarily stimulative. During the financial turbulences and recessions that took place in the aftermath of the Penn-Central debacle (1969-70), the Franklin-National bankruptcy (1974-75), and the Hunt-Bache silver speculation (1980), a combination of lender-of-last-resort intervention by the Federal Reserve and a stimulative fiscal policy prevented a plunge into a cumulative debt-deflation. Thus, over the past decade and a half, monetary interventions and fiscal policy have succeeded in containing financial crises and preventing a deep depression—even though they failed to sustain employment, growth, and price stability. This simultaneous success and failure are but two sides of the same process. What the Federal Reserve and the Treasury do to contain crises and abort deep depressions leads to inflation, and what the Federal Reserve and the Treasury do to constrain inflation leads to financial crises and threats of deep depressions.

The success in dampening and offsetting the depression-inducing repercussions of financial disturbances after 1965 stands in sharp contrast to the failure after 1929. What has followed financial disturbances since 1965 differs from what followed the disturbance of 1929 because of differences in the structure of the economy. The post-World War II economy is qualitatively different from the economy that collapsed after 1929 in three respects.

1. The relative size of the government is immensely larger. This implies a much greater deficit once a downturn occurs.

2. There is a large outstanding government debt which increases rapidly when there are deficits. This both sets a floor to liquidity and weakens the link between the money supply and business borrowing.

3. The Federal Reserve is primed to intervene quickly as a lender-of-last-resort whenever a financial crisis threatens——or at least has been so primed up to now. This prevents a collapse of asset values, because asset holders are able to refinance rather than being forced to sell out their position.

The actual past behavior of the economy is the only evidence economists have available to them when they build and test theories. The observed instability of capitalist economies is due to (1) the complex set of market relations that enter into the investment process; and (2) the way the liability structure commits the cash flows that result from producing and distributing output. To understand investment by a capitalist enterprise it is necessary to model the intertemporal relations involved in investment behavior.

## The financial nature of our economy

We live in an economy in which borrowing and lending, as well as changes in equity interests, determine investment. Financing arrangements enter into the investment process at a number of points: the determination of prices for both financial and capital assets and the furnishing of cash for investment spending are two such points. A financial innovation which increases the funds available to finance asset holdings and current activity will have two effects that tend to increase investment. The first is that the market price of existing assets will rise. This raises the demand price for outputs that serve as assets (investment). The second is that by lowering the cost of financing for production, financial innovations lower the supply price of investment output. If financing relations are examined within a framework which permits excess demand for financing at existing interest rates to lead to both higher interest rates and financial innovations, then theoretical constructions which determine important economic variables by ignoring monetary and financial relations are not tenable. For a theory to be useful for our economy, the accumulation process must be the primary concern, and money must be introduced into the argument at the beginning.

Cash flows to business at any time have three functions: they signal whether past investment decisions were apt; they provide the funds by which business can or cannot fulfill payment commitments as they come due; and they help determine investment and financing conditions. In a cash-flow analysis of the economy, the critical relation that determines system performance is that between cash payment commitments on business debts and current business cash receipts due to present operations and contract fulfillment. This is so because the relation between cash receipts and payment commitments determines the course of investment and thus of employment, output, and profits.

Much investment activity depends on financing relations in which total short-term debt outstanding increases because the interest that is due on earlier borrowings exceeds the income earned by assets. I call this "Ponzi financing." Rapidly rising and high interest rates increase Ponzi like financing activity. A rapid run-up of such financing almost guarantees that a financial crisis will emerge or that concessionary refinancing will be necessary to hold off a crisis. The trend over the postwar period is for the proportion of speculative (or rollover) financing, as well as Ponzi arrangements that involve the capitalizing of interest, to increase as the period without a serious depression is extended.

However, in spite of the deterioration of balance sheets, the near breakdowns of the financial system in a variety of crunches, and the extraordinarily high nominal and price-deflated interest rates, no serious depression has occurred in the years since 1966. This is due to two phenomena: the willingness and ability of the Federal Reserve to act as a lender of last resort; and the deficits incurred by the government.

As the ratio of short-term debt and debt that leads to a capitalization of interest increases relative to the gross capital income of business, there is an increase in the demand for short-term financing because of the need to refinance debt. Investment activity is usually financed by short-term debt. Thus when an investment boom takes place in the context of an enlarged need to refinance maturing debt, the demand "curve" for short-term debt increases (shifts to the right) and becomes steeper (less elastic). Under these circumstances, unless the supply of finance is very elastic, the short-term interest rate can increase very rapidly. In a world where part of the demand for short-term financing reflects the capitalization of interest, a rise in short-term interest rates may increase the demand for short-term financing, and this can lead to further increases in short-term interest rates. The rise in short-term interest rates produces higher long-term interest rates, which lowers the value of capital assets.

### Lender of last resort interventions

Rising short-term interest rates combined with rising long-term interest rates increase the cost of production of investment output with significant gestation periods, even as they lower the demand price for the capital assets that result from investment. This tends to decrease investment. The same interest rate changes affect the liquidity, profitability, and solvency of financial institutions. This process of falling asset values, rising carrying costs for asset holdings, and decreasing profits will compromise the liquidity and solvency of business units and financial institutions. A break comes when the net worth and the liquidity of some significant set of units are such that market participants will not, or may not, roll over or refinance maturing debt. In these circumstances the Federal Reserve and the government's deposit insurance organizations, along with private banks, are faced with the choice of either forcing "bankruptcy" on the units in question or acceding to concessionary, extra-market refinancing.

When concessionary, extra-market refinancing is undertaken by the Federal Reserve or by an agency acting with the "protection" of the Federal Reserve, then a lender-of-last-resort operation can be said to have taken place. Inasmuch as the Federal Reserve's participation can be interpreted as an exchange of "questionable assets" for Federal Reserve liabilities, this type of rescue action leads to an infusion of reserve money into the financial system.

Whereas the Federal Reserve stood aside through most of the banking crises of the 1929-33 epoch, in the sense that it did not engage in the wholesale refinancing of failing institutions, the Federal Reserve has intervened quite aggressively both on its own account and as an "organizer and guarantor" of intervention by others in the various crises since 1966. As a result, asset values did not fall as far as they would have under free market conditions, and the reserve position of banks improved in the aftermath of each refinancing "crisis." The maintenance of asset values and the infusion of liquidity by such lender-of-last-resort interventions is one set of factors that has brought about the speedy halt to the downturn and the prompt recovery that has characterized cycles after 1966.

## Profits in our economy

Only as history made available data on the behavior of income by type, investment, government deficits, and the balance of trade over the years since 1966 did it become clear that the formation and allocation of profits, in the sense of gross capital income, are central to an understanding of our economy. Gross capital income is the cash flow due to income production that is available to business to fulfill commitments on outstanding financial instruments. The ability of a unit to put out additional debt or to use debt to gather funds to pay debt depends upon the level and expected path of profits as here defined. In the conventional view, government spending is an ingredient in a Kuznets-Keynes definition of demand. As evidence accumulated on how crises are aborted and thrusts to deep depressions are contained, it became clear that a Kalecki-Keynes view, one that builds on a theory of how the composition of demand determines profits is more appropriate for our economy. In the Kalecki-Keynes view profits are not the result of the technical productivity of capital but are due to the types and sources of financed demand.

The great insight into the determination of profits in our economy that is associated with Kalecki—is that profits arise out of the impact of the accumulation process on prices. The money value of investment over a period is the basic determinant of money profits over that same period. Profits arise in consumption goods production because of the need to ration that which is produced by part of the labor force—the part that produces consumption goods—among all who consume. Rationing by price implies that the mark-up on unit labor costs in the realized prices of consumer goods reflects demands that are financed by sources other than wage incomes earned in the production of consumer goods. The sum of these mark-ups equals profits in consumer goods production. Under assumptions which though heroic, nevertheless reveal the processes that determine income distribution profits in consumer goods production equals the wage bill in investment goods production and total profits equals investment.

Whereas in the small government economy of the 1920s profits were well nigh exclusively dependent on the pace of investment, the increase in direct and indirect state employment along with the explosion of transfer payments since World War II means that the dependence of profits on investment has been greatly reduced. With the rise of big government, the reaction of tax receipts and transfer payments to income changes implies that any decline in income will lead to an explosion of the government deficit. Since it can be shown that profits are equal to investment plus the government's deficit, profit flows are sustained whenever a fall in investment leads to a rise in the government's deficit. A cumulative debt deflation process that depends on a fall of profits for its realization is quickly halted when government is so big that the deficit explodes when income falls. The combination of refinancing by lender-of-last-resort interventions and the stabilizing effect of deficits upon profits explain why we have not had a deep depression since World War II. The downside vulnerability of the economy is significantly reduced by the combination of these types of "interventions."

If stabilization policy is to be successful, it must stabilize profits. Expansion can take place only as expected profits are sufficient to induce increasing expenditures on investments. Current profits provide the cash flows that enable business to meet financial commitments that are embodied in debt even as expected profits determine the ability of business to issue debt to both finance expenditures and roll over maturing debt.

The monetary system is at the center of the debt creation and repayment mechanism. Money is created as banks lend—mainly to business—and money is destroyed as borrowers fulfill their payment commitments to banks. Money is created in response to businessmen's and bankers' views about prospective profits, and money is destroyed as profits are realized. Monetary changes are the result, not the cause, of the behavior of the economy, and the monetary system is "stable" only as profit flows enable businesses that borrow from banks to fulfill their commitments.

Central Bank interventions and the stabilization of profits by government deficits mean that liability structures that derive from innovations in finance during periods of expansion are validated during crises and recessions. Because Central Bank interventions to refinance exposed financial positions lead to an increase of Central Bank deposits, currency or guarantees, lender-of-last-resort interventions provide a base of reserve money for a rapid expansion of credit after the recession is halted. The progressively higher rates of inflation that followed the resolution of the financial crises of 1966, 1969-70, 1974-75, and 1980 reflect the way profits and liquidity were improved by the interventions that overcame the crises.

### Policy options

A simple two-by-two "truth table" of policy options in the aftermath of a financial crisis helps explain why our recent experience was unlike that of 1929-33. Managing a financial crisis and a recession involves two distinct steps: one is refinancing the markets or institutions whose perilous position defines the crisis; and the other is assuring that the aggregate of business profits does not decline. (Because a financial crisis reveals that some particular financing techniques are "dangerous," one consequence of a crisis is that debt financing of private demand decreases. Inasmuch as debt-financed demand is largely investment, and investment yields profits, a crisis leads to a reduction in profits.) Thus the two "parameters" to crisis management are the lender-of-last-resort intervention and the behavior of the government deficit when the economy is in recession.

## "Truth Table" of Policy Options

Lender-of-last-resort intervention

|  |  | Yes | No |
|---|---|---|---|
| **Government deficit** | **Yes** | Yes-Yes | Yes-No |
| | **No** | No-Yes | No-No |

When a crisis threatens, the Federal Reserve can intervene strongly to refinance organizations, which is "Yes" for central bank intervention, or it can hold off, which is a "No." When income declines, the federal government can run a deficit (because of automatic budget reactions or discretionary policy), which is "Yes," or it can try to maintain a balanced budget, which is "No." The active Federal Reserve intervention in the Franklin National Bank crisis of 1974-75 along with the discretionary tax rebates and unemployment insurance measures taken by Congress meant that the policy mix in 1974-75 was "Yes-Yes." This led to both a quick recovery and, with a lag, an increased rate of inflation. The Federal Reserve's abdication of responsibility in 1929-32, along with the small size of government and the commitment to a balanced budget, places the 1929-32 reactions in the "No-No" cell. The Great Depression was not "necessary," but it was inevitable in the ideological and institutional framework of that period.

In addition to the pure policy mixes of "Yes-Yes" and "No-No," there are mixed policies of "Yes-No" (a large government deficit without Central Bank intervention) and "No-Yes" (in which the government tries to run a balanced budget even as the Federal Reserve intervenes as a lender of last resort). The "No-Yes" policy mix was a possible policy option in 1930 and 1931. Government was so small that the government deficit could not make a large contribution to profits unless new large-scale spending programs were undertaken. The Federal Reserve could have been daring in 1930 and 1931 and refinanced a broad spectrum of institutions, sustaining a wide array of asset prices and thereby flooding member banks with reserves. Such a policy can succeed in halting a depression if the flooding of the system with reserves occurs before a collapse in investment, and therefore profits, takes place. While there would have been significantly greater recession with a "No-Yes" strategy than with a "Yes-Yes" strategy, the full disaster of the Great Depression would have been avoided if lender-of-last-resort interventions had come early enough in the contraction. Because of today's big government, a "No-Yes" policy mix is not possible.

In the 1980s, a "Yes-No" policy mix will be available. No matter how much taxes and government spending are cut, it is difficult, especially in light of the proposed military programs, to envisage government spending falling below 20 percent of the Gross National Product. The Reagan fiscal reforms significantly decrease the income elasticity of the government's budget posture. The government deficit will be smaller for any given downside deviation from a balanced budget level of GNP than was true for the tax and spending regime that ruled in 1980. This means that the gap between actual income and the balanced-budget level will have to be greater in order to achieve any given profit-sustaining deficit. But a greater gap implies that the excess capacity constraint upon investment will be greater. This will, in turn, decrease the effectiveness of a deficit-induced improvement in business income and balance sheets in triggering an expansion. The "Yes" part of a "Yes-No" strategy will be less effective with Reagan-style tax and spending programs than with programs that are more responsive to income changes.

The "No" part of a possible "Yes-No" mix is always conditional. It is to be hoped that the Federal Reserve will never again stand aside as the liquidity and solvency of financial institutions are thoroughly compromised. A "No" lender-of-last-resort strategy can only mean that the Federal Reserve will not intervene as quickly as it has since the mid-1960s. In particular it means that the Federal Reserve will not engage in preemptive strikes as it did in the spring of 1980 when a speculation by the Hunts and Bache & Co. went bad. A "Yes-No" strategy means that that the Federal Reserve will intervene only when it believes that a financial collapse is imminent.

A "No" lender-of-last-resort strategy will lead to bankruptcies and declines in asset values, which will induce financially conservative behavior by business, households, and financial institutions. The transition to a conservative liability structure by business, households, and financial institutions requires a protracted period in which income and profits are sustained by deficits while units restructure their liabilities. A "Yes-No" strategy should eventually lead to a period of tranquil growth, but the time interval may be so great that once tranquil progress has been achieved, the financial experimentation that led to the current turbulence will be resumed.

Big government prevents the collapse of profits which is a necessary condition for a deep and long depression, but with big government, as it is now structured, the near-term alternatives are either: the continuation of the inflation-recession-inflation scenario under a "Yes-Yes" strategy; or a long and deep recession while inflation is "squeezed" out of the economy even as private liabilities are restructured in the aftermath of bankruptcies, under a "Yes-No" strategy. However, even if a "Yes-No" strategy is followed, the propensity for financial innovation will mean that the tranquil expansion that follows the long recession will not be permanent. Substantial improvement is possible only if the spending side of government and the domain of private investment are restructured.

## Can we do better?

No matter how industry and government finances are structured, as long as the economy remains capitalist and innovation in industry and finance continues, there will be business cycles. Furthermore, as long as the financial structure is complex and long-lived capital assets are privately owned, a deep and long depression is possible. However, a closer approximation to a tranquil expanding economy may be attained if the nature of big government changed.

Our big government is "big" because of transfer payments and defense spending. The basic shortcomings of a capitalist economy that lead to business cycles are related to the ownership, creation, and financing of capital assets. Aside from the government's involvement in education and research, the basic spending programs of government either support private consumption or provide for defense, which is "collective consumption." Even as our federal government spends more than 20 percent of GNP, much of the physical and intellectual infrastructure of the economy is deteriorating. Very little of the government's spending creates capital assets in the public domain that increase the efficiency of privately owned capital. A government which is big because it engages in resource creation and development will encourage a greater expansion of output from private investment than is the case for a government which is big because it supports consumption. An economy in which a government spends to assure capital formation rather than to support consumption is capable of achieving a closer approximation to tranquil progress than is possible with our present policies. Thus while big government virtually ensures that a great depression cannot happen again, the resumption of tranquil progress depends on restructuring government so that it enhances resource development. While thoroughgoing reform is necessary, the Reagan road is unfortunately not the right way to go.

# CAN "IT" HAPPEN AGAIN?

# 1

Can "It"
Happen Again?

In the winter of 1933 the financial system of the United States collapsed. This implosion was an end result of a cumulative deflationary process whose beginning can be conveniently identified as the stock-market crash of late 1929. This deflationary process took the form of large-scale defaults on contracts by both financial and nonfinancial units, as well as sharply falling income and prices.[1] In the spring of 1962 a sharp decline in the stock market took place. This brought forth reassuring comments by public and private officials that recalled the initial reaction to the 1929 stock-market crash, as well as expressions of concern that a new debt-deflation process was being triggered. The 1962 event did not trigger a deflationary process like that set off in 1929. It is meaningful to inquire whether this difference is the result of essential changes in the institutional or behavioral characteristics of the economy, so that a debt-deflation process leading to a financial collapse cannot now occur, or merely of differences in magnitudes within a financial and economic structure that in its essential attributes has not changed. That is, is the economy truly more stable or is it just that the initial conditions (i.e., the state of the economy at the time stock prices fell) were substantially different in 1929 and 1962?

## I. General considerations

The Council of Economic Advisers' view on this issue was stated

Reprinted from Dean Carson, ed., *Banking and Monetary Studies* (Homewood, Illinois: Richard D. Irwin, 1963), pp. 101-111, by arrangement with the publisher. © 1963 by Richard D. Irwin, Inc.

when they remarked, while discussing fiscal policy in the 1930's, that ". . . whatever constructive impact fiscal policy may have had was largely offset by restrictive monetary policy and by institutional failures—failures that could never again occur because of fundamental changes made during and since the 1930's."[2] The Council does not specify the institutional changes that now make it impossible for instability to develop and lead to widespread debt-deflation. We can conjecture that this lack of precision is due to the absence of a generally accepted view of the links between income and the behavior and characteristics of the financial system.

A comprehensive examination of the issues involved in the general problem of the interrelation between the financial and real aspects of an enterprise economy cannot be undertaken within the confines of a short paper.[3] This is especially true as debt-deflations occur only at long intervals of time. Between debt-deflations financial institutions and usages evolve so that, certainly in their details, each debt-deflation is a unique event. Nevertheless it is necessary and desirable to inquire whether there are essential financial attributes of the system which are basically invariant over time and which tend to breed conditions which increase the likelihood of a debt-deflation.

In this paper I will not attempt to review the changes in financial institutions and practices since 1929. It is my view that the institutional changes which took place as a reaction to the Great Depression and which are relevant to the problem at hand spelled out the permitted set of activities as well as the fiduciary responsibilities of various financial institutions and made the lender of last resort functions of the financial authorities more precise. As the institutions were reformed at a time when the lack of effectiveness and perhaps even the perverse behavior of the Federal Reserve System during the great downswing was obvious, the changes created special institutions, such as the various deposit and mortgage insurance schemes, which both made some of the initial lender of last resort functions automatic and removed their administration from the Federal Reserve System. There should be some concern that the present decentralization of essential central bank responsibilities and functions is not an efficient way of organizing the financial control and protection functions; especially since an effective defense against an emerging financial crisis may require coordination and consistency among the various units with lender of last resort functions.

The view that will be supported in this paper is that the essential characteristics of financial processes and the changes in relative magnitudes during a sustained expansion (a period of full-employment growth interrupted only by mild recessions) have not changed. It will be argued that the initial conditions in 1962 were different from those of 1929 because the processes which transform a stable into an unstable system had not been carried as far by 1962 as by 1929. In addition it will be pointed out that the large increase in the relative size of the federal government has changed the financial characteristics of the system so that the development of financial instability will set off compensating stabilizing financial changes. That is, the federal government not only stabilizes income but the associated increase in the federal debt, by forcing changes in the mix of financial instruments owned by the public, makes the financial system more stable. In addition, even though the built-in stabilizers cannot by themselves return the system to full employment, the change in the composition of household and business portfolios that takes place tends to increase private consumption and investment to levels compatible with full employment.

In the next section of this paper I will sketch a model of how the conditions compatible with a debt-deflation process are generated. I will then present some observations on financial variables and note how these affect the response of the economy to initiating changes. In the last section I will note what effect the increase in the relative size of the federal government since the 1920's has had upon these relations.

## II. A sketch of a model

Within a closed economy, for any period

$$(1) \qquad\qquad I - S = T - G$$

which can be written as:

$$(2) \qquad\qquad (S - I) + (T - G) = 0$$

where $S - I$ is the gross surplus of the private sectors (which for convenience includes the state and local government sector) and $T - G$ is the gross surplus of the federal government. The surplus of each sector $\zeta_j (j = 1 \ldots n)$ is defined as the difference between its gross cash receipts minus its spending on consumption and gross real investment, including inventory accumulations. We therefore have

$$(3) \qquad\qquad \sum_{j=1}^{n} \zeta_j = 0$$

Equation 3 is an *ex post* accounting identity. However, each $\zeta_j$ is the result of the observed investing and saving behavior of the various sectors, and can be interpreted as the result of market processes by which not necessarily consistent sectoral *ex ante* saving and investment plans are reconciled. If income is to grow, the financial markets, where the various plans to save and invest are reconciled, must generate an aggregate demand that, aside from brief intervals, is ever rising. For real aggregate demand to be increasing, given that commodity and factor prices do not fall readily in the absence of substantial excess supply, it is necessary that current spending plans, summed over all sectors, be greater than current received income and that some market technique exist by which aggregate spending in excess of aggregate anticipated income can be financed. It follows that over a period during which economic growth takes place, at least some sectors finance a part of their spending by emitting debt or selling assets.[4]

For such planned deficits to succeed in raising income it is necessary that the  market processes which enable these plans to be carried out do not result in offsetting reductions in the spending plans of other units. Even though the *ex post* result will be that some sectors have larger surpluses than anticipated, on the whole these larger surpluses must be a result of the rise in sectoral income rather than a reduction of spending below the amount planned. For this to take place, it is necessary for some of the spending to be financed either by portfolio changes which draw money from idle balances into active circulation (that is, by an increase in velocity) or by the creation of new money.[5]

In an enterprise economy the saving and investment process leaves two residuals: a change in the stock of capital and a change in the stock of financial assets and liabilities. Just as an increase in the capital-income ratio may tend to decrease the demand for additional capital goods, an increase in the ratio of financial liabilities to income (especially of debts to income) may tend to decrease the willingness and the ability of the unit (or sector) to finance additional spending by emitting debt.

A rise in an income-producing unit's debt-income ratio decreases the percentage decline in income which will  make it difficult, if not impossible, for the unit to meet the payment commitments stated on its debt from its normal sources, which depend upon the unit's income. If payment commitments cannot be met from the normal sources, then a unit is forced either to borrow or to sell assets. Both borrowing on unfavorable terms and the forced sale of assets usually result in a capital loss for the affected unit.[6] However, for any unit, capital losses and gains are not symmetrical:

there is a ceiling to the capital losses a unit can take and still fulfill its commitments. Any loss beyond this limit is passed on to its creditors by way of default or refinancing of the contracts. Such induced capital losses result in a further contraction of consumption and investment beyond that due to the initiating decline in income. This can result in a recursive debt-deflation process.[7]

For every debt-income ratio of the various sectors we can postulate the existence of a maximum decline in income which, even if it is most unfavorably distributed among the units, cannot result in a cumulative deflationary process, as well as a minimum decline in income which, even if it is most favorably distributed among the units, must lead to a cumulative deflationary process. The maximum income decline which *cannot* is smaller than the minimum income decline which *must* lead to a cumulative deflationary process, and the probability that a cumulative deflationary process will take place is a nondecreasing function of the size of the decline in income between these limits. For a given set of debt-income ratios, these boundary debt-income ratios are determined by the relative size of the economy's ultimate liquidity (those assets with fixed contract value and no default risk) and the net worth of private units relative to debt and income as well as the way in which financial factors enter into the decision relations that determine aggregate demand.

If the financial changes that accompany a growth process tend to increase debt-income ratios of the private sectors or to decrease the relative stock of ultimate liquidity, then the probability that a given percentage decline in income will set off a debt-deflation increases as growth takes place. In addition, if, with a given set of debt-income ratios, the  net worth of units is decreased by capital or operating losses, then both the maximum decline in income which cannot and the minimum decline in income which must generate a debt-deflation process will decrease. If the economy generates short-term declines in income and decreases in asset values in a fairly routine, regular manner then, given the evolutionary changes in financial ratios, it is possible for an initiating decline in income or a capital loss, of a size that has occurred in the past without triggering a severe reaction, to set off a debt-deflation process.

A two sector (household, business) diagram may illustrate the argument. Assume that with a given amount of default-free assets and net worth of households, a decline in income of $\Delta Y_1$ takes place. For $\Delta Y_1$ there is a set of debt-income ratios for the two sectors that trace out the maximum debt-income ratios that cannot generate a debt-deflation process. There is another set of larger debt-income ratios which trace out the minimum debt-income

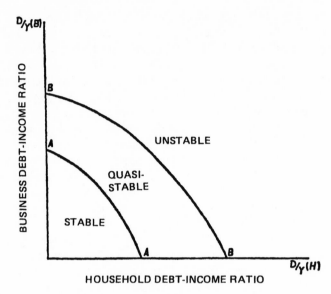

Figure 1

Debt-Income Ratios and the Stability of Reactions Given the
Decline in Income

ratios which must generate a debt-deflation process when income
declines by $\Delta Y_1$. For every debt-income ratio between these limits
the probability that a debt deflation will be set off by a decline in
income of $\Delta Y_1$ is an increasing function of the debt-income ratio.

The isoquants as illustrated in Figure 1 divide all debt-income
ratios into three sets. Below the curve $A$-$A$ are those debt-income
ratios for which a decline in income of $\Delta Y_1$ cannot lead to a debt
deflation. Above the line $B$-$B$ are those debt-income ratios for
which a decline in income of $\Delta Y_1$ must lead to a debt-deflation.
Between the two lines are those debt-income ratios for which the
probability of a debt-deflation following a decline in income of
$\Delta Y_1$ increases with the debt-income ratio. We can call these stable,
unstable, and quasi-stable reactions to an initiating change.

For $\Delta Y_j > \Delta Y_1$ both the maximum debt-income ratios which
cannot and the minimum debt-income ratios which must lead to a
debt-deflation process are smaller than for $\Delta Y_1$. Therefore, for
every pair of debt-income ratios, $D/_{Y(H)}\lambda$, $D/_{Y(B)}\lambda$ there exists a
$\Delta Y_\alpha$ for which these debt-income ratios are a maximal pair and another $\Delta Y_\beta$ for which these debt-income ratios are a minimal pair,
and $\Delta Y_\alpha < \Delta Y_\beta$. For every decline in income between $\Delta Y_\alpha$ and
$\Delta Y_\beta$ the probability that a debt-deflation process will occur with
$D/_{Y(H)}\lambda, D/_{Y(B)}\lambda$ is greater than zero, less than one, and increases
with the size of the decline in income.

The above has been phrased in terms of the reaction to an initial decline in income, whereas the problem we set was to examine how a sharp stock-market decline can affect income—in particular, whether it can set off a cumulative debt-deflation. The positions of the boundaries between debt-income ratios which lead to stable, quasi-stable, and unstable system behavior in response to a given decline in income depend upon the ultimate liquidity of the community and the net worth of households. A sharp fall in the stock market will decrease the net worth of households and also because of the increase in the cost of at least one type of financing —new issue equity financing—will operate to decrease business investment. In addition, the decline in net worth will also decrease household spending. Hence, the decline in net worth will both shift the boundaries of the reaction regions downward and lead to an initiating decline in income. The behavior of the system depends upon the location of the boundaries between the behavior-states of the system, after allowing for the effects of the initial capital losses due to the stock market crash, and the size of the initial decline in income.

### III. A look at some evidence

On the basis of the argument in the preceding section, the relative size of ultimate liquidity and the debt-income ratios of households and business are relevant in determining the likelihood that an initial shock will trigger a debt-deflation process. We will examine some evidence as to the trends of these variables between 1922-29 and 1948-62 as well as the values of the relevant ratios in 1929 and 1962.

The ultimately liquid assets of an economy consist of those assets whose nominal value is independent of the functioning of the economy. For an enterprise economy, the ultimately liquid assets consist of the domestically owned government debt outside government funds, Treasury currency, and specie. We will use gross national product divided by the amount of ultimate liquidity as our measure of relative ultimate liquidity. This is a velocity concept—what I call Pigou velocity—and we can compare its behavior over time with that of conventional velocity defined as gross national product divided by demand deposits plus currency outside banks.

In Figure 2 both Pigou and conventional velocity from 1922 to 1962 are presented. Conventional velocity exhibited a slight trend between 1922-29 (rising from around 3.5 to around 4.0), fell sharply until 1946 (to 1.9), and has risen since 1946. In 1962 conventional velocity was once again at the levels it had reached in the 1920's. Pigou velocity rose rapidly from 1922 to 1929 (from 2.8

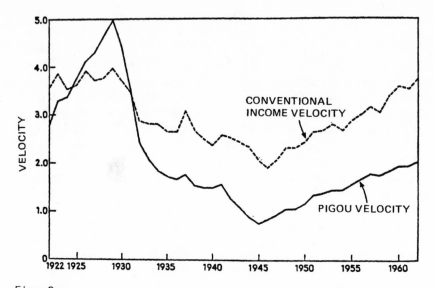

Figure 2

Velocity of Money, Conventional Income,
and Pigou, 1922-62

to 5.0), then fell drastically to 1945 (reaching a low of .8), and has
risen steadily since; in 1962 Pigou velocity was 2.1. That is, although the direction of change of Pigou and conventional velocity
has been the same since 1922, their relative values in 1929 and
1962 were quite different. In 1929 Pigou velocity was 25 percent
greater than conventional velocity whereas in 1962 Pigou velocity
was about 50 percent of conventional velocity. As Pigou velocity
was approximately 40 percent of its 1929 value in 1962, the stock
of ultimate liquidity relative to income was much greater in 1962
than in 1929.

As shown in Table 1, the debt-income ratios for both households
and corporate nonfinancial business rose during the sustained expansion of 1922-29 and 1948-62. However, the 1962 household
debt-income ratio was larger than in 1929, while the corporate
nonfinancial business ratio was considerably smaller. Inasmuch as
the nature of mortgage debt changed markedly between 1929 and
1962, the larger household debt-income ratio in 1962 may not indicate a greater sensitivity to a shock.

In Table 2 the rates of growth of these debt-income ratios for
1922-29 and 1948-62 are shown. The rate of growth of corporate
nonfinancial sector debt is much greater for 1948-57 and 1948-62
than for 1922-29, whereas the rates of growth of household debt
for these periods are of the same order of magnitude. It is inter-

Table 1

Liabilities-Income Ratio
Corporate Nonfinancial, and Consumer Sectors
1922-29 and 1948-62

| | Years | | | | |
|---|---|---|---|---|---|
| | 1922 | 1929 | 1948 | 1957 | 1962 |
| Corporate liabilities-income ratio | 5.701 | 6.082 | 3.56 | 4.97 | 4.66 |
| Consumers' liabilities-income ratio | .3811 | .6214 | .273 | .561 | .694 |

Table 2

Rates of Growth of Liabilities-Income Ratios
Corporate Nonfinancial, and Consumer Sectors
1922-29 and 1948-62

| | Intervals | | | |
|---|---|---|---|---|
| | 1922-29 | 1948-57 | 1957-62 | 1948-62 |
| Corporate nonfinancial sector | .9 | 3.8 | −1.3 | 1.9 |
| Consumers' sector | 7.2 | 8.4 | 4.3 | 6.9 |

Sources for Table 1 and 2: 1922, 1929: R. Goldsmith, *A Study of Saving in the United States* (Princeton, N. J.: Princeton University Press, 1956), Tables N-1, W 22, W 31.

1948, 1957: Federal Reserve System, *Flow of Funds/Savings Accounts 1946-60, Supplement 5*, December 1961, Tables 4 and 8.

1962: *Federal Reserve Bulletin*, April, 1963, "Flow of Funds/Savings Tables."

esting to note that the alleged retardation of the rate of growth of income since 1957 shows up in a lower rate of growth of the debt-income ratios for both households and corporate business. It is also interesting to note that a nonsustainable relative rate of growth of debt to income for the corporate nonfinancial sector, which existed between 1948-57 was broken in 1957-62 even though the 1957 debt-income ratio (5.0) was lower than the 1929 debt-income ratio for this sector.[8]

## IV. Conclusion: the role of the
    federal government

It seems that the trends in the debt-income ratios of households and corporate nonfinancial business, and in the ultimate liquidity-income ratio in the sustained boom  of the postwar period, are similar to the trends of these variables in the sustained boom of the interwar period. However, both the nonfinancial corporate sector's debt-income ratio and Pigou velocity were smaller in 1962 than in 1929, whereas the household debt-income ratio was of the same order of magnitude in the two periods. Even if we ignore the changes in the structure of debts and the nature of the contracts, the initial conditions in 1962 were much more conducive to a stable reaction to a stock-market crash than the initial conditions in 1929. Our tentative conclusion is that the observed differences in system behavior between the two periods is not necessarily due to any change in the financial processes associated with a boom dominated by private sector demand; rather the observed differences in the reaction to a sharp fall in stock prices can be imputed to the marked differences in the state of the system at the time the fall in prices occurred.

However, in one respect the economy is really quite different in 1962 from what it was in 1929. Federal government purchases of goods and services was 1.2 percent of GNP in 1929 and 11.3 percent of GNP in 1962. This enormous increase in the relative size of the federal government, combined with the reaction of tax receipts and spending to a decline in GNP means that today, much more so than in the 1920's, the federal government tends to stabilize income. In addition, once a decline in income results in a deficit, the stock of ultimate liquid assets increases, and the rate of increase of the stock of ultimately liquid assets increases with the size of the deviation from the balanced budget income. Hence, by diminishing the realized change in income due to an initial disturbance and by increasing the public's stock of ultimate liquidity markedly once income turns down, the increase in the relative size of the federal government makes the economy better able to withstand a deflationary shock such as the sharp fall in stock-market prices that occurred in 1962.

## Notes

1. I. Fisher, *Booms and Depressions* (New York: Adelphi Co., 1932); Staff, *Debts and Recovery* 1929-37 (New York: Twentieth Century Fund, 1938).

2. *Economic Report of the President* (Washington, D.C.: U.S. Government Printing Office, January, 1963), p. 71.

3. J. G. Gurley and E. S. Shaw, *Money in a Theory of Finance* (Washington, D.C.: The Brookings Institution, 1960).

4. *Ibid.*

5. H. Minsky, "Monetary Systems and Accelerator Models, " *American*

*Economic Review*, XLVII:859-83 (December, 1957).

6. J. Dusenberry, *Business Cycles and Economic Growth* (New York: McGraw-Hill Book Co., Inc., 1958).

7. I. Fisher, *op. cit.*; J. Dusenberry, *op. cit.*

8. H. Minsky, "Financial Constraints upon Decisions, An Aggregate View," *1962 Proceedings of the Business and Economic Statistics Section, American Statistical Association.*

## 2

*Finance and Profits:*
*The Changing Nature*
*of American*
*Business Cycles*

## I. Historical perspective

The great contraction of 1929-33 was the first stage of the Great Depression that continued until the end of the 1930s. Although economic turbulence has been evident since the mid-1960s, nothing that has happened in recent years even remotely resembles the economic disaster of the Great Depression. Furthermore, the first part of the era since World War II——the years between 1946 and the middle of the 1960s——were a great success. Between 1946 and 1965 the American economy exhibited consistent and fundamentally tranquil progress; these years were characterized by a close approximation of both full employment and price level stability. Although it was far from a utopia, during these twenty years the American economy was successful, in that substantial and widespread improvements in the economic dimensions of life were achieved. Furthermore similar economic progress took place in the other "advanced " capitalist economies during these years.

Since the middle 1960s the economy has been much more turbulent, and the turbulence seems to be increasing. Both unemployment and inflation showed an upward trend through the 1970s. Measures to manage demand which were deemed responsible for the success of the tranquil years have not been successful in containing the turbulence of the 1970s. Furthermore since the mid-1960s crises have occurred quite regularly in financial markets, and the dollar-based international monetary system set up after

Reprinted from *The Business Cycle and Public Policy, 1929-80,* Joint Economic Committee, Congress of the United States, U.S. Government Printing Office, Washington, D.C., 1980.

World War II has been destroyed. In the mid-1960s an era of mild cycles in income and employment, general price stability, financial strength, and international economic tranquility came to an end. It has been followed by an era of increasingly severe business cycles, growth retardation, accelerating inflation, financial fragility, and international economic disarray. However, even though the American economy has performed poorly in recent years, in comparison with what happened in the 1930s this performance is "not bad": we have not had another "great" or even serious depression.

Over the twenty or so years of on the whole tranquil progress after World War II cumulative changes in the financial structure occurred. In 1966-67 the stability of the financial structure was tested and the Federal Reserve found it necessary to intervene as a lender-of-last-resort. Since the middle 1960s two additional episodes occurred—in 1969-70 and 1974-75—in which the Federal Reserve intervened as a lender-of-last-resort. In early 1980 the Bache/Hunt silver crisis showed that there were serious domains of potential instability in the economic structure.

The thesis underlying this book is that an understanding of the American economy requires an understanding of how the financial structure is affected by and affects the behavior of the economy over time.

The time path of the economy depends upon the financial structure. The financial relations that generated the instability of 1929-33 were of minor importance during 1946-65—hence the economy behaved in a tranquil way. However over 1946-65 the financial structure changed because of internal reactions to the success of the economy. As a result of cumulative changes, financial relations became conducive to instability. The dynamic behavior of the American economy since the middle 1960s reflects the simultaneous existence of a structure of financial relations conducive to the generation of instability such as ruled after 1929, alongside a structure of government budget commitments and Federal Reserve interventions that prevent the full development of a "downward" cumulative process. The result has been a business cycle characterized by six stages:

(1) An accelerating inflation,

(2) A financial crisis,

(3) A sharp thrust toward lower income,

(4) Intervention (automatic and discretionary) by the Government through its budget and the Federal Reserve (and other financial agencies of Government) through lender-of-last-resort action.

(5) A sharp braking of the downturn, and

(6) Expansion.

Stage 6, expansion, leads to stage 1, accelerating inflation. Since 1966 the cycle seems to take from three to six years and economic policy seems able to affect the duration and severity of particular stages but only at a price of exacerbating other stages.

In this paper I will address the following questions that arise out of the above broad brush perspective:

(1) Why haven't we had a great or even a serious depression since 1946?

(2) Why was 1946-66 a period of tranquil progress and why has it been followed by turbulence?

(3) Is stagflation, as characterized by higher unemployment rates associated with a trend of higher rates of inflation, the price we pay for success in avoiding a great or serious depression?

(4) Are there feasible policies short of accepting a deep and long depression that will lead to a resumption of tranquil progress such as took place in the first post-World War II epoch?

## II. Financing and instability

The above questions deal with the overall stability of our economy. To address these questions we need an economic theory which explains why our economy is sometimes stable and sometimes unstable. In recent years the discussion about economic policy for the United States has been dominated by a debate between Keynesians and monetarists. Even though Keynesians and monetarists differ in their policy proposals, they use a common economic theory; they are branches of a common economic theory, which is usually called the neoclassical synthesis. Instability, of the kind that we have identified and which leads to the questions we are aiming to answer, is foreign to the economic theory of the neoclassical synthesis; it cannot happen as a normal result of the economic process.

It is self-evident that if a theory is to explain an event, the event must be possible within the theory. Furthermore if a theory is to guide policy that aims at controlling or preventing an event, the event must be possible within the theory.

Within the neoclassical synthesis a serious depression cannot occur as a result of internal operations of the economy. In this theory a serious depression can only be the result of policy errors or of non-essential institutional flaws. Thus a monetarist explanation of the Great Depression holds that it was the result of Federal Reserve errors and omissions and a Keynesian explanation holds that it was the result of an exogenously determined decline of investment opportunities or a prior unexplained decline in consumption activity.[1,2]

The neoclassical synthesis treats the complex system of financial institutions and instruments that are used to finance ownership of capital assets in a cavalier way. A detailed analysis of the behavior of financial institutions and the way the interrelations between financial units and operating units affect the performance of the economy is absent from the core of standard theory. Neither the standard Keynesianism nor any of the varieties of monetarism integrate the financial structure of our economy into the determination of income, prices, and employment in any essential way.

In both variants of the neoclassical synthesis the financial structure is represented by "money." Monetarists use money as a variable that explains prices and Keynesians use money as a variable that affects aggregate nominal demand, but in both money is an outside variable; the amount of money in existence is not determined by internal processes of the economy.

In our economy money is created as bankers acquire assets and is destroyed as debtors to banks fulfill their obligations. Our economy is a capitalist economy with long-lived and expensive capital assets and a complex, sophisticated financial structure. The essential financial processes of a capitalist economy center around the way investment and positions in capital assets are financed. To the extent that the various techniques used to finance capital asset ownership and production lead to banks acquiring assets, money is an end product of financial arrangements. In a capitalist economy investment decisions, investment financing, investment activation, profits and commitments to make payments due to outstanding debts are linked. To understand the behavior of our economy it is necessary to integrate financial relations into an explanation of employment, income, and prices. The performance of our economy at any date is closely related to the current success of debtors in fulfilling their commitments and to current views of the ability of today's borrowers to fulfill commitments.

Financing arrangements involve lenders and borrowers. The deals between lenders and borrowers are presumably a good thing for both. In our economy the proximate lender to an owner of capital assets and to investing units is a financial institution. Financial institutions are typically highly levered organizations. This means that any loss on the assets owned will lead to an amplified loss of the owner's equity. Because of leverage and the obvious desire of lenders to protect their capital, loans are made on the basis of various margins of safety. To understand our economy we need to know how an economy behaves in which borrowing and lending take place on the basis of margins of safety. The borrowing and lending of particular concern is that used to finance investment and the ownership of capital assets.

Borrowing and lending are also used to finance household spending and asset holdings. From time to time governments run deficits. Thus there are household and government debts in portfolios that need to be serviced by cash from household income and government taxes. In what follows it will become evident that household and government borrowing is not the critical element making for instability, although the overall stability of an economy can be affected by household and government borrowing.

To borrow is to receive money today in exchange for promises to pay money in the future. As a result of past borrowing, there are payments which have to be made over every short period. Furthermore, if the economy functions well during every short period, new borrowings take place which become promises to pay in the future. Our economy has a past, which is present today in maturing payment commitments, and a future, which is present today in debts that are being created.

### III. The significance of finance

A framework for analyzing the relations between cash payment commitments due to outstanding liabilities and the cash receipts of organizations with debts is needed if financial relations are to be fully integrated into the theory of income and price determination. Financial instability is a fact and any theory that attempts to explain the aggregate behavior of our economy must explain how it can occur. As financial instability is one facet of the serious business cycles of history, a theory that explains financial instability will enable us to understand why our economy is intermittently unstable.

Cash payment commitments on outstanding instruments are contractual commitments (1) to pay interest and repay the principal on debts and (2) to pay dividends—if earned—on equity shares. These cash payment commitments are money flows set up by the financial structure. A structure of expected money receipts underlies the various commitments to make payments on existing debts. Each economic unit—be it a business firm, household, financial institution, or government—is a money-in-money-out device. The relation among the various sources and uses of cash for the various classes of economic units determines the potential for instability of the economy.

Our economy is one that employs complex, expensive, and long-lived capital assets and which has a sophisticated and complex financial structure. The funds that are needed to acquire control over the expensive capital assets of the economy are obtained by a variety of financial instruments such as equity shares, bank loans, bonds, mortgages, leases, and rentals. Each financial instrument is created by exchanging "money today" for commitments to pay "money later." The payments during any period on outstanding financial instruments are the "money later" parts of contracts entered into in prior periods. We can summarize the above by the statement that firms may and do finance positions in capital assets by complex sets of financial obligations. The financial obligations outstanding at any date determine a series of dated cash payment commitments.

The legal form that business takes determines the debts that can be used to finance ownership of capital assets. The modern corporation is essentially a financial organization. The alternatives to using corporations as the legal form for private business are sole proprietorships and partnerships. In these alternatives the debts of the organization are debts of the individual owner or partners and the life of the organization is limited to the life of the partners. As a result of their limited lives and constrained debt carrying powers, proprietorships and partnerships are poor vehicles for owning and operating long-lived and special purpose capital assets. There is a symbiotic relation between the corporate form of organizing business and the emergence of an industrial and commercial structure in which debt is used to finance the construction of and determine the control over complex, special purpose and long-lived capital assets.

In addition to the ordinary business firms that own the capital assets of our economy there are financial firms (banks, etc.) that mainly own financial instruments. These institutions finance the assets they own (what will be called their position) by some combination of equity (capital and surplus) and debts. The typical position of the various types of financial institutions will include debts of capital asset owning firms, households, governments, and other financial institutions. In addition, some financial institutions own equity shares.

Thus there exists a complex network of commitments to pay money. The units that have entered into these commitments must have sources of money. When a financial contract is created, both the buyer (lender) and the seller (borrower) have scenarios in mind by which the seller acquires the cash needed to fulfill the terms of the contract. In a typical situation there is a primary and some secondary or fall-back sources of cash. For example, in an ordinary home mortgage the primary source of the cash needed to fulfill the contract is the income of the homeowner. The secondary or fallback source of cash is the market value of the mortgaged property. For an ordinary business loan at a bank, the expected difference between gross receipts and out of pocket costs is the primary source of cash. Secondary sources would include the value of collateral, borrowings, or the proceeds from selling assets. Expected cash receipts are due to contributions to the production and distribution of income, the fulfillment of contracts, borrowing and selling assets. In addition, payment commitments can be fulfilled by using what stocks of cash a unit may have on hand.

Our economy therefore is one in which borrowing and lending on the basis of margins of safety is commonplace. Today's payments on outstanding financial instruments are the result of commitments that were made in the past—even as today's transactions create financial contracts which commit various organizations to make payments in the future. The balance sheets at any moment of time of units that make up the economy are "snapshots" of how one facet of the past, the present, and the future are related.

Commercial banks are one set of financial institutions in our economy. Demand deposits, which are part of the money stock, are one of a number of liabilities that commercial banks use to finance their position in financial assets. In turn the financial assets of banks are debts of other units, which use these debts to finance positions in capital assets or financial instruments. As we peer through the financing veil of the interrelated set of balance sheets, it becomes evident that the money supply of the economy is like a bond, in that it finances positions in capital assets. Before one can speak securely of how changes in the money supply affect economic activity, it is necessary to penetrate the financing veil to determine how changes in the money supply affect the activities that are carried out.

Each financing transaction involves an exchange of money today for money later. The parties to the transaction have some expectations of the uses to which the receiver of money today will put the funds and how this receiver will gather the funds by which to fulfill the money-tomorrow part of the bargain. In this deal, the use by the borrower of the funds is known with a considerable assurance; the future cash receipts which will enable the borrower to fulfill the money-tomorrow parts of the contract are conditional upon the performance of the economy over a longer or shorter period. Underlying all financing contracts is an exchange of certainty for uncertainty. The current holder of money gives up a certain command over current income for an uncertain future stream of money.

Just as there is no such thing as a free lunch, there is no such thing as a certain deal involving the future. Every investment in capital assets involves giving up something certain in exchange for something conjectural in the future. In particular, any set of capital assets acquired by a firm is expected to yield cash flows over time whose sum exceeds by some margin the cash paid for the capital asset. These expectations are, however, conditional upon the state of particular markets and of the economy in the various futures in which cash receipts are to be collected. In making money-today—money-tomorrow transactions, whether the transaction be a financial transaction, such as issuing or buying bonds, or an investment transaction, in which current resources are used to create capital assets, assumptions about the intrinsically uncertain future are made. The assumptions often are that the intrinsically uncertain future can be represented by a probability distribution of, say, profits, where the probability distribution is assumed to be like the probability distributions that are used to represent outcomes at a roulette table. However, the knowledge of the process that determines the probabilities is much less secure for economic life than it is for fair roulette wheels. Unforeseen and unlikely events occur in gambling games and in economic life. Unlikely events will not cause a radical change in the estimates of the frequency distribution of outcomes at the roulette table whereas they are quite likely to cause marked change in the expectation of the future that guides economic activity.

The financial structure of our economy can be viewed as apportioning among various units the potential gains and losses from various undertakings in which the outcome is uncertain. By the very nature of uncertainty, the actual results are quite likely to deviate markedly from anticipated results. Such deviations will lead to capital gains and losses. Experience with capital gains and losses will lead to changes in the terms upon which a certain command over resources will be exchanged for a conjectural future command over resources. The prices of capital assets and financial instruments will change as history affects views about the likelihood of various outcomes.

Households, businesses, government units, and various types of financial institutions issue financial liabilities. Each issuer of financial instruments has a main source of cash which is expected to accrue so that the financial instruments it has outstanding can be validated. The primary source of cash for households is wages, for business firms it is gross profits, for government units it is taxes, and for financial institutions it is the cash flow from owned contracts. In addition each unit can, in principle, acquire cash by selling assets or by borrowing. Although the normal economic activity of many units depends upon borrowing or selling assets to obtain cash we will consider such financial transactions as a secondary source of cash—where the term secondary does not necessarily carry any pejorative connotations.

Household wage income, business profit flows, and government tax receipts are related to the performance of the economy. The primary cash flows that validate household, business, and government debts depend upon the level and distribution of nominal income. In our type of economy one link between financial markets on the one hand and income and output production on the other is that some of the demand for current output is financed by the issuance of financial instruments, and a second is that wage, profit, and tax flows need to be at a certain level to meet a standard that is determined by the payment commitments on financial instruments if financial asset prices and the ability to issue financial instruments are to be sustained. A capitalist economy is an integrated financial and production system and the performance of the economy depends upon the satisfaction of financial as well as income production criteria.

## IV. Hedge, speculative, and Ponzi finance

Three financial postures for firms, households, and government units can be differentiated by the relation between the contractual payment commitments due to their liabilities and their primary cash flows. These financial postures are hedge, speculative, and "Ponzi." The stability of an economy's financial structure depends upon the mix of financial postures. For any given regime of financial institutions and government interventions the greater the weight of hedge financing in the economy the greater the stability of the economy whereas an increasing weight of speculative and Ponzi financing indicates an increasing susceptibility of the economy to financial instability.

For hedge financing units, the cash flows from participation in income production are expected to exceed the contractual payments on outstanding debts in every period. For speculative financing units, the total expected cash flows from participation in income production when totaled over the foreseeable future exceed the total cash payments on outstanding debt, but the near term payment commitments exceed the near term cash flows from participation in income production, even though the net income portion of the near term cash flows, as measured by accepted accounting procedures, exceeds the near term interest payments on debt. A Ponzi finance unit is a speculative financing unit for which the income component of the near term cash flows falls short of the near term interest payments on debt so that for some time in the future the outstanding debt will grow due to interest on existing debt. Both speculative and Ponzi units can fulfill their payment commitments on debts only by borrowing (or disposing of assets). The amount that a speculative unit needs to borrow is smaller than the maturing debt whereas a Ponzi unit must increase its outstanding debts. As a Ponzi unit's total expected cash receipts must exceed its total payment commitments for financing to be available, viability of a representative Ponzi unit often depends upon the expectation that some assets will be sold at a high enough price some time in the future.

We will first examine the cash flow, present value, and balance sheet implications of hedge, speculative, and Ponzi financial postures for business firms. The financing of investment and positions in capital assets by debts is a distinguishing attribute of our type of economy. This makes the cash flows and balance sheets of business of special importance. As our focus is upon the payment commitments due to business debts, the cash receipts of special interest are the gross profits net of taxes but inclusive of interest payments, for this is the cash flow that is available to fulfill payment commitments. The generation and distribution of this broad concept of profits is the central determinant of the stability of an economy in which debts are used to finance investment and positions in capital assets.

The validation through cash flows of the liabilities of households and governments is of great importance to the operation of today's capitalist economies. Household and government financing relations affect the stability of the economy and the course through time of output, employment, and prices. However, the essential cyclical path of capitalist economies was evident when household debts were small and government, aside from times of war, was small. Household and government debt creation and validation modify but do not cause the cyclical behavior of capitalist economies. It will be evident in what follows that if the debt generation and validation by government becomes large relative to the debt generation and validation by business the basic path of the economy is likely to be affected.

*Business firms*

The fundamental variables in analyzing the financial structure of business firms are the cash receipts and payments of economic units over a relevant time period. The total receipts of a business firm can be divided into the payments for current labor and purchased inputs and a residual, gross capital income,[3] that is available to pay income taxes, the principal and interest on debts and for use by the owners.

We therefore have:

Gross Capital Income = Total Receipts From Operations
− Current Labor and Material Costs

and

Gross Capital Income = Principal and Interest Due on Debts
+ Income Taxes + Owners "Income."

In terms of the data available in National Income and Flow of Funds accounts, gross capital income equals gross profits before taxes plus interest paid on business debts. In analyzing the viability of a financial structure and the constraints it imposes, gross capital income as here defined is the key receipts variable.

The cash payments made by a unit over a relevant time period equal the spending on current labor and purchased inputs, tax payments, the remittance due to debts that fall due, and dividends. Over any particular interval cash payments may exceed, equal, or fall short of cash receipts. Of the payments the critical items are current input costs, taxes, and payments required by outstanding debts. As current costs and taxes are subtracted from current receipts to yield after tax capital income the key relation becomes that between after tax capital income (or gross profits after taxes broadly defined) and the payment commitments on debts. The relation has two facets:

(1) Each relevant period's (quarter, month, year) relation between gross capital income and payment commitments due to debts.

(2) The relation over an open horizon of the sum of expected gross capital income and the sum of payment commitments now on the books or which must be entered on the books if the expected gross capital income is to be achieved.

A necessary though not sufficient condition for the financial viability of a unit is that the expected gross capital income exceed the total payment commitments over time of debts now on the books or which must be entered upon if this capial income is to be forthcoming.

Gross capital income reflects the productivity of capital assets, the efficacy of management, the efficiency of labor, and the behavior of markets and the economy. The debt structure is a legacy of past financing conditions and decisions. The question this analysis raises is whether the future profitability of the business sector can support the financial decisions that were made as the current capital-asset structure of the economy was put into place.

## Hedge financing

A unit is hedge financing at a particular date when at that date the expected gross capital income exceeds by some margin the payment commitments due to debts in every relevant period over the horizon given by the debts now on the books and the borrowings that must be made if expected gross capital income is to be earned. The liabilities on the books at any time are the result of past financing decisions. As such they are entered into on the basis of margins of safety. One of the margins of safety is an excess of anticipated receipts over cash payment commitments. However the anticipated gross capital income for any date is uncertain. The holder and user of capital assets, the banker who arranges the financing and the owner of the liabilities expect the actual receipts to exceed the payment commitments due to debt by a substantial margin. One way to treat this is to assume that the owners of the capital assets, the bankers, and the owners of the debt assume there is a lower limit of the gross capital income which is virtually certain and that financing decisions and capitalized values are based upon this lower limit to earnings which are deemed to be virtually certain.

If we capitalize the cash payment commitments and the receipts that capital assets are deemed to be assured of earning at common interest rates we will get the present value of the enterprise that is expected to yield the specified gross capital income. In the case of the hedge unit the difference between these assured receipts and the payment commitments is positive in every period. Thus the capitalized value of the flow of gross capital income will exceed the capitalized value of payment commitments at *every* interest rate. Inasmuch as a unit is solvent only as the value of its assets exceeds the value of its debts, changes in interest rates cannot affect the solvency of a unit that hedge finances.

It is important to emphasize that, for a hedge unit, conservatively estimated expected gross capital income exceeds the cash payments on debts from contracts for every period in the future. The present value of this stream is the sum of the capitalized value of the cash flows net of debt payments for each period; inasmuch as each period's net cash flow is positive the sum will be positive. In particular a sharp rise in interest rates cannot reverse the inequality in which the present value of capital assets exceeds the book value of debts. For hedge finance units insolvency cannot result from interest rate increases.

Even though a hedge financing unit and its bankers expect that cash flows from operations will generate sufficient cash to meet payment commitments on account of debts, further protection for borrowers and lenders can exist by having a unit own excess money or marketable financial assets—i.e., it is convenient (as an implicit insurance policy) to hold assets in the form in which debts are denominated. A balance sheet of a hedge investor will include money or money market assets in addition to the capital assets.

A hedge unit's financial posture can be described by the excess of cash receipts over contractual payment commitments in each period, an excess of the value of capital assets over debt and the holding of cash or liquid assets. We can further divide the assets and liabilities. In particular we can note that the cash can be held in the form of various financial assets such as Treasury debt, commercial paper, and even open lines of credit. Similarly the debts of a unit can be short term, long term, or even non-debts like commitments on leases.

A unit that has only equities on the liability side of its balance sheet or whose only debts are long term bonds with a sinking fund arrangement where the payments to the sinking fund are well within the limits set by expected cash flows is engaged in hedge financing. A hedge financing unit is not directly susceptible to adverse effects from changes in financial markets. The only way a hedge financing unit can go bankrupt is if its revenues fall short of its out of pocket costs and commitments.

## Speculative financing

A unit speculates when for some periods the cash payment commitments on debts exceed the expected gross capital income. The speculation is that refinancing will be available when needed. This speculation arises because the commitments provide for the repayment of debt at a faster rate than the gap between revenues and costs allows for the recapturing of the money costs of capital assets. We restrict the term speculative to a liability structure in which the income portion of gross profits exceeds the income portion of payment commitments.

The liability structure of a speculative unit leads to a series of cash payments and the operations of the unit will lead to a series of cash receipts. The sum of the payment commitments is less than the sum of the cash receipts *but* in some periods the payment commitments are larger than the expected cash receipts; there are deficits. These "deficit" periods are typically closer in time from the "today" at which the balance sheet is being characterized; the deficits for the speculative unit are mainly because the unit has engaged in short term financing so that the principal of debts falling due exceeds the recapture of capital-asset commitments in these early periods. Even as the debt is being reduced in these early periods, the cash flow prospects of later periods include receipts due to the recapture of principal even as there is no need to reduce the principal of outstanding debts. Thus a speculative unit has near term cash deficits and cash surpluses in later terms.

The present value of an organization equals the present value of the gross capital income minus the present value of the cash payment commitments. This is equivalent to the present value of the series of cash deficits and surpluses that a speculative unit is expected to earn. For a speculative unit the shortfalls of these receipts relative to payment commitments occur early on in the future and the positive excess of receipts over payments occurs later: a speculative unit finances a long position in assets by short run liabilities. Higher interest rates lower the present value of all cash receipts, however the decline is proportionately greater for the receipts more distant in time. Thus a dated set of cash flows which yields a positive excess of asset values over the value of debts at low interest rates may yield a negative excess at high interest rates: a present value reversal, from positive to negative present values, can occur for speculative financing relations and not for hedge financing units.

In a speculative financing arrangement the unit, its bankers, and the holders of its debts are aware that payment commitments can be fulfilled only by issuing debt or by running down cash balances during periods in which the payment commitments exceed the relevant receipts. The financing terms at those dates when it is necessary to borrow to pay debts can affect the spread between gross capital income and cash payment commitments. In particular refinancing can make cash commitments at some later date, which initially were expected to be positive, negative. The ability of a firm that engages in speculative finance to fulfill its obligations is susceptible to failures in those markets in which it sells its debts.

A speculative unit will also carry cash kickers. As the near term payments exceed the expected cash flows from income, for a given value of debt the cash balance of a speculative unit can be expected to be larger than that for a hedge unit. However because speculative units are active borrowers it is likely that lines of credit and access to markets will be a part of the cash position of such units, albeit this part will not be visible on the balance sheet.

The gross cash flows due to operations that a unit receives are broken down by accounting procedures into an income portion and a recapture of the value of the investment in capital assets; the recapturing is called depreciation or capital consumption. The payment commitments on debts are usually separated into the interest due and the repayment of principal. For a speculative financing unit in the periods when there is a cash flow deficit the receipts allocated to income exceed the interest payments even as the receipts allocated to the repayment of principal fall short of the principal amount due on the debt. Thus the speculative unit is earning a net profit and is in a position to decrease its indebtedness by allocating a portion of the excess of income over debt payments to lowering the debts.

## Ponzi financing

Ponzi units are speculative units with the special characteristic that for some if not all near term periods cash payment commitments to pay interest are not covered by the income portion of the expected excess of receipts over current labor and material costs. These units must borrow in order to pay the interest on their outstanding debt: their outstanding debt grows even if no new income yielding assets are acquired.

Obviously asset owners, bankers, and debt holders participate in Ponzi finance only if the present value of the sum of all future expected cash receipts and payments is positive. Therefore the positive present value of cash receipts minus payments in later periods must offset the negative present value of cash receipts minus payments in early periods. An extreme example of Ponzi finance is borrowing to hold assets which yield no or little income in the expectation that at some date the market value of the object held will yield enough to clear debt and leave a sizeable gain. The low margin stock exchange of the 1920s and the margin financing of the Hunt position in silver in 1980 are examples of Ponzi financing.[4] The REITs of the early 1970s, which paid dividends on the basis of interest accruals, were engaging in Ponzi finance. A unit that is heavily involved in building capital assets can be engaging in Ponzi finance.

It is obvious that a Ponzi finance unit's present value depends on interest rates and the expectations of cash flows in the future. Rising interest rates increase the rate of increase of outstanding debts and can transform positive present values into negative present values. Inflation will often lead to financing relations which can be validated only if inflation continues. Acquiring assets because of inflationary expectations bids up the price of favored assets and the financing bids up interest rates. A decline in inflation expectations will lead to a drop in these asset prices which can lead to the debts exceeding the value of assets.

The stability of an economy depends upon the mixture of hedge, speculative, and Ponzi finance. Over a period of good years the weight of short term debt in the business financial structure increases and the weight of cash in portfolios declines. Thus there is a shift in the proportion of units with the different financial structures—and the weight of speculative and Ponzi finance increases during a period of good years.

It should be noted that a decline in expected gross capital income, or a rise in the income protection required for hedge financing can make hedge units speculative units; and a decline in expected gross capital income, a rise in the income protection requried for speculative financing or a rise in financing costs can make speculative units Ponzi units. Such changes can lead to the value of debts exceeding the capitalized value of these excess receipts. There are two facets to financial instability. In the first the cost of debt and the need to roll over ever larger debt structures leads to a break in asset values as units try (or are forced to try) to decrease their debt dependency; the second is when gross capital income falls because the determinants of profits have fallen. A deep recession requires that such financial markets and cash flow effects occur.

At this point it is worth noting that the level and pattern of interest rates do not affect the solvency even though it affects the size of the positive net worth of a hedge finance unit. However the solvency—i.e., a shift of net worth from positive to negative and back again—of speculative and Ponzi finance units is affected by interest rate changes. In a world dominated by hedge finance the authorities can disregard the course of interest rates. But in a world dominated by hedge finance, the interest inelastic demand for finance from units that must refinance positions and finance commitments will not exist—i.e., in a world dominated by hedge finance interest rates do not change by much.

On the other hand, for speculative and especially for Ponzi finance units a rise in interest rates can transform a positive net worth into a negative net worth. If solvency matters for the continued normal functioning of an economy, then large increases and wild swings in interest rates will affect the behavior of an economy with large proportions of speculative and Ponzi finance. Furthermore speculative and especially Ponzi finance give rise to large increases in an interest inelastic demand for finance, i.e., speculative and Ponzi finance create market conditions conducive to large swings in interest rates. In a world where speculative and Ponzi finance is important the authorities cannot disregard the effect of policies on the level and volatility of interest rates.

## Households

For households, the cash flow income that is mainly relevant to the financial structure is the difference between wage income as the major component of household disposable income and cash payment commitments on household debt.[5] The secondary household financial relation of importance, which is especially relevant for the various forms of "to the asset" (mortgage, conditional sales) contracts, is between the value of the hypothecated asset and the face or book value of the outstanding debt.

Household debts are either fully amortized, partially amortized, or unamortized. In a fully amortized contract a series of payments is specified and at the end of the time the contract is fully paid. In a partially amortized contract there is a payment due at the end of the contract which is a portion of the original principal. An unamortized contract has the full original principal due at its end.

The cash flow relation for a fully amortized contract assumes that the payment commitments are less than the expected wage incomes. Thus a fully amortized contract conforms to the definition of hedge financing. Partially amortized and unamortized contracts can have payments due at some dates that exceed the anticipated wage incomes. The cash flow relations for partially amortized contracts conform to that of speculative financing except that the cash deficit comes late in the sequence of payments rather than early.

Consumer and mortgage debt can become Ponzi-like only if actual wage income falls short of anticipated and other sources of disposable income, for example, unemployment insurance, do not fill the gap. Such shortfalls can occur because of personal events or overall economic events. Various types of insurance premiums added to the cash payment commitments take care of the health and accident portions of the personal risk. Large scale and persistent unemployment can lead to reversal of the inequality for a substantial number of initial hedge units and the subsequent foreclosures and repossession of the hypothecated asset can lead to a fall in asset prices relative to the outstanding debt. This can occur only if a substantial decline in income and employment has taken place. The typical financing relation for consumer and housing debt can amplify but it cannot initiate a downturn in income and employment.

However a part of household financing is often Ponzi; this is the financing of holdings of securities and some types of collectable assets. A typical example is the financing of ownership of common stocks or other financial instruments by debts. In principle a separate cash flow account for such assets within the household accounts could be set up. Debts for carrying a fixed portfolio of securities would increase whenever the income earned by the securities falls short of interest payments on the debt. If we set up the cash flow relation for a margin account for common stock we find that if the dividend/price ratio exceeds the interest rate then the financing is speculative, mainly because the underlying debt is nominally short term. If the interest payments exceed the dividend then the financing is Ponzi. Hedge financing disappears as a classification for stock market financing except if the term to maturity of the debt is so long that the borrowing unit does not have to refinance its positions.

Why would any rational man enter upon and a rational banker finance a security holding in which the carrying costs exceed the cash flow from dividends? The obvious answer is that the dividend yield is not the full yield; the full yield will include appreciation (or depreciation) of asset values. Thus in household finance we find that the payment commitments can exceed the dividends and be less than the total asset return including the appreciation of the price of the assets. In the extreme case—which applies to stock market booms and speculative manias (such as the 1979-80 Gold and Silver episode), the cash income from assets approaches zero; the only return is from appreciation. In these cases, if there is a margin between the price in the market of the assets and the value of the debt used to carry the assets, the cash due on debt is acquired by a rise in debt. This rise in debt finances the interest income of the lenders (bankers). Income is earned even though the payor pays no cash.

Household finance can be destabilizing if there is a significant portion of Ponzi finance in the holding of financial and other assets. A speculative boom exists whenever a substantial and growing portion of outstanding payment commitments can be fulfilled only if an appreciation of asset values takes place. In such a boom the current and near term expected cash flows from participating in the production and distribution of income are not sufficient to meet even the income portion of the payment commitments. In this situation some of the unrealized capital gains are transformed into incomes, thus financing demand for output. A speculative boom, as exemplified by a growth in Ponzi financing of asset holdings by households, can induce a rise in current output prices, even as the basis of the Ponzi financing of asset ownership is the anticipation by debtors and their financing agents of inflation in the prices of the assets being financed.

Debt-financing of asset ownership and consumption spending

by households has increased over the era since World War II. The increase of the items that can be financed by debt and of the ease with which households can debt-finance has meant that the link between household wage income and household consumption is not as close as in the past. When households can readily purchase consumer goods by promising to pay a portion of future wage incomes, a close link between this period's income and demand for output is broken. Symmetrically when a household's payments on debt contracts exceed the interest due, the household "saves." Thus a buildup of consumer debt will lead to a high ratio of consumption to household income; a decrease in the amount outstanding will lead to a low ratio of consumption to household income. The achieved ratio of savings to wage income in a modern economy reflects the course of outstanding household debts.

To recapitulate, household debt-financing and cash payment commitments on account of debt can be broken into two categories: the financing of consumption and the financing of ownership of assets, mainly financial assets. [Housing is in part a consumption good and in part an asset; other consumer durables such as automobiles, etc. are not valued as assets even though they may have a resale value.] The cash flows that will validate consumption financing are mainly household disposable income which is largely wages. The cash flows that will validate the debt-financing of assets are either dividends and interest or the result of selling out the position at an appreciated price. Household debt-financing of consumption is almost always hedge financing; only a fall in income (wages) can transform such contracts into examples of Ponzi financing. Housing is typically financed by hedge financing. Positions in common stocks and collectables, such as gold, are often financed in a Ponzi fashion.

Because consumption and housing debts of households are primarily hedge financing, the contracts will tend to be validated unless there is a prior fall in wage income. Household financing of asset ownership can be Ponzi in nature. As a result a rise in interest rates applicable to future prices of the assets or to future income can lead to a sharp fall in the price of assets in position. Such a sharp fall in price means that the margin of safety in asset values falls and the expected appreciation of asset values which enable cash to be raised to satisfy payment commitments is not realized. These effects can determine the markets in which changes in relative prices initiate financial and economic stability.

## Government

Government units also have payment commitments on debts. These payment commitments will be validated by some combination of an allocation of tax payments and new borrowing. Government units are often speculative financing units which operate by rolling over short term debt. As long as the total future expected cash flows exceed the total future cash payment commitments on the current outstanding debt, this proves no special problem. However if the expected tax take or expected current operating expenses misbehave then roll-over problems can arise. Government financial policies are not typically initiating forces in the instability that is due to market forces. But government units can mismanage their affairs and individually get into trouble. In particular government units with large floating (short term) debts can find the cost of carrying debts rising relative to the taxes net of current expenses available for servicing debt. High interest rates can make government units into Ponzi units.

## Summing up

The distinction between hedge, speculative and Ponzi finance defines both the sets of markets that need to be functioning normally for payment commitments to be validated and the potential sources of difficulty. If units engage in adequately protected hedge finance their financial difficulties cannot be an initiating factor in instability. Units which initially are hedge financing can become speculative and even Ponzi financing units as their income deteriorates and thus amplify initial disturbances.

Speculative financing units can fulfill their commitments as long as their longer term income prospects are favorable and as long as funds are forthcoming at non-punitive terms from the markets in which they finance and refinance their positions. Speculative finance units are vulnerable to both income and financial market disturbances. Furthermore shortfalls in income and increases in financing charges can transform speculative units into Ponzi units.

The viability of units which engage in Ponzi finance depends upon the current expectations of future prices of capital assets or financial instruments. These future prices depend upon profits in the more distant future. The viability of Ponzi finance units is dependent upon discount rates, on future cash flows and expectations of future profitability and prices. Obviously too great an admixture of Ponzi and near-Ponzi speculative finance is conducive to instability.

We can conceive of a scale of financial robustness—financial fragility which depends upon the mixture of hedge, speculative and Ponzi finance outstanding. As the proportion of hedge financing decreases the financial structure migrates toward fragility.

## V. The level and distribution of income and the validation of the financial structure

A debt is validated when maturing commitments to pay are fulfilled and expectations are sustained that future remaining commitments will be fulfilled. By extension a debt structure, either in total or for various subdivisions of the economy, is validated when on the whole maturing commitments to pay are fulfilled and when expectations are that future receipts by debtors will enable payment commitments that extend over time to be fulfilled. The qualifying phrase "on the whole" is needed because a debt structure will be validated even if some payment commitments are not fulfilled. Debt-financing organizations anticipate that some (small) percentage of debtors will not fulfill their commitments.

The validation of debt depends upon various components of income being large enough so that the payment commitments can be fulfilled either out of the income flows or by refinancing. Thus for the Flow of Funds category Non-Financial Corporate Business, capital income as measured by the sum of interest payments and gross profits after taxes during any period must be large enough to enable maturing commitments to be satisfied either out of this grossest of profits or out of the proceeds of new debts issued in roll-over or funding operations. But access to roll-over or funding finance depends upon anticipated future cash flows. Therefore at all times the emerging evidence on business profitability must lead to anticipated profit flows that enable refinancing to take place. In addition business profits have to be large enough so that when current and recent business profits are fed into whatever logic determines expected profits, the capitalized value of such expected profits is large enough to validate the price paid in the past for capital assets and induce current decisions to produce capital assets, i.e., to invest.

Wages and taxes need to meet standards set by household and government spending and payments due on outstanding debts if commitments on household and government debts are to be met and if new debts are to be negotiated. However, the wage bill and the tax take (once the tax schedule is determined) result from rather than determine aggregate demand. There is no link between the current and past levels of wages and taxes as inputs to anticipated future levels, that feeds back and determines a part of current demand, such as exists between current profits, anticipated profits, and current investment demand. Profits are critical in a capitalist economy because they are a cash flow which enables business to validate debt *and* because anticipated profits are the lure that induces current and future investment. It is anticipated profits which enable business to issue debts to finance investment and positions in capital assets. Any theory that aims to explain how an investing capitalist economy works must focus upon the determination of total profits and the division of total profits among debt servicing, household disposable income, and retained earnings.

In neoclassical economic theory profits equal the marginal productivity of capital times the quantity of capital. In our economy fluctuations in employment, output, and profits occur which cannot be explained by changes in the quantity or productivity of capital. Furthermore the concept of a quantity of capital is ambiguous; it is questionable if any meaning can be given to the concept that is independent of expected future profits and the capitalization rate on profits. There is an unambiguous meaning to the price at which investment output enters the stock of capital assets, but that price has little or no significance in determining the price of that item as a capital asset.

In equilibrium the depreciated value of investment output equals the capitalized value of future profits. In most of economic analysis the depreciated value of investment output is used as the value of capital—therefore implicitly assuming the economy is in equilibrium. But an economic theory that assumes that the economy is always in equilibrium cannot explain fluctuations. If the value of capital always equals the depreciated value of investment goods then even large scale exogenous shocks cannot affect the equilibrium values determined within the system.[6]

In neoclassical theory the price level and money are always outside the system that determines outputs and relative prices. Within this system of thought change in the money supply is an exogenous shock variable that will change money prices without changing relative prices—and price deflated profits. The neoclassical theory cannot be of help in explaining fluctuating profits. Therefore it is of no use in helping us understand how the financial structure of a capitalist economy affects the economy's behavior.

In a capitalist economy the total value of output or of any subset of outputs equals the sum of wages and capital income. Thus for consumer goods we find that the value of output (price times quantity) equals the wage bill plus profits. Similarly the value of investment output (price times quantity) equals the wage bill plus profits. Let us make a heroic but not unreasonable "first approximation" assumption that all of wages are spent on consumption and none of profits are so spent. This means that the wage bill in consumption plus the wage bill in investment equals the value of consumption output which in turn equals the wage bill in consumption plus the profits in consumption. The wage bill in consumption enters both demand and costs, subtracting it from both sides of the equation leads to

Profits in consumption goods production = The wage bill in investment goods production.

If we add profits in investment goods production to both sides of the above we get

Profits = Investment.

These simple formulas, which are true for a model based upon heroic abstractions, tell us a great deal about our economy.[7] The result that profits in consumption goods production equals the wage bill in investment goods production is no more than the proposition that the price system operates so that consumption goods are rationed by price among various consumers. It also asserts that workers in consumption goods production cannot buy back what they produce; if they did then workers in investment goods production would starve.

The "profits equal investment" result is based upon the identity that profits in investment goods production equal profits in investment goods production. To improve upon this tautology it is necessary to integrate the financing of investment goods production into the model of price determination. Investment output is often special purpose and produced to order. The production of an investment good usually takes time and in the case of modern investment output—let us take a jumbo jet plane or a nuclear power plant as our examples—production often takes the form of a sequenced assemblage of specialized components. The production of investment goods typically involves money being spent on a dated schedule and a receipt of money when the investment good is finished and it becomes a capital asset. In the construction industry this payment sequence takes the form of interim or construction financing while the project is being built and permanent or take out financing for the completed project.

In investment production the funds used are often borrowed. When borrowed funds are used both the borrower and lender alike expect sales proceeds to be sufficient to cover payment of the debts with a margin of safety. Given the contingencies that can arise the margins of safety required by borrowers and lenders can be large. Thus it is the financing conditions for investment in process—and the recognition that owned funds must yield what could be earned in financing other endeavors—that lead to the value of investment exceeding out of pocket labor cost. To the extent that labor costs represent all current costs (purchased materials, etc.) the supply price of investment output is given by a markup on wage costs where the markup reflects interest charges and the margins of safety required by lenders and borrowers.

The supply price of investment goods depends upon conditions in financial markets and various protections desired by producers and lenders. If production takes time and lenders and borrowers recognize that they live in an uncertain world and therefore want protection then the relative prices of different outputs depend upon particular financing terms and protections desired by borrowers and lenders.

It is worth noting that the supply price of the investment goods produced during a period will be paid only if the demand price of the investment good as a capital asset is equal to or greater than the supply price of investment as output. But the demand price is the capitalized value of future profits. We therefore find that investment will take place only if the capitalized value of future profits exceeds the supply price of investment output.

The proposition that profits equal investment can be opened up to allow for demands for consumption goods in addition to that which is financed by wages in the production of consumption and investment goods. It is particularly important to determine how the government budget and the international accounts affect the generation of profits. We first consider only the Federal Government.

The government hires workers, buys outputs, and pays transfers. Government spending is equal to the sum of the wage bill for government employees, purchases from private industry, and transfer payments (including interest on government debt). As government purchases equal a wage bill and profits, government spending equals the sum of direct and indirect wages, profits on government contracts, and transfer payments.

The government collects taxes. For simplicity we assume that all taxes are income taxes and that tax receipts—the tax take—are a percentage of the total wage bill plus a percentage of profits.

The government budget posture is the difference between government spending and the tax take. If the government budget is integrated into the determination of profits we find that

After Tax Profits = Investment + The Government Deficit.

This result is critical in understanding why we have not had a deep depression in the postwar period.

An implication of the result that after tax profits equal investment plus the deficit is that taxes on profits do not affect after tax profits unless such taxes affect the sum of investment and the deficit. However, a shift in taxes from wages to profits can be inflationary. The rise in disposable wage income raises demand and the rise in profit taxes will increase the pre-tax profits needed to achieve equality with investment plus the deficit. Pre-tax profits are the product of per unit profits times the number of units. A rise in pre-tax profits can be the result of greater output or a higher markup per unit of output. Inasmuch as the greater output response is only possible from the industries in which suppliers have market power and are willing to accept a reduction in their market power, the presumption has to be that prices in all production will tend to rise when taxes are shifted to profits.

The profit generating process can be opened up to allow for exports, imports, savings out of wage income, and consumption out of profits income. Imports minus exports equals the balance of trade deficit and if we allow for exports and imports the profits equation becomes

After Tax Profits = Investment + The Government Deficit — The Balance of Trade Deficit.

This equation shows that a trade surplus is good for domestic profits and a trade deficit is bad.

Expanding our analysis to allow for savings out of wages and consumption out of profits the profits equation becomes

After Tax Profits = Investment + The Government Deficit — The Balance of Trade Deficit + Consumption Out of Profit Income — Saving Out of Wage Income.

Profits are positively related to investment, the government deficit, and consumption out of profit income and negatively related to a balance of payments deficit and savings out of wages.[8]

For the purposes of this paper the simple equation

After Tax Profits = Investment + The Government Deficit

is of central importance. To understand how our economy functions we can first explore the meaning of the simple equation and then trace out the impact upon the behavior of the economy due to the initially neglected balance of payments, savings out of wages, and consumption out of profits items.

If we are to build a complete model of the economy on the basis of this profit equation, like the various econometric models used by business and government, we need to explain investment and the deficit.

Investment can be explained by interpreting the influence of expected profit flows, existing and anticipated debt servicing flows, the current prices of investment output and financial instruments, and the supply price of capital assets. In addition the state of uncertainty that determines the leverage ratios for current interim and position financing needs to be considered. Leverage ratios integrate borrower's and lender's risk (uncertainty) into the determination of current output.

The deficit is the difference between government spending and the tax take. Government spending is a policy variable that takes the form of government employment, transfer payment schemes, and purchases from private industry. The tax take reflects policy decisions as to tax schedules and the operation of the economy.

Total employment (labor demand) is the sum of employment in government, investment goods production, and consumer goods production. Inasmuch as government and investment goods production are given, the demand for labor in these two sectors is given. Given investment and the deficit as a schedule of the tax take, after tax profits are known. Profits in producing consumer goods are determined by subtracting profits in investment goods and in producing for government, from total profits.

Consumer goods production is carried to the point where profits in consumer goods production equals total profits minus those in investment goods production and in producing for government. We can think of two types of consumer goods production. In one type the price is fixed (profit margins per unit of output are fixed) and the output and thus employment varies. A second source of profits is from the sales and production of flexibly priced output. In this production the wage bill is fixed and the markup varies. The wage bill is divided by the preference system into spending for fixed price goods and spending for flexibly price goods. Wage income will expand by means of increased employment in fixed price outputs and this wage income will be divided between fixed and flexible-price outputs until the sum of the two types of profits in consumer goods production equals the profits to be earned in consumer goods production.[9]

If there is a deficit in the balance of trade then profits to be earned in consumption goods production need to be adjusted for the deficit (or surplus). As imports may be a function of consumption, the profits to be earned in consumption goods production may decrease as employment increases. Similarly consumption out of profits and savings out of wages will affect the employment in consumer goods production associated with each level of investment plus the government deficit.

The fundamental vision in this argument is that private employment is determined by profit opportunities. The aggregate profit opportunities in the economy are in the skeletal and essential analysis determined by investment and the government deficit. Investment and government spending generate profit opportunities in specific production, and wage income (or more generally consumers' disposable income) generates profit opportunities in the production of consumer goods. Unlike investment goods production, where banking considerations enforce a split of aggregate investment spending between wages and profits, profits in consumption goods production are determined by a variable markup on preestablished wage costs for flexibly priced outputs, and by variable employment and fixed markups for fixed price outputs. The preference systems of households determine how each level of aggregate employment (and total wage bill) is related to profits earned in industries characterized by flexible and fixed prices.

## VI. Profit determination and the validation of the financial structure

Profits are the cash flow that do or do not validate any particular structure of business debt. The expected level and stability of profits determines the debt structure that businessmen, their bankers, and the ultimate holders of the economy's assets will accept. In particular in an economy where there are serious consequences to default on financial obligations the potential downside deviation of profits from expected levels is an important determinant of acceptable debt structures.

The various profit formulas we have identified:

(1)              Profits = Investment

(2)   After Tax Profits = Investment + the Government Deficit

(3)   After Tax Profits = Investment + the Government Deficit
      − the Balance of Trade Deficit

(4)   After Tax Profits = Investment + the Government Deficit
   − the Balance of Trade Deficit + Consumption Out of Profit
      Income − Saving Out of Wage Income

are important in determining the currently acceptable debt structure and thus the current debt financing of demand, for they define the potential stability of profits. Each of Equations 1 through 4 represents a different structure of the economy and each structure will have a different expected behavior of profits over time.

The first case, Profits = Investment, represents a closed economy with a small government, an impoverished labor force, and a "puritanical" and efficient business class which constrains its consumption, in order to preserve and augment its capital, and runs a "tight ship" insofar as business overheads are concerned. In such an economy the amplitude of fluctuations in profits will be the same as the amplitude of fluctuations in investment.

The second case represents a closed economy with a substantial government in the sense that the in-place government spending and taxing schedules can lead to government deficits that are significant in relation to investment. If such government deficits are negatively correlated with investment, then the amplitude of the variations in after tax profits will be substantially smaller than the amplitude of fluctuations in investment.

The third case represents an open economy with a big government. In such an economy the flow of profits depends upon the course of the balance of trade as well as the course of investment and the government deficit. This indicates that the mercantilist perception—that a favorable balance of trade is good for an economy—has merit.

The fourth case represents an open economy with big government in which workers' income is high and stable enough so that workers can save and finance consumption through debt, and in which the administrative structure of business is bureaucratized and expensive so that a large part of profits is assigned to paying salaries and financing ancillary activities such as advertising. Salaries and advertising, in turn, finance consumption. Today's American economy is of this type.

In a closed economy with a small government (the first case) the ability of debtors to validate the debt structure by profit flows depends upon current investment. The use of debt to finance positions in capital assets is constrained by the expected volatility of investment. As investment depends upon the availability of external finance and short term financing is available on favorable terms (because of asset preferences and the institutional [banking] structure), fluctuations in financing terms and in profit expectations will lead to fluctuations in investment and in the validation of debts: an economy of the first type will tend to be cyclically unstable. The evolution of financial markets which facilitate the use of short term debt tends to build liability structures which can be sustained only if total investment increases at a rate that cannot for long be sustained. Frequent mild recessions and periodic deep depressions occur in such an economy. During recessions and depressions, payment commitments on the inherited debt structure are decreased through contract fulfillment, default, or refinancing.

The first case can be interpreted as representing the American economy before the Roosevelt era reforms and the Great Depression. The total federal government budget was small relative to the gross national product, working class savings were tiny and business was mainly entrepreneurial rather than highly bureaucratized. In these circumstances the volatility of investment was transformed into the volatility of the cash flows that enable business to validate debts. Whenever profits decreased hedge finance units became speculative and speculative units became Ponzi. Such induced transformations of the financial structure lead to falls in the prices of capital assets and therefore to a decline in investment. A recursive process is readily triggered in which a financial market failure leads to a fall in investment which leads to a fall in profits which leads to financial failures, further declines in investment, profits, additional failure, etc. This process was well described by Irving Fisher in 1933 and economists of the early thirties were aware that such a mode of operation was likely to occur.[10] The Federal Reserve System owes its existence to a felt need for a lender of last resort to prevent such cumulative deflationary processes from operating.

The second case can be considered as the essential or skeletal relation for an economy in which government is so big that the changes in the deficit can offset the effect of swings in investment on profits. In particular if government spending increases and revenues decrease when investment falls, then the flow of profits will tend to be stabilized. In such an economy if a financial disturbance leads to changes in acceptable financing terms the resulting fall in investment will lead to a fall in profits. This fall in profits will lead to shifts in inherited financial postures, so that the weight of speculative and Ponzi finance in the financial structure increases. This in turn leads to a further fall in asset prices and investment. However, as this is going on tax receipts decrease and government spending (today largely transfer payments) increases, i.e., the deficit increases. Whereas the decline in investment tends to lower profits the rising deficit tends to increase profits. The downside potential for profits is diminished. With profits sustained and increased by the government deficit, the shift of the debt structure toward increased weight of speculative and Ponzi finance ceases and is reversed. With gross profit flows stabilized, the reduction, funding, and otherwise restructuring of outstanding debts proceeds.[11]

In standard economic analysis the emphasis is upon how government spending affects aggregate demand and thus employment. Thus in the standard formulation, $Y = C + I + G$, the effects of government spending increasing and taxes decreasing would be felt in higher $C$, $I$, and $G$, leading to greater employment than would have ruled if government was small. In the analysis just sketched this income and employment effect of government is reinforced by a profits effect of government, especially big government.[12]

Much has been written of stabilization policy. The question that needs to be addressed is "What is it that needs to be stabilized if a threat of a recession/depression is to be contained and if a cumulative decline is to be halted?" The proposition that follows from the argument is that profits have to be stabilized in the sense that the downside variability of profits must be constrained. Big government and the deficits which can occur in an economy with big government are important in stabilizing the economy because they stabilize profit flows.

It should be noted that this stabilizing effect of big government has destabilizing implications in that once borrowers and lenders recognize that the downside instability of profits has decreased there will be an increase in the willingness and ability of business and bankers to debt-finance. If the cash flows to validate debt are virtually guaranteed by the profit implications of big government then debt-financing of positions in capital assets is encouraged. An inflationary consequence follows from the way the downside variability of aggregate profits is constrained by deficits.

The third type of economy is an open economy with a big government. For the balance of payments deficit to be a significant determinant of the course of profits the level of exports or imports must be of the same order of magnitude as investment. If profits determine the willingness of domestic producers to invest and the ability of investors to debt-finance then a favorable balance of trade will make for a rapidly developing economy. It should also be noted that an economy whose domestic profits depend upon a large balance of trade surplus is very vulnerable to whatever may cause a reversal of its surplus.

In some ways the Japanese economy is an example of a highly vulnerable open economy. Japanese manufacturing businesses use a great deal of debt-financing and export a large proportion of their output. Any reversal of the Japanese balance of trade surplus, unless it is accompanied by a burst in the government deficit, will lead to failures to validate debt.[13]

It is worth noting that the profit equation of an open economy with small government is

(3a)     Profits = Investment − The Balance of Trade Deficit.

In such an economy any sharp rise in the balance of trade deficit— or a decrease in the surplus—will lead to a deterioration of profits and the possibility of a deterioration of the financial structure.[14]

Although the fourth case is the most realistic statement of the profit determining relations for the American economy, data on the ratio of savings to wages and consumption to profits are not available. While this is a useful framework for analyzing the behavior of the American economy, its content depends to a large extent upon interpreting consumption out of profit income as largely due to the allocations of profits to salaries, research, advertising, and "business style" expenditures. What the full fourth case emphasizes is that the allocation of profits to consumption follows from the building of a bureaucratic business style, which, like inherited debt, may lead to current period "uncontrolled" expenditures.

## VII. Some data

To understand why our economy has behaved differently since 1946 than it did prior to 1939 we have to appreciate how the broad contours of demand have changed. In order to understand why our economy has behaved differently since the middle 1960s than it has earlier in the post-World War II epoch we have to appreciate how the broad contours of the financial structure have changed. The changes in the broad contours of demand have changed the reaction of aggregate profits to a change in investment and therefore have changed the cyclical behavior of the ability of business to validate its debts. The changes in the financial structure have increased the proportion of speculative and Ponzi finance in the total financial structure and therefore increased the vulnerability of the financial system to refinancing and debt validating crises. As a result since the middle 1960s there has been an increased need for Federal Reserve lender of last resort interventions and for contracyclical fiscal policy by which government deficits sustain business profits.

### The broad contours of demand

The great contraction of 1929-1933 took place in an environment of small government. In the prosperity year of 1929 gross national product was $103.4 billion and total Federal Government expenditures, combining both the purchases of goods and services and transfer payment to persons, were $2.6 billion. In the same year investment was $16.2 billion. In 1933, the year in which the great contraction bottomed out and in which the New Deal was started (Roosevelt was elected in November 1932 and took office in March 1933) gross national product was $55.8 billion and total Federal Government expenditures were $4.0 billion. Investment was $1.4 billion in 1933.

Recall that profits equal investment plus the deficit. There is no way a Federal Government that spent $4.0 billion in total can offset by its deficit the effect on business profits of a $14.8 billion drop in private investment. In 1929 business gross retained earnings were $11.7 billion. In 1933 they were $3.2 billion. Inasmuch as the debts of 1933 were largely a legacy of earlier years, the financial problem of business was to meet the payment commitments on debts entered into in prosperous years by cash flows generated by depression incomes.

With investment at $16.2 billion and a government of $2.6 billion (as in 1929) there was no way an automatic or semi-automatic response of government spending or taxation could offset the drop of investment. Between 1929 and 1933 gross investment fell by $14.8 billion (from $16.2 to $1.4 billion) and government expenditures rose by $1.4 billion (to $4.0 from $2.6 billion). Business Gross Retained Earnings—a measure of the internal funds available to finance investment and meet payment commitments on account of the principal amount due on debts—fell from $11.7 billion in 1929 to $3.2 billion in 1933.

The recession of 1973-75 was the longest and deepest recession of the postwar period. Of course it is not at all comparable to the great contraction of 1929-33, but it is the best we can do for comparative purposes. This contraction took place in the context of big government. In 1973 gross national product was $1306.6 billion and total Federal Government expenditures were $265.0 billion. Federal Government expenditures were some 20.3 percent of gross national product. Investment in 1973 was $220.6 billion.

The behavior of investment, government expenditures, and profits over the 1973-75 recession stands in sharp contrast to the 1929-33 behavior. In terms of the index of industrial production the drop from 125.6 in September 1974 to 109.9 in May of 1975 was very steep indeed; the rise in unemployment from about 5 million in July of 1974 to a peak of 8.25 million in May of 1975 was a great shock to the nation—within a year the unemployment rate jumped from the neighborhood of 5 to 9 percent. In spite of the steepness of the decline in industrial production, Business Gross Retained Earnings increased substantially between 1973 and 1975. Between 1973 and 1975 gross investment fell from $220.2 billion to $190.9 billion—a decline of some $29.3 billion. Over the same years government expenditures rose from $265.0 billion to $356.8 billion (mainly but not exclusively in transfer payments), a rise of $91.8 billion. As a result, in spite of the rise in unemployment rates and the substantial decline in industrial production, business gross retained profits rose from $140.2 billion in 1973 to $176.2 billion

Table I

## Gross National Product and Its Major Components, Selected Years 1929 through 1979
### (In billions of dollars)

| Year | Gross national product | Consumption | Investment | Government purchase | | | Transfer payments to persons | Exports | Federal Government expenditures | Business gross retained earnings |
| | | | | Total | Federal | State and local | | | | |
|---|---|---|---|---|---|---|---|---|---|---|
| 1929 | 103.4 | 77.3 | 16.2 | 8.8 | 1.4 | 7.4 | 0.9 | 7.0 | 2.6 | 11.7 |
| 1933 | 55.8 | 45.8 | 1.4 | 8.3 | 2.1 | 6.2 | 1.5 | 2.4 | 4.0 | 3.2 |
| 1939 | 90.8 | 67.0 | 9.3 | 13.5 | 5.2 | 8.3 | 2.5 | 4.4 | 8.9 | 8.8 |
| 1949 | 258.0 | 178.1 | 35.3 | 38.4 | 20.4 | 18.0 | 11.7 | 15.9 | 41.3 | 31.4 |
| 1959 | 486.5 | 310.8 | 77.6 | 97.6 | 53.9 | 43.7 | 25.2 | 23.7 | 91.0 | 58.5 |
| 1969 | 935.5 | 579.7 | 146.2 | 207.9 | 97.5 | 110.4 | 62.7 | 54.7 | 188.4 | 101.7 |
| 1973 | 1,306.6 | 809.9 | 220.2 | 269.5 | 102.2 | 167.3 | 113.5 | 101.6 | 265.0 | 140.2 |
| 1974 | 1,412.9 | 889.6 | 214.6 | 302.7 | 111.1 | 191.5 | 134.9 | 137.9 | 299.3 | 137.9 |
| 1975 | 1,528.8 | 979.1 | 190.9 | 338.4 | 123.1 | 215.4 | 170.6 | 147.3 | 356.8 | 176.2 |
| 1979 | 2,368.5 | 1,509.8 | 386.2 | 476.1 | 166.3 | 309.8 | 241.9 | 257.4 | 508.0 | 276.0 |

Source: Economic Report of the President January 1980, table B1 p. 203, except Government transfer payments to persons table B18 p. 223, Federal Government expenditures, table B72 p. 288, and gross retained earnings, table B8 p. 213.

Table II

## Gross National Product and Its Major Components, Selected Years 1929 through 1979
(As a percentage of gross national product)

| Year | Gross national product | Consumption | Investment | Government purchase Total | Government purchase Federal | Government purchase State and local | Transfer payments to persons | Exports | Federal Government expenditures | Business gross retained earnings |
|------|------|------|------|------|------|------|------|------|------|------|
| 1929 | 100.0 | 74.8 | 15.7 | 8.5 | 1.2 | 7.2 | 0.1 | 6.8 | 2.5 | 11.3 |
| 1933 | | 82.1 | 2.5 | 14.9 | 3.8 | 11.1 | 2.7 | 4.3 | 7.2 | 5.7 |
| 1939 | | 74.2 | 10.3 | 15.0 | 5.8 | 9.2 | 2.8 | 4.8 | 9.8 | 9.7 |
| 1949 | | 69.0 | 13.7 | 14.9 | 7.9 | 7.0 | 4.5 | 6.2 | 16.0 | 12.2 |
| 1959 | | 63.9 | 16.0 | 20.1 | 11.1 | 9.0 | 5.2 | 4.9 | 18.7 | 12.0 |
| 1969 | | 62.0 | 15.6 | 22.2 | 10.4 | 11.8 | 6.7 | 5.8 | 20.1 | 10.9 |
| 1973 | | 62.0 | 16.9 | 20.6 | 7.8 | 12.8 | 8.7 | 7.8 | 20.3 | 10.7 |
| 1974 | | 62.9 | 15.2 | 21.4 | 7.9 | 13.5 | 9.5 | 9.8 | 21.2 | 9.8 |
| 1975 | | 64.0 | 12.5 | 22.1 | 8.1 | 14.1 | 11.2 | 9.6 | 23.3 | 11.5 |
| 1979 | | 63.7 | 16.3 | 20.1 | 7.0 | 13.0 | 10.2 | 10.9 | 21.4 | 11.7 |

Source: Table I.

in 1975—a rise of $36 billion or 25.7 percent.

The budget deficit rather than government spending enters the profit equation. In 1929 the Federal Government ran a surplus of $1.2 billion and in 1933 the deficit was $1.3 billion, a swing of $2.5 billion or 2.4 percent of the 1929 Gross National Product. In 1973 the deficit was $6.7 billion, in 1975 it was $70.6 billion, an increase of $63.9 billion; the swing in the deficit was 4.7 percent of GNP. But more important the swing in the deficit of $60.7 billion more than compensated for the swing in investment of $29.3 billion.

In standard policy analysis the impact of big government and the government deficit on profits and therefore on the ability of business to fulfill its financial liabilities is overlooked. If business cannot meet its commitments on debts then the financing loop, by which funds are made available to business, is broken. Furthermore if the rate at which business fails to meet its obligations increases then the risk premiums that enter into the calculations of business and financial organizations increase. If profits are sustained and increased even as business investment falls then the balance sheets of business are improved at a rapid rate. The quick recovery from the decline of 1973-75 can be in good measure imputed to the enormous government deficit. If in 1973-75 the Congress and the Administration had tried to hold back the explosive growth of the deficit then the recession would have been deeper and longer, and the rate of inflation would have been much lower in 1979 and 1980 than in fact it is.

### The broad contours of the financial structure, 1950-1975

In order to understand why our economy has been much more unstable in the years since the mid-1960s than earlier in the postwar era we have to examine the changes in the financial structure. An exhaustive and in detail study of the evolution of the United States financial structure that uses the analytical foundation of this paper would be useful; however this paper is not the place for it.

A thorough research study should examine the changing composition of the assets and liabilities of the various sectors and the implications of this changing structure, as well as changes in financing terms, for the cash flows of the various sectors of the economy. The cash flow structure due to liabilities need then be integrated with the cash flow from assets and the various cash flows due to income production. In particular the changing relations between cash receipts and payment obligations and between payment obligations and the margins of safety need be understood.

In the absence of such a thorough study we will examine some time series for nonfinancial corporations, households, and commercial banking—the three sectors that would constitute a simple economy with finance. The sectors and the data are from the Board of Governors Flow of Funds Accounts.

## Nonfinancial corporations

In Chart I the ratio of Gross Fixed Investment to Gross Internal Funds for nonfinancial corporations for the years 1950-1979 is shown. The data on this chart show the extent to which fixed investment was being financed by gross internal flows and the extent to which there was a dependence on external funds. The evidence from the first fifteen years shows a mild cycle in this ratio, along with a downward trend. Ignoring 1950, the maximum ratio was 1.15 in 1951. If we look at the years 1958-1967 we see that fixed investment was at a maximum 1.05 of internal funds and in 6 of the 10 years fixed investment was less than internal funds.

In the years since 1967 this ratio has exhibited both increasing fluctuations and an apparent strong upward trend. The cycles of the period show up strongly in this series. In 1970 the ratio hit 1.30 and dropped to 1.15 in 1972. In 1974 the ratio was greater than 1.5 and in 1975 it barely exceeded 1.0, in 1976 it dropped below 1, and it exceeded 1.25 by 1979. The time series on Fixed Investment/Internal Funds indicates that there was a change in the

Chart I

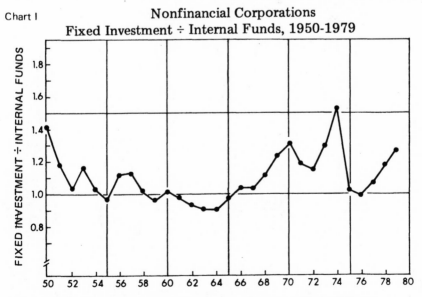

Nonfinancial Corporations
Fixed Investment ÷ Internal Funds, 1950-1979

*Source*: Board of Governors Federal Reserve System—Flow of Funds Accounts

mode of operation of the economy in the mid-1960s. Prior to the mid-1960s corporations seem to have been internally financing their fixed investment whereas the data indicate that there was an increased dependency on external finance after the middle 1960s.

Chart II measures the ratio of Total Liabilities to Internal Funds of nonfinancial corporations. This chart is indicative of the trend of payment commitments of business on account of debt relative to the funds available to pay such debts. The liabilities are a proxy for the payment commitments; of course the length of maturity of the liabilities and the interest rate on the liabilities would determine the cash flows required per period. Furthermore the internal funds should be augmented by interest and dividends paid to get a measure of gross capital income after taxes, which is the true variable that measures the ability of cash flows to validate a debt structure.

This crude approximation to what truly should be measured indicates that the middle 1960s saw a break in the relationships that determine this data. Up to 1967 the ratio exhibited mild fluctuation around a somewhat downward trend; since those dates the data show a strong cycle and upward trend. The ratio of liabilities to internal funds was mainly in the range of 6.2 to 7.2 from 1950 through 1967. After 1967 the ratio began to rise and exhibit sharp fluctuation, hitting 9.4 in 1970, 8.3 in 1972, and 10.75 in 1974 be-

Chart II

Nonfinancial Corporations
Total Liabilities ÷ Internal Funds, 1950-1979

*Source*: Board of Governors Federal Reserve System——Flow of Funds Accounts

fore falling to 7.2 in 1977. It then increased to 8.5 in 1979. The high peaks hit in 1970 and again in 1974 indicate that at the tail end of the recent business cycle expansions the ability of business cash flows to sustain debt may well have been under pressure.

Charts I and II showed the ratio of a flow (in Chart I, gross fixed investment) and a stock (in Chart II, total liabilities) to a flow (internal funds) that is one measure of business profitability and ability to meet payment commitments. Chart III shows the time series for total liabilities divided by demand deposits and for open market paper divided by total liabilities. Both series in Chart III measure an aspect of the quality of the balance sheets of nonfinancial corporations. The liability/demand deposit ratio measures the extent to which payment commitments can be met by cash on hand if there is an interruption of cash flows in the form of gross profits. The other ratio reflects an attempt to measure the extent to which business is financing its activities by tapping volatile or exotic sources. The class "open market paper" includes commercial paper—a volatile source—and borrowings from finance companies —a generally expensive source.

Even though the series measure quite different variables they show a remarkably similar pattern: a rather mild upward trend in the 1960s, a pause between 1960 and 1964 or 1966, and then an upward thrust that is stronger than the thrust before the middle

Chart III                  Nonfinancial Corporations
Total Liabilities ÷ Demand Deposits and Open
Market Paper, etc. ÷ Total Liabilities, 1950-1979

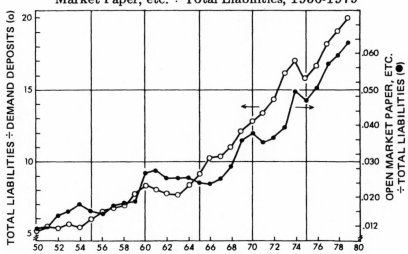

Source: Board of Governors Federal Reserve System——Flow of Funds Accounts

1960s. The first fifteen years of the time series are quite different in the rate of growth they indicate as taking place. It is interesting to note that the break in 1974 shows up in both series.

The data presented for nonfinancial corporations indicate that something changed in the middle 1960s. The ratios of debt to internal funds, of liabilities to demand deposits, and of open market paper to total liabilities indicate that the corporate sector not only now has greater debt payments to make relative to cash flows but also that the margin of safety for debt in cash on hand has decreased, and the reliance by business on volatile and relatively uncertain sources of financing has increased. The difference between the two indicates that the liability structure of nonfinancial corporations can not only amplify but even initiate a disturbance in financial markets.

## Households

The ratios of liabilities of households to income and to cash on hand (demand deposits and currency) tell a story of something changing in the middle 1970s. Once again the data examined is a proxy for the desired but unavailable data on the payment commitments due to debt.

The payment commitments on household liabilities will typically be paid by disposable personal income. Between 1950 and 1965

Chart IV    Households Liabilities Divided by
1. Disposable Personal Income
2. Demand Deposits & Currency, 1950-1979

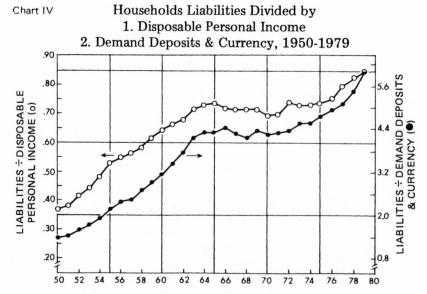

*Source*: Board of Governors Federal Reserve System——Flow of Funds Accounts

the ratio of liabilities to consumer disposable income increased monotonically from .37 to .74—the ratio doubled. From 1965 until 1975, this ratio fluctuated between .74 and .69. In 1976 it stood at .76, in 1977 at .80, in 1978 at .83, and in 1979 at .85. The era of financial turbulence that began in the mid-1960s saw little movement in the ratio of liabilities to disposable personal income until after the mid-1970s when the ratio resumed its rise.

As is evident from Chart IV, the ratio of total household liabilities to demand deposits and currency showed virtual parallel development to that of the ratio of household liabilities to disposable personal income.

The data for households indicates that the turbulence of the mid-1960s to mid-1970s was not mainly due to household debt being an ever increasing burden. The rise in the ratios in the late 1970s can be interpreted as a reaction to inflationary expectation; however if it is so interpreted then it took a long period of inflation combined with instability to affect expectations.

*Commercial banking*

The data for commercial banking does not show the sharp changes in the mid-1960s that are so striking for both nonfinancial corporate business and households. In Chart V it is evident that the ratio of financial net worth to total liabilities rose through the 1950s reaching a peak in 1960 and then began a decline which with few

Chart V    Commercial Banking Financial Net Worth and
Protected Assets as Ratio to Total Liabilities, 1950-1979

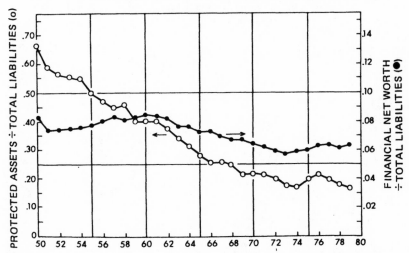

*Source*: Board of Governors Federal Reserve System——Flow of Funds Accounts

interruptions lasted until 1973. The evidence indicates that the difficulties of 1974-75 led to a rise in the ratio, which seems to have been transitory.

The ratio of protected assets [U.S. government securities, vault cash, and member bank reserves] to total liabilities—also in Chart V—shows a steady decline from 1950 to 1974. It appears as if there was a slight decrease in the steepness of the decline in the mid-1960s. The banking trauma of 1974-75 shows up in the rise of protected assets relative to liabilities.

In Chart VI two ratios—that of demand deposits and bought money to total liabilities—are exhibited [bought money is the sum of large negotiable certificates of deposit, deposits at foreign banking offices, Federal funds, security repurchase agreements, and open market paper]. The ratio of demand deposits to total liabilities showed a steady decline from almost .70 to .25 over 1950-79. The behavior of demand deposits relative to total liabilities is striking evidence of the change in the character of banking that has taken place in the postwar period. In the beginning of the postwar era the commercial banking system mainly owned protected assets and it financed these asset holdings by demand deposits. In recent years the commercial banking system's ownership of protected assets has fallen to below 20 percent of total liabilities even as its demand deposits have fallen to about 25 percent of liabilities. Today the commercial banking system mainly holds private debts and it finances this ownership by liabilities other than demand deposits.

Chart VI    Commercial Banking Demand Deposits and Bought Money ÷ Total Liabilities, 1950-1979

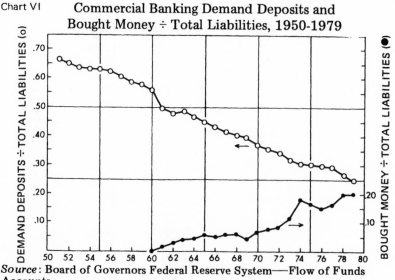

Source: Board of Governors Federal Reserve System—Flow of Funds Accounts

Beginning in 1960—and at an accelerating rate after 1969—bought money in the form of large negotiable certificates of deposit (CDs), deposits at foreign banking offices, Federal funds purchased, security repurchase agreements, and open market paper became significant bank liabilities. Of these liabilities, deposits at foreign banking offices existed throughout the postwar period but they were a trivial fraction of total commercial bank liabilities in the early years.

The introduction and rapid growth of negotiable CDs after 1960 marked the introduction of bought money and liability management as a significant factor in banking. Since then there has been a virtual proliferation of instruments only a few of which can be identified in the flow of funds data. For example the flow of funds data do not enable us to isolate bankers' acceptances or the money market rate time deposits at commercial banks. Nevertheless even with this truncated list, by 1979 bought money was virtually as significant as demand deposits as a source of bank funds.

## VIII. The answers to the initial questions

Our analysis leads to a result that the way our economy functions depends on the level, stability, and prospects of profits. Profits are the lure that motivates business and they are the flow that determines whether decisions taken in the past are apt in the light of the way the economy is functioning now. The flow of aggregate profits is the link between the past and the present and the lure of future profits determines the flow of current profits.

The quest for profits has a side effect in that investments result in capital assets and the capital assets that come on stream determine the changes in the production process that are available to produce output. Thus the aptness of the details of the investments undertaken determines the course of useful productive capacity and changes in the ratio of useful output to labor used, i.e., productivity. If on the whole investment is apt then the improvement in techniques that result yield a large enough margin over labor costs to induce sufficient investment to sustain profits. If the incremental outputs—or the outputs that are produced with the inherited capital stock—are not apt then the flow of profits will be attenuated. This tends to decrease investment. Similarly as the foreign balance deteriorates or the savings ratios of households increase the flow of profits decreases. A decrease in the flow of profits can start a recursive process that decreases total investment, profits, etc.

In our current "big government" capitalism, this recursive process is soon halted by the impact of government deficits in sustaining profits. Whenever the deficit explodes (as in 1975 II) the aggregate flow of profits to business increases. Investment turns out to be profitable even if the investments that come on stream are inept. The impact on profits of the deficits that big government generates can override the failure of investments to increase the productivity of labor; big government is a shield that protects an inefficient industrial structure. When aggregate profits are sustained or increased, even as output falls and the ratio of output to man hours worked does not increase, prices will rise. Thus the generation of sustained and rising profits by government deficits is inflationary whereas rising profits that are due to increases in output when labor productivity increases relative to money wages can be associated with falling prices.

Thus the current policy problem of inflation and declining rates of growth of labor productivity are not causally related but rather they are the result of a common cause, the generation of profits by means of government deficits where the government deficits do not result from spending that leads to useful output.

The answer to the first question—"Why haven't we had a great or even serious depression since 1946?"—is that our big government that is in place has made it impossible for profits to collapse as in 1929-1933. As the government deficit now virtually explodes whenever unemployment increases business profits in the aggregate are sustained. The combined effects of big government as a demander of goods and services, as a generator—through its deficits—of business profits and as a provider to financial markets of high-grade default-free liabilities when there is a reversion from private debt means that big government is a three way stabilizer in our economy and that the very process of stabilizing the economy sets the stage for a subsequent bout of accelerating inflation.

There is a second reason for our not having a serious depression since 1946. Once the interrelations involved in financing a sustained expansion led to the emergence of a fragile financial structure in the mid-1960s, the Federal Reserve has intervened strongly as a lender of last resort whenever a financial crisis threatens. This intervention by the Federal Reserve both helps stop the plunge to a deep depression and assures that the subsequent recovery from the rather mild depression that does take place will be inflationary.

The shift from the tranquil progress of 1946-65 to the turbulence of recent years is mainly due to the change in the financing relations of business, households, and financial institutions. At the end of World War II the financial structure that was a legacy of war finance and the portfolio preferences that reflected the great depression led to a regime of conservative finance. There is no way that a financial crisis could develop in an economy in which bank protected assets, mainly U.S. Government debt, were 60 percent of total liabilities. Similarly household and business balance sheets and liability-income relations were such that business could readily fulfill its payment commitments.

The analysis indicates that stagflation is the price we pay for the success we have had in avoiding a great or serious depression. The techniques that have been used since the mid-sixties to abort the debt-deflations have clearly been responsible for the stepwise acceleration in the inflation rates. The argument we have put forth indicates that stepwise accelerating inflation has been a corollary of the validation of an inept business structure and poorly chosen investments by government deficits and thus inflation has been associated with a decline in the rate of growth. The continuing taut liability structures due to the ever greater reliance on debt has led to the shortening of business horizons. The very turbulence of the economy operates against prudent investment and finance. The general economic tone since the mid-sixties has been conducive to short-run speculation rather than to the long-run capital development of the economy.

The final conclusion that emerges is that the problems as evident in the American economy since the mid-1960s are not due to vagaries of budget deficits or to errors in controlling the money supply: the problems reflect the normal way our type of economy operates after a run of successful years. If we are to do better it is necessary to reform the structure of our economy so that the instability due to a financial structure heavily weighted with debt is diminished.

## Notes

1. Milton Friedman and Anna J. Schwartz. *A Monetary History of the United States 1867-1960* (Princeton: National Bureau of Economic Research. 1963).

2. Peter Temin, *Did Monetary Forces Cause the Great Depression?* (New York: W. W. Norton & Co., Inc., 1976).

3. In the economic literature, following Marshall and Keynes, this residual is called quasi-rent.

4. As this was being prepared a magnificent example of Ponzi financing became "public property" in the problems of the Hunts and their margin financing of positions in silver.

5. In an economy with massive transfer payment schemes, significant dividend and interest income, and significantly high income taxes, the relevant household income might well be consumer disposable income.

6. This is a "quick and dirty summary" of a key position in the Two

Cambridge Debate. See G. H. Harcourt, *Some Cambridge Controversies in the Theory of Capital* (Cambridge: Cambridge University Press, 1972).

7. The proposition about profits and investment is by Kalecki. See M. Kalecki, *Selected Essays on the Dynamics of the Capitalist Economy 1933-1970* (Cambridge: Cambridge University Press, 1971).

8. These propositions about profits were in Kalecki, op cit. See also Hyman P. Minsky, "The Financial Instability Hypothesis: A Restatement" (*Thames Papers in Political Economy*: Thames Polytechnic, 1978). See Chapter 5, below, pp. 90-116.

9. In sundry recent writings J. R. Hicks has been making much about fixed and flexible price outputs. See *The Crisis in Keynesian Economics* (New York: Basic Books, 1974).

10. Irving Fisher, "The Debt Deflation Theory of Big Depression," *Econometrica* 1 (1933).

11. It is estimated that in the current (1980) United States economy, each percentage point increase in the measured unemployment rate is associated with a $27 to $30 billion increase in the deficit. Thus if the prospective budget is balanced at a 7 percent unemployment rate a 10 percent unemployment rate will be associated with a deficit of $80 to $90 billion even if Congress takes no expansionary tax or spending actions.

12. The econometric models used in forecasting by the various government departments and private forecasting services are built on $Y = C + I + G$. Once this base is selected then financial considerations can only play a peripheral role in determining system behavior. As far as I know debts, and the need of profits to validate a debt structure and the market price of assets, are not integrated into the structure of existing forecasting and simulation models in any essential way. Such models are at best relevant to an era of financial tranquility like that which ruled in 1946-65.

13. This is what happened in 1974-75. The rise in the price of oil and the recession in the United States led to an enormous deficit in Japan's trade balance and a wave of business failures. The Japanese economy was inflated out of that crisis.

14. The Smoot-Hawley tariff led to change in the balance of payments of many countries with small government and therefore exacerbated the developing international depression. While Smoot-Hawley was not the cause of the Great Depression it was a factor that amplified what, even so, was a large downturn.

# 3

The Financial
Instability Hypothesis:
An Interpretation of
Keynes and an Alternative
to "Standard" Theory

## Introduction

Professor Jacob Viner of the University of Chicago wrote a long and serious review of Keynes's *General Theory*—the only review which drew a rebuttal by Keynes. Professor Viner maintained that the *General Theory* really did not make a sharp break with traditional economics and that Keynes achieved novel results because velocity was allowed to vary and prices and wages were assumed to be rigid.[1] Professor Viner's review pointed toward the neoclassical synthesis, which can be said to have reached maturity with Patinkin's work at Chicago.[2]

In his rebuttal Keynes rejected Professor Viner's interpretation and offered a concise statement of the *General Theory*.[3] Once Keynes's rebuttal to Viner is used as a key to disentangle the new from the old, an interpretation of the *General Theory* as "a theory of why output and employment are so liable to fluctuations" emerges.[4] The interpretation of the *General Theory* that follows from Keynes's argument is inconsistent with both the Hicks-Hansen formulation of Keynesian theory and the neoclassical synthesis.[5] Furthermore, the interpretation of the *General Theory* that is consistent with Keynes's rebuttal to Viner leads to a theory of the capitalist economic process that is more relevant and useful for understanding our economy than the standard neoclassical theory. This theory, which builds upon an interpretation of Keynes, is the "financial instability hypothesis."[6]

The main objective of this paper is to state succinctly the finan-

Reprinted from the *Nebraska Journal of Economics and Business*, Winter 1977, Vol. 16, No. 1, by arrangement with the publisher.

cial instability hypothesis, and to indicate briefly why it is better suited to our economy than the dominant neoclassical synthesis. Before proceeding to the statement of the financial instability view, a brief argument is essayed to show how an interpretation of the *General Theory* that rests upon Keynes's rebuttal to Viner leads to the financial instability hypothesis.

The legitimacy of the financial instability hypothesis as an interpretation of Keynes is not as important as the relevance of this hypothesis to our economy. The connection between Keynes and the financial instability hypothesis is emphasized because the author's version of the financial instability hypothesis did arise out of an attempt to understand Keynes in light of the crunches and other financial disturbances of the past decade. Even though extreme financial disturbances took place during the gestation period of the *General Theory*, subsequent interpretative literature has ignored financial instability.

### Interpretation of the *General Theory* in light of Keynes' rebuttal to Professor Viner

From the perspective of the standard economic theory of Keynes's day and the presently dominant neoclassical theory, both financial crises and serious fluctuations of output and employment are anomalies: the theory offers no explanation of these phenomena. In the *General Theory* Keynes developed a theory of the capitalist process which was able to explain financial and output instability as the result of market behavior in the face of uncertainty. Unfortunately, the statement of this new theory is often obscured by vestiges of the old theory. A clear and precise statement of the new was not achieved by Keynes until his rebuttal to Viner. The view of the *General Theory* that emerges, once the reply to Viner is used as a key, is markedly different from the standard interpretation.

The new theory that emerges focuses upon the investment decision within the context of capitalist financial practices as the key determinant of aggregate activity. In his rebuttal to Viner, Keynes insisted that the main propositions of the *General Theory* center around the disequilibrating forces that operate in financial markets. These disequilibrating forces directly affect the valuation of capital assets relative to the prices of current output, and this price ratio, along with financial market conditions, determines investment activity. The *General Theory* is thus concerned with how these two sets of prices (capital and financial assets on the one hand, and current output and wages on the other) are determined in different markets and by different forces in our economy, and why such an economy is "so given to fluctuations."

Construction of standard economic theory——the neoclassical synthesis——starts by examining bartering, such as might take place at a village fair, and proceeds by adding production, capital assets, money, and financial assets to the basic model. Such a village fair paradigm shows that a decentralized market mechanism can lead to a coherent result, but it cannot explain the periodic rupturing of coherence as an endogenous phenomenon. In Keynes's view, the rupturing of coherence originates in financial usages and spreads by way of investment activity. In order to explain how this takes place, it is necessary to abandon the village fair paradigm and the definition of money as merely an expediter of transactions.

In the *General Theory* Keynes adopts a City or a Wall Street paradigm: the economy is viewed from the board room of a Wall Street investment bank. Theorizing starts by assuming a monetary economy with sophisticated financial institutions. In such an economy, money is not just a generalized ration point that makes the double coincidence of wants unnecessary for trading to take place; money is a special type of bond that emerges as positions in capital assets are financed. Keynes clearly stated this conception of money in a 1931 essay:

> There is a multitude of real assets in the world which constitutes our capital wealth——buildings, stocks of commodities, goods in the course of manufacture and of transport, and so forth. The nominal owners of these assets, however, have not infrequently borrowed *money* in order to become possessed of them. To a corresponding extent the actual owners of wealth have claims, not on real assets, but on money. A considerable part of this "financing" takes place through the banking system, which interposes its guarantee between its depositors who lend it money, and its borrowing customers to whom it loans money wherewith to finance the purchase of real assets. The interposition of this veil of money between the real asset and the wealth owner is a specially marked characteristic of the modern world. [7]

This conception of money, as a financing veil between the "real asset and the wealth owner," is a natural way for a banker to view money, and is fundamental to understanding both Keynes and our economy. [8]

To Keynes, we live in a world ". . . in which changing views about the future are capable of influencing the quantity of employment." [9] The current variables most directly affected by changing views about the future are financial variables, such as the market valuation of capital assets, the prices of financial assets, and behavior with respect to liability structures both by businessmen and by their bankers. Once a financial perspective is adopted, time cannot be interpreted away as just adding additional commodities to the economy. In Keynes's theory, "time" is calendar time and the future always is uncertain.[10] Thus investment and financing decisions are made in the face of intractable uncertainty, and uncertainty implies that views about the future can undergo marked changes in short periods of time. In particular, changing views of the future affect the relative price of various capital assets and financial instruments, as well as the relation between capital-asset price and the price of current output.[11]

In Keynes's view, the financial attributes of a capitalist economy lead to the observed unstable behavior. In an economy with a sophisticated financial system, the financing veil encompasses many more financial instruments than any narrow—or even extended—money concept includes. In particular, Keynes's financing view of money means that ". . . money enters into the economic scheme in an essential and peculiar manner. . . ."[12] This is in marked contrast to the classical and today's standard neoclassical economic theory, for, in both, money does not affect the essential behavior of the economy.

There are interesting problems in the history of ideas revolving around the loss of those aspects of Keynes's *General Theory* that point to the business cycle interpretation of that seminal work, but these will not be considered here. Instead, the rest of this article will be concerned with a statement of the "financial instability hypothesis" as a theory which endeavors to explain "the phenomena of the Trade Cycle."[13] This hypothesis is one among a number of interpretations of Keynes which differ from the standard interpretation.[14] The claim to "legitimacy" of this interpretation will not be documented further: the hypothesis will be put forth not as an interpretation of Keynes but rather as an alternative to current standard neoclassical theory.

## The financial instability view of our economy

The first twenty years after World War II were characterized by financial tranquility. No serious threat of a financial crisis or a debt-deflation process (such as Irving Fisher described[15]) took place. The decade since 1966 has been characterized by financial turmoil. Three threats of financial crisis occurred, during which Federal Reserve interventions in money and financial markets were needed to abort the potential crises.

The first post-World War II threat of a financial crisis that required Federal Reserve special intervention was the so-called "credit crunch" of 1966. This episode centered around a "run" on bank-negotiable certificates of deposit. The second occurred in 1970, and the immediate focus of the difficulties was a "run" on the commercial paper market following the failure of the Penn-Central Railroad. The third threat of a crisis in the decade occurred in 1974-75 and involved a large number of over-extended financial positions, but perhaps can be best identified as centering around the speculative activities of the giant banks. In this third episode the Franklin National Bank of New York, with assets of $5 billion as of December 1973, failed after a "run" on its overseas branch.

Since this recent financial instability is a recurrence of phenomena that regularly characterized our economy before World War II, it is reasonable to view financial crises as systemic, rather than accidental, events. From this perspective, the anomaly is the twenty years after World War II during which financial crises were absent, which can be explained by the extremely robust financial structure that resulted from a Great War following hard upon a deep depression. Since the middle sixties the historic crisis-prone behavior of an economy with capitalist financial institutions has reasserted itself. The past decade differs from the era before World War II in that embryonic financial crises have been aborted by a combination of support operations by the Federal Reserve and the income, employment, and financial effects that flow from an immensely larger government sector. This success has had a side effect, however; accelerating inflation has followed each success in aborting a financial crisis.

Looking at the economy from a Wall Street board room, we see a paper world——a world of commitments to pay cash today and in the future. These cash flows are a legacy of past contracts in which money today was exchanged for money in the future.[16] In addition, we see deals being made in which commitments to pay cash in the future are exchanged for cash today. The viability of this paper world rests upon the cash flows (or gross profits after out-of-pocket costs and taxes) that business organizations, households, and governmental bodies, such as states and municipalities, receive as a result of the income-generating process.

The focus will be on business debt, because this debt is an essential characteristic of a capitalist economy. The validation of business debt requires that prices and outputs be such that almost all firms earn large enough surpluses over labor and material costs either to fulfill the gross payments required by debt or to induce refinancing. Refinancing takes place only if gross profits are expected to be large enough to either validate the new debt or induce further refinancing.

Gross profits in the production of consumer goods depend upon the expenditures on consumer goods by wage earners in consumption and investment goods production and by those who receive income from other than the production process. If the simplifying assumption is made that wage income is received only from the production of consumer and investment goods, that only wage income is spent on consumption goods, and that all of wage income is so spent, then the markup on labor costs in the production of consumer goods will be the wage bill in the production of investment goods.[17] This simple formula can be expanded to allow for wage income from state employment, income received from transfer payments, consumption spending out of profits, and savings by receivers of income. Total spending on consumer goods yields a realized markup on labor costs in the production of consumer goods. The markup on labor costs generates the gross profits from operations.

Profit margins in the production of investment goods are not determined in as direct a manner as for consumption goods. Profit flows are always determined, however, by the relative scarcity of specific capital assets. The relative scarcity of capital assets used to produce investment goods, and thus the difference between gross revenues and wage costs in the production of investment goods, depands upon the pace of investment. The funds that are available to meet commitments on debts of both consumer- and investment-goods producers are a function of investment. It follows that present acceptable liability structures reflect current speculations on the course of future investment.

Not only are gross profits after taxes the funds available for the validation of the debts which were used to finance control over capital assets, but the excess of gross profits after taxes over debt payment commitments is the cash flow that accrues to equity share holders. Equity share prices are the result of capitalizing the expected residual cash flows. Equity share prices—which fluctuate in a world with Wall Street—are a determinant of the market valuation of capital assets as collected in firms. The market value of capital assets affects the demand price for investment goods, which, together with supply conditions of investment goods and conditions in financial markets, determines investment.

If our world includes government purchases of goods and services and transfer payments, then gross profits in the production of consumer and investment goods also depend upon government deficits. In our present world, a sharp shift to government deficit financing—as occurred in the four quarters 1974 IV-1975 III—not only sustains demand but also sustains and may even increase business profits. The business profits implications of big government offset a tendency for the debt-sustaining capacity of business to diminish whenever financial market distrubances induce a decline in consumer and business spending. The economy has behaved differently in the postwar period than in earlier epochs, mainly because of the increase in the relative size of the federal government, not necessarily because of any greater skill of policy makers.

The behavior of our economy therefore depends upon the pace of investment. In a capitalist economy the valuation that is placed upon capital assets, which determines current investment, and the ability to fulfill contractual commitments, which determines financing possibilities, depend critically upon the pace of gross profits. Gross profits, in turn, are largely determined by investment. Thus the ability to debt finance new investment depends upon expectations that future investment will be high enough so that future cash flows will be large enough for the debts that are issued today to be repaid or refinanced.

An economy with private debts is especially vulnerable to changes in the pace of investment, for investment determines both aggregate demand and the viability of debt structures. The instability that such an economy exhibits follows from the subjective nature of expectations about the future course of investment, as well as the subjective determination by bankers and their business clients of the appropriate liability structure for the financing of positions in different types of capital assets. In a world with capitalist financial usages, uncertainty—in the sense of Keynes—is a major determinant of the path of income and employment.

The natural starting place for analyzing the relation between debt and income is to take an economy with a cyclical past that is now doing well.[18] The inherited debt reflects the history of the economy, which includes a period in the not too distant past in which the economy did not do well. Acceptable liability structures are based upon some margin of safety so that expected cash flows, even in periods when the economy is not doing well, will cover contractual debt payments. As the period over which the economy does well lengthens, two things become evident in board rooms. Existing debts are easily validated and units that were heavily in debt prospered; it paid to lever. After the event it becomes apparent that the margins of safety built into debt structures were too great. As a result, over a period in which the economy does well, views about acceptable debt structure change. In the deal-making that goes on between banks, investment bankers, and businessmen, the acceptable amount of debt to use in financing various types of activity and positions increases. This increase in the weight of debt financing raises the market price of capital assets and increases investment. As this continues the economy is transformed into a boom economy.

Stable growth is inconsistent with the manner in which investment is determined in an economy in which debt-financed ownership of capital assets exists, and the extent to which such debt financing can be carried is market determined. It follows that the fundamental instability of a capitalist economy is upward. The tendency to transform doing well into a speculative investment boom is the basic instability in a capitalist economy.

Innovations in financial practices are a feature of our economy, especially when things go well. New institutions, such as Real Estate Investment Trusts (REITs), and new instruments, such as negotiable Certificates of Deposits, are developed and old instruments, such as commercial paper, increase in volume and find new uses. But each new instrument and expanded use of old instruments increases the amount of financing that is available and which can be used for financing activity and taking positions in inherited assets. Increased availability of finance bids up the prices of assets relative to the prices of current output, and this leads to increases in investment. The quantity of relevant moneys in an economy in which money conforms to Keynes's definition, is endogenously determined. The money of standard theory——be it the reserve base, demand deposits and currency, or a concept that includes time and savings deposits——does not catch the monetary phenomena that are relevant to the behavior of our economy.[19]

In our economy it is useful to distinguish between hedge and speculative finance. Hedge finance takes place when the cash flows from operations are expected to be large enough to meet the payment commitments on debts. Speculative finance takes place when the cash flows from operations are not expected to be large enough to meet payment commitments, even though the present value of expected cash receipts is greater than the present value of payment commitments. Speculating units expect to fulfill obligations by raising funds by new debts. By this definition, a "bank" with demand and short-term deposits normally engages in speculative finance. The REITs, airlines, and New York City engaged in speculative finance in 1970-73. Their difficulties in 1974-75 were due to a reversal in present values (the present value of debt commitments exceeding the present value of expected receipts), due both to increases in interest rates and a shortfall of realized over previously anticipated cash flows.

During a period of successful functioning of the economy, private debts and speculative financial practices are validated. However, whereas units that engage in hedge finance depend only upon the normal functioning of factor and product markets, units which engage in speculative finance also depend upon the normal functioning of financial markets. In particular, speculative units must continuously refinance their positions. Higher interest rates will raise their costs of money even as the returns on assets may not increase. Whereas a money supply rule may be a valid guide to policy in a regime dominated by hedge finance, such a rule loses its validity as the proportion of speculative finance increases. The Federal Reserve must pay more attention to credit market conditions whenever the importance of speculative financing increases, for the continued viability of units that engage in speculative finance depends upon interest rates remaining within rather narrow bounds.

Units that engage in speculative finance are vulnerable on three fronts. One is that they must meet the market as they refinance debt. A rise in interest rates can cause their cash payment commitments relative to cash receipts to rise. The second is that, as their assets are of longer term than their liabilities, a rise in both long- and short-term interest rates will lead to a greater fall in the market value of their assets than of their liabilities. The market value of assets can become smaller than the value of their debts. The third front of vulnerability is that the views as to acceptable liability structures are subjective, and a shortfall of cash receipts relative to cash payment commitments anyplace in the economy can lead to quick and wide revaluations of desired and acceptable financial structures. Whereas experimentation with extending debt structures can go on for years and is a process of gradual testing of the limits of the market, the revaluation of acceptable debt structures, when anything goes wrong, can be quite sudden.

In addition to hedge and speculative finance there is Ponzi finance—a situation in which cash payments commitments on debt are met by increasing the amount of debt outstanding.[20] High and rising interest rates can force hedge financing units into speculative financing and speculative financing units into Ponzi financing. Ponzi financing units cannot carry on too long. Feedbacks from revealed financial weakness of some units affect the willingness of bankers and businessmen to debt finance a wide variety of organizations. Unless offset by government spending, the decline in investment that follows from a reluctance to finance leads to a decline in profits and in the ability to sustain debt. Quite suddenly a panic can develop as pressure to lower debt ratios increases.

There is, in the financial instability hypothesis, a theory of how a capitalist economy endogenously generates a financial structure which is susceptible to financial crises, and how the normal functioning of financial markets in the resulting boom economy will trigger a financial crisis.

Once endogenous economic processes take the economy to the brink of a crisis, Federal Reserve intervention can abort the development of a full-fledged crisis and a debt deflation. Experience in the past decade has shown that the decline in investment and consumer debt-financed spending that follows after an aborted debt deflation leads to a decline in income. In today's economy, positive fiscal actions and the built-in stabilizers lead to massive government deficits as income falls. Such deficits sustain income, sustain or increase corporate profits, and feed secure and negotiable financial instruments into portfolios hungry for safety and liquidity. As a result, the economy recovers rather quickly from the recession but, because the Federal Reserve intervention has protected various financial markets, the recovery can soon lead to a resumption of an inflationary boom.

## Conclusion

The controversy over the interpretation of Keynes is not as important as the question of whether today's standard economic theory —the neoclassical synthesis—is a valid tool for analyzing and prescribing for our economy. The cyclical behavior and financial instability of our economy can be viewed as the "critical experiment" that refutes the validity of the neoclassical synthesis. Once it is accepted that the neoclassical synthesis "won't do," the question becomes: "What will do?"—"What is an apt economic theory for our economy?"

The construction of new theory is difficult. The task becomes much more feasible if one can stand on the shoulders of giants. Keynes addressed the question of whether standard theory "will do" in an era characterized by strong business cycles and financial instability. He came to the conclusion that inherited theory would not do, and he proposed an alternative theory. Over the past forty years one interpretation of Keynes's theory, which virtually ignored Keynes's concern with financial markets and financial usages, has been largely assimilated to standard theory. Now that the problems of economic and financial instability loom large in the world, the question is relevant as to whether those parts of Keynes's theory that point toward a financial and cyclical view of the economy (which were largely ignored in constructing today's standard theory) can serve as a basis for the needed new theory.

The financial instability hypothesis is an attempt to build a theory that is relevant for a financially sophisticated capitalist economy and to show why such an economy is unstable. This theory builds upon Keynes by deemphasizing those parts of the *General Theory* that were seized upon in the integration of Keynes and the classics, and emphasizing those parts that were largely ignored. Because Keynes, in his rebuttal to Viner, emphasized the parts of the *General Theory* that look toward the effect of financial usages in a capitalist framework upon the stability of the economy, the financial instability hypothesis has a strong claim to legitimacy.

Legitimate or not as "Keynesian doctrine," the financial instability hypothesis fits the world in which we now live. In a world with sharp turnabouts in income, such as that experienced in 1974-75, the rise and fall of interest rates, and the epidemic of financial restructuring, bailouts, and outright bankruptcy, there is no need to present detailed data to show that a theory which takes financial instability as an essential attribute of the economy is needed and is relevant.

Policy implications follow from the financial instability hypothesis. One is that fine-tuning, except as a transitory phenomenon, is impossible within the existing financial framework. Another is that policies which work in one financial regime, such as the robust finance of 1946-65, may not be effective in another regime, such as the fragile finance that has ruled in the past decade. A third is that, in order to do better than hitherto, we have to establish and enforce a "good financial society" in which the tendency by business and bankers to engage in speculative finance is constrained.

## Notes

1. Jacob Viner, "Mr. Keynes on the Causes of Unemployment," *Quarterly Journal of Economics*, November 1936.

2. Don Patinkin, *Money Income and Prices* (Evanston, Ill.: Row, Peterson, 1956; 2nd ed., New York: Harper and Row, 1965).

3. J. M. Keynes, "The General Theory of Employment," *Quarterly Journal of Economics*, February 1937.

4. Ibid., p. 221.

5. John R. Hicks, "Mr. Keynes and the Classics, A Suggested Interpretation," *Econometrica*, April 1937; and Alvin H. Hansen, *Fiscal Policy and Business Cycles* (New York: W. W. Norton & Co., 1941).

6. G. L. S. Shackle has long maintained that Keynes's *Quarterly Journal of Economics* article is the "ultimate distillation" of Keynes's thought on money. See G. L. S. Shackle, *Keynesian Kaleidics* (Edinburgh: Edinburgh University Press, 1974). Also see Hyman P. Minsky, *John Maynard Keynes* (Columbia University Press, 1975), for a detailed argument about the legitimacy of this alternative interpretation.

7. J. M. Keynes, "The Consequences to the Banks of the Collapse of Money Values," in *Essays in Persuasion*, vol. IX of the *Collected Writings of John Maynard Keynes* (London and Basingstoke: MacMillan, St. Martins Press, for the Royal Economic Society, 1972), p. 151.

8. Dudley Dillard, "The Theory of a Monetary Economy," in K. K. Kurihara, ed., *Post-Keynesian Economics* (London: George Allen and Unwin, 1955). Dillard offers an interpretation of Keynes which goes far toward the interpretation offered here. Unfortunately, Dillard's article did not have a major impact.

9. J. M. Keynes, *The General Theory of Employment, Interest and Money* (New York: Harcourt, Brace, 1936), p. vii.

10. John R. Hicks, "Some Questions of Time in Economics," in *Evolution, Welfare and Time in Economics: Essays in Honor of Nicholas Georgesca-Roegen* (Lexington, Mass.: Lexington Books, 1976), pp. 135-151. In this essay Hicks finally repudiates the potted equilibrium version of Keynes embodied in the IS-LM curves: he now views IS-LM as missing the point of Keynes and as bad economics for an economy in time.

11. Keynes, *Quarterly Journal of Economics*.

12. Keynes, *The General Theory*, p. vii.

13. Ibid., p. 313.

14. Paul Davidson, *Money and the Real World* (London: MacMillan, 1972): Sidney Weintraub, *Classical Keynesianism, Monetary Theory and the Price Level* (Philadelphia: Chilton, 1961); and Axel Leijonhufvud, *On Keynesian Economics and the Economics of Keynes* (New York: Oxford University Press, 1968).

15. Irving Fisher, "The Debt-Deflation Theory of Great Depressions," *Econometrica*, 1933.

16. The $q$, $c$, and $l$ of Chapter XVII, "The Essential Properties of Interest and Money," *The General Theory* [Keynes, op. cit.], are best interpreted as cash flows or cash flow equivalents. See H. P. Minsky, *John Maynard Keynes* (New York: Columbia University Press, 1975), ch. 4, "Capitalist Finance and the Pricing of Capital-Assets."

17. Michal Kalecki, *Theory of Economic Dynamics* (London: Allen and Unwin, 1965).

18. Actually all that has to be assumed is that the economy has not always been in equilibrium and that the memory of disequilibrium "lingers." In general equilibrium theory the assumption is made, by means of recontracting or Walras's peculiar auctioneer, that all economic action occurs in equilibrium. The theory that is designed to demonstrate that decentralized markets lead to coherence (equilibrium) is based upon a postulate that the economy is now and has always been in equilibrium. The disequilibrium of neoclassical theory is a "virtual," not an "actual," disequilibrium.

19. Hyman P. Minsky, "Central Banking and Money Market Changes," *Quarterly Journal of Economics*, May 1957.

20. Charles Ponzi was a Boston "financial wizard" who discovered that by offering high returns on "deposits" he could acquire a large amount of "deposits." As long as his total borrowing grew at a faster rate than his promised "interest," he could fulfill his commitments by increasing his debts. Once his deposits began to grow at a slower rate than his interest obligations, he could not meet his commitments. Inasmuch as debts are used to pay interest (or dividends), a Ponzi scheme eventually collapses. Any time present cash returns to liability earners are paid on the basis of expected future cash flows, then the financing has "Ponzi" aspects. By the above criteria, many REITs engaged in Ponzi finance when they paid dividends on the basis of accruals.

# 4

Capitalist Financial
Processes and
the Instability of
Capitalism

In the following quotation, Henry Simons, a founder of the Chicago School, recognizes the endogenous nature of money and the impossibility of managing money by trying to control the quantity of some specific set of debts, especially in an economy in which the lure of potential profits induces innovations in financial practices.

> Banking is a pervasive phenomenon, not something to be dealt with merely by lesiglation directed at what we call banks. The experience with the control of note issue is likely to be repeated in the future: many expedients for controlling similar practices may prove ineffective and disappointing because of the reappearance of prohibited practices in new and unprohibited forms. It seems impossible to predict what forms the evasion might take or to see how particular prohibitions might be designed in order that they might be more than nominally effective.[1]

Simons followed the logic of his insight into the endogenous and evolutionary nature of money by advocating strict limitations on the permissible liabilities of enterprises and binding constraints upon the permitted activities of financial institutions.

In Simons's view, control over money requires strict limitations upon "large scale financing at short terms."[2] Simons therefore proposed to eliminate the financing, through banks and other intermediaries with short-term liabilities, of positions in capital assets and in investment in the process of production. Unfortunately for Simons's prescription, bank and other short-term financing of activity is a major link in the investment process under capitalism. Whereas titles to capital assets may be financed long, the producing

Reprinted from the *Journal of Economic Issues*, Vol. XIV, No. 2, June 1980, by arrangement with the publisher.

of investment output, like other production activity, is a short-term affair that naturally calls for short-term financing.

An essential attribute of modern capitalism is that positions in both capital assets and investment in process are financed by a combination of debts and commitments of the liquid capital of the proximate owners or producers, that is, of corporations.[3] Debts are best interpreted as commitments to make payments over time. The flow of cash resulting from firms' operations is used to pay current costs, fulfill explicit payment commitments on debts, and yield a cash position for the firm and income to its owners. The debts of firms state the minimum profits, broadly defined, that must be generated if commitments as stated on the liabilities are to be fulfilled either by the flow of profits or by funds obtained by a refinancing arrangement. Entering into and repaying debts are essential processes of capitalism: Both depend upon profits, expected or realized.

If debts are to banks, then the payments which fulfill commitments on debts destroy "money." In a normally functioning capitalist economy, in which money is mainly debts to banks, money is constantly being created and destroyed. Economic theory that focuses only on the exchanges that create money, or which assumes that money is "the non-interest paying debt of some agency outside the formal system,"[4] induces no need to examine how borrowers are able to fulfill their commitments and the economic consequences of systemically induced failures to meet them.

In contrast, if money is viewed as a "veil" that "camouflages" ultimate ownership of wealth, then the major concern of monetary theory becomes the expected profits that induce debt creation and the realized profits that lead to the validation of debt. The transition from abstract economics to the economic analysis of capitalism depends upon defining money as a "product" of financial interrelations. This was well understood by J. M. Keynes:

> There is a multitude of real assets in the world which constitute our capital wealth—buildings, stock of commodities, goods in course of manufacture and of transport and so forth. The nominal owners of these assets, however, have not infrequently borrowed *money* in order to become possessed of them. To a corresponding extent the actual owners of wealth have claims, not on real assets, but on money. A considerable part of this "financing" takes place through the banking system, which imposes its guarantee between its depositors who lend it money and its borrowing customers to whom it loans money with which to finance the purchase of real assets. The interposition of this veil of money between the real asset and the wealth owner is a specially marked characteristic of the modern world [emphasis in original].[5]

Any economic theory which ignores this "specially marked characteristic of the modern world" cannot serve as an effective instrument for the design of policies. In particular, today's standard economic theory—the neoclassical synthesis—which ignores the "financing veil" aspects of money and persists in viewing money only as a "bartering veil," cannot explain how instability is a normal functioning result in a capitalist economy. As a result, neoclassical theory is a defective instrument to use in the formulation of policies that aim at controlling or attentuating instability. If we are to do better in controlling unemployment and inflation, we have to return to the insights of Simons and Keynes and build an economic theory that fully accepts the financing veil characteristic of money.

The current significance of Simons and Keynes is not surprising, for their insights and analysis were born out of the observed instability of capitalism. Our current difficulties in economics and in the economy stem from our failures to understand and deal with instability. If we are to do better, we must accept being forced back to the square one of the 1930s.

## Finance and the behavior of a capitalist economy

Finance affects the behavior of a capitalist economy in three ways. First, positions in the existing stock of capital assets need to be financed. Second, activities, that is the production and distribution of consumption and investment goods, need to be financed. Third, payment commitments, as stated on financial contracts, need to be met.

The techniques available for financing positions in capital assets affect asset prices. In a capitalist economy, assets are priced. The prices reflect the relation between the cash flows, or quasi-rents, that capital assets are expected to earn as they are used in production and the payment commitments that have to be agreed upon in order to finance ownership. A debt involves an exchange of money today for promises to pay money in the future. The smaller the amount of future money that has to be promised in order to receive current money to finance a position in a capital asset with some given expected cash flow, the greater the demand for such capital assets.

In the short term, the supply of capital assets is fixed; therefore, an increase in demand will lead to an increase in the price. Innovations in mobilizing funds through intermediation and in the contracts used for financing ownership of assets will tend to raise the prices of assets. The various "innovations" in housing finance have led to higher prices of housing, the acceptance of a heavier weight of debt in corporation balance sheets has sustained the price of capital assets, and the explosive growth of money market funds has increased the availability of short-term finance to business.

Borrowing and lending take place on the basis of margins of safety. The fundamental margin of safety is the excess of the expected quasi-rents from operating capital assets over the cash flow committed by financial contracts. Two time series—the expected receipts and the contractual commitments—summarize the financial position of units. When Simons delivered his strictures against short-term financing, he was railing against arrangements in which payment commitments exceed the expected quasi-rents from operations for the near term. If businessmen and their bankers agree upon such arrangements, then they must envisage that there are sources of cash to debtors other than the flow of quasi-rents from operations, that is, cash can be obtained by refinancing. A secondary margin of safety is the breadth, depth, and resilience of markets in which refinancing can take place.

The financial relations of units owning capital assets depend upon the views of borrowers and lenders as to the assuredness of cash flows, the appropriate margin of safety, and the availability of alternative sources if cash from operations falls short of expectations. Expectations with regard to cash flows depend upon the history of cash flows, the margin of safety that is deemed appropriate depends upon the adequacy of past margins, and the willingness to rely upon refinancing depends upon the history and institutional structure of the markets in which refinancing may take place. During tranquil years, success combined with institutional evolution make borrowers and lenders more assured of the cash flows from operations, confident that success is compatible with smaller margins of safety, and secure in cash flow arrangements which require refinancing. Trends in financing reflect changes in views of how the economy normally functions and in the preference system of "operators." The liability structures used to finance positions in capital assets reflect subjective views as to the acceptable chance of illiquidity occurring. The essential liquidity preference in a capitalist economy is that of bankers and businessmen, and the observable phenomena that indicate the state of liquidity preference are the trends of business and banker balance sheets.

An immediate effect of a change in liquidity preference is upon the money price of capital assets. A decrease in liquidity preference allows an increase in the ratio of near-term payment commitments to near-term expected quasi-rents to take place. This leads to an increase in the money price of capital assets. An increase in liquidity preference, which typically occurs when quasi-rents fail to validate debt structures or financial markets fail to refinance positions, will force attempts to reduce near-term payment commitments relative to expected quasi-rents. This will lead to a fall in the money price of capital assets.

In addition to positions in capital assets, the production and distribution of consumption and investment goods need to be financed. The cash that enables the "producers" of consumer goods to fulfill their commitments to bankers is derived from sales proceeds, which, if we abstract from consumer debt, depend upon consumer disposable income (largely wages and salaries). The cash that enables producers of investment goods to fulfill their commitments to their bankers is also derived from sales proceeds, but the "cash" used by the buyers of investment goods is derived from a combination of retained earnings and external finance. The financing of investment goods production leads to debts by investment goods producers. These debts are repaid when capital asset buyers pay. Such buyers typically borrow at least part of their needed funds. In the investment process, a continued funding of debt occurs, albeit it is the short-term debt of the producers of investment goods that is "funded" by the financing arrangements of the purchasers of investment goods as capital assets.

A capitalist economy is characterized by a layered set of payment commitments that are stated in financial contracts. These commitments will be fulfilled either by the flow of cash from operations—for business the flow is an "enlarged" gross profits—or by issuing debt. The ability to issue debt rests upon borrowers' and lenders' expectations of future cash flows, that is, of future profits. Thus, central to an understanding of the functioning of a capitalist economy is an understanding of how the flow of gross profits measured in money is determined.

### An aside on "money funds"

The points about banking being a pervasive phenomenon and that profit opportunities from borrowing and lending lead to financial innovations are beautifully illustrated by the growth and evolution of money market funds in the past several years. These funds, which first emerged in the high interest rate days of 1974-1975 and stagnated during the lower interest stagflation of 1975-1977, grew at an explosive rate in 1978-1979, when the assets they managed increased by a factor of ten. In addition, the percentage of their funds invested in open market paper and miscellaneous assets rose from an estimated 16.2 percent in 1975 to an estimated 46.2 percent in 1979; these funds are now direct suppliers of short-term financing.

Any analysis of these funds which looks at the assets they own and the liabilities they issue *must* identify the institutions as banks and their liabilities as money. Because of their success, we now have a two-tier monetary system; part of the money supply has the protection of bank equity, established channels for refinancing through the central bank, and deposit insurance, and another part lacks these margins of safety. When a money supply consists of instruments that differ in their yield and risk characteristics, then runs, in which holders of one type of money try to change quickly to another type, are possible. If there is no provision for supplying the desired money to the institutions which have the undesired money as liabilities, a run can have disasterous consequences. As financial markets replicate our experience of 1966, 1969-1970, and 1974-1975 and drive toward the brink of a financial crisis, some lender of last resort intervention, because of the money market funds, is likely to be needed.

Money market funds are but the latest in  a series of financial market and banking innovations that have changed the nature of the financial system over the past several decades. Beginning with

---

Table 1

## Money Market Funds

|  | 1973 | 1974 | 1975 | 1976 | 1977 | 1978 | 1979[a] |
|---|---|---|---|---|---|---|---|
| Total assets | 0 | 2.4 | 3.7 | 3.7 | 3.9 | 10.8 | 39.6 |
| Demand deposits and currency | 0 | – | – | – | – | .4 | .3 |
| Time deposits | 0 | 1.6 | 2.1 | 1.5 | 1.8 | 5.3 | 14.2 |
| Credit market instruments | 0 | .8 | 1.5 | 2.1 | 1.9 | 5.1 | 24.1 |
| U.S. government securities | 0 | .1 | .9 | 1.1 | .9 | 1.5 | 7.1 |
| Open market paper | 0 | .6 | .5 | .9 | 1.1 | 3.7 | 17.1 |
| Miscellaneous | 0 |  | .1 | .1 | .1 | .3 | 1.2 |
| Shares outstanding | 0 | 2.4 | 3.7 | 3.7 | 3.9 | 10.8 | 39.6 |
| Open market paper – miscellaneous as a share of totals, in percentage |  | 25.0 | 16.2 | 27.0 | 30.8 | 37.0 | 46.2 |

*Source*: Board of Governors, Federal Reserve System, *Flow of Funds Accounts* (Washington, D.C.: quarterly).

[a]Extrapolated at 1979 rate of change.

the emergence of the federal funds market in the mid-1950s, changes such as certificates of deposits, the explosive growth of commercial paper, the rise and fall of REIT's, the internationalization of banking, and the wide use of repurchase agreements have occurred. The changes have been in response to profit opportunities, and these have resulted from changing interest rate differentials due to demand for financing growing at a faster pace (at each set of terms for financing from traditional sources) than the supply of financing from traditional sources.[6]

### Federal reserve operations to constrain inflation

A major portion of the traditional supply of financing comes from banks. Federal Reserve operations to constrain inflation first constrain the ability of commercial banks to finance asset acquisition by expanding their reserve-absorbing liabilities. Financial innovation and evolution are stimulated by the interest rate effects of such Federal Reserve constraining action. Innovation and evolution offset a part, all, or even more than all of the constraint upon financing through banks caused by the initiating Federal Reserve actions.

This evolutionary response makes the rate of increase of activity that is financed greater than the rate of increase of commercial bank liabilities that absorb bank reserves: The velocity of money (narrowly defined as currency and reserve-absorbing liabilities of banks) rises. Such an increase of velocity to offset Federal Reserve constraint is a normal occurrence in financial markets. The limit on the offset through changes in institutions and usages of monetary constraint is determined by the effect of the cash payment commitments due to the increments of finance upon the cash flow relations of various asset and liability combinations. Monetary constraint does not lead to an immediate or smooth deceleration of an inflationary expansion. In the face of an accelerating inflationary expansion, monetary constraint initially leads to a sharp increase in financing outside normal banking channels. With a variable lag, this is followed by a sharp rise in payments required by debts relative to business profits. Monetary constraint in a situation in which ongoing investment activity leads to a rising demand for finance is effective only as it forces a sharp break in asset values caused by market pressures to liquidate or fund positions. Ever since the 1960s, monetary constraint has been effective only as it succeeded in pushing the economy to the brink of a debt deflation. This is shown by the credit crunch of 1966, the liquidity squeeze of 1969-1970, and the debacle of 1974-1975.[7]

The complex and evolving financial structure of a modern capitalist economy enables businessmen and their bankers to offset monetary constraint until it forces the economy to a crisis that threatens to lead to a deep depression. The fundamental instability of capitalism is upward. Attempts by central banks to constrain upward expansion, or endogenous limits of the financial system, lead to present values and cash flow relations that break rather than attenuate the expansion. Once the break occurs, the effect on capital asset prices of expected higher nominal profits is removed. This implies that capital asset prices will tend to decline sharply, which will lead to a fall in the demand price and the available financing for investment. Once the price of capital assets reflects inflationary expectations, an end to those expectations will lead to a sharp fall in investment. The upward instability of capitalism is a necessary precondition for the possibility of a deep depression.

## Asset prices, investment, and financing

In a brilliant, incisive, and unfortunately neglected article published in 1955, Dudley Dillard noted that, to Keynes, the "problem of economics" was the analysis of the behavior of a monetary production economy.[8] Dillard argues that in the *General Theory*, and in the interpretative literature that followed, the emphasis is upon the way in which money enters into the determination of interest rates. As I have pointed out,[9] in the *General Theory* and in later pieces clarifying it,[10] Keynes treated liquidity preference as a relation between money and the price level of capital assets.

Although a money-interest rate relation and a relation between money and the "price level" of capital assets can be made formally identical,[11] in truth they lead to quite different perspectives on how a capitalist economy works. Once an interest rate-money supply relation is accepted as the theoretical correlative of how financial markets affect the operations of the economy, the way is clear for the monetarist counterrevolution in which the liquidity preference function becomes a demand function for money. The stability of the latter function and the exogenous determination of the supply of money are the rocks upon which the secularist monetarist faith rests.[12]

The price level of capital assets and the interest rate statements of liquidity preference lead to quite different views of the economic process. The perception that the quantity of money determines the price level of capital assets, for any given set of expectations with respect to quasi-rents and state of uncertainty, because it affects the financing conditions for positions in capital assets, implies that in a capitalist economy there are two "price levels," one of current output and the second of capital assets. A fundamental insight of Keynes is that an economic theory that is relevant to a capitalist economy must explicitly deal with these two sets of prices. Economic theory must be based upon a perception that there are two sets of prices to be determined, and they are determined in different markets and react to quite different phenomena. Thus, the relation of these prices—say, the ratio—varies, and the variations affect system behavior.[13] When economic theory followed Sir John Hicks and phrased the liquidity preference function as a relation between the money supply and the interest rate,[14] the deep significance of Keynesian theory as a theory of behavior of a capitalist economy was lost.

The demand for current output consists of the demand for consumption and investment outputs in the "no government" case. The demand for investment depends upon the price of capital assets, the supply price of investment output, and the financing condition and availability of internal finance for investment output.

In Figure 1, the investment and financing relations of a representative firm are set out. $P_K$, the money price of capital assets, is the demand price of investment output. $P_K$ depends upon what Keynes called the state of long-term expectations which leads to current views about future profits; the financing conditions that are available for positions in capital assets; and the supply of

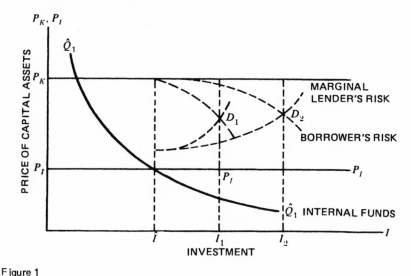

Figure 1

The Determination of Investment

money, defined as the default-free assets that yield only liquidity.

$P_I$ is the supply function of gross investment. The "position" of $P_I$ depends upon the short-run profit expectations of the producers of investment goods. The supply curve of investment output states the minimum price at which particular outputs of investment goods would be produced given current money wages, the carrying interest costs of investment goods as they are produced, and the cost of purchased inputs.

The existing liability structure of firms determines the cash payment commitments. The sum of gross profits after taxes and interest paid on debts as reported in the national income accounts is the gross capital income. This income minus gross payments on debts and dividends yields the gross internal finance. The price multiplied by the quantity of investment goods that can be internally financed yields a rectangular hyperbole ($Q_1$ in the diagram) which defines the combinations that can be so financed. The intersection of the expected internal finance and the supply function of investment goods yields the amount of investment that it is expected can be financed internally. In the diagram this is labelled $\bar{I}$.

External finance is required if investment is to exceed $\bar{I}$. Given that $P_K > P_I$, there will be a demand for external finance to acquire investment. The supply price of investment output has to be modified by the  cost of debt financing, which reflects the premiums upon a constant interest rate that reflect lenders' risk. Furthermore, the demand price for investment will fall away from the price of capital assets to reflect borrowers' risk. Investment will be carried to the point at which the price of capital, as affected by borrowers' risk, equals the supply price of investment output, as augmented to reflect lenders' risk. In Figure 1, let us say that $I_1$ of investment will be undertaken, of which $\bar{I}$ is internally financed and $I_1 - \bar{I}$ is externally financed.

As a result of the gross investment of $I_1$, $P_I(I_1 - \bar{I})$ of debt becomes part of the liability structure of firms. The extent of leverage in the financing of investment is given by the ratio of $I_1$ to $\bar{I}$. This ratio depends upon the excess of $P_K$ over $P_I$, the available financing contracts, and the evaluation of and attitude toward risk of lenders and borrowers. Whereas lenders' risk becomes, in part, an objective phenomenon, in the form of interest rates and contract provisions, borrowers' risk is largely a subjective phenomenon which sets limits on the ratio of payment commitments to gross profits.

The evolution of financial institutions and usages, such as was discussed earlier, will tend to increase the feasible leverage. The success of business in fulfilling payment commitments due to past financing will increase the "subjectively acceptable" external financing over a run of tranquil good times. The flow-of-funds data for the first three decades after World War II bear this out. With an increase in leverage relative to gross profits, the ratio of payment commitments (because of liabilities) to gross profits rises; the margins of safety in cash flows are eroded. As this occurs, the financial system becomes fragile.

Once financial considerations are integrated into the investment decision, it is evident that capitalism as we know it is endogenously unstable. As Dillard points out, in Keynes the proposition "that employment depends upon investment" leads to a general critique of the whole capitalist process. Contradictions and tensions associated with the accumulation of wealth come to the forefront of the analysis. Instability becomes normal rather than abnormal.[15]

### Investment, profits, and the validation of business debts

Once debts exist, some of the cash receipts of debtors are committed to the fulfillment of contracts. Thus, the cash receipts of debtors must meet some minimal standard if the debts are to be validated. Furthermore, debts finance only a portion of the positions in capital assets and investment in process. There is some minimum standard that the cash receipts attributed to capital assets have to meet if the debts and the prices paid for capital assets are to be validated. The validating cash receipts are gross capital income (profits, broadly defined). The successful functioning of a capitalist economy requires that the present and expected gross capital income be large enough so that past decisions to invest and to finance are validated.

In a capitalist economy, present views about future profits determine current investment and financing decisions, even as present achieved profits determine whether what was done in the past is validated. An economic theory that is relevant to a capitalist economy cannot evade the issues involved in unidirectional historical time by assuming recontracting or the existence of universal systems of future, or contingent, contracts. The essence of capitalism is that units have to take positions in an uncertain world.[16]

In a world in which investment is taking place, the heroic assumptions that workers spend all of their wage income on consumption goods and capitalists do not consume yields the result that[17]

(1) $$C = W_c N_c + W_I N_I;$$

(2) $$\pi_c = P_c Q_c - W_c N_c = W_I N_I; \text{ and}$$

(3) $$\pi_I = P_I Q_I - W_I N_I = \pi_I.$$

Since $\pi_c + \pi_I = \pi$, and $P_I Q_I = I$, we have

(4) $$\pi = W_I N_I + \pi_I = I.$$

As is well known, the simple Kalecki result can be expanded to

(5) $$\pi = I + Df$$

if government is introduced,

(6) $$\pi = I + Df + C\pi - sW$$

if consumption out of profits and savings out of wages are allowed, and

(7) $$\pi = I + Df + C\pi - sW + BPS$$

if the economy is open.[18]

Given that investment is determined by a complex interplay which involves present expectations of future performance, the simple Kalecki relation can be interpreted as meaning that profits are determined by investment. As the Kalecki relation is extended, the logic of running from investment to profits is reinforced by the structural and policy determinants of the government deficit, the balance of payments, savings by households, and consumption by receivers of capital income.

Investment is carried to the point at which the adjusted price of capital assets (as a function of expected profits and the available financing conditions for holding capital and financial assets) equals the adjusted supply price of investment output (as a function of the money wage), where the adjustments reflect uncertainty and financing conditions. The evolution of financial markets affects investment both through the pricing of capital assets and the financing available for investment. Normal functioning of the financial system is a necessary condition for investment to be sustained so that profits are forthcoming to validate debt and induce future investment. Any break in the financial system—such as occurred on a massive scale between 1929 and 1933, and on a minor or contained scale in 1966, 1969-1979, and 1974-1975—will disrupt the economy. If institutional change and central bank behavior allow available financing to expand rapidly, then an inflationary boom is likely to result: if a financial crisis compromises the ability and willingness of institutions to provide credit, or if central bank actions constrain credit, a debt deflation and deep depression are likely to occur.

In Figure 1, the extent of debt financing as determined by lender and borrower risk and the evolving structure of financial relations were shown to affect the level of investment. During a tranquil era, the development of new institutions and new usages leads to an increase in the leveraging ratio. As $I_1$ "drifts" to the right relative to expected $\bar{I}$, greater achieved investment ($I_2$) will lead to realized profits greater than anticipated profits. This will mean that internal finance will be greater and external finance smaller than anticipated. Even as investing units and their bankers attempt to increase debt financing, greater than expected profits will result in a shortfall of realized as compared to anticipated debts. During business cycle expansions, the "unused" or "open" borrowing capacity of business and owners of wealth increases.

A rise in investment, due to improved financing terms, leads to an increase in profits. As the level and trend of profits enter into the determination of the price of capital assets, the "evolutionary" expansion of financing forms increases the prices of capital assets in two ways: It increases both expected quasi-rents and the price that will be paid in the market for given time series of expected quasi-rents.

The path of a capitalist economy in historic time depends upon the transactions between businessmen and bankers as they finance capital asset ownerships and investment. During good times, these transactions increasingly reflect underestimation by borrowers and lenders of the risks of external finance. This means that such an economy is unstable. The path of this basic instability is "upward" from periods of tranquil expansion to those of "inflationary" boom.

As the leverage ratio for new investment increases, "underlevered" positions in the inherited stock of capital assets are refinanced to conform to the emerging standards. Such refinancing leads to debts growing at a faster rate than both the capital stock and profits. Even if interest rates on financial contracts do not increase, the ratio of payment commitments to profits increases.

Financial innovation, combined with the interactions by which increased investment leads to increased profits, implies that current output prices rise.[19] Either because the central bank attempts to restrict financing available through banks or because the pace of the demand for financing outraces the availability of finance, the rise in investment in the "pipeline" will lead to a rise in interest rates. Because investment decisions lead to a sequence of investment demands, a run of tranquil behavior leads to a rising inelastic demand for financing for the production of investment goods. Given this inelasticity, any emerging inelasticity in the supply of finance will lead to a sharp rise in interest rates. Such a rise, by initially lowering the price of capital assets, lowers the demand price of investment even as it raises the supply price of investment output. As a result, the ratio of planned investment demand to expected internal funds will fall; the thrust toward ever higher profits due to increasing investment reflecting ever higher leverage ratios will cease.

The financial processes of a capitalist economy introduce instability by making a tranquil state unstable in an upward direction and set flexible limits to this upward expansion. However, the limit to external finance requires that weak or fragile financial situations emerge. A decrease in investment will decrease profits, thus increasing the ratio of payment commitments on outstanding debt to gross funds available for such payment and also increasing the proportion of current investment that must be financed externally. Just as rising profits frustrate the attempts of bankers and businessmen to debt finance investments, so falling profits frustrate their attempts to decrease their indebtedness.

The debt deflation process can be limited if the financial system is robust. From time to time in history, a financial system has proved so fragile that deep depressions, such as that in 1929-1933, have occurred. In the era since World War II, no such debt deflation and deep depression have taken place.

In the years since the mid-1960s there have been three episodes —1966, 1969-1970, and 1974-1975—when the economy was on the verge of a debt deflation. Nevertheless, it did not occur. In part this was because the Federal Reserve quickly intervened and bolstered the system with its guarantee to protect banks and other financial institutions; in part it was because a huge government deficit substitutes for investment in sustaining deficit profits. With profits sustained, a debt deflation process cannot gain momentum.

From equation (5) we have $\pi = I + Df$. If a decline in investment and employment triggers an explosion of the government deficit so that the increase in the deficit offsets the decline in investment, then profits will not fall. If profits are sustained, then the gross cash flow to capital owners is sustained. This means that outstanding debts and the prices that were paid for capital assets tend to be validated.

The combination of automatic stabilizers, lagged adjustments to past inflation in various government transfer payment schemes, and discretionary fiscal intervention means that when financial stringency is followed by a fall in investment, a massive government deficit occurs. Profits are sustained even as business activity and employment decrease. As a result, the business sector is able to validate its debts. The interactions among investment, profits, and financial markets which constitute the downward spiral of a deep depression do not occur.

The aggregate demand effect of big government, especially government that expands dramatically when income and employment fall, sustains and increases the markup on labor costs.[20] Inasmuch as transfer payment schemes sustain money wages in the face of excess supply of labor, and the deficit tends to sustain, if not increase, the markup on money wages, prices do not fall; they even rise when unemployment increases. Stagflation is truly a result of big government, but so is the absence of a deep depression in the years since 1966.

There is no free lunch; we have eliminated deep depressions, but the price has been first chronic and now accelerating inflation.

## Conclusion

Once we shift from an abstract economy and turn to analyzing the behavior of a capitalist economy with expensive capital assets and a sophisticated financial system, the equilibrium, equilibrating, and stability properties derived in standard economic theory are not relevant. Such a capitalist economy is unstable due to endogenous forces which reflect financing processes. These processes transform a tranquil and relatively stable system into one in which a continued accelerating expansion of debts, investment, profits, and prices is necessary to prevent a deep depression.

A comparison of 1929-1933 with 1966, 1969-1970, and 1974-1975 makes it clear that when a financial crisis is imminent, the structure of the economy and discretionary intervention by the authorities determine what happens. At such a juncture, policy does matter. If, as in 1929, aggregate federal government spending is small relative to investment, and if the Federal Reserve takes a narrow view of its responsibilities, then a debt deflation and a deep depression will follow financial trauma. If, as in 1966, 1969-1970, and 1974-1975, aggregate government spending is large relative to investment, and if the Federal Reserve takes a broad view of its responsibilities, then stagflation and a stepwise accelerating inflation will follow financial trauma.

Whereas the period 1946-1966 shows that an extended run of capitalism without instability is possible, it should be recognized that these years are a special case. The memory of 1929-1939 made "balance sheet conservatism" a dominant characteristic when World War II ended. The available ability to spend, which was a legacy of war finance, was gradually transformed into actual spending. A long tranquil period of expansion and relative price stability resulted; however, as was evident even in the mid-1960s, the basis of this stability was gradually being eroded.[21]

Both the Great Depression and the great inflation and intermittent stagnation of 1966-1979 are symptoms of the underlying instability of capitalism. A great depression is the outcome when government is small and the central bank is timid. A great stagflation is the outcome when government is big and the central bank intervenes forcefully.

Given the fragility of our financial system, we will soon experience another crisis period reminiscent of the more recent ones. This time, however, big government will not be as quick nor as able (because of international financial relations) to pour money into the economy, as in 1974-1975. In addition, the Federal Reserve will be reluctant to intervene and increase the monetary base and extend broad guarantees. The prospect is that the next time financial instability occurs, the policy response will be slower and more modest than in 1974-1975. The subsequent recession will be both longer and deeper.

The current institutional structure offers us unappetizing alternatives; we need to alter it, recognizing that the essential critical flaw in capitalism is instability, and that instability is due to the way capital asset holding and accumulation are financed. Simons was correct: Banking, that is, the financing of capital asset ownership and investment, is the critical destabilizing phenomenon. But, as Simons realized, control of banking—money, if you wish—is not enough; the liability structures available to units that own the massive capital assets of the economy must be constrained.

The fundamental dilemma in economic organization is how to preserve the vitality and resilience of decentralized decisions without the instability accompanying decentralized financial markets. Keynes's solution—the socialization of investment—may be a way of attenuating, although not eliminating, financial instability by removing the financing of the most capital-intensive processes and expensive capital assets from private debt markets. The substitution of government for private financing of capital-intensive investment, along with limitations on the liability structure of private business, could decrease the domain of instability of a capitalist economy.

The economics of Simons of Chicago and Keynes of Cambridge have much in common, but this is not surprising. Both Keynes's *General Theory* and Simons's *Rules versus Authorities* were responses to the same real world situation. However, Simons never broke with inherited economic theory, whereas Keynes saw that one aspect of the crisis of his time was that the inherited theory was incapable of explaining what was happening.

In many ways, today's many crises of economics—in performance, policy, and theory—are reminiscent of those of the 1930s. Once again, the discipline is divided between those who view the inherited theory as an adequate basis for future progress of both the economy and the discipline and those who hold that inherited standard theory will not do. Today, just as in the 1930s, the control of systemic instability is the critical problem in performance and policy, and instability is the phenomenon that renders inherited theory suspect.

## Notes

1. Henry Simons, "Rules versus Authorities in Monetary Policy," *Journal of Political Economy* 44 (February 1936): 1-39, reprinted in *H. Simons' Economic Policy for a Free Society* (Chicago: University of Chicago Press, 1948), p. 172. "Rules versus Authorities" was written in the same years of intellectual ferment that gave rise to *The General Theory* and reflects a similar concern with understanding the fundamental rules of behavior of a capitalist economy.

2. Ibid., p. 171.

3. In all that follows, "corporations" or "firms" will be the proximate owners of the capital assets of the economy. This institutional specification simplifies the exposition and does not do grave violence to reality.

4. Kenneth Arrow and Frank Hahn, *General Competitive Analysis* (San Francisco and London: Holden-Day, 1971), p. 346.

5. J. M. Keynes, "The Consequences to the Banks of the Collapse of Money Value," in *Essays in Persuasion*, vol. 9, *The Collected Writings of John Maynard Keynes* (New York: Macmillan, for The Royal Economic Society, 1971), p. 151.

6. Hyman P. Minsky, "Central Banking and Money Market Changes," *Quarterly Journal of Economics* 71 (May 1957): 171-87. See Chapter 7, below, pp. 162-178.

7. Irving Fisher, "The Debt Deflations Theory of Great Depressions," *Econometrica* 1 (October 1933): 337-57.

8. Dudley Dillard, "Theory of a Monetary Economy," in *Post Keynesian Economics*, edited by L. K. Kurihara (London: 1955).

9. Hyman P. Minsky, *John Maynard Keynes* (New York: Columbia University Press, 1975).

10. J. M. Keynes, "The General Theory of Employment," *Quarterly Journal of Economics* 51 (February 1937): 209-33.

11. Minsky, *Keynes*, chapter 4, "Capitalist Finance and the Pricing of Capital Assets."

12. Milton Friedman, "The Quantity Theory of Money: A Restatement," in *Studies in the Quantity Theory of Money*, edited by Milton Friedman (Chicago: University of Chicago Press, 1956).

13. When neoclassical theory is extended to deal with problems of accumulation and growth, in one form or another, the assumption is made that the depreciated value of historical investments equals the value of the capital stock as determined by the present value of future profits: that is, two sets of

prices are equal. But this assumption is an attribute of an investing economy in equilibrium. Neoclassical general equilibrium theory, when extended to investing capitalist economies, proves the existence of equilibrium by first assuming the economy is in equilibrium. See G. C. Harcourt, *Some Cambridge Controversies in the Theory of Capital* (Cambridge: Cambridge University Press, 1972). This point is very clear in the writings of Jan Kregal: see especially *The Reconstruction of Political Economy* (New York: Wiley, 1973).

14. J. R. Hicks, "Mr. Keynes and the Classics," *Econometrica* 5, no. 1 (1937): 147-59.

15. Dillard, "Theory," pp. 22-23.

16. Kregal, *Reconstruction*; and Paul Davidson, *Money in the Real World* (New York: Wiley, 1972).

17. $C$ = consumption; $W_c$, $W_I$ = wages in consumption and investment production; $N_c$, $N_I$ = employment in consumption and investment production; $\pi_c$, $\pi_I$, $\pi$ = profits in consumption, investment, and total production; $Df$ = government deficit; $C$ = consumption coefficient out of profits; $s$ = saving coefficient out of wages, and $BPS$ = surplus in the balance of payments. See Michal Kalecki. *Selected Essays on the Dynamics of the Capitalist Economy* (1933-1970) (Cambridge: Cambridge University Press, 1971). Chapter 7, pp. 78-92. "The Determinants of Profits," is a reprint of a paper that first appeared in 1942.

18. There is a formal equivalence between $Y = C + I$, and so forth, and $\pi = I + Df$, and so forth; the difference is in the treatment of received income as a homogeneous glob in the $Y = C - I$ (and so forth) formulation and the differentiation by source of income in the $\pi = I + Df$ (and so forth) formulation. The emphasis upon $\pi$ as the especially relevant attribute of a capitalist economy is important once the financial structure is specified, and once it is recognized that it is the flow of profits that determines whether past financing and asset values are to be validated.

19. From the Kalecki relations we have

$$P_c Q_c = W_c N_c + W_I N_I,$$

which yields

$$P_c = \frac{W_c}{(Q_c/N_c)}\left(1 + \frac{W_I N_I}{W_c N_c}\right),$$

or

$$P_c = \frac{W_c}{A_v}\left(1 + \frac{W_I N_I}{W_c N_c}\right),$$

where $A_v$ is the average productivity of labor in the production of consumer goods. The higher the ratio of $N_I$ to $N_c$, the higher the price level of consumer goods.

20. $\hat{P}_c Q_c = W_E N_E + W_I N_I + Df;$

$$P_c = \frac{W_c N_c}{Q_c}\left[1 + \frac{W_I N_I}{W_c N_c} + \frac{Df}{W_c N_c}\right]; \text{ and}$$

$$P_c = \frac{W_c}{A_v}\left[1 + \frac{W_I N_I}{W_c N_c} + \frac{Df}{W_c N_c}\right].$$

The markup on labor is

$$\frac{WN + Df}{W_c N_c}.$$

21. Hyman P. Minsky, "Longer Waves in Financial Relations; Financial Factors in the More Severe Depressions," *American Economic Review* 54 (May 1964): 324-32.

# 5

## The Financial Instability
## Hypothesis:
## A Restatement

## I. Introduction

It is trite to acknowledge that the capitalist economies are "not behaving the way they are supposed to." However, most economists—especially the policy-advising establishment in the United States—refuse to accept that at least part of the fault lies in the "supposed to." As a result, one source of the troubles of the capitalist economies is that the economic theory that underlies economic policy, which defines the "supposed to," just won't do for these economies at this time.

In this paper the salient features of an economic theory that is an alternative to today's standard theory are put forth. Within this theory, which I call the financial instability hypothesis, the recent behavior of the capitalist economies is not an anomaly: these economies have been behaving the way capitalist economies with sophisticated financial institutions are supposed to behave once economic intervention prevents fragile financial relations from leading to debt deflations and deep depressions. Because the financial instability hypothesis leads to a different view of the normal functioning of capitalist economies it has implications for economic policy that differ from those of the standard economic theory of our time.

We are in the midst of three closely related crises in economics: in performance, policy, and theory. The crisis in performance is that inflation, financial disturbances, chronically high unemployment rates, and instability of international exchanges are not de-

Reprinted from *Thames Papers in Political Economy*, Autumn 1978, by arrangement with the publisher.

sirable attributes of an economy and yet they now characterize not only the American economy but also well nigh all the more affluent capitalist economies.

The crisis in policy is that both monetary and fiscal policy seem to be ineffective, not only because of the "trade off" between inflation and unemployment that is summarized by the Phillips curve, but more significantly because of a strong tendency for an expansion to become an inflationary expansion which, in turn, leads to an incipient financial crisis. With the current structure of the economy and policy reactions an incipient financial crisis leads to an inflationary recession: what is now called stagflation. In the years since the mid-1960s financial crises have emerged as clear and present, though intermittent, dangers. In the present structure of the economy and policy an inflationary "floating off" of inherited debt has become part of the process that has enabled capitalist economies to avoid deep and prolonged depressions.

The crisis—in economic theory—has two facets: one is that "devasting logical holes" have appeared in conventional theory; the other is that conventional theory has no explanation of financial crises. The logical flaw in standard economic theory is that it is unable to assimilate capital assets and money of the kind we have, which is created by banks as they finance capital asset production and ownership. The major propositions of neo-classical theory, which are that a *multi-market full employment equilibrium exists* and that *this equilibrium will be sought out by market processes*, has not been shown to be true for an economy with capital assets and capitalist financial institutions and practices. Furthermore, the financing of investment and capital asset holdings within a modern banking environment makes the effective money supply endogenous; endogenous money implies that there is a great deal of deviation amplifying complementarity among markets. Furthermore "too much" complementarity means that no equilibrium exists for multi-market interdependent systems. From time to time, especially during strong economic expansions and contractions, complementarity due to financial interactions becomes a dominant though transitory trait of our economy. Monetary theory cannot assume that monetary changes occur within an economy that always has strong equilibrium tendencies. The very definition of equilibrium that is relevant for a capitalist economy with money differs from the definition used in standard "Walrasian" theory.[1]

The second failure of standard theory is that it has no explanation of financial instability. Three times in the past dozen years 1966, 1969/70, and 1974/75 financial instability loomed large in the United States. From the point of view of standard theory, that which was happening in, let us say, 1974/75 just could not happen as a normal functioning result of the economic process. The financial instability hypothesis is an alternative to the neo-classical synthesis, i.e., to today's standard economic theory. It is designed to explain instability as a result of the normal functioning of a capitalist economy. Instability of financial markets—the periodic crunches, squeezes, and debacles—is the observation. The theory is constructed so that financial instability is a normal functioning internally generated result of the behavior of a capitalist economy.

The financial instability hypothesis is rich. It not only offers an explanation of serious business cycles but it also offers explanations of stagflation that goes beyond the money supply, the fiscal posture of the government, or trade union misbehavior. It integrates the formation of relative prices with the composition of aggregate demand. In the financial instability hypothesis the pervasive role of profits in the functioning of a capitalist economy is made clear. Profits are that part of prices that supports the financial system and the structure of financial relations by providing the cash flows that validate past financial commitments. Profits are also the signals for investments and current financial commitments. Furthermore, because they differ in how they generate profits, the weighting of competition and monopoly markets in the economy affects the system's reactions to monetary and fiscal policy measures. But more important than these in detail results is the "big theorem" that emerges: this theorem is that a *capitalist economy with sophisticated financial institutions is capable of a number of modes of behavior and the mode that actually rules at any time depends upon institutional relations, the structure of financial linkages, and the history of the economy.*

The financial instability hypothesis has policy implications that go beyond the simple rules for monetary and fiscal policy that are derived from the neo-classical synthesis. In particular the hypothesis leads to the conclusion that the maintenance of a robust financial structure is a precondition for effective anti-inflation and full employment policies without a need to hazard deep depressions. This implies that policies to control and guide the evolution of finance are necessary.

## II. The place of the financial instability hypothesis in economic theory

The financial instability hypothesis is a variant of post-Keynesian economics. The interpretation of Keynes that has descended from the formalizations by Hicks, Hansen, Modigliani, and Patinkin of the *General Theory* has always been of questionable legitimacy.[2] The interpretation of Keynes that is developing under the rather unfortunate label of post-Keynesian economics emphasizes the importance of time and uncertainty, especially as they relate to capital-asset pricing, investment, and the liability asset structures of households, business, and financial institutions, to an understanding of Keynes. One focal point of the emerging post-Keynesian theory is the proposition that the liquidity preference function of the neo-classical synthesis is both a poor representation of Keynes' thought and an inept way to examine how money and finance affect the behavior of a capitalist economy.[3]

In the interpretation of Keynes used in the neo-classic synthesis the liquidity preference function is interpreted as a demand for money function. In the rebuttal to Viner's outstanding review of the *General Theory*, Keynes denied the validity of such an interpretation.[4] Keynes argued that with a given set of long run expectations (and with given institutional arrangements and conventions in finance) the supply and demand for money affects the price level of capital assets. In particular Keynes argued against any view that the effect of the quantity of money was mainly on the price level of output or even the money value of output. Keynes argued that the supply and demand for money determines the price level of capital assets. This objection by Keynes has been ignored and the neo-classical model builders continue to interpret liquidity preference as a demand equation for money. The revival of the quantity theory by Professor Friedman rests upon a stable demand for money function which permits the money supply to be the main determinant of the money value of total output.[5] It is but a small step from Friedman's construct to the pre-Keynesian view that the supply and demand for labor yields output and the quantity of money yields the price level.

The current dominant thrust in economic theory, which holds that the Walrasian theoretical scheme of a system of interdependent equations in which relative prices are the only argument, is valid and that the main proposition of this theory, which is that the economy will follow a full employment growth path, is valid, has taken economic theory full circle back to the 1920s and 30s. This time however, the neo-classical theory is buttressed against the objections raised by Keynes by what specialists in the philosophy of science characterize as degenerative and ad hoc assumptions. In the light of the current state of capital theory it is known that the proposition that an investing economy with money and capital assets generates a growth equilibrium rests upon a prior assumption that investment goods and capital-asset prices are always equal.[6] This equality assumption is equivalent to assuming that the economy is now and always will be in equilibrium. Assuming the "result" that a theory is "designed" to prove is clearly not admissible. The buttressing of neo-classical theory by the assumption that capital-asset prices are equal to investment goods prices reduces neo-classical theory to a tautology.

The view that Keynes advanced in his rebuttal to Viner (a view which appears in the *General Theory*) is that money, along with liability structure preferences, the mix of available capital assets, and the supply of financial assets, generates the prices of capital assets. In Keynes' view, each capital and financial asset is a combination of quick cash and future income. Furthermore, each liability is a dated demand or contingent commitment to pay cash. As a result of the nature of debts and contracts there will always be a subjective return from holding quick cash. The quantity of money determines the amount of quick cash that will be held and thus the subjective returns from holding money. The money prices of those assets which can be exchanged or pledged for quick cash only at a cost and with varying degrees of certainty but which yield cash income streams will have prices that adjust to the standard set by the subjective return on money. In contrast to the way in which the price system for capital-assets is set the price system of current output (both consumption and investment output) is set by the short run profit expectations of firms, demand conditions, and the cost of producing output.

In the aggregate, and in a closed economy, the costs of using capital assets to produce current output are mainly labor costs. The price system of current output is keyed to the money wage rate as the main determinant of relative unit costs of different outputs.

A capitalist economy, therefore, is characterized by two sets of relative prices, one of current output and the other of capital assets. Prices of capital assets depend upon current views of future profit (quasi-rent) flows and the current subjective value placed upon the insurance against uncertainty embodied in money or quick cash: these current views depend upon the expectations that are held about the longer run development of the economy. The prices of current output are based upon current views of near term demand conditions and current knowledge of money wage rates. Thus the prices of current output—and the employment offered in producing output—depend upon shorter run expectations. Capital-asset and current output prices are based upon expectations over quite different time horizons: capital asset prices reflect long run expectations and current output prices reflect short run expectations.

The alignment of these two sets of prices, which are based upon quite different time horizons and quite different proximate variables, along with financing conditions, determines investment. Furthermore current investment demand, along with other factors, such as consumption out of profit income, savings out of wages income, the way government taxes and spending respond to income, and the foreign trade balance yields aggregate effective demand. The aggregate effective demand for consumption, investment, government, and export output yields employment.

The financial instability hypothesis starts with the determinants of each period's effective demand. It takes into account the financial residue or legacy from past financing activity and how this legacy both imposes requirements upon the current functioning of the economy and conditions the future behavior of the economy. The financial instability hypothesis forces us to look beyond the simple accounting relations of the Gross National Product tables to the flows of funds in a capitalist economy where cash payment commitments exist because they are a legacy from past financing decisions.

The financial instability hypothesis which is rooted in Keynes differs from what is explicit in Keynes and other post-Keynesian economists in that financial institutions and usages are integrated into the analysis. Furthermore, because of the emphasis upon finance and the way in which changes in relative prices of current output and capital assets are brought about the financial instability hypothesis is more clearly a theory of the cyclical behavior of a capitalist economy than the economic theory of other post-Keynesian economists. That is, the financial instability hypothesis leads to an investment theory of the business cycle and a financial theory of investment.

## III. Investment, consumption, and
### the theory of effective demand[7]

The distinction between investment and consumption demand and the differences in the variables, markets, and considerations that affect these demands are crucial to an understanding of:

1. Why a theory of effective demand is necessary,

2. The concept of equilibrium that is relevant for the understanding of an investing capitalist economy and how the relevant concept differs from the concept as used in standard economic

theory, i.e., the difference between Keynesian and Walrasian ideas of equilibrium, and

3. The behavior of a capitalist economy that uses expensive capital assets in production and which has complex, sophisticated, and evolving financial institutions and practices.

In recent years a considerable literature on the interpretation and true meaning of Keynes has been produced.[8] Part of this literature consists of interpreting "Keynesian Economics" as a "disequilibrium state" within the framework provided by static Walrasian general equilibrium theory. In these interpretations assumptions about market behavior, in the form of sticky prices, are introduced so that "short side" sales or "rationing" characterizes the equilibrium. The "short side outcome" or "rationing" of jobs yields unemployment as an equilibrium of a constrained system. In these models wage, price, and interest rate rigidities are constraints which lead to the unemployment result. The unemployment result is taken to characterize Keynesian analysis.[9]

This disequilibrium approach completely misses the central problem that was identified by Keynes, which is that in a capitalist economy the variables and markets which determine investment demand are different from the variables and markets that determine the extent to which labor is applied to existing capital assets to produce "current output." Keynes worked with interdependent markets, but the interdependence stretched back and forth through time and the variables and markets that are relevant to one set of time dependent decisions are not the same as those that affect other sets. In these interdependent markets the signals from current utilization rates to investment demand can be apt, non-existent, weak, or perverse depending upon relations and institutions that reflect the history of the economy.

The main issue in the controversy about what Keynes really meant is not the discovery of the true meaning of the "Master's" text. The main issue is how to construct a theory that enables us to understand the behavior of a capitalist economy. Hopefully understanding how a capitalist economy behaves will give us knowledge that will enable us to control and change it so that its most perverse characteristics are either eliminated or attenuated. In this quest Keynes provides us with the "shoulders of a giant" on which we can stand as we do our little bit. Therefore an attempt to understand Keynes is a valid scientific endeavor.

To understand Keynes it is necessary to recognize that Keynes' analysis was not solely given to explaining unemployment. True the massive and continuing unemployment of the 1930s was a "critical experiment" thrown up by history which forced a reconsideration of the validity of the inherited economic theory. However, Keynes, while allowing for and explaining the time to time appearance of deep and persistent unemployment, did not hold that deep depressions are the usual, normal, or everlasting state of a capitalist economy. The collapse of the world's financial order over 1929-1933 was another "critical experiment" that forced a reconsideration of inherited economic theory. Keynes' special theory argued that in a particular conjunction, where a financial crisis and a debt deflation process had just occurred, endogenous market processes were both inefficient and quite likely perverse, in that they would tend to make matters worse with regard to eliminating unemployment. This state of things would not last forever, but would last long enough to be politically and socially relevant.

Keynes' *General Theory* viewed the progress of the economy as a cyclical process; his theory allowed for transitory states of moderate unemployment and minor inflations as well as serious inflations and deep depressions. Although cyclical behavior is the rule for capitalist economies, Keynes clearly differentiated between normal and traumatic cycles. In a footnote Keynes noted that "it is in the transition that we actually have our being."[10] This remark succinctly catches the inherently dynamic characteristics of the economy being studied.

Disequilibrium theorists such as Malinvaud persist in forcing the analysis of inherently dynamic problems into their static general equilibrium framework. In this framework constraints and rigidities are introduced to determine the characteristics of the "equilibrium." In doing this Malinvaud hides the interesting and relevant economics in the market and social processes that determine the constraints. The disequilibrium theorists may construct logically sound models that enable them to demonstrate some degree of theoretical virtuosity, but at the price of making their economics trivial.

Keynes' novelty and relatively quick acceptance as a guide to policy were not due to his advocacy of debt financed public expenditures and easy money as apt policies to reverse the downward movement and speed recovery during a depression. Such programs were strongly advocated by various economists throughout the world. Part of Keynes' exasperation with his colleagues and contemporaries was that the policies they advocated did not follow from their theory. In the United States economists such as Professor Paul Douglas, Henry Simon, and even Jacob Viner, all of whom were at the University of Chicago, advocated what would now be called expansionary fiscal policies well before the *General Theory* appeared. Before Herbert Hoover was president of the

United States he was Secretary of Commerce. As such he sponsored commissions and, reports which advocated a budget that was balanced over the business cycle rather than annually, i.e., under his auspices contra-cyclical fiscal policies were advocated. However these economists and politicians did not have and hold a theory of the behavior of capitalist economies which gave credence to their policies: their policy advice was divorced from their theory. Keynes' contribution can be interpreted as providing a theory that made activist expansionary policy a "logical inference from a tightly knit theory."[11]

The concept of "effective" or aggregate demand and the market processes that determine each transitory equilibrium of effective demand and supply are central to Keynesian theory and central to an understanding of the dynamic processes that determine the behavior of the economy. Significant and serious market failures occur because market processes do not assure that effective demand will be sufficient to achieve full employment. Furthermore when effective demand is sufficient, so that full employment is first achieved and then sustained, market processes will take place which lead to a "speculative" investment and financial boom that cannot be sustained.

Effective or aggregate demand is the sum of two demands: consumption demand and investment demand. (Government and the rest of the world are ignored for now.) Businesses offer employment and thus produce output on the basis of the profits they expect to earn by using labor and the existing capital assets to produce and distribute consumption and investment output. In production and distribution demand for labor to use with existing capital assets depends upon what Keynes identified as "short run expectations." In determining the price at which shoes will be offered to American and German distributors for the "next" season, Italian producers need to estimate their labor and material costs over this relatively short horizon. The American and German wholesale and retail firms have to estimate next summer's market for shoes in their country—which mainly depends upon their expectations of income, employment, and price developments. Similar short run considerations centering around investment projects under way, authorizations to spend on investment approved by business, and financing arrangements being made affect the employment and output decisions of the producers of goods used in investment. Employment offered in the construction industry, where projects are undertaken on the basis of "orders in hand," also relates to short run expectations. Thus it is short run expectations that lead to the production of consumer and investment goods. Standard gross national product statistics measure the result over a period of time of a set of short run expectations.

In addition to deciding how to use existing capacity business has to decide whether and how to expand capacity. Whereas the utilization of existing capacity is determined by price, cost, and therefore profit expectations over a relatively short run (six months, one or two years) the decision to expand capacity is determined by profit expectations over a much longer time horizon: ten, twenty, and even forty years. Thus uncertainty, in the sense that there is a need to decide and act on the basis of conjectures about future economic and political situations which in no way can be encompassed by probability calculations, enters in an essential way into the determination of that part of today's effective demand that is derived from investment behavior.

Investment demand is financed in a different manner than consumption demand. It is true that in a world with consumer credit, banks and financial relations affect consumption demand, but consumer demand mainly depends upon income plus the demand for capital assets, while investment truly depends upon the conditions under which short and long term external finance are available. Thus the demand for investment output is affected by the long run expectations not only of businessmen but also of the financial community. Finance and financial markets enter in an essential way in generating the effective demand for investment output.

The distinction between the external financing of household demand—consumer financing and the financing of home ownership—and of investment demand and capital-asset ownership by business centers around the time horizon of the credits and the expected source of the funds that will fulfill the debt obligations. Aside from the financing of housing, consumer debt is typically short run. While the banking system does provide business with short term financing, typically for activity based upon short run expectations, the financing of investment and of capital-asset ownership involves longer term equity and debt instruments.

The cash required to fulfill consumer debt and housing finance obligations normally is received as wages and other household incomes. The cash required to fulfill obligations on the instruments used to finance business debt will be generated by profits and the way in which longer run profit expectations are transformed into asset prices. The role of debt financing and the considerations bankers need take into account are different for household and business debts.

Investment demand determines whether the short run profit expectations of businessmen who made decisions to utilize the existing production capacity are or are not validated. If investment demand is at the appropriate level then the various outputs produced with existing productive capacity will generate the profits that were expected. If such a result occurs then business will be induced to offer the same employment to produce the same output, provided that the intervals between the first and subsequent production decisions are so small that the ongoing investments do not significantly affect production possibilities and the liabilities issued to finance investment do not significantly affect cash payment commitments.

Inasmuch as aggregate profits are generated by the way demand affects the utilization of existing capacity, the validation of short run profit expectations by realized profits depends upon the level of investment activity. It is financed investment demand that forces aggregate effective demand, by means of the multiplier, to the level at which savings equals investment. If investment is stabilized then the aggregate flow of profits is determined and, eventually, by a process of market adjustments, employment will settle at the level that is determined by correctly anticipating the volume of profits that follows from the hypothetically stabilized investment. Thus to each state of long run expectations there corresponds a level of investment, and if short run expectations adjust to the profits implicit in that investment level then there will be a level of employment to which the economy will settle. This level of employment, which is consistent with the state of long term expectations, is the "virtual" equilibrium of the system that Keynes considered: it is an implicit rather than an achieved equilibrium, for in truth the effects of investment and financing upon production capacity and payment commitments that were placed in the "ceteris paribus" bag will be taking place and these cumulated effects will change the implicit equilibrium of the system. Furthermore, if the short run equilibrium implicit in the state of long run expectations is attained and then sustained a "stable" or a "tranquil" behavior of the economy will result. Such a stable or tranquil state of the economy, if sustained for a while, will feed back and affect long term expectations about the performance of the economy. This will affect views of the uncertainties involved which, in turn, will affect asset values and permissible liability structures.

For the economy to sustain a virtual equilibrium of employment in which short run profit expectations are consistent with financed investment, the profit flows must be sufficient to validate debts, i.e., businesses will be able to fulfill their cash payment commitments embodied in their liability structure. But such fulfillment of debt commitments will affect the willingness to debt finance by bankers and their customers: the value of the insurance embodied in money decreases as the economy functions in a tranquil way. Stability—or tranquility—in a world with a cyclical past and capitalist financial institutions is destabilizing.

If a transitory equilibrium defined by the existing short run expectations differs from full employment the question arises as to whether labor, product, or financial market reactions to the ruling situation will affect either short or long run expectations in such a way that a movement toward full employment takes place. Keynes' answer was that this depends upon how the market adjustments affect the state of long run expectations that guide businessmen and their bankers as they hold and finance positions in capital assets and as they plan and finance investment spending. In the years of the great contraction 1929-33 it seems clear that responses in labor, product, and financial markets to unemployment, excess supply, and difficulty in meeting financial commitments made things worse, not better. Falling wages and product prices, by increasing the burden of cash payment commitments due to existing debts relative to profit flows which depend upon current prices, outputs, and wages, made the state of long run expectations of businessmen and bankers less, not more, favorable to ordering investment output.

Thus there is a problem of effective demand failures in a capitalist economy that is not due to wages, price or interest rate rigidities. To recognize that such a problem exists it is necessary to specify that we are dealing with an investing capitalist economy that has sophisticated financial institutions. In such an economy employment is offered on the basis of short run profit expectations whereas investment demand, which depends upon long run profit expectations, determines the profits that in fact are realized. Only if market reactions to unemployment change long run expectations so that investment increases and if market reactions to excess aggregate demand change long run expectations so that investment decreases can the system be considered as self-equilibrating with its "equilibrium" in the neighborhood of full employment.

The financial instability hypothesis by emphasizing the way in which investment demand is generated by the combination of the valuation of the stock of assets, the financing available from internal funds and financial markets, and the supply price of investment output shows how a collapse of asset values, that occurs because of position making problems of units engaged in speculative and Ponzi[12] finance, leads to a collapse of investment. Such a collapse of investment will lead to a short fall in the profit flows generated by capital assets, which in turn makes the fulfillment of business financial commitments more difficult if not impossible. Financial structures and financial interrelations are the phenomena in a capitalist economy that make the development of those long term expectations that lead to a collapse of investment an endogenous phenomenon in the particular circumstances that in fact arise in the aftermath of a sustained expansion.

## IV. A restatement of the financial instability hypothesis

The financial instability hypothesis is rooted in the analysis of the two sets of prices that exist in capitalism, those of current output, which reflect short run or current considerations, and those of capital assets which reflect long run expectations.[13] Thus it is a variant of Keynesian theory.

However the financial instability hypothesis goes beyond what is explicit in the *General Theory* by integrating the liability structure and the cash payment commitments they imply into the analysis of the determination of capital asset prices and the financing of investment. The view of the economy is from "Wall Street" or "The City." Economic activity is seen as generating business cash flows. A part of these cash flows is applied to validate debt. Anticipated cash flows from business operations determine the demand for and supply of "debts" to be used to finance positions in capital assets and the production of new capital assets (investment output). Money is mainly created as banks finance business and acquire other assets and money is destroyed as debts to banks are repaid or as banks sell assets.[14]

The "Wall Street" or "City" view looks upon the exchange of money today for money later as the key economic transaction. The money today part may involve a financial instrument, an existing capital asset, or investment output. The money tomorrow part may be interest, dividends, repayment of principal, *or* the gross profits after taxes from the use of capital assets in production. Acquiring capital assets in general and investment in particular are money today-money tomorrow transactions. Debt financed positions in capital-assets and investments involve two sets of money today-money tomorrow transactions: one set consists of the promises to pay on the debt instrument, the other consists of the returns that will be earned as the capital-asset or completed investment good is used in production.

An economy with a Wall Street cannot be static. Yesterday's debts and capital asset acquisitions have to be validated by today's cash flows; today's cash flows are largely determined by today's investment; today's investment will or will not be validated depending upon the cash flows that are generated tomorrow. Therefore the economic theory that is relevant for an economy with a Wall Street cannot be static; it cannot abstract from time.

The cash flows that validate debt and the prices that were paid, in the past, for capital assets are profits. These profits are capital's share in gross national product, not the net profits of financial reports. The critical question for an economy with a Wall Street is "what determines profits."

The answer that neo-classical theory gives is that the technical marginal productivity of capital generates profits. This obviously won't do in a world where output fluctuates and market power exists. Once the dynamic and cyclical character of the economy is accepted, the production function construct will not do as the basis for the theoretical analysis of either output or of relative factor renumerations.

The existing set of short-run cost curves, which reflect technical capabilities as embodied in capital assets, is the appropriate starting point for the analysis of profit flows. These cost curves state the in fact relation between out-of-pocket costs and output. When cost curves are combined with market conditions, variations in demand curves (that reflect variations in aggregate demand) translate into variations in gross profits. If gross profits are large enough, the debt structure and past investment decisions are validated.

If, with Kalecki,[15] we assume that workers spend all they earn on consumption and profit receivers do not consume, we get

1. $$\pi = I \text{ (profits equal investment).}$$

This is nothing more than a restatement of $S = I$ (savings equals investment). However, $I$ is a function of $(P_K, P_I(I), E\pi, \text{Ext. Finance})$ where $P_K$ = price of capital assets, $P_I(I)$ = supply price of investment goods as functions of investment price, $E\pi$ = expected profits and Ext. Finance = external financing conditions. Thus

1'. $I \mapsto \pi$. The causation runs from investment to profits.

Investment calls the tune and finance affects investment. It can readily be shown that

2. $$\overset{*}{\pi} = I + DF,$$

when $DF$ is the government deficit and $\overset{*}{\pi}$ is after-tax profits. Furthermore,

3. $$\overset{*}{\pi} = I + DF - BPDF,$$

where $BPDF$ is the deficit in the balance of payments. The Kalecki model can also allow for consumption out of profits $C\overset{*}{\pi}$ and savings by workers $SW$ which leads to:

4. $\qquad \overset{*}{\pi} = I + DF - BPDF - SW + C\overset{*}{\pi}$ so that

5. $\quad \overset{*}{\pi} = \dfrac{1}{1-C} (I + DF - BPDF - SW)$. Profits rather than being

determined by technology, as in the neo-classical synthesis where production functions rule the roost, are determined by the economic, political, social, and psychological relations that determine $I, DF, BPDF, W, SW$, and $C\overset{*}{\pi}$.[16]

This view of profits as the result of the way the economy in fact functions clearly identifies profits as a cash flow. Viewing profits as a cash flow quite naturally leads to an analysis of the different roles played by profits in a capitalist economy. Realized profits in a capitalist economy are: (1) the cash flows that may (or may not) validate debts and the prices paid for capital assets: (2) the mark-up on labor costs that assures that what is produced by part of the labor force is allocated to all of the labor force. (This allocating of what is produced by a part to the whole is a device for generating a surplus); and (3) the signals whether accumulation should continue and where the surplus should be used.

Profits, especially profits relative to the cash payment commitments on debts, affect the long run expectations of business and bankers. Profits are the critical link to time in a capitalist economy: they are determined by the existing size and structure of aggregate demand, they determine whether the past debts and prices paid for capital assets are validated, and they affect the long run expectations of businessmen and bankers that enter into investment and financing decisions. We are dealing with a capitalist economy with a past, a present, and a future. In such an economy the extent to which present profits validate decisions taken in the past affects long run expectations and thus present investment and financing decisions; present investment and financing activity in turn determine the "parameters" within which future decisions will be made. By focusing on profits a theory based upon Kalecki's insights on how profit is generated clearly recognizes that we need build our theory to be relevant for an economy that exists in history.

A capitalist economy only works well as an investing economy, for investment generates profits. Profit expectations make debt financing possible and help determine the demand for investment output. Investment takes place because it is expected that capital assets will yield profits in the future, but these future profits will be forthcoming only if future investment takes place. Profits are the carrot and the stick that make capitalism work.

Profits result from an excess of prices over unit labor and purchased input costs. The price system for current output allocates profits to particular outputs and thus to particular in existence capital-assets. In the simple model where government and foreign trade are not taken into account, prices and outputs adjust so that profits equal financed investment. Relative price formation, production, and employment take place within aggregate economic conditions that are determined by the need for profits to equal investment.

The identification of profits as a flow determined by the income generating process is but one ingredient in the financial instability view. This ingredient leads to the proposition that current investment determines whether or not the financial commitments on business debts can be fulfilled. At a sufficiently low level of investment, income, employment, and thus profits, a significant proportion of the contractual commitments on business debts cannot be fulfilled from the normal sources. Attempts by debtors to raise funds needed to meet commitments by recourse to extraordinary sources, such as the sale of assets, are part of the mechanism by which an initial financial tautness is transformed into a financial crisis. Fluctuations in investment determine whether or not debts can be validated; the question that now has to be addressed is "why does investment fluctuate?"

To answer this question, we turn to the financial system and the debt structure.[17] Any "position" (i.e., a set of owned assets) needs to be financed. The instruments used to finance positions set up cash flow commitments even as the assets "in position" yield cash flows. We can distinguish three types of financial postures:

1. Hedge finance: The cash flows from assets in position are expected to exceed the cash flow commitments on liabilities for every period. As cash in exceeds cash out in every period the expected present value of a hedge finance unit is positive for every set of finite interest rates. The liability structure of a hedge unit consists mainly of long term debts and equity although short term commercial credits to finance work in progress are consistent with hedge financing.

2. Speculative finance: The cash flows from assets in the near term fall short of the near-term contracted payments, but the income portion of the near-term cash flows, measured by accepted accounting conventions, exceeds the interest cost of the debt, and the expected cash receipts in the longer term are expected to exceed cash payment commitments that are outstanding. A unit engaged in speculative finance needs to roll over or refinance debt

to meet its near-term financial commitments. The present value of the net cash flows of a speculative finance unit will be positive for one set of (low) interest rates and negative for other higher interest rates. Banks are speculative finance units.

3. "Ponzi" finance: The cash flows from assets in the near-term fall short of cash payment commitments and the net income portion of the receipts falls short of the interest portion of the payments. A "Ponzi" finance unit must increase its outstanding debt in order to meet its financial obligations. Presumably, there is a "bonanza" in the future which makes the present value positive for low enough interest rates. Although "Ponzi" finance is often tinged with fraud, every investment project with a long gestation period and somewhat uncertain returns has aspects of a "Ponzi" finance scheme. Many of the real estate investment trusts that came upon hard times in 1974/75 in the United States were, quite unknowing to the household investors who bought their equities, involved in "Ponzi" schemes. Many of these trusts were financing construction projects that had to be sold out quickly and at a favorable price if the debts to the trusts were to be paid. A tightening of mortage credit brought on slowness of sales of finished construction, which led to a "present value reversal" (to be defined on page 108) for these projects.

The mix of hedge, speculative, and Ponzi finance in existence at any time reflects the history of the economy and the effect of historical developments upon the state of long term expectations. In particular during a period of tranquility, in which the economy functions at a reasonably close approximation to full employment, there will be a decline in the value of the insurance that the holding of money bestows. This will lead to both a rise in the price of capital assets and a shift of portfolio preference so that a larger admixture of speculative and even Ponzi finance is essayed by business and accepted by bankers. In this way the financial system endogenously generates at least part of the finance needed by the increased investment demand that follows a rise in the price of capital assets.[18]

As the ratio of speculative and Ponzi finance units increases in the total financial structure of an economy, the economy becomes increasingly sensitive to interest rate variations. In both speculative and Ponzi finance units the expected cash flows that make the financial structure viable come later in time than the payment commitments on outstanding debt. At high enough short term interest rates speculative units become Ponzi units and for Ponzi units the accumulated carrying charges at high interest rates on their outstanding short term debts can lead to cash flow requirements that exceed the cash flow expectations that made the initial position viable—that is the initial short run cash flow deficit is transformed into a permanent cash flow deficit by high interest rates.

External finance and interest "rates" enter the investment process at two quite different stages. The production of investment takes time and the early-on costs are compounded at the short-term interest rate in determining the costs of investment output. This is beautifully illustrated in the way construction is financed in the United States. The financing of a construction project leads to the drawing down of funds made available by a bank; obviously the interest charges on such funds have to be recovered in the "delivered price" of the investment good. The delivered price of an investment good is a positive function of the (short term) interest rate.

An investment good, once delivered and "at work" in a production process, is a capital-asset. As a capital-asset, its value is the present value of the anticipated gross profits after taxes (quasi-rents) that are imputed to its participation in economic activity. The present value of a capital asset is an inverse function of the (long term) interest rate.

A rising investment demand leads to an increase in investment in process. As investment in process increases, an inelastic component of the demand curve for financing rises. If the supply curve of finance is infinitely elastic, then finance costs do not rise as investment increases. As more investment leads to greater profits, the prices of capital assets, at constant interest rates, increase. Such an increase is an incentive for more investment: the run up of prices and profits that characterizes a boom will result. However, the internal workings of the banking mechanism or Central Bank action to constrain inflation will result in the supply of finance becoming less than infinitely elastic—perhaps even approach zero elasticity. A rising inelastic demand curve for finance due to the investment in process combined with an inelastic supply curve of finance leads to a rapid increase in short-term interest rates.

Sharp increases in the short-term interest rate increase the supply price of investment output. Sharp increases in short-term interest rates lead to a rise in long-term interest rates. This leads to a fall in the present value of gross profits after taxes (quasi-rents) that capital assets are expected to earn. Rising interest rates shift the supply curve of investment upward even as they shift the demand curve for investment, which is derived from the price of capital assets, downward. These shifts in the conditions of investment supply and demand lead to a fall in investment, which lowers current and near-term expected profits. Lower profit expectations lower the price of capital-assets, and thus the price that business is willing to pay for investment output.

The fall in profits means that the ability of business to fulfill financial commitments embodied in debts deteriorates. In particular when profits fall some hedge units become speculative units and some speculative units become Ponzi units. The rise in long term interest rates and the decline in expected profits play particular havoc with Ponzi units, for the present value of the hoped for future bonanza falls sharply. The prior Ponzi units find they must sell out positions in assets to meet payment commitments only to discover that their assets cannot be sold at a price that even comes near to covering debts. Once the selling out of positions rather than refinancing becomes prevalent, asset prices can and do fall below their cost of production as an investment good.

What has been sketched is the route to a financial crisis. Whether a full-fledged financial crisis takes place depends upon the efficacy of central bank lender of last resort behavior and whether gross profit flows are sustained by an increase in the government deficit or changes in the balance of payments. However, even if a full-fledged financial crisis does not take place, the long run expectations of business, bankers, and the ultimate holders of financial assets will be affected by these developments. The risk premiums associated with investment projects will increase and businessmen and bankers will move toward balance sheet structures that involve less speculative finance.

The recursive process between profits and the effective discount rate for business assets can continue even onto a "present value reversal"; i.e., the supply curve of investment output can rise above the demand curve for investment output so that investment, and, with investment, profits collapse. Once profits collapse, the cash flows to validate even initially hedge financing arrangements will not be forthcoming. (These relations are illustrated in Figures 1 and 2.)[19]

In Figure 1 the "normal" situation is illustrated. The demand and supply conditions for investment, taking financial conditions into account, might lead to investment shifting back and forth between $I_1$ and $I_2$ as profits, risk premiums, and costs of production of investment output vary. In Figure 2 the situation in which the repercussions of a "debt-deflation" have affected both profits and effective financing terms is sketched. In this case the fall of profits has lowered the demand price for capital-assets even as the rise in "lenders' risk" has raised the supply price of investment output for any given level of money wages. What is sketched is the ex-

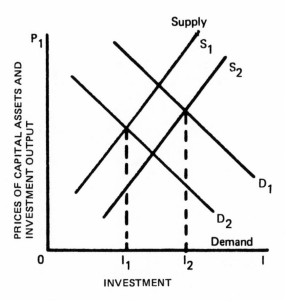

Figure 1

treme case in which the supply curve "everywhere" lies above the demand curve.

In Figure 1 the shifts in the supply and demand curves for investment reflect changes in the variables that enter as proximate determinants of aggregate demand and supply even as the variables that enter into the determination of long run expectations are unaffected. This in particular means that even though there have been variations in earned profits and in the terms upon financing contracts, the current expectations of longer term profits, interest rates and acceptable financial structures have not been changed. In Figure 1 a shift to the left of the supply and demand curves can be offset by minor changes in money market conditions, the government fiscal posture, and money wages rates.

In Figure 2 the position of the supply and demand curves for investment output reflect changes in the long run expectation about profits and desirable financing structure. The shift from the situation illustrated in Figure 1 to that of Figure 2 reflects the type of unfavorable experience with inherited liability structures that we sketched in the discussion of hedge, speculative, and Ponzi finance. In the situation in Figure 2, short term changes in proximate profits, market interest rates, money wages, and the government fiscal posture might sustain income and employment but will not have a quick effect upon the supply and demand for investment output. In particular in a regime of small government, such as existed when Keynes wrote the *General Theory*, neither wage deflation nor money market ease could quickly transform what is sketched in Figure 2 into that of Figure 1. In fact because a key element in the emergence and continuation of the situation sketched in Figure 2 is the shortfall of profits relative to the financial obligations on inherited debt a decline in money wages which leads to an expected decline in the "dollar" value of profits will make things worse.

That is, whereas variation in market variables that are determined by "supply and demand" conditions in product, labor, and money markets are effective governors of the rate of investment when long run expectations are conducive to investment, variations in these same variables are not effective governors of investment once the shift in long run expectations that occurs with and after a financial crisis has taken place.

Once a situation resembling that sketched in Figure 2 exists, the economy is well on its way to or already in a deep depression. However, whether such a situation fully develops and if it does, how long it lasts, depends upon the government's involvement in the economy; how promptly the government intervenes and how effective the intervention. In 1929/1933 government intervention was minute and late. In particular in the United States the Federal Reserve virtually abdicated its responsibilities as a lender of last resort, which is to assure that those speculative and Ponzi financial

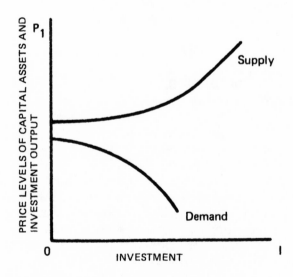

Figure 2

positions, which would be validated by longer term cash flows at the current (pre-crisis) price level, at a reasonable approximation to full employment income, and at interest rates short of the rates that rule at the peak of the investment boom, receive prompt refinancing.

In 1974/1975 the emerging threats of a financial debacle were met by extensive lender of last resort interventions by the Federal Reserve System and a virtual explosion of the Federal Government deficit——which sustained aggregate business profits. The U.S. economy——and with it the world economy——exhibited more resilience in 1974/75 than in 1929/33 because the government's involvement in the economy was much greater and more effective.

The essence of the financial instability hypothesis is that financial traumas, even onto debt deflation interactions, occur as a normal functioning result in a capitalist economy. This does not mean that a capitalist economy is always tottering on the brink of disaster. There are situations where the short term debt financing of business and households is modest; this leads to robust financial markets which are not susceptible to debt deflation processes. There are also fragile financial structures which include a great deal of speculative and Ponzi finance of business and households. The normal functioning of an economy with a robust financial situation is both tranquil and, on the whole, successful. Tranquillity and success are not self-sustaining states, they induce increases in capital asset prices relative to current output prices and a rise in (1) acceptable debts for any prospective income flow, (2) investment, and (3) profits. These concurrent increases lead to a transformation over time of an initially robust financial structure into a fragile structure. Once a financial structure includes a sufficiently large weight of speculative and "quasi-Ponzi" finance (of the interim financing of long gestation period investments) a run-up of short-term interest rates, as the demand for short-term financing increases rapidly, can occur. This will lead to "present value reversals," especially if it is accompanied by a rise in the value of liquidity as some units fail to meet financial obligations. As the cost of investment output becomes greater than the value of capital assets being produced, take-out financing will not be forthcoming. This leads to a "collapse" of asset values even further below the supply price of investment output, which further decreases investment. But decreases in investment by decreasing profits makes things worse. The immediate market reactions to a decline in income in the context of a financial structure that is heavily weighted by Ponzi and speculative finance make things worse; the set of interrelated markets is unstable.

## V. Policy implications

The financial instability hypothesis has serious implications for policy. First of all, it points out that there are inherent and inescapable flaws in capitalism. That capitalism is flawed does not necessarily mean that one rejects capitalism. The financial instability hypothesis emphasizes the importance of institutions and the ability of institutions to modify the behavior of the economy; thus, there are varieties of capitalism. The question may very well be which variety is better, not necessarily for all time, but for now.

In a capitalist economy with a small government, $\pi = I$, so that a collapse in asset values, which lowers $I$, not only decreases income and employment but it also lowers profits. This not only means that the value of capital assets falls, but it also means that outstanding debt payment commitments, especially by units that are "into" speculative and Ponzi finance, cannot be fulfilled.

On the other hand, in a capitalist economy with a big government, $\overset{*}{\pi} = I + DF$; after tax profits equals investment plus the deficit. If a decrease in $I$ is offset by a rise in the deficit, then profit flows need not fall; in fact, if the increase in the deficit is large enough, profits will rise. This is what happened in 1975 in the United States. The enormous government deficit in the first two quarters of that year helped abort a serious debt deflation process by sustaining gross profits after taxes even as investment fell.

An implication of the proposition that prices must be such as to generate profits equal to investment is that any increase in the ratio of the total wage bill in the production of investment output to the total wage bill in the production of consumption goods is inflationary. Furthermore, any increase in spending on consumption goods financed by transfer payments or profit income is inflationary. As wages that are paid for overhead labor and ancillary business services such as advertising are best considered as allocations of profit, a rise in spending on advertising, executive suites, product research and development is inflationary. Thus, the emphasis upon growth through investment, the bias toward bigness in business, business styles that emphasize advertising and overheads, and the explosion of transfer payments are main causes of our current inflation.

From the perspective of the financial instability hypothesis, inflation is one way to ease payment commitments due to debt. In the 1970s a big depression has been avoided by floating off untenable debt structures through inflation. Stagflation is a substitute for a big depression. However, the floating off of debt through inflation is a "game" that can be played only a number of times; the propensity to expand into a boom will be atrophied as bankers became wary of Ponzi schemes. Alternatively, government intervention to sustain investment can become so overpowering that the "sharp pencils" needed to assure that investment yields real rather than nominal, social rather than private, benefits become blunted.

Every businessman and banker knows that for every investment project worth undertaking there are literally an infinite number that are losers. Once the doctrine of salvation through investment becomes deeply ingrained into our political and economic system the constraints on foolish investment are relaxed. This is especially so if the government stands ready to guarantee particular investors or investment projects against losses. A capitalism with a big government that is dedicated to full employment through ostensibly private investment can approach the inefficiencies of a Stalinist economy that refuses to use present value calculations.

In the aggregate the foolishness of bankers, businessmen, and government guarantors is floated off by massive government deficits that lead to profits which validate aggregate past investment and overall business liabilities, albeit at a price in inflation and increasingly inefficient business techniques. The inefficiency of the chosen techniques is reflected by the unemployment that accompanies inflation: stagflation is a symptom of an underlying inept set of capital-assets.

Given that instability is due to the emphasis upon investment and that inflation is due to the emphasis upon investment, transfer payments, and the need to bail out the threatened financial structure, the financial instability hypothesis indicates that an economy that is oriented toward the production of consumption goods by techniques that are less capital intensive than those now being induced by policy will be less susceptible to financial instability and inflation. This suggests that the policy emphasis should shift from the encouragement of growth through investment to the achievement of full employment through consumption production. The financial instability hypothesis suggests that a simplification of financial structures is a way of achieving greater stability, although being rooted in an analysis of the historical dynamics of the financial structure, it also recognizes that the enforcement of simplicity in financial arrangements will be difficult.

The financial instability hypothesis also suggests that while there are better ways of running our economy than the way it has been run in the recent past, there is no economic organization or magic formula which, once achieved and set in motion, solves the problem of economic policy for all times. Economies evolve, and with the internal evolution of the economic mechanism the apt structure of legislated institutions and policy operations change: there is no way one generation of economists can render their successors obsolete. I am afraid economists can never become mere technicians applying an agreed-upon theory that is fit for all seasons within an institutional structure that does not and need not change.

## Notes

1. Of the mathematical economists, perhaps F. H. Hahn has been most open about the limitations of mathematical theory. See F. H. Hahn, "On Some Problems of Proving the Existence of an Equilibrium in a Monetary Economy," in B. Clower (ed.) *Monetary Theory* (Penguin, 1969), "Professor Friedman's Views on Money," *Economica*, February 1971, 38(149): 61-80, *On the Notions of Equilibrium in Economics* (Cambridge: Cambridge University Press, 1973). Also see: K. Arrow and F. H. Hahn, *General Competitive Analysis* (San Francisco: Holder Day, 1971), especially Chapter 14, The Keynesian Model, pp. 347-369. In introducing their discussion they note that in their earlier proof that a temporary equilibrium always exists they ". . . supposed that at the moment an equilibrium was shown to exist, economic agents had no commitments left from the past . . ." i.e., there are no debts and no capital assets as we know capital assets. It is interesting to note that Arrow and Hahn head Chapter 14 with a quotation from W. B. Yeats', "The Second Coming," "Things fall apart, the centre does not hold."

2. Perhaps the best references are: J. R. Hicks, "Mr. Keynes and the Classics: A Suggested Interpretation," *Econometrica* 5(1937): 147-159, A. Hansen, *Monetary Theory and Fiscal Policy* (New York: McGraw-Hill, 1949), F. Modigliani, "Liquidity Preference and the Theory of Interest and Money," *Econometrica*, 12(1944), D. Patinkin, *Money Interest and Prices* (Evanston, Ill.: Row-Peterson and Co., 1956).

3. Among the "key works" in the emerging post-Keynesian synthesis are: Joan Robinson, *Economic Heresies* (London: MacMillan, 1971), P. Davidson, *Money and the Real World* (New York: John Wiley & Sons, 1972), J. A. Kregal, *The Reconstruction of Political Economy* (London: MacMillan, 1973), S. Weintraub, *A Keynesian Theory of Employment, Growth and Income Distribution* (Philadelphia, Chilton, 1966), Victoria Chick, *The Theory of Monetary Policy* (London: Gray-Mills Publishing Ltd., 1973).

4. J. Viner, "Mr. Keynes and the Causes of Unemployment," *Quarterly Journal of Economics* (November 1936): 147-167, J. M. Keynes, "The General Theory of Employment," *Quarterly Journal of Economics* (February 1937): 209-223.

5. M. Friedman, "The Quantity Theory of Money—A Restatement," in M. Friedman (ed.) *Studies in the Quantity Theory of Money* (Chicago: University of Chicago Press, 1956).

6. This is the outcome of the two Cambridge debates on Capital Theory, although the standard discussion and summary of the debate, G. C. Harcourt, *Some Cambridge Controversies in the Theory of Capital* (Cambridge: Cambridge University Press, 1972) does not make this clear.

7. This section reflects discussions with Jan Kregal and Ignazio Musu and my reading of some of their work in progress.

8. R. W. Clower, "The Keynesian Counter-revolution: A Theoretical Ap-

praisal" in F. H. Hahn and F. C. R. Brechling (eds.), *The Theory of Interest Rates* (London: MacMillan, 1965), and A. Leijonhufvud, *On Keynesian Economics and the Economics of Keynes* (London: Oxford University Press, 1968), are non-post-Keynesians who had a part in triggering the discussion of what Keynes "truly meant."

9. E. Malinvaud, *The Theory of Unemployment Reconsidered*, Yrjo Johnsson Lectures (Oxford: Basil Blackwell, 1977), is a sophisticated statement of this approach.

10. J. M. Keynes, *The General Theory of Employment, Interest and Money* (London: MacMillan, 1936), p. 343.

11. M. Blaug, "Kuhn versus Lakatos on Paradigms versus Research Programmes in the History of Economic Thought," in Spiro Latsis (ed.), *Method and Appraisal in Economics* (Cambridge: Cambridge University Press, 1976), p. 164.

12. The label "Ponzi" refers to a Boston event soon after World War I in which a "pyramid" financing scheme swept through the working class and even affected "respectable" folk.

13. H. P. Minsky, *John Maynard Keynes* (New York: Columbia University Press, 1975).

14. Malinvaud (op. cit.) introduces money as follows: "Let us consider an economy with $r$ commodities ($h = 1,2. . . ., r$), the last one being money;. . ." (p. 18). Arrow and Hahn in Chapter 14 of their *The Keynesian Model* write, "Let the subscript "$n$" stand for money that we now regard as the non-interest-paying debt of some agency outside our formal system, say the government," p. 349. It is clear that "money" in Malinvaud and Arrow/Hahn has no relevant resemblance to the "money" of those economies whose behavior we are trying to understand when we "do" ecnomic theory. Arrow and Hahn recognize that they are violating reality in their definition and offer apologies for the "primitive monetary ideas" they explore. Malinvaud does not articulate any recognition of the "heroic" nature of his abstractions, even as he offers his work as being "relevant" to the analysis of policy.

15. M. Kalecki, *Selected Essays on the Dynamics of the Capitalist Economy* (1933-1970) (Cambridge: Cambridge University Press, 1971), Chapter 7, "The Determinants of Profits," pp. 78-92. The financial instability hypothesis identifies profits, determined as Kalecki shows, as a cash flow that does or does not validate past financial commitments: it integrates Kalecki's vision of the dynamic determination of profits with the capitalist institutional fact of a liability structure inherited from the past that commits current and future profits. (Incidentally the paper by Kalecki first appeared in 1942.)

16. See Thanos Skouras *Government Activity and Private Profits*, Thames Papers in Political Economy (London: Thames Polytechnic, Summer 1975).

17. H. P. Minsky, "The Modelling of Financial Instability: An Introduction," *Modelling and Simulation*, Vol. 5, Proceedings of the Fifth Annual Pittsburgh Conference, Edited by William G. Vogt and Merlin H. Mickle. School of Engineering, University of Pittsburgh, 1974. "Suggestions for a Cash Flow Oriented Bank Examination," *Conference on Bank Structure and Competition*, Federal Reserve Bank of Chicago, December 1975.

18. The shift toward speculative and even Ponzi finance is evident in the financial statistics of the United States as collected in the Flow of Funds accounts. The movement to "bought money" by large multinational banks throughout the world is evidence that there are degrees of speculative finance: all banks engage in speculative finance but some banks are more specu-

lative than others. Only a thorough cash flow analysis of an economy can indicate the extent to which finance is speculative and where the critical point at which the ability to meet contractual commitments can break down is located. See H. P. Minsky, "Suggestions for a Cash Flow Oriented Bank Examination" (op. cit.). The Flow of Funds reference is: Board of Governors of the Federal Reserve System, *Flow of Funds Accounts 1946-1975* (Washington, D.C., December 1976).

19. H. P. Minsky, "A Theory of Systemic Fragility," in E. Altman, A. W. Sametz, *Financial Crises* (New York: Wiley Interscience, 1977).

# 6

*Financial Instability*
*Revisited:*
*The Economics*
*of Disaster*

## I. Introduction

A striking characteristic of economic experience in the United
States is the repeated occurrence of financial crises——crises that
usher in deep depressions and periods of low-level economic stagnation. More than 40 years have passed since the financial shock
that initiated the Great Depression of the 1930s, a much longer
period of time than between the crises and deep depressions of the
previous century.[1] Is the experience since the Great Depression
the result of fundamental changes in the economic system and of
our knowledge so that crises and deep depressions cannot happen,
or are the fundamental relations unchanged and our knowledge
and power still inadequate so that crises and deep depressions are
still possible?

This paper argues that the fundamentals are unchanged; sustained
economic growth, business cycle booms, and the accompanying financial developments still generate conditions conducive to disaster
for the entire economic system.

Every disaster, financial or otherwise, is compounded out of initial displacements or shocks, structural characteristics of the system, and human error. The theory developed here argues that the

The original draft of this paper was written in the fall of 1966 and it was revised in January 1970. I wish to thank Maurice I. Townsend, Lawrence H.
Seltzer, and Bernard Shull for their comments and encouragement. Needless
to say, any errors of fact or fancy are my responsibility.

Abridged by the author for this volume. From *Reappraisal of the Federal
Reserve Discount Mechanism* (Washington, D.C.: the Board of Governors of
the Federal Reserve System, June 1972).

structural characteristics of the financial system change during periods of prolonged expansion and economic boom and that these changes cumulate to decrease the domain of stability of the system. Thus, after an expansion has been in progress for some time, an event that is not of unusual size or duration can trigger a sharp financial reaction.[2]

Displacements may be the result of system behavior or human error. Once the sharp financial reaction occurs, institutional deficiencies will be evident. Thus, after a crisis it will always be possible to construct plausible arguments——by emphasizing the triggering events or institutional flaws——that accidents, mistakes, or easily corrected shortcomings were responsible for the disaster.[3]

In previous work, I have used an accelerator-multiplier cum constraining ceilings and floors model to represent the real economy. Within this model the periodic falling away from the ceiling, which reflects parameter values and hence is an endogenous phenomenon, is not the unusual event that can trigger the "unstable" financial reaction——if a "proper" financial environment or structure exists. The financial reaction in turn lowers the effective floor to income. Once the gap between floor and ceiling incomes is large enough, I assumed that the accelerator coefficient falls to a value that leads to a stagnant behavior for the economy. In this way a set of parameter values that leads to an explosive income expansion is replaced by a set that leads to a stagnant economy. I assumed that the gap between floor and ceiling income is a determinant of the accelerator coefficient and that the immediate impact of financial instability is to lower the floor income, because financial variables——including the market value of common stocks——determine the position of a conventional Keynesian consumption function.[4]

This view neglects decision-making under uncertainty as a determinant of system behavior. A special type of uncertainty is inherent in an enterprise system with decentralized decisions and private ownership of productive resources due to the financial relations. The financial system of such an economy partitions and distributes uncertainty. A model that recognizes the problems involved in decision-making in the face of the intrinsically irrational fact of uncertainty is needed if financial instability is to be understood. A reinterpretation of Keynesian economics as just such a model, and an examination of how monetary constraint——whether due to policy or to behavior of the economy——works, are needed before the stability properties of the financial system and thus of the economy can be examined. It turns out that the fundamental instability of a capitalist economy is a tendency to explode——to enter into a boom or "euphoric" state.

This paper will not present any empirical research. There is, nevertheless, need to: (1) examine updated information of the type analyzed in earlier studies, (2) explore additional bodies of data, and (3) generate new data (see Section VII). Only with this information can the problem be made precise and the propositions tested.

There is a special facet to empirical work on the problems at issue. Financial crises, panics, and instability are rare events with short durations.[5] We have not experienced anything more than unit or minor sectoral financial distress since the early 1930s. The institutions and usages in finance, due to both legislation and the evolution of financial practices, are much different today from what they were before the Great Depression. For example, it is necessary to guess the power of deposit insurance in order to estimate the conditions under which a crisis can develop from a set of initial events.[6] The short duration of crises means that the smoothing operations that go into data generation as well as econometric analysis will tend to minimize the importance of crises.

Because of such factors it might be that the most meaningful way to test propositions as to the cause and effect of financial instability will be through simulation studies, where the simulation models are designed to reflect alternative ways that financial instability can be induced.[7]

In this paper, Section II discusses differences between an economy that is simply growing steadily and one that is booming. The characteristics of a euphoric economy are identified. This section develops the proposition that, in a boom or euphoric economy, the willingness to invest and to emit liabilities is such that demand conditions will lead to tight money markets—defined in terms of the level and rate of change of interest rates and other financing terms—independently of the rate of growth of the money supply.

Section III focuses upon cash flows due to income production, balance sheet relations, and transactions in real and financial assets. The likelihood of financial instability occurring is dependent upon the relationship between cash payment commitments and the normal sources of cash, as well as upon the behavior of markets that will be affected if unusual sources of cash need to be tapped.

Section IV develops the role of uncertainty as a determinant of the demand for investment within a framework of Keynesian economics.

Section V examines alternative modes of operation of monetary constraint. In a euphoric economy, tight money, when effective, does not operate by inducing a smooth movement along a stable investment schedule; rather it operates by shifting the liquidity preference function. Such shifts are typically due to a liquidity crisis of some sort.

Section VI explores the domains of stability both of the financial system and of the economy. These domains are shown to be endogenous and to decrease during a prolonged boom. In addition, the financial changes that take place during a euphoric period tend also to decrease the domain of stability and the feedbacks from euphoria tend to induce sectoral financial difficulties that can escalate to a general financial panic. If such a panic occurs, it will usher in a deep depression; however, the central bank can abort a financial crisis. Nevertheless, the tensions and tremors that pass through the financial system during such a period of near crisis may lead to a reconsideration of desired portfolio composition by both financial institutions and other economic units. A rather severe recession may follow such a reconsideration.

Sections VII and VIII, which are omitted in this reprinting, deal with two special topics, bank examinations and regional impacts. In Section VII it is argued that a bank examination procedure centering around cash flows as determined by balance sheet and contractual relations would be a valuable guide for Federal Reserve policy and an important instrument for bank management. Such an examination procedure would force financial-unit managers and economic policy-makers to consider the impact upon financial units of the characteristics of both the real economy and the financial system.

The discussion of the regional impact of Section VIII centers around the possibility that there is a concentration of financially vulnerable units within one region. In these circumstances, the escalation of financial constraint to a financial crisis might occur though financially vulnerable units, on a national basis, are too few to cause difficulty.

Section IX sets forth some policy guidelines for the Federal Reserve System. It is argued that the discount window should be open to selected money market position takers (dealers) and that the Federal Reserve should move toward furnishing a larger portion of the total reserves of banks by discounting operations. This policy strategy follows from the increased awareness of the possibility of a financial crisis and of the need to have broad, deep, and resilient markets for a wide spectrum of financial instruments once a financial crisis threatens so that the effects of such a crisis can be moderated.

## II. The economics of euphoria

In the mid-1960s the U.S. economy experienced a change of state.

Political leaders and official economists announced that the economic system had entered upon a new era that was to be characterized by the end of the business cycle as it had been known.[8] Starting then, cycles, if any, were to be in the positive rate of growth of income. The doctrine of "fine tuning" went further and asserted that even recessions in the rate of growth of income could be avoided. Contemporary business comments were consistent with these official views.

The substance of the change of state was an investment boom: in each year from 1963 through 1966 the rate of increase of investment by corporate business rose.[9] By the mid-1960s business investment was guided by a belief that the future promised perpetual expansion. An economy that is ruled by such expectations and that exhibits such investment behavior can properly be labeled euphoric.

Consider the value of a going concern. Expected gross profits after taxes reflect the expected behavior of the economy, as well as expected market and management developments. Two immediate consequences follow if the expectation of a normal business cycle is replaced by the expectation of steady growth. First, those gross profits in the present-value calculations that had reflected expected recessions are replaced by those that reflect continuing expansion. Simultaneously there is less uncertainty about the future behavior of the economy. As the belief in the reality of a new era emerges, the decrease in the expected down or short time for plant and equipment raises their present values. The confident expectation of a steady stream of prosperity gross profits makes portfolio plunging more appealing to firm decision-makers.

A sharp rise in expected returns from real capital makes the economy short of capital overnight. The willingness to assume liability structures that are less defensive and to take what would have been considered in earlier times, undesirable chances in order to finance the acquisition of additional capital goods means that this shortage of capital will be transformed into demand for financial resources.

Those that supply financial resources live in the same expectational climate as those that demand them. In the several financial markets, once a change in expectations occurs, demanders, with liability structures that previously would in the view of the suppliers have made them ineligible for accommodations, become quite acceptable. Thus, the supply conditions for financing the acquisitions of real capital improve simultaneously with an increase in the willingness to emit liabilities to finance such acquisitions.

Such an expansionary new era is destabilizing in three senses.

One is that it quite rapidly raises the value of existing capital. The second is an increase in the willingness to finance the acquisition of real capital by emitting what, previously, would have been considered as high-cost liabilities, where the cost of liabilities includes risk or uncertainty borne by the liability emitter (borrower's risk). The third is the acceptance by lenders of assets that earlier would have been considered low-yield——when the yield is adjusted to allow for the risks borne by the asset acquirer (lender's risk).[10]

These concepts can be made more precise. The present value of a set of capital goods collected in a firm reflects that firm's expected gross profits after taxes. For all enterprises there is a pattern of how the business cycles of history have affected their gross profits. Initially the present value reflects this past cyclical pattern. For example, with a short horizon

$$V = \frac{Q_1}{1 + r_1} + \frac{Q_2}{(1 + r_2)^2} + \frac{Q_3}{(1 + r_3)^3}$$

where $Q_1$ is a prosperity, $Q_2$ is a recession, and $Q_3$ is a recovery gross profits after taxes, $(Q_2 < Q_3 < Q_1)$. With the new era expectations $Q_2'$ and $Q_3'$, prosperity returns replace the depression and recovery returns. As a result we have: $V$ (new era) $> V$ (traditional). This rise in the value of extant capital assets as collected in firms increases the prices that firms are willing to pay for additions to their capital assets.

Generally, the willingness to emit liabilities is constrained by the need to hedge or to protect the organization against the occurrence of unfavorable conditions. Let us call $Q_2''$ and $Q_3''$ the gross profits after taxes if a possible, but not really expected, deep and long recession occurs. As a risk averter the portfolio rule might be that the balance sheet structure must be such that even if $Q_2''$ and $Q_3''$ do occur no serious consequences will follow; $Q_2''$ and $Q_3''$——though not likely——are significant determinants of desired balance sheet structure.[11] As a result of the euphoric change in "state," the view grows that $Q_2''$ and $Q_3''$ are so unlikely that there is no need to protect the organization against them. A liability structure that was expensive in terms of risk now becomes cheap when there were significant chances of $Q_2''$ and $Q_3''$ occurring. The cost of capital or of finance by way of such liability structures decreases.

Financial institutions are simultaneously demanders in one and suppliers in another set of financial markets. Once euphoria sets in, they accept liability structures——their own and those of borrowers——that, in a more sober expectational climate, they would have rejected. Money and Treasury bills become poor assets to hold with the decline in the uncertainty discount on assets whose returns depend upon the performance of the economy. The shift to euphoria increases the willingness of financial institutions to acquire assets by engaging in liquidity-decreasing portfolio transformations.

A euphoric new era means that an investment boom is combined with pervasive liquidity-decreasing portfolio transformations. Money market interest rates rise because the demand for investment is increasing, and the elasticity of this demand decreases with respect to market interest rates and contractual terms. In a complex financial system, it is possible to finance investment by portfolio transformations. Thus when a euphoric transformation of expectations takes place, in the short run the amount of investment financed can be independent of monetary policy. The desire to expand and the willingness to finance expansion by portfolio changes can be so great that, unless there are serious side effects of feedbacks, an inflationary explosion becomes likely.

A euphoric boom economy is affected by the financial heritage of an earlier, more insecure time. The world is not born anew each moment. Past portfolio decisions and conditions in financial markets are embodied in the stock of financial instruments. In particular, a decrease in the market value of assets which embody protections against states of nature that are now considered unlikely to occur will take place, or alternatively there is a rise in the interest rate that must be paid to induce portfolios to hold newly created assets with these characteristics. To the extent that such assets are long lived and held by deposit institutions with short-term or demand liabilities, pressures upon these deposit institutions will accompany the euphoric state of the economy. In addition the same change of state that led to the investment boom and to the increased willingness to emit debt affects the portfolio preferences of the holders of the liabilities of deposit institutions. These institutions must meet interest rate competition at a time when the market value of the safety they sell has decreased; that is, their interest rates must rise by more than other rates.

The rising interest rate on safe assets during a euphoric boom puts strong pressures on financial institutions that offer protection and safety. The linkages between these deposit institutions, conventions as to financing arrangements, and particular real markets are such that sectoral depressive pressures are fed back from a boom to particular markets; these depressive pressures are part of the mechanism by which real resources are shifted.

The rise in interest rates places serious pressures upon particular financial intermediaries. In the current (1966) era the savings and loan associations and the mutual savings banks, together with the closely related homebuilding industry, seem to take a large part of the initial feedback pressure. It may be that additional feedback pressures are on life insurance and consumer finance companies.

A little understood facet of how financial and real values are linked centers around the effect of stock market values.[12] The value of real capital rises when the expectation that a recession will occur diminishes and this rise will be reflected in equity prices. The increased ratio of debt financing can also raise expected returns on equities. Inasmuch as owners of wealth live in the same expectational climate as corporate officers, portfolio preferences shift toward equities as the belief in the possibility of recession or depression diminishes. Thus, a stock market boom feeds upon and feeds an investment boom.

The financing needs of the investment boom raise interest rates. This rise lower the market value of long-term debt and adversely affects some financial institutions. Higher interest rates also increase the cost of credit used to finance positions in equities. Initially, the competition for funds among various financial sectors facilitates the rapid expansion of the economy; then as interest rates rise it constrains the profits of investing units and makes the carrying of equities more expensive. This first tends to lessen the rate of increase of equity prices and then to lower equity prices.

All in all, the euphoric period has a short lifespan. Local and sectoral depressions and the fall in equity prices initiate doubts as to whether a new era really has been achieved. A hedging of portfolios and a reconsideration of investment programs takes place. However, the portfolio commitments of the short euphoric era are fixed in liability structures. The reconsideration of investment programs, the lagged effects upon other sectors from the resource-shifting pressures, and the inelasticity of aggregative supply that leads to increases in costs combine to yield a shortfall of the income of investing units below the more optimistic of the euphoric expectations.

The result is a combination of cash flow commitments inherited from the burst of euphoria and of cash flow receipts based upon lower-than-expected income. Whether the now less-desirable financial positions will be unwound without generating significant shocks or whether a series of financial shocks will occur is not known. In either case, investment demand decreases from its euphoric levels. If the boom is unwound with little trouble, it becomes quite easy for the economy once again to enter a "new era";

on the other hand, if the unwinding involves financial instability, then there are prospects of deep depressions and stagnation.

The pertinent aspects of a euphoric period can be characterized as follows:

1. The tight money of the euphoric period is due more to runaway demand than to constraint upon supply. Thus, those who weigh money supply heavily in estimating money market conditions will be misled.

2. The run-up of short- and long-term interest rates places pressure on deposit savings intermediaries and disrupts industries whose financial channels run through these intermediaries. There is a feedback from euphoria to a constrained real demand in some sectors.

3. An essential aspect of a euphoric economy is the construction of liability structures which imply payments that are closely articulated directly, or indirectly via layerings, to cash flows due to income production. If the impact of the disruption of financing channels occurs after a significant build-up of tight financial positions, a further depressive factor becomes effective.

## III. Cash flows

Financial crises take place because units need or desire more cash than is available from their usual sources and so they resort to unusual ways to raise cash. Various types of cash flows are identified in this section, and the relations among them as well as between cash flows and other characteristics of the economy are examined.

The varying reliability of sources of cash is a well-known phenomenon in banking theory. For a unit, a source of cash may be reliable as long as there is no net market demand for cash upon it, and unreliable whenever there is such net demand upon the source. Under pressure various financial and nonfinancial units may withdraw, either by necessity or because of a defensive financial policy, from some financial markets. Such withdrawals not only affect the potential variability of prices in the market but also may disrupt business connections. Both the ordinary way of doing business and standby and defensive sources of cash can be affected.

Withdrawals on the supply side of financial markets may force demanding units that were under no special strain and were not directly affected by financial stringencies to look for new financing connections. An initial disturbance can cumulate through such third-party or innocent-bystander impacts. Financial market events that disrupt well-established financing channels affect the present value and cash flows of units not directly affected.[13]

For most consumers and nonfinancial (ordinary) business firms the largest source of cash is from their current income. Wages and salaries are the major source of cash to most consumers and sales of output are the major source for business firms. For financial intermediaries other than dealers, the ordinary cash flow to the unit can be derived from its financial assets. For example, short-term business debts in a commercial bank's portfolio state the reserve money that borrowers are committed to make available to the bank at the contract dates. A mortgage in a savings and loan association's portfolio states the contractual "cash flow to" for various dates. For financial market dealers cash receipts usually result from the selling out of their position, rather than from the commitments as stated in their inventory of assets. Under ordinary circumstances dealers as going concerns do not expect to sell out their positions; as they sell one set of assets they proceed to acquire a new set.

The ordinary sources of cash for various classes of economic units will be called cash flow from operations. All three types of cash flow from the operations described——income, financial contracts, and turnover of inventory——can be considered as functions of national income. The ability to meet payment commitments depends upon the normal functioning of the income production system.

In addition to cash flow from the sale of assets, dealers——and other financial and non-financial units——can meet cash drains due to the need to make payments on liabilities by emitting new liabilities. This second source of cash is called the refinancing of positions.

Furthermore, liquidating, or running off, a position is the third possible way for some units to obtain cash. This is what retailers and wholesalers do when they sell inventories (seasonal retailers actually do liquidate by selling out their position).

The financial assets and liabilities of an economic unit can be transformed into time series of contractual cash receipts and payments. The various items in these contractual receipts and payments depend upon national income: the fulfillment of the terms of mortgage contracts depends upon consumer disposable income and so forth.[14] Estimates of the direct and indirect impact of variations in national income upon the ability of units in the various sectors to meet their financial commitments can be derived.[15]

Each economic unit has its reserve, or emergency, sources of cash. For many units the emergency source consists of positions in some marketable or redeemable assets. Savings bonds and time deposits are typical standby sources of cash for consumers. A corporation may keep a reserve in Treasury bills or other money market instruments to meet either unusual needs for cash or an unexpected shortfall in cash receipts. Hoards of idle cash serve this purpose for all units. Cash has the special virtue that its availability does not depend upon the normal functioning of any market.

In principle the normal and secondary sources of cash for all units can be identified and their ratio to financial commitments can be estimated. By far the largest number of units use their income receipts to meet their financial commitments. Mortgage and consumer installment payments for consumers and interest and sinking fund payments for businesses would be financed normally by income cash flows.

The substitution of a deposit by customer B for a deposit from customer A in a bank liability structure may be viewed as the refinancing of a position. The typical financial unit acquires cash to meet its payment commitments, as stated in its liabilities, not from any cash flow from its assets or by selling assets but rather by emitting substitute liabilities. (The only financial organizations that seem to use cash flows from assets to meet cash flow commitments are the closed-end investment trusts, both levered and unlevered.)

When a unit that normally meets its financial commitments by drawing upon an income cash flow finds it necessary, or desirable, to refinance its position, additional pressures may be placed upon financial institutions.

Some financial relations are based upon the periodic liquidation of positions—for example, the seasonal inventory in retailing. Capital market dealers or underwriters liquidate positions in one set of assets in order to acquire new assets. However, if organizations that normally finance their payments by using cash from either income or refinancing of positions should instead attempt to sell their positions, it may turn out that the market for the assets in position is thin: as a result a sharp fall in the price of the asset occurs with a small increase in supply. In the market for single-family homes a sale is usually not a forced sale, and to a large extent sellers of one house are buyers or renters of another. If homeowners as a class tried to sell out their houses, the market would not be able to handle this without significant price concessions. But significant price concessions mean a decline in net worth—not only for the selling unit but for all units holding this asset. More particularly, a fall in price may mean that the offering units may be unable to raise the required or expected cash by dealing in the affected asset.

As an empirical generalization, almost all financial commitments are met from two normal sources of cash: income flows and refinancing of positions. For most units—especially those that have real capital goods as their asset—the selling out of their position is not feasible (no market exists for a quick sale); for others, aside from marginal adjustments by way of special money markets, it is an unusual source of cash.

A further empirical generalization is that asset prices—prices of the stock—can fall much more rapidly than income prices—prices of the flow.[16] Any need or desire to acquire cash that leads to attempts to sell out positions in reproducible assets will result not only in large-scale decreases in net worth but also in market prices for reproducible assets that are far below their current cost of production.

Even in the face of a widespread need or desire to acquire cash by selling assets, not all assets are allowed to fall in price. The price of some assets will be stabilized by central bank purchases or loans (refinancing positions); such assets can be called protected assets.

Financial instability occurs whenever a large number of units resort to extraordinary sources for cash. The conditions under which extraordinary sources of cash have to be tapped—which for financial units means mainly the conditions in which positions have to be liquidated (run off or sold out)—are the conditions that can trigger financial instability. *The adequacy of cash flows from income relative to debt, the adequacy of refinancing possibilities relative to position, and the ratio of unprotected to protected financial assets are determinants of the stability of the financial system.* The trend or evolution of the likelihood of financial instability depends upon the trend or evolution of the determinants of financial stability.

## IV. Financial instability and income determination

The essential difference between Keynesian and both classical and neoclassical economics is the importance attached to uncertainty.[17] Basic propositions in classical and neoclassical economics are derived by abstracting from uncertainty; the most that uncertainty does is to add some minor qualifications to the propositions of the theory. The special Keynesian propositions with respect to money, investment, and underemployment equilibrium, as well as the treatment of consumption, can be understood only as statements about system behavior in a world with uncertainty. One defense against some possible highly undesirable consequences of some possible states of the world is to make appropriate defensive portfolio choices.[18]

In an attempt to make precise his view of the nature of uncertainty and what his "General Theory" was all about, Keynes asserted that in a world without uncertainty, no one, outside a lunatic asylum, would use money as a store of wealth.[19] In the world as it is, money and Treasury bills are held as assets. Portfolios reflect the choices that sane men make as they attempt to behave in a rational manner in an inherently irrational (unpredictable) universe. This means that a significant proportion of wealth holders try to arrange their portfolios so that they are reasonably well protected irrespective of which one of a number of alternative possible states of the economy actually occurs.

In making portfolio choices, economic units do not accept any one thing as a proven guide to the future state of the economy. Unless there are strong reasons for doing otherwise, they often are guided by extrapolation of the current situation or trend, even though they may have doubts about its reliability.[20] Because of this underlying lack of confidence, expectations and hence present values of future incomes are inherently unstable; thus a not unusual event, such as a "salad oil scandal" or a modest decline in income, if it occurs in a favorable environment, can lead to a sharp revaluation of expectations and thus of asset values. It may lead not only to a sharp change in what some particular rational man expects but also to a marked change in the consensus as to the future of the economy.

Conceptually the process of setting a value upon a particular long-term asset or a collection of such assets can be separated into two stages. In the first the subjective beliefs about the likelihood of alternative states of the economy in successive time periods are assumed to be held with confidence. A second stage assesses the degree of "belief" in the stated likelihoods attached to the various alternatives.

When beliefs about the actual occurrence of various alternative states of the economy are held with perfect confidence, the standard probability expected value calculation makes sense. The present value of a long-term asset reflects its (subjective) expected yield at each state-date of the economy and the assumed likelihood of these state-dates occurring. Under stable conditions, the expected gross profit after taxes (cash flow) of the $i^{th}$ asset at the $t^{th}$ date, $Q_{it}$, will equal $\Sigma\ p_{st}Q_{si}$ where $Q_{si}$ is the gross profit after taxes of the $i^{th}$ asset if the $s^{th}$ state of nature occurs (assumed independent of date, could be modified to $Q_{sit}$, the $s^{th}$ state of nature at the $t^{th}$ date) and $p_{st}$ is the (subjective) probability that the $s^{th}$ state will occur at the $t^{th}$ date. The $s$ states are so defined that for each $t$, $\Sigma\ p_{st} = 1$. These $Q_{it}$, discounted at a rate appropriate to the assumed perfect certainty with which the expectations are held, yield the present value of the $ith$ assets, $V_i$.[21]

Assume that $S$ is a set of mutually exclusive and exhaustive states of nature. At date $t$, one of the $S$, $s_j$ will occur; the $\Sigma\ p_{sj} = 1$. However, the probabilities, $p_{sj}$, which must be attached to the alternative outcomes in order to compute the expected gross profit and the cash flow for date $t$, can be accepted with varying degrees of rational belief. The value of the $ith$ asset will vary, not only with the expected payoffs at various state-dates of nature and the probabilities attached to these payoffs, but also with the confidence placed in the probabilities attached to the occurrence of these various state-dates of nature. That is, $Q_{it} = \emptyset\ (\Sigma\ p_{st}Q_{si})$ where $0 \leqslant \emptyset \leqslant 1$ and $\emptyset$ reflects the confidence with which the particular weights are attached to the likelihood of various states of nature occurring.

In other words, there are at least two conjectural elements in determining the expected payoffs, $Q_{it}$ and hence $V_{it}$: one is that the $Q_{si}$ are conjectures; the other that the probability distribution of possible states of nature, as reflected in the $p_s$, is not known with certainty. Obviously, events that affect the confidence placed in any assumed probability distribution of the possible alternative states may also affect the confidence placed in the assumed expected payoff if state $s$ occurs, $Q_{si}$. A computed present value of any asset $V_i$ may be accepted with a wide range of confidence—from near certainty to a most tenuous conjecture. This degree of acceptance affects the market price of the asset.

The relevant portfolio decisions for consumers, firms, and financial concerns are not made with respect to individual assets; rather, they are made with respect to bundles of assets. The problem of choosing a portfolio is to combine assets whose payoffs will vary quite independently as the states of nature vary in order to achieve the unit's objective; which for a risk averter might be a minimal satisfactory state in any circumstance. This might be stated as follows: a portfolio is chosen so as to maximize $V$ given a specified valuation procedure subject to the constraint that $V_s > V_{min}$ for every likely state of nature.[22]

The assets available are both inside and outside assets: the outside assets consist of money and Government debt.[23] The nominal value of a monetary asset (money plus Government debt) is independent of the state of the economy. Government debt can exhibit variability in its nominal value due to interest rate variations, but in conditions where business cycles occur, its nominal value is not highly correlated with the expected nominal value of inside assets.

We assume that two types of periods can be distinguished: one in which beliefs are held with confidence concerning the likelihood of alternative states of nature occurring within some horizon period and the second in which such beliefs are most insecure. In the second situation bets are placed under duress. During these second periods—when what can be called higher-order uncertainty rules—markedly lower relative values are attached to assets whose nominal value depends upon the economy's performance. Periods of higher-order uncertainty will see portfolios shift toward assets that offer protection against large declines in nominal values. Even though flexibility is almost always a virtue, the premium on assets that permit flexibility will be larger in such periods of higher-order uncertainty. For many questions a rational man has the option of saying "I don't know" and of postponing a decision. As a wealth owner he must assess the worth of various assets even when conditions are so fluid that he would rather not make a decision.

Keynesian liquidity preference encompasses both confidence conditions. Expectations as to the likelihood of different states of nature may be held with varying degrees of confidence. During periods of stable expectations, portfolios are managed so that the outcome will be tolerable regardless which state of nature rules. Most units tend to weigh heavily the avoidance of disasters, such as a liquidity crisis for the unit. Assets that offer protection against a liquidity crisis or temporarily disorganized asset markets would be part of a rational portfolio under all circumstances. In addition a preferred market may exist for assets that obviate against capital losses. Thus liquidity preference is defined as a rational person's demand for money as an asset; this leads to a determinate demand function for money for any value of higher-order uncertainty.[24]

In addition to periods when the likelihood of various states of nature appears stable, there are troubled periods when the subjective estimates as to the likelihood of various states of nature are held with much less confidence. The risk-averter reaction to a decline in confidence is to attempt to increase the weight of assets that yield flexibility in portfolio choices, in other words, to increase the value not only of money but also of all assets that have broad, deep, and resilient markets. Any increase in uncertainty shifts the liquidity preference function, and this shift can be quite marked and sudden.

Obviously, the reverse—a decrease in uncertainty—can occur. If risk-averters are dominant, then an increase in uncertainty is likely to be a rapid phenomenon, whereas a decrease will require a slow accretion of confidence. There is no need for a loss in confidence to proceed at the same pace as a gain in confidence.

Rapid changes in desired portfolios may be confronted with short-period inelastic supplies of primary assets (real capital and government liabilities). As a result, the relative prices of different assets change. An increase in uncertainty will see the price of inside assets—real capital and equities—fall relative to the price of outside assets -government debt—and money; a decrease in uncertainty will see the price of inside assets rise relative to that of outside assets.

The nominal money supply in our fractional reserve banking system can be almost infinitely elastic. Any events that increase uncertainty on the part of owners of real wealth will also increase uncertainty of commercial bankers. Unless prices of inside assets are pegged by the central bank, a sharp increase in uncertainty will result in the price of inside assets falling relative to both money and the price of default-free or protected assets.

In a decentralized private-enterprise economy with private commercial banks, we cannot expect the money supply to increase sufficiently to offset the effects of a sharp increase in uncertainty upon inside asset prices. Conversely, we cannot expect the money supply to fall sufficiently to offset the effects of a sharp decrease in uncertainty. We should expect the private, profit-maximizing, risk-averting commercial banks to behave perversely, in that with a decrease in uncertainty they are willing and eager to increase the money supply and with an increase in uncertainty they act to contract the money supply.[25]

Portfolios must hold the existing stocks of private real assets, Treasury debt, and money. Even during an investment boom the annual increment to the stock of real capital is small relative to the total stock. However, in time the stock of reproducible capital is infinitely elastic at the price of newly produced capital goods. Thus there is a ceiling to the price of a unit of the stock of real capital in the current market. This ceiling price allows for an expected decline in the price of the stock to the price of the flow of newly produced units.

The current return on real capital collected in firms reflects the current functioning of the economy, whether prosperity or depression rules. During an investment boom current returns are high. Because a ceiling on the price of units in the stock of capital is imposed by the cost of investment, a shift in the desired composition of portfolios toward a greater proportion of real capital cannot lower very far the short-run yield on real capital valued at market price; in fact because of prosperity and greater capacity utilization this yield may increase. As the outside assets—Treasury debt and so forth —are now less desirable than in other more uncertain circumstances, their yield must rise toward equality with the yield on inside or real assets. To paraphrase Keynes ". . . in a world without uncertainty no one outside of a lunatic asylum . . ." will hold Treasury bills as a store of wealth unless their yield is the same as that on real assets.

As the implicit yield on money is primarily the value of the implied insurance policy it embodies, a decrease in uncertainty lowers this implicit yield and thus lowers the amount desired in portfolios. As all money must be held, as bankers are eager to increase its supply, and as its nominal value cannot decline, the money price of other assets, in particular real assets, must increase.

In a euphoric economy it is widely thought that past doubts about the future of the economy were based upon error. The behavior of money and capital market interest rates during such a period is consistent with a rapid convergence of the yield upon default-free and default-possible assets. This convergence takes place by a decline in the price of—the rise in the interest rate on—default-free assets relative to the price of—yield on—the economy's underlying real capital.

In addition to default-free—government debt plus gold—and default-possible—real capital, private debts, equities—assets, there are protected assets. Protected assets in varying degrees and from various sources carry some protection against consequences that would follow from unfavorable events. Typical examples of such assets are bonds and savings deposits.

The financial intermediaries—including banks as they emit money—generate assets that are at least partially protected. A rise in intermediation and particularly a rise in bank money, even if the asset acquired by the bank carries default possibilities, may unbalance portfolios in favor of default-free assets. The ability of banking, through the creation of money, to stimulate an economy rests upon the belief that banks and the monetary authorities are able to give such protection to their liabilities. The liabilities of other financial intermediaries are protected, but not so much as bank money; thus their stimulative effect, while not negligible, is smaller. In a euphoric economy the value of such protection decreases, and these instruments also fall in price relative to real assets or equities.[26]

To summarize, the relative prices of assets are affected by portfolio imbalance that follows from changing views as to uncertainty concerning future states of the economy. A decrease in the uncertainty will raise the price of units in the stock of real inside assets for any given supply of money, other outside assets, and assets that are in all or in part protected against the adverse behavior of the economy; an increase in uncertainty will lower these prices. For a given state of uncertainty and stock of real capital assets, the greater the quantity of money, other outside assets, and protected assets, the greater the price of units in the stock of real capital. Investment consists of producing substitutes for items in the stock of real capital; the price of the units in the stock is the demand price for units to be produced. To the extent that the supply of investment responds positively to its demand price, the pace of investment flows from portfolio imbalance.

The investment process can be detailed as (1) the portfolio balance relation that states the market price for capital assets as a function of the money supply (Figure 1), and (2) the investment supply function that states how much investment output will be produced at each market price for capital assets (Figure 2). It is assumed that the market price for capital assets is the demand price for investment output. The supply curve of investment output is positively sloped. At some positive price the output of investment goods becomes zero. The market price of capital assets as determined by portfolio preferences is sensitive to the state of expectations or to the degree of uncertainty with respect to the future.[27]

In Figure 1, I have chosen to keep the stock of capital constant. Thus $V = P_k \bar{K} + M$, where $V$ is wealth, $P_k$ is price level of capital, $\bar{K}$ is the fixed stock of capital, and $M$ is outside money. As $M$ increases, $V$ increases because of both the rise in $M$ and a rise in $P_k$. If $M$ increases as manna from heaven, it would be appropriate for the consumption function to include a $W/P_y$ variable ($P_y$ is the price level of current output). This would, by today's conventions, add an upward drifting consumption function to the mechanism by which a rise in $M$ affects output.[28]

If $C = f(Y)$ and $Y = C + I$, then the above diagram determines income as a function of $M$.[29]

It is impossible in this view to generate an investment function $I = f(r)$ that is independent of the portfolio adjustments of the liquidity preference doctrine; investment is a speculative activity in a capitalist economy that is only peripherally related to productivity.

Two phenomena can be distinguished. If $M$ remains fixed as capital is accumulated, a slow downward drift of the $Q(M, \bar{K})$ function (Figure 1) will take place. A rise in $M$ is needed to maintain real asset prices in the face of the rise in the stock of real capital.[30] Alternatively, if portfolio preferences change, perhaps because of a change in uncertainty, then, independently of the impact of real accumulation, the $Q(M, \bar{K})$ function will shift. It is the

# 1 | STOCK

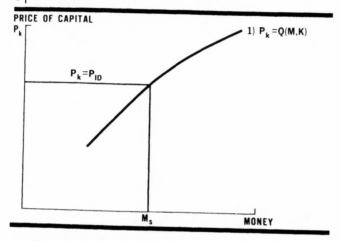

**PRICE OF CAPITAL**

$P_k$

1) $P_k = Q(M,K)$

$P_k = P_{ID}$

$M_s$   MONEY

# 2 | FLOW

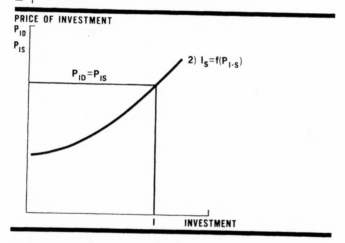

**PRICE OF INVESTMENT**

$P_{ID}$
$P_{IS}$

2) $I_s = f(P_{I \cdot s})$

$P_{ID} = P_{IS}$

I   INVESTMENT

second type of shift that occupies center stage in the Keynesian view of the world. This has been neglected in both monetary and investment analysis.

At all times investment demand has to take into account the returns received during various expected states of the economy. As the result of a shock, the weight attached to depression returns may increase. As the dust settles there is gradual easing of the views on the likelihood of unfavorable states of nature. The weight attached to liquidity is decreased and a gradual increase of investment will take place.

Hopefully we know enough to supplement investment by honorary investments (Government spending) so that the expected returns from capital will not again reflect large-scale excess capacity. Nevertheless, if a shock takes place, some time elapses before its effects wear off. In these circumstances honorary investment may have to carry the burden of maintaining full employment for an extended period.

The essence of the argument is that investment activity may be viewed as an offshoot of portfolio preferences, and that portfolio preferences reflect the attempt by rational men to do well in a world with uncertainty. Any shock to portfolio preferences that leads to a sharp drop in investment results from experiences with portfolios that have gone sour. On a large scale, portfolios go sour in the aftermath of a financial crisis.

## APPENDIX TO SECTION IV: A MODEL

The model can be written as follows:

$$(1) \qquad Y = C + I$$
$$(2) \qquad C = C(Y)$$
$$(3) \qquad I = I(P_{IS}, \overline{W})$$
$$(4) \qquad P_K = L(M, \overline{K})$$
$$(5) \qquad P_{I \cdot D} = P_K$$
$$(6) \qquad P_{IS} = P_{I \cdot D}$$
$$(7) \qquad M_D = M_S$$

$M_S$ (Money), $\overline{K}$(capital stock), and $\overline{W}$(wages) are all exogenous, $P_M = 1$.

Symbols have their usual meaning: we add $P_{IS}$ as the supply price of a unit of investment, $P_K$ as the market price of a unit of existing real or inside capital, and $P_{I \cdot D}$ is the demand price of a unit of investment.

$$(3) \qquad \frac{dI}{dP_{IS}} > 0, \frac{P_{IS}}{I \rightarrow 0} > 0, \frac{dP_{IS}}{dW} > 0$$

$$(4) \qquad \frac{dP_K}{dM} > 0, \frac{dP_K}{dK} < 0$$

Equation 4 is unstable with respect to views as to uncertainty; it shifts "down" whenever uncertainty increases. This portfolio balance equation (the liquidity preference function) yields a market price for the units in the stock of real capital for each quantity of money.

Given $W$, $I$ adjusts so that $P_{IS} = P_K$ (equations 3, 5, and 6). Once $I$ is given $C$ and $Y$ are then determined (equations 1 and 2). Nowhere in this model does either the interest rate or the productivity of capital appear. "Liquidity preference" (equation 4) determines the market price of the stock of real assets. A shift in liquidity preference means a shift in equation 4, not a movement along the function.

In the model, the tune is called by the market price of the stock of real capital. Given a cost curve for investment that has a positive price for zero output, it is possible for the demand price to fall below the price at which there will be an appreciable production of capital goods. Thus, the complete collapse of investment is possible.

Of course, productivity in the sense of the expected quasi-rents is almost always an element in the determination of the market price of a real asset or a collection of assets. However, this formulation minimizes the impact of productivity as it emphasizes that the liquidity attribute of assets may at times be of greater significance in determining their market price than their productivity. The perspective in this formulation is that of business cycles, not of a full-employment steady state.

Productivity of capital takes the form of expected future earnings (gross profits after taxes) of a collection of capital goods within a producing unit. In any real world decision, the earnings on specific items or collections of capital must be estimated, and the heterogeneity of the capital stock must be taken into account.

Once earnings are estimated, then given the current market price, a discount rate can be computed. That is, we have

$$(7) \qquad P_K \cdot \bar{K} = \sum_{i=1}^{n} \sum_{t=1} Q_i/(1 + r_i)t$$

which states the arithmetic relation that the value of the capital stock is of necessity equal to the discounted value of some known stream of returns, $Q_i$. If the current market determines $P_k \cdot K$ and if a set of $Q_i$ is estimated, an interest rate can be computed. If it is wished, equation 4 can be suppressed by using equation 7, that is,

$$(4') \qquad \frac{1}{K} \sum_{i,t=1}^{n} \frac{Q_i}{(1 + r_i)t} = L(M,K)$$

If a transaction demand for money is added, if the $Q_i$ are interpreted as a function of $Y$, if all $r_i$ are assumed equal, and if $K$ is suppressed as being fixed in the short run then

$$(4'') \qquad M_D = L(r,Y)$$

may be derived.

For the investment decision, we may assume that the future return of the increment to capital is the same as to the stock of capital. With the $Q_i$ known and assumed independent of the short-run pace of investment, then

$$(3') \qquad P_{is} = \frac{1}{K} \sum_{i,t=1}^{n} \frac{Q}{(1 + r_i)t}$$

Thus given the fact that the supply price of investment rises with investment (constant $W$), greater investment is associated with a lower interest rate. That is,

$$(3'') \qquad\qquad I = I(r,Y) \text{ and } \frac{dI}{dr} < 0$$

Both equations $4''$ and $3''$ are arithmetic transformations of 4 and 3. Equations 4 and 3 represent market phenomena, whereas $4''$ and $3''$ are computed transformations of market conditions.

For financial contracts such as bonds the $Q_i$ are stated in the contract. Even so the yield to maturity is a computed number—the market number is the price of the bond.

When the interest rate is not computed, the investment decision and its relation to liquidity preference are viewed in a more natural way. Of course, for real capital the $Q_i$ reflects the productivity in the form of cash flows, current and expected. But the productivity of capital and investment affect present performance only after they are filtered through an evaluation of the state of the irrational, uncertain world that is the positioning variable in the liquidity preference function. Productivity and thrift exist, but in a capitalist economy their impact is always filtered by uncertainty.

## V. How does tight money work?

Tight money, defined as rising nominal interest rates associated with stricter other terms on contracts, may work to restrain demand in two ways.[31] In the conventional view tight money operates through rationing demand by means of rising interest rates. Typically this has been represented by movements along a stable negatively sloped demand curve for investment (and some forms of consumption) that is drawn as a function of the interest rate. An alternative view that follows from the argument in Section IV envisages tight money as inducing a change in expectations, in the perceived uncertainty, due to an episode such as a financial crisis or a period of financial stringency. This within Figures 1 and 2 can be represented by a downward shift in the infinitely elastic demand curve for investment.

The way in which tight money operates depends upon the state of the economy. In a non-euphoric expanding economy, where liability structures are considered satisfactory, monetary restraint will likely operate by way of rationing along a stable investment demand curve. In a booming euphoric economy, where high and rising prices of capital are associated with a willingness on the part of firms to "extend" their liability structures and of financial intermediaries to experiment with both their assets and their liabilities, tight money will be effective only if it brings such portfolio, or financial structure, experimentation to a halt. A reconsideration of the desirability of financial experimentation will not take place without a triggering event, and the reaction can be both quick and disastrous. A euphoric boom is characterized by a stretching, or thinning out, of liquidity; the end of a boom occurs when desired liquidity quickly becomes significantly greater than actual liquidity.

In a euphoric economy, with ever-increasing confidence, there is an increase in the weights attached to the occurrence of states of nature favorable to the owning of larger stocks of real capital. Thus, an upward drift in the price of the real capital-money supply function occurs (Figure 1, p. 135).

This shift means that for all units both the expected flows of cash from operations and the confidence in these expectations are rising. Given these expectations, an enterprise assumes that with safety it can undertake (1) to emit liabilities whose cash needs will be met by these now-confidently-expected cash flows and (2) to undertake projects with the expectation that the cash flows from operations will be one of the sources of finance. In a euphoric economy the weight attached to the necessity for cash reserves to ease strains due to unexpected shortfalls in cash flows is ever decreasing.

In a lagless world—where all investment decisions are taken with a clean slate, so to speak—current investment spending is related to current expectations and financial or money market conditions. In world when today's investment spending reflects past decisions, the needs for financing today can often be quite inelastic with respect to today's financing conditions: and today's financing conditions may have their major effect upon investment spending in the future. Thus, there exists a pattern of lags between money and capital market conditions and investment spending conditions. This lag pattern is not independent of economic events. A dramatic financial market event, in particular a financial crisis or widespread distress, can have a quick effect.

For units with outstanding debts, tight money means that cash payment commitments rise as positions are refinanced. This is true not only because interest rates are higher but also because other terms of the units' borrowing contracts are affected. In addition, if projects are undertaken with the expectation that they would be financed in part by cash generated by ongoing operations, and if the available cash flows fall short of expectations—due perhaps to the increased cost of the refinanced inherited debt—then a larger amount will need to be financed by debt or by the sale of financial assets. This means that the resultant balance sheet can be inferior to and the cash flow commitments larger than the target envisaged when the project was undertaken. Conversely, if gross profits rise faster than costs, so that a smaller-than-expected portion of investment is financed by debt, the resultant balance sheet will be superior to that expected when projections were made. In this way, investment may be retarded or accelerated by cash flow and balance sheet considerations.[32]

Deposit financial institutions are especially vulnerable to tight money if their assets are of significantly longer term than their debts; they are virtually refinancing their position daily by offering terms that are attractive to their depositors. A rapid rise in their required cash flows due to interest costs may take place, which can lead to a sharp reduction in their net income.

Thus, during a euphoric expansion the effects of tight money are more than offset for units holding real capital, whereas for other units, such as savings banks, tight money means a significant deterioration in their financial position whether measured by liquidity or net worth.

In a euphoric economy the willingness to hold money or near money decreases. The observed tightness of money—the rise in interest rates on near monies and other debts—is not necessarily caused by any undue constraint upon the rate of increase of the money supply; rather it reflects the rapid increase in the demand for financing. An attempt by the authorities to sate the demand for finance by creating bank credit will lead to rapidly rising prices: inflationary expectations will add to the euphoria. Euphoric expectations will not be ended by a fall in income, as the strong investment demand that is calling the tune is insensitive to the rise in financing terms.

In a euphoric economy characterized by an investment boom, cash payments become ever more closely articulated to cash receipts; the speculative stock of money and near monies is depleted. Two phenomena follow from this closer articulation. The size decreases of both the shortfall in cash receipts and of the overrun in cash payments due to normal operations, that will result in insufficient cash on hand to meet payments decreases. The frequency with which refinancing or asset sales are necessary to meet payment commitments increases. Units become more dependent upon the normal functioning of various financial markets.

Under these emerging circumstances there is a decrease in the size of the dislocation that can cause serious financial difficulties to a unit, and an increase in the likelihood that a unit in difficulty will set other units in difficulty. Also, even local or sectoral financial distress or market disruptions may induce widespread attempts to gain liquidity by running off or selling out positions in real or financial assets (inventory liquidation). This action in turn may depress incomes and market prices of real and financial assets. We may expect financial institutions to react to such developments by trying to clean up their balance sheets and to reverse the portfolio changes entered into during the recent euphoric period. The simultaneous attempt by financial institutions, consumers, and firms to improve their balance sheets may lead to a rupture of what had been normal as well as standby financing relations. As a result losses occur, and these, combined with the market disruptions, induce a more conservative view as to the desired liability structure.

The view that, in conditions of euphoria, tight money operates by causing a re-evaluation of the uncertainties carried by economic units is in marked contrast to the textbook analysis of tight money seen as operating by constraining expenditures along a stable investment function. If an expansion is taking place in the absence of a transformation—by way of euphoric expectations—of preferred portfolios and liability structures then the system can operate by rationing along a stable investment relation. Then tight money may lead to a decline in investment and a relaxation of monetary constraint may reverse this decline: conventional monetary policy can serve as an economic steering wheel.

But once the expansion is associated with the transformation of asset and liability structures that have been identified as characteristic of a euphoric economy, tight money will constrain demand only if it induces a shift either in the demand function for money or in the price function for capital goods. For this to happen the expansion must continue long enough for balance sheets to be substantially changed. Then some triggering event that induces a reconsideration of desired balance sheets must occur. A financial crisis or at least some significant amount of financial distress is needed to dampen the euphoria. The fear of financial failure must be credible in order to overcome expectations built on a long record of success.

During an emerging euphoric boom, the improvement in expectations may overwhelm rising interest rates. As a result of the revision of portfolio standards, the supply of finance seems to be almost infinitely elastic at stepwise rising rates. Typically, this "infinitely" elastic supply is associated with the emergence of new financial instruments and institutions,[33] such as the use of Federal funds to make position, the explosive growth of negotiable CD's, and the development of a second banking system. Under these circumstances, a central bank will see its restriction of the rate of growth of the money supply or the reserve base overwhelmed by the willingness of consumers, business firms, and financial institutions to decrease cash balances: increases in velocity overcome restrictions in quantity. The frustrated central bank can try to compensate for its lack of success in constraining expansion by further decreasing the rate of growth of the money supply, thus forcing a more rapid development of a tightly articulated cash position. Such a further tightening will occur within a financial environment that is increasingly vulnerable to disruption. The transition will not be from too-rapid economic expansion to stability by way of a slow deceleration, but a rapid decline will follow a sharp braking of the expansion.

With some form of a financial crisis likely to occur after a euphoric boom, it becomes difficult to prescribe the correct policy for a central bank. However, the central bank must be aware of this possibility and it must stand ready to act as a lender of last resort to the financial system as a whole if and when a break takes place. With the path of the economy independent in its gross terms of the rate of increase of the money supply and of the relative importance of bank financing, the central bank might as well resist the temptation to further tighten its constraints if the initial extent of constraint does not work quickly. The central bank should sustain the rate of growth of the reserve base and the money supply at a rate consistent with the long-term growth of the economy. This course should be adopted in the hope, however slight, that the rise in velocity—deterioration of balance sheet phenomena described earlier—will converge, by a slow deceleration of the euphoric expectations, to a sustainable steady state.

In particular during a euphoric expansion the central bank should resist the temptation to introduce constraining direct controls on that part of the financial system most completely under its control—the commercial banks. The central bank should recognize that a euphoric expansion will be a period of innovation and experimentation by both bank and nonbank financial institutions. From the perspective of picking up the pieces, restoring confidence, and sustaining the economy, the portion of the financial system that the central bank most clearly protects should be as large as possible. Instead of constraining commercial banks by direct controls, the central bank should aim at sustaining the relative importance of commercial banks even during a period of euphoric expansion; in particular, the commercial banks should not be unduly constrained from engaging in rate competition for resources.

## VI. The theory of financial stability

In Section IV it was concluded that normal functioning requires that the price level, perhaps implicit, of the stock of real capital assets be consistent with the supply price of investment goods at the going-wage level. The euphoric boom occurs when portfolio preferences change so that the price level of the stock rises relative to the wage level, causing an increase in the output of investment goods. A sharp fall in the price level of the stock of real assets will lead to a marked decline in investment and thus in income: a deep depression can occur only if such a change in relative prices takes place.

*Attributes of stability*

In the discussion of uncertainty, we identified one element that could lead to a sharp lowering of the price level of the existing stock of capital. A sharp change in the desired composition of assets in portfolios—due to an evaporation of confidence in views held previously as to the likelihood of various alternative possible state-dates of the economy—will lower the value of real assets relative to both the price level of current output and money. Such a revaluation of the confidence with which a set of expectations is held does not just happen.

The event that marks the change in portfolio preferences is a period of financial crisis, distress, or stringency (used as descriptive terms for different degrees of financial difficulty). However, a financial crisis—used as a generic term—is not an accidental event, and not all financial structures are equally prone to financial instability. Our interest now is in those attributes of the financial system that determine its stability.

We are discussing a system that is not globally stable. The economy is best analyzed by assuming that there exist more than one stable equilibrium for the system. We are interested in the determinants of the domain of stability around the various stable equilibria. Our questions are of the form: "What is the maximum displacement that can take place and still have the system return to a particular initial equilibrium point?" and "Upon what does this 'maximum displacement' depend?"

The maximum shock that the financial system may absorb and still have the economy return to its initial equilibrium depends upon the financial structure and the linkages between the financial structure and real income. Two types of shocks that can trigger large depressive movements of financial variables can be identified: one is a shortfall of cash flows due to an overall drop in income, and the second is the distress of a unit due to "error" of management. But not all recessions trigger financial instability and not every financial failure, even of large financial units, triggers a financial panic or crisis. For not unusual events to trigger the unusual, the financial environment within which the potential triggering event occurs must have a sufficiently small domain of stability.

The contention in this paper is that the domain of stability of the financial system is mainly an endogenous phenomenon that depends upon liability structures and institutional arrangements. The exogenous elements in determining the domain of financial stability are the government and central banking arrangements: after mid-1966 it is clear that the exogenous policy instrument of deposit insurance is a powerful offset to events with the potential for setting off a financial crisis.

There are two basic attributes of the financial system that determine the domain of stability of the financial system: (1) the extent to which a close articulation exists between the contractual and customary cash flows from a unit and its various cash receipts and (2) the weight in portfolios of those assets that in almost all circumstances can be sold or pledged at well nigh their book or face value. A third element, not quite so basic, that determines vulnerability to a financial crisis is the extent to which expectations of growth and of rising asset prices have affected current asset prices and the values at which such assets enter the financial system.[34] The domain of stability of the financial system is smaller the closer the articulation of payments, the smaller the weight of protected assets, and the larger the extent to which asset prices reflect both growth expectations and realized past appreciations. The evolution of these attributes of the financial structure over time will affect the size of the domain of stability of the financial system. An hypothesis of this, as well as the earlier presentations of these ideas, is that when full employment is being sustained by private demand, the domain of stability of the financial system decreases.

In addition to the impact of such full employment a euphoric economy with its demand-pull tight money will be accompanied by a rapid increase in the layering of financial obligations, which also tends to decrease the domain of stability. For as layering increases, the closeness with which payments are articulated to receipts increases and layering increases the ratio of inside assets to those assets whose nominal or book value will not be affected by system behavior.[35] A euphoric economy will typically be associated with a stock market boom and an increase in the proportion of the value of financial assets that is sensitive to a sharp revaluation of expectations.

Even though a prolonged expansion, dominated by private demand, will bring about a transformation of portfolios and changes in asset structures conducive to financial crises, the transformations in portfolios that take place under euphoric conditions sharply accentuate such trends. It may be conjectured that euphoria is a necessary prelude to a financial crisis and that euphoria is almost an inevitable result of the successful functioning of an enterprise economy.

Thus, the theory of financial stability takes into account two aspects of the behavior of a capitalist economy. The first is the evolution of the financial structure over a prolonged expansion, which affects the nature of the primary assets, the extent of financial layering, and the evolution of financial institutions and usages. The second consists of the financial impacts over a short period due to the existence of a highly optimistic, euphoric economy; the euphoric economy is a natural consequence of the economy doing well over a prolonged period. Over both the prolonged boom and the euphoric period portfolio transformations occur that decrease the domain of stability of the financial system.

Financial instability as a system characteristic is compounded of two elements. How are units placed in financial distress and how does unit distress escalate into a systemwide crisis?

## The "banking theory" for all units

It is desirable to analyze all economic units as if they were a bank —or at least a financial intermediary. The essential characteristic of such a financial unit is that it finances a position by emitting liabilities. A financial institution does not expect to meet the commitments stated in its liabilities by selling out its position, or allowing its portfolio to run off. Rather, it expects to refinance its position by emitting new debt. On the other hand every unit, including banks and other financial units, has a normal functioning cash flow from operations. The relation between the normal functioning cash flow and the refinancing opportunities on the one hand and the commitments embodied in the liabilities on the other determine the conditions under which the organization can be placed in financial distress.

It is important for our purpose to look at all organizations from the *defensive* viewpoint: "What would it take to put the organization in financial distress?"

*Solvency and liquidity constraints.* All economic units have a balance sheet. Given the valuation of assets and liabilities one may derive a net worth or owner's equity for the unit. The conditional maximization of owner's equity may be the proximate goal of business management—the condition reflecting the need to protect some minimum owner's equity under the most ádverse contingency as to the state of the economy.

A unit is solvent—given a set of valuation procedures—when its net worth is positive.[36] A unit is liquid when it can meet its payment commitments. Solvency and liquidity are two conditions that all private economic organizations must always satisfy. Failure to satisfy either condition, or even coming close to failing, can lead to actions by others that affect profoundly the status of the organization.

Even though textbooks may consider solvency and liquidity as independent attributes, the two are interrelated. First of all, the willingness to hold the debt of any organization depends in part upon the protection to the debt holder embodied in the unit's net worth. A decline in net worth—perhaps the result of revaluation of assets—can lead to a decreased willingness to hold debts of a unit and hence to difficulties when it needs to refinance a position. A lack of liquidity may result from what was initially a solvency problem.

Similarly, a net drain or outflow of cash from an organization may lead to a need to do the unusual—to acquire cash by selling assets. If, because of the thinness of the market, a sharp fall in the asset price occurs when such sales are essayed, then a sharp drop in net worth takes place, especially if the organization is highly levered.

We can identify, therefore, three sources of a decline in the price level of the stock (capital), relative, of course, to the flow (income and investment). One is a rise in the weight attached to those possible states of the society that make it disadvantageous to hold real assets and financial assets whose value is closely tied to that of real assets. The second is the fall in asset values due to a rise in the discount caused by uncertainty. The third is a decline in asset values as the conditions change under which a position in these assets may be financed. In particular, whenever the need to meet the cash payment commitments stated by liabilities requires the selling out of a position, there is the possibility of a sharp fall in the price of the positioned asset. Such a fall in asset prices triggers a serious impact of financial markets upon demand for current output.

*The need for cash for payments.* Cash is needed for payments, which are related to financial as well as income transactions. The layering of financial interrelations affects the total payments that must be made. To the extent that layering increases at a faster rate than income, over a prolonged boom, or in response to rising interest rates, or during a euphoric period, the payments/income ratio will rise. The closer the articulation by consumers and business firms of income receipts with payments due to financial contracts, the greater the potential for financial crisis.

Each money payment is a money receipt. As layering increases, the importance of the uninterrupted flow of receipts increases. The inability of one unit to meet its payment commitments affects the ability of the would-be recipient unit to meet its payment commitments.

Three payment types can be distinguished: income, balance sheet, and portfolio, each of which can in turn be broken down into subclasses.[37] These payment types reflect the fact that economic units have incomes and manage portfolios.

The liabilities in a portfolio state the payment commitments. These contractual payment commitments can be separated into dated, demand, and contingent commitments. To each liability some penalty is attached for not meeting the commitment: and the payment commitments quite naturally fall into classes according to the seriousness of the default penalty. In particular, the payment commitments that involve the pledging of collateral are important——for they provide a direct and quick link between a decline in market value of assets and the need to make cash payments. That is, they are a type of contingent payment commitment that involves the supply of additional collateral or cash whenever a market price falls below some threshhold. This margin or collateral maintenance payment commitment can be a source of considerable disorganization and can lead to sharp declines in asset prices.

Another aspect of balance sheet payment commitments is the source of the cash that will be used to make the payments. Three sources can be distinguished: the flow due to the generation of income; the flow due to the assets held in a portfolio; and the flow due to transactions in assets, either the emission of new liabilities or the sale of assets.

For each unit, or class of units, the trend in payment commitments relative to actual or potential sources of cash generates the changing structure of financial interrelations. The basic empirical hypothesis is that over a prolonged expansion——and in particular during a euphoric period——the balance sheet commitments to make payments increases faster than income receipts for private units (layering increases faster than income) and so total financial commitments rise relative to income. In addition, during euphoric periods, portfolio payments (transactions in assets) increase relative to both income and financial transactions. The measured rise in income velocity during an expansion underestimates the increase in the payment load being carried by the money supply.[38]

*Modes of system behavior*

Three modes of system behavior can be distinguished depending upon how *ex post* savings are in fact offset by *ex post* investment. The offsets to saving that we will consider are investment in real private capital and Government deficits. For convenience, we will call real private capital inside assets and the accumulated total of Government deficits outside assets. Thus, the consolidated change in net worth in an economy over a time period equals the change in the value of inside assets plus the change in the value of outside assets.

At any moment in time the total private net worth of the system equals the consolidated value of outside plus inside assets. Assuming the value of outside assets is almost independent of system behavior, the ratio of the value of outside to the value of total or inside assets in the consolidated accounts is one gross measure of the financial structure.

The savings of any period are offset by outside and inside assets. The ratio of outside to inside assets in the current offset to savings as compared to the initial ratio of outside to inside assets will determine the financial bias of current income. If the Government deficit is a larger portion of the current offset to savings than it is of the initial wealth structure, then the period is biased toward outside assets; if it is smaller, the period is biased toward inside assets; if it is the same, then the period is neutral.

Over a protracted expansion the bias in financial development is toward inside assets. This bias is compounded out of three elements: (1) Current savings are allocated to private investment rather than to Government deficits; (2) capital gains raise the market price of the stock of inside assets; and (3) increases in interest rates lower the nominal value of outside, income-earnings assets. Thus, the vulnerability of portfolios to declines in the market price of the constituent assets increases.[39]

In the long run, portfolio balance has been maintained by cycles in the relative weights of primary assets accumulated: historically the portfolio cycle centered around business cycles of deep depressions. However, to judge what is happening over time it is necessary to evaluate the significance of changes in financial usages. The existence of effective deposit insurance makes the inside assets owned by the banking system at least a bit outside. The same is true for all other Government underwritings and endorsements of private debt. Thus, with the growth of Government and Government agency contingent liabilities even growth that is apparently biased toward the emission of private liabilities may in fact be biased toward outside assets. An attempt to enumerate—and then evaluate—the various Government endorsements and underwritings of various asset and financial markets in these terms is necessary when estimating the potential of an economy for financial instability.

## Secondary markets

The domain of stability of the system depends upon the ratio of the value of those assets whose market value is independent of system behavior to the value of those assets whose market value reflects expected system behavior. The value of a particular asset can be independent of system behavior either because its market is pegged or because the flow of payments that will be made does not depend upon system performance and its capital value is largely independent of financial market conditions.

For secondary markets to be an effective determinant of system stability, they must transform an asset into a reliable source of cash for a unit whenever needed. This means that the secondary market must be a dealer market; in other words, there needs to be a set of position takers who will buy significant amounts for their own account and who sell out of their own stock of assets. Such position takers must be financed. Presumably under normal functioning the position taker is financed by borrowing from banks, financial intermediaries, and other private cash sources. However, a venturesome, reliable position taker must have adequate standby or emergency financing sources. The earlier argument about refinancing a position applies with special force to any money market or financial market dealer.

The only source of refinancing that can be truly independent of any epidemics of confidence or lack of confidence in financial markets is the central bank. Thus if the set of protected assets is to be extended by the organization of secondary markets, the stability of the financial system will be best increased if the dealers in these secondary markets have guaranteed access to the central bank.

It might be highly desirable to have the normal functioning of the system encompass dealer intermediaries who finance a portion of their position directly at the Federal Reserve discount window.

If a Federal Reserve peg existed in the market for some class of private liabilities, these liabilities would become guaranteed sources of cash at guaranteed prices. Such assets are at least in part outside, and they would increase the domain of stability of the system for any structure of other liabilities.

The extension of secondary markets to new classes of assets and the associated opening of the discount window to new financial intermediaries may compensate at least in part—or may even more than compensate—for the changes in financial structure due to the dominance of private investment in the offsets to saving during a prolonged boom.

## Unit and system instability

Financial vulnerability exists when the tolerance of the financial system to shocks has been decreased due to three phenomena that cumulate over a prolonged boom: (1) the growth of financial—balance sheet and portfolio—payments relative to income payments; (2) the decrease in the relative weight of outside and guaranteed assets in the totality of financial asset values; and (3) the building into the financial structure of asset prices that reflect boom or euphoric expectations. The triggering device in financial instability may be the financial distress of a particular unit.

In such a case, the initiating unit, after the event, will be adjudged guilty of poor management. However, the poor management of this unit, or even of many units, may not be the cause of system instability. System instability occurs when the financial structure is such that the impact of the initiating units upon other units will lead to other units being placed in difficulty or becoming tightly pressed.

One general systemwide contributing factor to the development of a crisis will be a decline in income. A high financial commitment-income ratio seems to be a necessary condition for financial instability; a decline in national income would raise this ratio and would tend to put units in difficulty. Attempts by units with shrunken income to meet their commitments by selling assets adversely affects other initially quite liquid or solvent organizations and has a destabilizing impact upon financial markets. Thus, an explosive process that involves declining asset prices and income flows may be set in motion.

The liabilities of banks and nonbank financial intermediaries are considered by other units (1) as their reservoirs of cash for possible delays in income and financial receipts and (2) as an asset that will never depreciate in nominal value. Bank and financial intermediary failure has an impact upon many units—more units hold liabilities of these institutions than hold liabilities of other private-sector organizations. In addition such failures, by calling into question the soundness of the asset structure of all units, tend to modify all desired portfolios. A key element in the escalation of financial distress to systemwide instability and crisis is the appearance of financial distress among financial institutions. Without the widespread losses and changes in desired portfolios that follow a disruption of the financial system, it is difficult for a financial crisis to occur. The development of effective central banking, which makes less likely a pass-through to other units of losses due to the failure of financial institutions should decrease the likelihood of the occurrence of sweeping financial instability that has characterized history.

From this analysis of uncertainty it appears that, even if effective action by the central bank aborts a full-scale financial crisis by sustaining otherwise insolvent or illiquid organizations, the situation that made such abortive activity necessary will cause private liability emitters, financial intermediaries, and the ultimate holders of assets now to desire more conservative balance sheet structures. The movement toward more conservative balance sheets will lead to a period of relative stagnation.

The following propositions seem to follow from the preceding analysis:

1. The domain of stability of the financial system is endogenous and decreases during a prolonged boom.

2. A necessary condition for a deep depression is a prior financial crisis.

3. The central bank does have the power to abort a financial crisis.

4. Even if a financial crisis is aborted by central bank action, the tremor that goes through the system during the abortion can lead to a recession that, while more severe than the mild recessions that occur with financial stability, can be expected nevertheless to be milder and significantly shorter than the great depressions that have been experienced in the past.[40]

## IX. Central banking

The modern central bank has at least two facets: a part of the stabilization and growth-inducing apparatus of Government and the lender of last resort to all or part of the financial system. These two functions can conflict.

For the United States, central bank functions are decentralized among the Federal Reserve System, the various deposit insurance and savings intermediary regulatory bodies, and the Treasury. The decentralization of central banking functions and responsibilities makes it possible for "buck passing" to occur. One result of this decentralization, along with the fact of usage and market evolution, is that there exists a perennial problem of defining the scope and functions of the various arms of the central bank. The behavior of the various agencies in mid-1966 indicates that *ad hoc* arrangements among the various agencies can serve as the *de facto* central bank. However, even though central banking functions are distributed among a number of organizations, the fact that the Federal Reserve System appears first among them should not be obscured. The Federal Reserve may have to make markets in the assets or liabilities of the other institutions if they are to be able to carry out their assigned subroutines.

The Federal Reserve System undertook, when the peg was removed from the Government bond market, to maintain orderly conditions in this market. Maintaining orderly conditions in a key asset market is an extension of the lender-of-last-resort functions in that it is a preventive lender of last resort. "If we allow the now disorderly conditions to persist, we will in fact have to be a lender of last resort" is the underlying rationalization behind such action. Maintaining orderly conditions in some markets serves to protect position takers in the instrument traded in these markets. This protection of position takers may be a necessary ingredient for the development of efficient financial markets.

The stabilizer and lender-of-last-resort functions are most directly in conflict as a result of such efforts to maintain orderly conditions. If constraining action, undertaken to stabilize income, threatens the solvency of financial institutions, the central bank will be forced to back away from the policy of constraint.

If a financial crisis occurs, the central bank must abandon any policy of constraint. Presumably the central bank should intervene before a collapse of market asset values that will lead to a serious depression. However, if it acts too soon and is too effective, there will be no appreciable pause in the expansion that made the policy of constraint necessary.

I have already discussed one way in which tight money can cause financial instability; that is, asset holders that are locked into assets bearing terms born in times of greater ease are forced into risky portfolio decisions. In addition the very rise in interest rates, which measures tight money, induces substitutions in portfolios that makes financial instability more likely. Thus, intervention on grounds of lender of last resort and responsibilities for maintenance of orderly conditions become more likely during such periods.

In exuberant economic conditions central banking has to determine, once distress appears, just how disorderly markets can become before the lender-of-last-resort functions take over and dominate its actions. Perhaps the optimal way to handle a euphoric economy is to allow a crisis to develop——so that the portfolios acceptable under euphoric conditions are found to be dangerous ——but to act before any severe losses in market values, such as are associated with an actual crisis, take place. If monetary conditions are eased too soon, then no substantial unlayering of balance sheets will be induced, and the total effect of monetary actions might very well be to reinforce the euphoric expansion. If conditions are eased after a crisis actually occurs——so that desired portfolios have been revised to allow for more protection——but the effective exercise of the lender-of-last-resort function prevents too great a fall in asset prices, then the euphoria will be terminated and a more sustainable relation, in terms of investment demand, between the capital stock and desired capital will be established.

If the lender-of-last-resort functions are exercised too late and too little, then the decline in asset prices will lead to a stagnation of investment and a deeper and more protracted recession. Given that the error of easing too soon only delays the problem of constraining a euphoric situation, it may be that the best choice for monetary policy really involves preventing those more severe losses in asset prices that lead to deep depressions, rather than preventing any disorderly or near-crisis conditions. If capitalism reacts to past success by trying to explode, it may be that the only effective way to stabilize the system, short of direct investment controls, is to allow minor financial crises to occur from time to time.

Note that the preceding is independent of the policies mix. If, as seems evident, the tight money of 1965-66 was due more to a rapid rise in the demand for money than to a decline in the rate of growth of the supply of money, a greater monetary ease combined with fiscal constraint would not have done the job. If we accept that a major expansionary element over this period was the investment boom and that the expenditures attributable to Vietnam only affected the degree, not the kind, of development, then an increased availability of finance would have resulted in increased investment and nominal income. A changed policy mix would have constituted further evidence of a new era. Of course, the fiscal constraint could have been severe enough to cause such a large decline in private incomes that existing commitments to make payments could not be met. A financial crisis or a close equivalent may be induced by too severe an application of fiscal constraint as well as by undue monetary constraint.

Within the Federal Reserve System, from the perspective of the maintenance of financial stability or at least the minimization of the impact upon income and employment of instability, a reversal may be in order of the trend that has led to the attenuation of the discount window. If secondary markets are to grow as a way of generating both liquidity while the system is functioning normally and protection while the system is in difficulty, then the dealers in these markets will need access to guaranteed refinancing. The only truly believable guaranty is that of the central bank.

However, a central bank's promise to intervene to maintain orderly conditions in some market will be credible only if the central bank is already operating in that market. If the central bank is not operating in the market, then it will not have working relations with market participants and it will not be receiving first-hand and continuous information as to conditions in the market; no regular channels that feed information about market conditions will exist as now exist for the Government bond market. Thus, the Federal Reserve will need to be a normal functioning supplier of funds to the secondary markets it desires to promote.

At present, only a small portion of the total reserve base of banks is due to discounting at the Federal Reserve System. Discounting can serve three functions—a temporary offset to money market pressures, a steady source of reserves, and the route for emergency stabilization of prices. In order to set the ground for the Federal Reserve System to function effectively in the event of a crisis that requires a lender of last resort, the Federal Reserve normally should be "dealing" or "discounting" in a wide variety of asset markets. One way to do this is to encourage the emergence of dealer secondary markets in various assets and to have the Federal Reserve supply some of the regular financing of the dealers. It might be that a much higher percentage of the bank's cash assets than at present should result from discounting, but the discounting should be by market organizations rather than by banks.

Monetary and fiscal constraint may not be enough once the Keynesian lessons have been learned. The monetary-fiscal steering wheel had assumed a mechanistic determination of decisions that center around uncertainty; the system's doing well may so affect uncertainty that an arsenal of stabilization weapons including larger rationing elements may be necessary.

Let us assume the present arsenal of policy weapons and objectives. The policy objectives will be taken to mean that the high-level stagnation of the 1952-60 period does not constitute an acceptable performance. Under these conditions, the lender-of-last-resort obligations of the Federal Reserve, redefined as allowing local or minor financial crises to occur while sustaining overall asset prices against large declines, become the most important dimension of Federal Reserve policy. The lender-of-last-resort responsibilities become also the arena where human error may play a

significant role in determining the actual outcome of
situations.

It is only in a taut, euphoric, and potentially explosive
that there is much scope for error by the central bank. Th
tance attached to human error under these circumstances is due to
a system characteristic—the tendency to explode—rather than to
the failings of the Board of Governors.

## REFERENCES

Ackley, G. *Macroeconomic Theory.* New York: Macmillan, 1961.

Arrow, K. J. "Aspects of the Theory of Risk Bearing." Yrjo Jahnsson lectures.
Helsinki: Yrjo Jahnssonin Säätio, 1965.

————. "Uncertainty and the Welfare Economics of Medical Care," *American Economic Review*, December 1963.

Clower, R. W. "An Investigation into the Dynamics of Investment," *American Economic Review*, March 1954.

*Economic Report of the President.* Washington, D.C.: U.S. Government Printing Office, 1969.

Fellner, W. "Average-Cost Pricing and the Theory of Uncertainty," *Journal of Political Economy*, June 1948.

————. "Monetary Policies and Hoarding in Periods of Stagnation," *Journal of Political Economy*, June 1943.

Fisher, I. "The Debt-Deflation Theory of Great Depressions," *Econometrica*, October 1933.

Friedman, M. "The Demand for Money: Some Theoretical and Empirical Results," *Journal of Political Economy*, August 1959.

Friedman, M., and Schwartz, A. J. *A Monetary History of the United States, 1867-1960.* Study by the National Bureau of Economic Research, N.Y. New Jersey: Princeton University Press, 1963.

————."Money and Business Cycles," *Review of Economics and Statistics,* Supplement, February 1963.

Galbraith, J. K. *The Affluent Society.* Boston: Houghton Mifflin, 1958.

Greenberg, E. "A Stock-Adjustment Investment Model," *Econometrica*, July 1964.

Gurley, J. G., and Shaw, E. *Money in a Theory of Finance.* Washington, D.C.: Brookings Institution, 1960.

Hicks, J. R. "Mr. Keynes and the 'Classics,' A Suggested Interpretation," *Econometrica*, April 1937.

Johnson, H. G. "The 'General Theory' after Twenty-five Years," *American Economic Review*, papers and proceedings, May 1961.

Kalecki, M. "The Principle of Increasing Risk," *Economica*, November 1937.

Keynes, J. M. "The General Theory of Employment," *Quarterly Journal of Economics*, February 1937.

_____. *The General Theory of Employment, Interest and Money.* New York: Harcourt, Brace, and Company, 1936.

Minsky, H. P. "A Linear Model of Cyclical Growth," *Review of Economics and Statistics*, May 1959; also in Gordon, R. A., and Klein, L. R., A.E.A. Readings in Business Cycles, vol. 10. Homewood, Ill.: Richard D. Irwin, Inc., 1965.

_____ (ed.). *California Banking in a Growing Economy: 1946-1975.* Berkeley, California: University of California, Institute of Business and Economic Research, 1965.

_____. "Central Banking and Money Market Changes," *Quarterly Journal of Economics*, May 1957.

_____. "Comment on Friedman and Schwartz's Money and Business Cycles," *Review of Economics and Statistics*. Supplement, February 1963.

_____. "Financial Crisis, Financial Systems, and the Performance of the Economy," in *Private Capital Markets*. Prepared for the Commission on Money and Credit, N.Y. Englewood Cliffs, N.J.: Prentice-Hall, Inc., 1964.

_____. "Financial Intermediation in the Money and Capital Markets," in Pontecorvo, G., Shay, R. P., and Hart, A. G. *Issues in Banking and Monetary Analysis.* New York: Holt, Rinehart and Winston, Inc., 1967.

Ozga, S. A. *Expectations in Economic Theory.* Chicago: Aldine Publishing Co., 1965.

Tobin, J. *The Intellectual Revolution in U.S. Economic Policy Making.* Noel Buxton lecture. Essex, England: The University of Essex, 1966.

_____. "Liquidity Preference as Behavior Towards Risk," *Review of Economic Studies*, February 1958.

Turvey, R. "Does the Rate of Interest Rule the Roost?" in Hahn, F. H., and Brechling, F. P. R. (eds.). *The Theory of Interest Rates.* New York: St. Martin's Press, 1965.

Viner, J. "Mr. Keynes on the Causes of Unemployment," *Quarterly Journal of Economics*, November 1936.

Witte, J. G., Jr. "The Microfoundations of the Social Investment Function," *Journal of Political Economy*, October 1963.

## Notes

1. For the chronology of mild and deep depression cycles see M. Friedman and A. J. Schwartz, "Money and Business Cycles."

In that chronology all clearly deep depression cycles were associated with a financial crisis and all clearly mild depression cycles were not. Friedman and Schwartz choose to ignore this phenomenon, preferring a monolithic explanation for both 1929-33 and 1960-61. It seems better to posit that mild and deep depressions are quite different types of beasts and the differences in length and depth are due to the absence or occurrence of a financial panic. See H. P. Minsky, "Comment on Friedman and Schwartz's 'Money and Business Cycles.'"

2. I. Fisher, "The Debt-Deflation Theory of Great Depressions."

3. See M. Friedman and A. J. Schwartz, *A Monetary History of the United States 1867-1960*, pp. 309 and 310, footnote 9, for a rather startling example of such reasoning.

4. H. P. Minsky, "Financial Crisis, Financial Systems, and the Performance of the Economy," and "A Linear Model of Cyclical Growth."
5. The large and long contraction of 1929-33 can be interpreted as a succession of crises compounding an initial disturbance.
6. Perhaps the financial history of 1966 can be interpreted as a test of the power of deposit insurance to offset the destabilizing aspects of financial constraint.
7. H. P. Minsky, "Financial Crisis, Financial Systems, and the Performance of the Economy," pp. 326-70, where a number of "primitive" simulations are presented.
8. J. Tobin, *The Intellectual Revolution in U.S. Economic Policy Making.*
9. Investment by nonfarm, nonfinancial corporations, 1962-66:

| Year | Purchase of physical assets | |
|------|------|------|
| | Billions of dillars | Growth rate (percent) |
| 1962 | 44.7 | — |
| 1963 | 76.7 | 4.5 |
| 1964 | 53.5 | 14.6 |
| 1965 | 64.9 | 21.3 |
| 1966 | 79.8 | 21.6* |

*Source: Economic Report of the President*, 1969, Table B73.
*The "crunch" of 1966 occurred in late August/early September; it put a damper on investment and the purchase of physical assets declined to $74.1 billion in 1967.

10. M. Kalecki, "The Principle of Increasing Risk."
11. W. Fellner, "Average-Cost Pricing and the Theory of Uncertainty," and "Monetary Policies and Hoarding in Periods of Stagnation," and S. A. Ozga, *Expectations in Economic Theory.*
12. R. Turvey, "Does the Rate of Interest Rule the Roost?" J. M. Keynes. *The General Theory of Employment, Interest and Money*, Chapter 12.
13. Thus the disruption of the southern California savings and loan mortgage markets in mid-1966 affected *all* present values and cash flow expectations in the economy.
14. This becomes the rationale for a cash flow bank examination. The deviation of actual from contractual cash flows depends upon the behavior of the economy.
15. The Minsky-Bonen experiments in H. P. Minsky, "Financial Crisis, Financial Systems, and the Performance of the Economy," were primitive attempts to do this.
16. This is the content of the alleged wage rigidity assumption of Keynesian theory. See H. G. Johnson, "The 'General Theory' after Twenty-five Years."
17. I include the conventional interpretation of Keynes under the rubric of neoclassical economics. This standard interpretation, which "took off" from J. R. Hicks' famous article—"Mr. Keynes and the 'Classics,' A Suggested Interpretation," and which since has been entombed in standard works like G. Ackley, *Macroeconomic Theory*—is inconsistent with Keynes' own succinct and clear statement of the content of the general theory in his rebuttal to

Viner's famous review ("Mr. Keynes on the Causes of Unemployment"). Keynes' rebuttal appeared with the title "The General Theory of Employment" and emphasized the dominance of uncertainty in the determination of portfolios, the pricing of capital, and the pace of investment.

18. J. K. Galbraith in *The Affluent Society* and K. J. Arrow in "Uncertainty and the Welfare Economics of Medical Care" take the view that various labor and product market deviations from competitive conditions reflect the need to constrain the likelihood that undesirable "states" of the world will occur. This Galbraith-Arrow view of the optimal behavior of firms and households seems to complement the view in Keynes' rebuttal to Viner. See also K. J. Arrow, *Aspects of the Theory of Risk Bearing*, Lecture 2: "The Theory of Risk Aversion," and Lecture 3: "Insurance, Risk and Resource Allocation."

19. J. M. Keynes, "The General Theory of Employment," pp. 209-23. The exact quotation, in full, is: "Money, it is well known, serves two principal purposes. By acting as a money of account it facilitates exchange without it being necessary that it should ever come into the picture as a substantive object. In this respect it is a convenience which is devoid of significance or real influence. In the second place it is a store of wealth. So we are told without a smile on the face. But in the world of the classical economy, what an insane use to which to put it! For it is a recognized characteristic of money as a store of wealth that it is barren: whereas practically every other form of storing wealth yields some interest or profit. Why should anyone outside a lunatic asylum wish to use money as a store of wealth?" p. 215.

20. The doubts can take the form of uncertainty as to what "inertia" should be attached: should it be attached to the level, the rate of change (velocity), or the rate of change of the rate of change (acceleration)?

21. If it is wished, to each outcome $Q_{it}$ a utility $U(Q_{it})$ can be attached. The probability and present value computation can be undertaken with respect to utilities. The risk-aversion character of a decision unit is represented by the curvature of the utility function. A change in confidence can be depicted by a change in curvature, decreased confidence being indicated by an increase in curvature. If preference systems can be assumed to reflect experience, then a long period without a deep depression will decrease the curvature and the occurrence of a financial crisis will increase the curvature of the preference system. The psychology of uncertainty and the social psychology of waves of optimism and pessimism are two points at which economists need guidance from the relevant sister social sciences. Throughout any discussion of uncertainty and of economic policy in the framework of uncertainty psychological assumptions must be made. At times the conclusions depend in a critical manner upon the psychological assumptions.

22. Alternatively, the desired portfolio objective can be stated in terms of cash flows; this less conventional view is examined in Section VI.

23. J. G. Gurley and E. Shaw, *Money in a Theory of Finance*.

24. See J. Tobin, "Liquidity Preference as Behavior Toward Risk," pp. 65-68.

25. The stagnant state that follows a deep depression has been characterized by very low yields—high prices—on default-free assets. One interpretation of the liquidity trap is that it reflects the inability to achieve a meaningful difference between the yields on real assets and on default-free assets by further lowering of the yield on default-free assets. An equivalent but more enlightening view of the liquidity trap is that circumstances occur in which it is not possible by increasing the stock of money to raise the price of the units

in the stock of existing capital so as to induce investment. In these conditions expansionary fiscal policy, especially government spending, will increase the cash flows that units in the stock of real capital generate. In otherwise stagnant conditions this realized improvement in earnings will tend to increase the relative price of inside capital, and thus help induce investment.

26. Incidentally, the phenomenon by which a decrease in the value of some protection affects observable market prices also exists in the labor market. Civil servants and teachers accept low money incomes relative to others with the same initial job opportunity spectrum in exchange for security; civil servants value security more than others. In a euphoric, full employment economy the value of such civil servant security diminishes. Hence in order to attract workers, their relative measured market wage will need to rise.

27. The investment argument builds upon R. W. Clower, "An Investigation into the Dynamics of Investment," and J. G. Witte, Jr., "The Microfoundations of the Social Investment Function." Both Clower and Witte emphasize the determination of the price per unit of the stock as a function of exogenously given interest rates: they are wedded to a productivity basis for the demand for real capital assets. The argument here emphasizes the portfolio balance or speculative aspects of the demand for real capital assets. Thus, interest rates are computed from the relation between expected flows and market prices, that is, the price of capital as a function of the money supply relation *is* the liquidity preference function.

28. Alternatively, the value of wealth can be kept constant; thus $\bar{V} = P_k K + M$. An increase in $M$ is initially an "open market operation" $\Delta M = P_k K$. However, as portfolios now hold more money and less capital goods, the price per unit of capital goods rises. Capital is expropriated so that $W$ remains fixed. This is a pure portfolio balance relation.

If, starting from an initial position, $V_0 = P_{k_0} K_0 + M_0$, $M$ is increased, then the $P_k$ of the second variant would lie above that of the first variant. If $M$ is decreased, the $P_k$ of the second variant will lie below that of the first. The constant wealth variant cuts the constant private capital stock variant from below. I have assumed constant capital stock $K$ in drawing Figure 1.

29. If we assume that the future expected returns from capital are known, then the equation $P_k = Q(M, \bar{K})$ can be transformed into $r = Q(M, \bar{K})$. With every quantity of $M$ a different price will be paid for the same future income stream; a larger quantity of money will be associated with a higher market price of existing capital and thus a lower rate of return on the market value of capital. In a similar way, *the investment relation* can be turned into an $I = I(r)$ relationship. This requires the same information on expected returns as is used in transforming the portfolio relation. In turn the $I = I(r)$ and the $r = Q(M)$ can be transformed into $I = Q(M)$. Because $\bar{K}$ and not $Y$ is an argument in the equation $P_k = Q(M, \bar{K})$, the $IS - LM$ construction is not obtained.

30. Underlying preferences need not be such that for $P_k$ to remain constant

$$\frac{dM}{M} = \frac{dK}{K} \text{ ; it may be that } \frac{dM}{M} < \frac{dK}{K} \text{ or even } \frac{dM}{M} > \frac{dK}{K}. \text{ See Arrow, "As-}$$

pects of the Theory of Risk Bearing." Friedman's well-known result is that

$$\frac{dM}{M} > \frac{dP_k K}{P_k K} \text{ . See M. Friedman, "The Demand for Money: Some Theoretical}$$

and Empirical Results," pp. 327-51.

31. "Tightness" of money refers to costs (including contract terms) for

financing activity by way of debt. High and rising interest rates plus more re-strictive other terms on contracts are evidence of tight money. Tightness has nothing directly to do with the rate of change of the money supply or the money base or what you will. Only as these money supply phenomena affect contract terms do they affect tightness.

Nonprice rationing by suppliers of finance means that the other terms in financing contracts for some demanders increase markedly. The tightness of money is not measured correctly when only one term in a contract, the inter-est rate, is considered.

32. For a more detailed analysis of how financial actualities may relate to project decisions, see H. P. Minsky, "Financial Intermediation in the Money and Capital Markets." See also E. Greenberg, "A Stock-Adjustment Invest-ment Model."

33. H. P. Minsky, "Central Banking and Money Market Changes."

34. Assets enter the financial system when they are used as collateral for borrowing. A newly built house enters the financial system through its mort-gage, which is based upon its current production costs. If the expectation takes over that house prices will rise henceforth at say 10 percent a year, the market value of existing houses will rise to reflect the expected capital gains. If mortgages are based upon purchase prices, once such a house turns over, the values in the portfolios of financial institutions reflect growth expecta-tions. This happens with takeovers, mergers, conglomerates, and so on. It is no accident that such corporate developments are most frequent during eu-phoric periods.

35. The relevant assets structure concept is outside assets as a ratio to the combined assets (or liabilities) of all private units, not the consolidated assets.

36. The common valuation procedures take book or market value. For purposes of both management and central bank decisions it would be better if valuation procedures were conditional, that is, of the form: if the economy behaves as follows, then these assets would be worth as follows.

37. *Income payments* are those payments directly related to the produc-tion of current income. Even though some labor costs are independent of cur-rent output, the data are such that all wage payments are in the income pay-ments class. All of the "Leontief" payments for purchased inputs are such in-come payments.

*Balance sheet payments* during a period are those payments that reflect past financial commitments. Lease, interest, and repayment of principal are among balance sheet payments. For a financial intermediary either withdraw-als by depositors or loans to policyholders are balance sheet payments.

*Portfolio payments* are due to transactions in real and financial assets.

Any payment may be of a different class when viewed by the payor or the payee. To the producer of investment goods the receipts from the sale of the good is an income receipt; to the purchaser it is a portfolio payment.

In addition to types, payments may be classified by "from whom" and "to whom."

If money consisted solely of depositors subject to check, then total pay-ments would be the total debits to accounts and total receipts would be cred-its to accounts. Hence, it is the implication for system stability of total clear-ings, where the financial footings are integrated with the income footings, that is being examined.

38. In various places, I have tried to estimate by proxies some of these re-lations. Empirical investigation of stability could begin with a more thorough and also an up-to-date examination of these payment relations. The relations

mentioned in this section are discussed in detail in my paper, "Financial Crisis, Financial Systems, and the Performance of the Economy."

39. This is, of course, an assertion as to the facts, and the truth of these statements can be tested. Perhaps with a government sector that is 10 percent of GNP, such statements are less true than with one that is 1 percent of GNP.

40. The above was written in the fall of 1966. If the crunch of 1966 is identified as an aborted financial crisis, then the events of 1966-67 can be interpreted as a particularly apt use of central bank and fiscal policy to first abort a financial crisis and then offset the subsequent decline in income. It is also evident from the experience since 1966 that if a crisis and serious recession are aborted, the euphoria, now combined with inflationary expectations, may quickly take over again. It may be that, for the boom and inflationary expectations evident in 1969 to be broken, the possibility of a serious depression taking place again must become a credible threat. Given the experience of the 1960s, it may also be true that the only way such a threat may be made credible is to have a serious depression.

# 7

*Central Banking*

*and*

*Money Market Changes*

## I. Introduction

The ability of a central bank to achieve its objectives depends upon how its operations affect the various elements that make up the money market. Hence, the efficacy of any particular technique of monetary policy depends upon the financial institutions and usages that exist. If financial institutions do not change significantly, then, once the efficacy of the various central bank operations is established, financial institutions can be ignored in discussions of monetary policy. However, if a period of rapid changes in the structure or in the mode of functioning of financial markets occurs, then the efficacy of central bank actions has to be re-examined.

Changes in financial institutions and money-market usages are the result of either legislation or evolution. Legislated changes typically are the result of some real or imagined malfunctioning of the monetary-financial system and hence they usually are accompanied by discussions of their impact. Evolutionary changes occur typically in response to some profit possibilities which exist in the money market. As the evolved changes often center around some technical detail of money-market behavior and as they usually start on a small scale, their significance for monetary policy is generally ignored at the time they first occur. Only if, at a later date, some malfunctioning of the financial system is imputed

The observations upon which Part II of this paper is based were made while I was in New York City on a fellowship sponsored by the Joint Committee on Education of the American Securities business. I wish to thank J. Margolis, R. Miller, and R. Roosa for helpful comments and suggestions.

Reprinted from *The Quarterly Journal of Economics*, Vol. LXXI, No. 2, May 1957, by arrangement with the publisher.

to such an evolved money-market institution will it be discussed, and then the discussion usually occurs as a prelude to "corrective" legislation. Awareness of the conditions which induce institutional changes in the money market and knowledge of the typical effects of such institutional changes should enable the Federal Reserve or the legislating authorities either to take preventive measures or to be ready to minimize the effects of a "crisis" when one occurs.

As evolutionary changes in financial institutions and usages are the result of profit-seeking activities, the expectation is that such financial changes will occur most frequently during periods of high or rising interest rates. Such rates are evidence of a vigorous demand for financing relative to the available supply. They act as a signal to money-market professionals to seek ways of using the available lending ability more efficiently.[1]

Essentially, the relations upon which the monetary authorities base their operations are predicated upon the assumption that a given set of institutions and usages exists. If the operations of the authorities have side effects in that they induce changes in financial institutions and usages, then the relations "shift." As a result, the effects of monetary operations can be quite different from those desired. To the extent that institutional evolution is induced by high or rising interest rates, this would be particularly significant when the central bank is enforcing monetary constraint in an effort to halt inflationary pressures.[2]

In the recent past (1954 to date) short-term interest rates in the United States have been relatively high and rising. During this period at least two changes in the American money market have occurred: the development and growth of the federal funds market; and the increase in the importance of nonfinancial corporations in financing government bond houses. In Section II these two evolved developments are described and examined, in Section III the implications of these particular changes for Federal Reserve policy are taken up, and in Section IV the implications for monetary policy of the expectation that money-market institutions will change are investigated.

## II. Two recent institutional changes

### A. The federal funds market

There is no single trading center where the full scope of the federal funds market can be observed. One brokerage house in New York has for many years, however, played an important role in the market.[3] The best possible view of the market, from any single vantage point, is probably that obtained by observing this firm's operations.

At the end of June, 1956, Garvin, Bantel and Company had some 79 commercial banks and 14 other financial institutions as clients for transactions in federal funds. Not all sales or loans of federal funds are cleared through the brokerage facilities of this firm. A substantial volume of transactions occurs, for example, through the network of correspondent relations among banks, at times in the form of direct loans between banks. However, for the transactions which do not pass through the worksheet of Garvin, Bantel and Company the rate is thought to be typically the same as that which emerges from the offerings and bids brought together through their office.[4]

Reserves at the Federal Reserve Banks are the commodity in which the federal funds market deals. The transaction is an unsecured overnight loan between banks.[5] Among New York City banks this is accomplished by an exchange of checks, the lending bank gives the borrowing bank a draft on the Federal Reserve Bank, and the borrowing bank gives the lending bank a check drawn on itself. As it takes one day for a check to clear, the borrowing bank's overnight balance at the Federal Reserve Bank is increased by this transaction.[6] For non-New York City banks, a telegraphic transfer of reserve balances in one direction today is offset by a telegraphic transfer of reserve balances in the opposite direction at the opening of the next business day. These reserve balances can be and are freely transferred between Federal Reserve districts.[7]

Obviously a loan of federal funds decreases the reserve balance of the lending bank and increases the reserve balance of the borrowing bank. During a period of negative free reserves,[8] a bank which actively participates in this market aims at not having excess reserves, over the averaging period, greater than the unit of transactions. Also a bank active in this market might not borrow from its Federal Reserve Bank unless there are no federal funds available. The benefit to the lending bank is obvious: it earns interest on what would have been an idle balance. The borrowing bank benefits in not having to borrow at its reserve bank. In contrast, for a bank not in the federal funds market, a reserve deficiency results in its either selling assets or borrowing at the reserve bank, and any short-run excess of reserves remains on its books.

The interest rate on federal funds is never greater than the discount rate. During periods when there are sizeable negative free reserves, the federal funds rate usually is equal to the discount rate. Most banks average their reserves over the assigned period by building an excess reserve position at the beginning of the averaging period and then allowing reserve deficits to accumulate during the latter part of the period so that, as a result of the dominance of the weekly reporting member banks in the federal funds market, a rate pattern has developed. During periods of sizeable negative free reserves, the federal funds rate is equal to the discount rate except, perhaps, on Wednesday when it often is lower than the discount rate. There is some evidence that by midyear 1956 some banks were beginning to play this interest rate pattern.

Of the 79 commercial banks which actively participate in the federal funds market by using the facilities of Garvin, Bantel and Company for all or part of their federal funds transactions, 24 are Central Reserve City Banks, 39 are Reserve City Banks and 16 are Country Banks. Of course, the largest and most active group of banks using Garvin, Bantel and Company's facilities are the 25 New York and Chicago banks.[9] The large number of Reserve City and Country banks participating is evidence that the market is national.

The effective limiting factor determining whether or not a bank will take part in the federal funds market is the size of the bank. It does cost something to take part: the time of an officer, phone calls, etc. The broker charges 1/16 of 1 percent "each way" to banks outside of New York City which do not use his facilities for stock and bond business. As the loan is an overnight loan, the interest at 2¾ percent on one million dollars for one day is $76.389 and the broker's commission on a one million dollar loan (1/16 of 1 percent each way) is $3.472. As a result of such considerations the unit of trading in midyear 1956 was around one-half million dollars, and each participating bank was expected to deal in several units. Since the maximum allowable loan to any one borrower (excluding the federal government) by a National Bank is 10 percent of the bank's capital and surplus, no National Bank with less than five million dollars of capital accounts can participate. An examination of the balance sheets of banks shows this to be the case.[10]

In addition to the capital limitation, the broker expects each bank either to borrow or lend, with some regularity, several such half-million dollar units. Thus a participating bank must often have a one or two million dollar excess or deficit reserve position. Of the 79 banks listed by Garvin, Bantel and Company only 4 had less than $100 millions in deposits and another 14 had deposits of between $100 and $200 millions. Six of these 18 smaller banks were in the New York metropolitan area and 4 were in Chicago.

The existence of the federal funds market makes a given volume of reserves more efficient in supporting deposits. If each bank deals with the Federal Reserve Bank on the basis of its own needs, then the excess reserves of some banks are not available to support deposits at deficit banks, which are forced either to borrow at the Federal Reserve Bank or to sell securities. If a perfectly functioning federal funds market existed, no borrowing from the Federal Reserve System would take place while there were excess reserves in any bank, and no bank would have excess reserves while some other bank was borrowing.

As a result of the development of the federal funds market a basic change has taken place in the operations of a part of the banking system. For a participating bank it is not its own reserve position which determines whether or not it will borrow at the Federal Reserve Bank, and no longer does borrowing by a particular bank imply that excess reserves are being generated in the system. To illustrate the argument, assume a 20 percent reserve requirement and Bank A to have a $10 million clearing loss to Bank B, so that Bank A has a deficit and Bank B an excess of $8 millions in reserves. Without participation by these banks in the federal funds market, Bank A would borrow $8 millions from its reserve bank and Bank B would make $8 millions of loans or investments: hence total demand deposits increase. However, if both Bank A and B participate in the federal funds market, then Bank A will borrow and Bank B will lend $8 millions through the market. If the market is tight, some residual deficit bank will end up borrowing at the Federal Reserve: but it is the market situation rather than the behavior of a particular bank which leads to this borrowing.[11]

## B. The financing of government bond houses: Sale and repurchase agreements with nonfinancial corporations

In midyear 1956 sale and repurchase agreements with nonfinancial corporations were a major source of funds for government bond houses. Although the contract between the bond house and the nonfinancial corporation is ostensibly a sale of government debt instruments with a tied repurchase agreement, in truth the transaction is a collateral loan callable both ways. The lending corporation does not earn the interest accruals on the "purchased" debt instruments, rather the corporation earns a stated contractual interest rate.

In addition to these sales and repurchase agreements with nonfinancial corporations, government bond houses can finance their inventory (position) by their own resources, by sales and repurchase agreements with the Federal Reserve System (presumably at the initiative of the open market committee), and by borrowing at commercial banks. The bond houses' own resources can finance only a small portion of their inventories; therefore the behavior of the bond houses and hence of the government bond market depends upon the characteristics of these different sources of funds.

A call loan to a government bond house, secured by government debt, is in many ways a superior asset to a Treasury bill. Hence, one would expect that the interest rate on sale and repurchase agreements between government bond houses and nonfinancial corporations would be lower than the rate on Treasury bills. This expectation is not borne out by the facts: the rate at which government bond houses borrow from nonfinancial corporations is greater than the bill rate, although it is lower than the rate at which government bond houses borrow from commercial banks.[12] Apparently, the rate charged by nonfinancial corporations is low enough so that the government bond houses do not lose on carrying issues with a higher yield than Treasury bills.

Sale and repurchase agreements between government bond houses and the Federal Reserve are almost always at the discount rate.[13] As the initiative is with the Federal Reserve, such accommodations are a privilege rather than a right of the government bond houses.[14] Hence, to the bond houses, such funds are unreliable and they will not make commitments in the expectation that they will be accommodated at the Reserve Banks.[15]

The bond houses always have lines of credit open at the large commercial banks: in fact these banks are the bond house's "lender of last resort." In midyear 1956 the interest rate charged bond houses by these commercial banks ranged from 3¼ percent to 3½ percent. This was a "penal" rate as it was approximately 1 percent greater than the yield on Treasury bills and ½ percent greater than the yield on other government debt. In this situation, when government bond houses financed their position by borrowing from banks, they would lose money on the carry. Hence by midyear 1956, government bond houses did not finance their position by borrowing at commercial banks unless they were forced to do so by the unavailability of other funds. In contrast, during the easy money days, government bond houses financed their position by borrowing at the giant commercial banks, and the interest rate structure was such that they made money on the carry.

In midyear 1956, the interest rate pattern relevant to the operations of government bond houses was (in order, beginning with the lowest interest rates):

(1) Treasury bills

(2) sales and repurchase agreements with nonfinancial corporations

(3) discount rate

(4) longer-term government debt

(5) bank loans to government bond houses (the lowest bank interest rate).

As the yield on Treasury bills was much lower than the interest rate charged bond houses by commercial banks, there was considerable pressure for bond houses to use and develop alternative sources of funds.

Due to the intermittent pattern of tax, dividend, and interest payments, giant nonfinancial corporations have periodic needs for large amounts of cash which they satisfy by accumulating "liquidity" out of earnings. Among the forms in which "liquidity" can be held are:

(1) demand deposits

(2) Treasury bills

(3) sale and repurchase agreements with government bond dealers

(4) loans to sales finance companies.

As commercial banks are forbidden to pay interest on demand deposits, such holdings yield no income. Given the very easy money position and the associated low short-term interest rates which ruled from 1935 to the early 1950s, the holding of demand deposits did not mean any substantial loss of income. The developing higher interest rate pattern of the 1950s means that increasingly the substantial cash balances of nonfinancial corporations have been invested in short-term liquid assets. As a result of the ability and willingness of nonfinancial corporations to hold Treasury bills, the holdings of Treasury bills by commercial banks have decreased from $7.0 billions in 1952 to $2.2 billions in 1956, as shown in Table 1.

On the other hand the holdings of other investors (which include the nonfinancial corporations) have increased from $12.5 billions in 1952 to $17.1 billions in 1956. The same trend is evident in the ownership of marketable securities maturing within one year (Table 2).

The nonfinancial corporations can also hold liquidity in the form of sales and repurchase agreements with government bond houses and the paper of sales finance companies. The paper of sales finance companies earns a higher yield and can be tailor-made to suit the needs of the lender, but it is neither so liquid nor so

Table 1

Ownership of Treasury Bills, 1952—1956[1]
(in billions of dollars)

| | | Held by | |
| | | | Other investors (includes |
| Date | Total outstanding | Commercial banks | nonfinancial corporations) |
| --- | --- | --- | --- |
| Dec. 31, 1952 | 21.7 | 7.0 | 12.5 |
| Dec. 31, 1953 | 19.5 | 4.4 | 11.4 |
| Dec. 31, 1954 | 19.5 | 4.4 | 12.1 |
| Dec. 31, 1955 | 22.3 | 3.6 | 16.0 |
| June 30, 1956 | 20.8 | 2.2 | 17.1 |

[1] Federal Reserve Bulletin: Table titled "Ownership of United States Government Marketable and Convertible Securities" (various issues).

Table 2

Ownership of Marketable Issues Maturing
Within One Year, 1952—1956[1]
(in billions of dollars)

| | | Held by | |
| | | | Other investors (includes |
| Date | Total outstanding | Commercial banks | nonfinancial corporations) |
| --- | --- | --- | --- |
| Dec. 31, 1952 | 57.0 | 17.0 | 23.5 |
| Dec. 31, 1953 | 73.2 | 25.1 | 29.0 |
| Dec. 31, 1954 | 62.8 | 15.7 | 26.3 |
| Dec. 31, 1955 | 60.6 | 7.7 | 30.8 |
| June 30, 1956 | 58.7 | 7.4 | 29.2 |

[1] Federal Reserve Bulletin (various issues).

respectable an asset for a nonfinancial corporation to hold as Treasury bills. Sales and repurchase agreements between nonfinancial corporations and bond houses are very liquid and can be tailor-made. The agreement does seem to be superior to an outright purchase of Treasury bills by the corporations, and it certainly is superior to their outright purchase of longer term issues. As was stated earlier, by midyear 1956 such corporation funds were, as far as could be judged, the major financing source for the government bond houses.

Both developments, the shift of short-term government debt and of the financing of government bond houses from commercial banks to nonfinancial corporations, have freed bank resources to finance other activities. As far as the ability of the banking system to finance expansion is concerned, these developments are equivalent to an increase in bank reserves.

Expansion of the bond houses' nonfinancial corporation sales and repurchase agreements seems likely to occur. If nonfinancial corporations should find loans to bond houses preferable to ownership of Treasury bills, then the rates on Treasury bills would increase and the rate on sales and repurchase agreements would decrease relative to other rates. The "fully developed" market would be in equilibrium when the rate on sales and repurchase agreements was fractionally lower than or equal to the bill rate. The discount rate would remain higher than the bill rate. In this event, the bond houses would be dealers.

What are the implications of the market structure detailed above? Any withdrawal of corporation money will force the government bond houses to borrow from commercial banks. With the present interest rate pattern, this contingency makes it risky for bond houses to take a position. In addition if corporate funds are withdrawn from bond houses because of economic conditions, this will be associated with the sale or the running down of corporation holdings of Treasury bills. As government bond houses are only guaranteed expensive commercial bank financing, they hesitate to take a position in a falling market. Hence, unless the Federal Reserve acts promptly to carry the bond houses or to buy Treasury bills, interest rates will rise rapidly. As the sale and running down of Treasury bills by nonfinancial corporations indicates that they desire increased liquidity (which could be associated with a downward shift in the investment schedule) such a rise in interest rates would occur at the "wrong" time. To counteract this, a money market which is based upon short-term lending by nonfinancial institutions requires a device which automatically feeds reserves into the system when the lenders desire increased liquidity, e.g., a mechanism is needed which automatically increases the quantity of money to compensate for a decrease in the velocity of money; and vice versa.

There are other considerable dangers in nonfinancial corporations financing the bond houses. Almost all government bond houses deal in other types of paper as well. Once nonfinancial corporations are habituated to making "loans" with government debt as collateral, the possibility exists that collateralized loans using nongovernment paper will develop.[16] Such a development would entail greater possibilities of capital losses in a liquidity crisis which, in turn, would affect the stability of the nonfinancial corporations.

A seemingly simple solution to the problems raised by nonfinancial corporations financing financial institutions with their idle balances is to allow commercial banks to pay interest on demand deposits. To eliminate the "dangers" of banks competing for deposits, the rate could be tied to the discount rate. A rate structure in which large demand deposits pay about 1 percent less than the rediscount rate (and there are a number of rates between the deposit and the rediscount rate) seems to be more conducive to financial stability than the existing rate structure. However, such a rate structure requires either a much higher Treasury bill rate or a special source of financing for government bond houses to replace the sale and repurchase agreements with nonfinancial corporations. As the development of a special financing setup for bond houses could entail institutional changes,[17] the seemingly simple solution to the problems raised by nonfinancial corporations financing bond houses has quite complex implications.

## III. Implications of these changes for monetary policy

Two conclusions stand out as a result of the institutional changes described in the preceding sections:

(1) a given volume of reserves now supports more deposits;
(2) a given volume of demand deposits now supports more bank loans to business.

These changes which have increased the volume of business activity that the banking system can finance have not resulted from legislation or Federal Reserve policy. Rather they have been the result of reactions to opportunities for profit in the money market.

Central bank constraint upon commercial bank reserves during a period diagnosed as inflationary is due to a belief that any increase of bank loans would feed inflation. Since at present rates the demand for loans is greater than the supply, these central bank constraints result in higher interest rates. The higher interest rates, in turn, induce institutional changes in the money market which have the effect of increasing lending ability. These institutional changes may or may not lead to a sufficient increase in financing ability to effect the same increase in financing as would have occurred if there had been no central bank constraint.

Within a stable institutional framework, a rise in interest rates tends to make households and business firms conserve their cash balances. As an increase in velocity increases loanable funds, it will at least in part offset the effects of a tight money policy; but, unless the economy is in a state of excess money supply of a liquid-

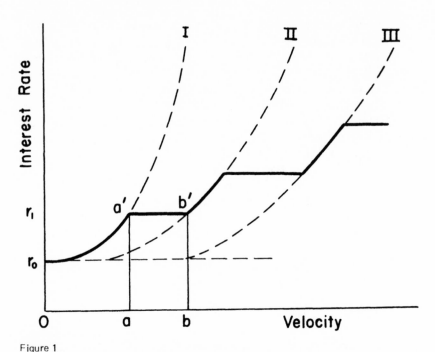

Figure 1

Institutional Changes and Velocity

ity trap type, this offset will not be complete. This can be represented as a positively sloped curve between velocity and the interest rate, and an increase in velocity represents a "permanent"
increase in lending ability. Hence, if the institutional framework is
stable, a tight money policy will be effective and the interest rate
will rise to whatever extent is necessary in order to restrict the demand for financing to the essentially inelastic supply.

However, the rise in interest rates feeds back upon the institutional framework. With rising interest rates the incentives to find
new ways to finance operations and new substitutes for cash assets
increase. The money market is highly competitive and, as large returns are almost always available from some new way to play differential interest rates, new ideas tend to get a hearing. Hence
there is a favorable environment for institutional innovations.
Since the significant institutional innovations during a period of
monetary constraint will be those which tend to increase velocity,
they can be represented as shifting the velocity-interest rate relation to the right.

The resultant velocity-interest rate relation is the sum of the effect of a change in interest rates within unchanging institutional
arrangements and the effects of changes in institutions. While an
institutional innovation in the money market is working its way

through the economy, the net effect is as if the velocity curve were infinitely elastic. The resultant velocity-interest rate relation is a step function, as in Figure 1. If $I$ is the original velocity-interest rate relation, a rise in the interest rate from the liquidity trap rate $r_0$ to $r_1$ will induce institutional innovation $I'$ which, in time, shifts the velocity-interest rate relation to $II$. As a result at a constant interest rate, the amount of additional lending associated with a rise in velocity from $a$ to $b$ will be effected during the time that it takes the institutional innovation to work its way through the economy. Of course, during this time, there may be short-run increases in the interest rate above $r_1$, if the short-run demand for financing increases by more than the increase in financing implicit in the rate at which the institutional framework is changing.[18]

Whenever such an institutional change in the money market is working its way through the economy, restrictive monetary policy, to be effective, must offset the rise in velocity by decreasing the quantity of reserves. Purely passive constraint which operates by not allowing the quantity of money to increase will not be effective in preventing inflation. Therefore, unless the central bank acts strongly to decrease the money supply, monetary policy has only a very limited domain of effectiveness in controlling inflationary pressures. The asserted asymmetry of monetary policy (that it is effective in constraining an inflation and ineffective in constraining a depression) is not true; monetary policy is of very limited effectiveness both in constraining an inflation and in counteracting a depression.

The reverse side of the coin to the increase in velocity is that every institutional innovation which results in both new ways to finance business and new substitutes for cash assets decreases the liquidity of the economy. That is, even though the amount of money does not change, the liquidity of the community decreases when government debt is replaced by private debt in the portfolios of commercial banks. Also, when nonfinancial corporations replace cash with government bonds and then government bonds with debts of bond houses, liquidity decreases. Such a pyramiding of liquid assets implies that the risks to the economy increase, for insolvency or even temporary illiquidity of a key nonbank organization can have a chain reaction and affect the solvency or liquidity of many organizations.

If, during a long prosperity, monetary policy is used to restrain inflation, a number of such velocity-increasing and liquidity-decreasing money-market innovations will take place.[19] As a result, the decrease in liquidity is compounded. In time, these compounded changes will result in an inherently unstable money market so that a slight reversal of prosperity can trigger a financial crisis.

## IV. Implications of the expectation
## that institutions will change

The argument thus far has shown that money-market institutions do evolve, especially under conditions associated with tight money, and that such developments in the money market tend to counteract a tight money policy. As a result during a strong boom, interest rates will not rise very much for the supply of financing is, in fact, very elastic. Associated with the ability of the money market to finance an inflationary expansion is a decline in the liquidity of households and firms. To the extent that either the most liquid assets leave the banking system for the portfolios of other financial institutions or the debts of the newly grown and developed financial institutions enter the portfolios of banks, the liquidity of the banking system declines.

Declining liquidity of banks, households, and business firms has two attributes. One is that the debt-net worth ratio rises. The other is that the vulnerability of money-market assets to a fall in value increases. The two attributes of declining liquidity reinforce each other so that the chances of insolvency and illiquidity increase simultaneously.

A major limiting factor to the decline in the value of any asset is the terms or the price at which it will be monetized by the central bank. However, the evolutionary changes in the money market result in both new kinds of assets and new kinds of financial institutions. One view of the central banks' money-market responsibilities limits them to the maintenance of the liquidity of the banking system and orderly conditions in the government bond market. A central bank with such a view of its money-market responsibilities would not stabilize the new assets either by purchasing or discounting them.[20]

On a priori grounds neither the operators in the money market nor the central bank authorities know the limitations of new institutions and paper. And, unfortunately, in a boom they are not particularly concerned with the possibility of a financial crisis. Hence the newly found profit opportunities will be exploited to such an extent that the money market becomes unstable. In an unstable market a slight deviation from equilibrium has widespread repercussions. Hence, once the money market evolves into such an unstable situation, a financial crisis can be expected. The collapse of a portion of the financial market results in both a loss of net worth and of liquidity by households, business firms, and other financial institutions. Even if the financial crisis is not generalized, economic units will revise their view and desire more liquidity. A tendency to use savings to liquidate debt and hence to increase the ratio of net worth to debt will arise; this has a depressing effect upon income. Thus the "shock" from the financial sector can create a situation which leads to a deep depression. The financing of an expansion by increasing velocity tends to create a situation in which both a financial crisis and a deep depression are possible.

The attitudes of both central bankers and other members of the money market during a boom can be characterized as a version of the Maginot line mentality. The defense against the imperfections of the financial mechanism that was revealed in previous depressions is now perfect, the money market is now working well, hence there is no need to worry.[21] However, the institutions of the money market are constantly changing and as a result of these institutional innovations, the next financial crisis will never be just like the last one. What is required to counteract the effects of such evolutionary developments is a broadened view of central bank responsibilities and a clear recognition that, in spite of corrective steps, the money market will always stretch liquidity to the breaking point during a boom.

To date the Federal Reserve System is a lender of last resort to a commercial bank in distress. It is not a lender of last resort to the money market. In contrast, the classical Bank of England position was as a lender of last resort to a financial intermediary, the discount houses, which, in terms of the paper available, deeply penetrated the British money market. A broad view of a central bank's responsibilities includes the maintenance of the stability of, and acting as a lender of last resort to, a broad segment of the financial market. Hence as new financial institutions develop and as new types of paper appear on the money market, such institutions and paper would not necessarily be ineligible for central bank aid in time of crisis. Hence the central bank would prevent the widespread loss of liquidity resulting from a crisis in one segment of the market.[22]

A policy of monetary constraint would still induce institutional innovations which would result in stretching liquidity. However even after the money market becomes unstable, the central bank, by monetizing the vulnerable asset, can prevent widespread repercussions from occurring. After stabilization, if a money-market institution or usage is considered undesirable because it inevitably leads to instability, then it could be got rid of by legislative or administrative measures.

That the effort by the central bank to control inflation abets the development of unstable conditions in the money market may seem to be a dismal conclusion. Actually, it is too much to expect that a trivial set of operations such as those labeled monetary policy or fiscal policy will always succeed in maintaining stability in a dynamic economy. Institutional innovation is one aspect of a dynamic economy and money-market innovations occur in response to the needs of a growing economy. That these changes will tend to undermine the effectiveness of stabilization policies is a by-product of growth.

However, the role of the central bank is not really diminished by the recognition of its ineffectiveness in preventing inflation as well as in stemming deflation. The central bank's function is to act as a lender of last resort and therefore to limit the losses due to the financial crisis which follows from the instability induced by the innovations during the boom. A combination of rapid central bank action to stabilize financial markets and rapid fiscal policy action to increase community liquidity will minimize the repercussions of the crisis upon consumption and investment expenditures. Thus a deep depression can be avoided. The function of central banks therefore is not to stabilize the economy so much as to act as a lender of last resort. This they are able to do.[23]

## Notes

1. "The basic functioning of financial institutions is the mobilization of the financial resources of the economy in support of economic activity, and I suggest that when credit conditions are tightened and the creation of new money through the banking system is restricted, the financial machinery of the country automatically begins to work in such a way as to mobilize the existing supply of money more effectively, thus permitting it to do most of the work that would have been done by newly created money had credit conditions been easier" (Warren L. Smith, "On the Effectiveness of Monetary Policy," *American Economic Review* XLVI [September 1956]: 601). Smith's point that the more effective utilization of a given monetary supply counteracts, at least in part, tight credit conditions is well taken. However, the assertions that it automatically begins to operate and that it occurs within an unchanging institutional framework are, I believe, incorrect.

2. "Moreover, any rise in interest rates brought about perhaps by a combination of restrictive monetary policy and accumulating debt creates the opportunities for non-bank intermediaries to offer more expensive attractions to creditors and hence to compete more actively with banks" (John G. Gurley and E. S. Shaw, "Financial Aspects of Economic Development," *American Economic Review* XLV [September 1955]: 532). Gurley and Shaw deal with the evolution of financial institutions in a growth context and hence they tend to take for granted the inducements to, and the facts of, institutional change.

3. I wish to thank George Garvin and Ralph de Paola of Garvin, Bantel and Company for their kindness in explaining their operations to an academician. The following analysis of the characteristics of their clients is based upon their worksheet. I wish to emphasize that only the segment of the national market which relies upon the brokerage facilities of that firm is described here. I alone am responsible for the reporting and the interpretation which follows.

For a good introduction to the mechanics of the federal funds market see Nadler, Heller, and Shipman, *The Money Market and Its Institutions* (New York: The Ronald Press, 1955).

4. A more comprehensive survey of the entire market was reportedly undertaken by a special committee of the Federal Reserve System some time in 1956. Pending the completion of that study, which has been kept on a confidential basis up to the time of this writing, it is difficult to generalize with any certainty about the market as a whole.

5. At times, government bond houses, as the result of a sale of bonds to the Federal Reserve System, will lend (sell) federal funds.

6. In computing reserve requirements, the deposits are taken as of the beginning of a business day whereas the reserves are calculated as of the close of the day.

7. When the discount rate is not the same in all districts, some banks will not lend reserves from low to high discount rate districts. Also some New York banks will not allow their federal funds to be loaned outside the New York district.

8. Free reserves are excess reserves minus borrowings at the Federal Reserve Banks.

9. Because of the peculiar Illinois unit banking law, some of the smallest banks (ranked by deposits) which participate in the federal funds market are in Chicago.

10. Information about the banks listed on Garvin, Bantel and Company's worksheet was obtained from *Moody's Bank and Financial Manual, 1956*, especially the table "The Three Hundred Largest Banks in the United States," pp. a 22-23.

All of the data cited about particular banks are as of December 31, 1955.

11. There are obvious similarities between the federal funds market and the classical London discount market and in particular in the part played by Garvin, Bantel and Company and by Gurneys. See W. T. C. King, *The History of the London Discount Market* (London, 1936).

12. My own explanation is that the premium rate on sales and repurchase agreements reflects both the newness of these agreements and the risk due to the lack of a guarantee that the bond houses can replace such call loans by tapping the Federal Reserve.

13. The authorization, as of August 2, 1955, by the Open Market Committee for sales and repurchase agreements between government bond houses and the Federal Reserve System provides that: "In no event shall [they] be at a rate below whichever is the lower of (1) the discount rate of the Federal Reserve Bank on eligible commercial paper, or (2) the average issuing rate on the most recent issue of three month Treasury bills, . . ." However, this is with the "understanding that the authority would be used sparingly in entering into repurchase agreements at rates below the discount rate" (*Forty-Second Annual Report of the Board of Governors of the Federal Reserve System*, pp. 102-3).

14. In July 1955, the Open Market Committee rejected a proposal to ". . . establish at the Federal Reserve Banks an open window for use in financing dealers at rates preferably above, but not lower than, the discount rate" (*ibid.*, pp. 100-1).

15. Around the end of June 1956, the Federal Reserve "opened the window" by letting it be known that it was willing to enter in sale and repurchase agreements with the government bond houses. My interpretation of this event is that at this time nonfinancial corporation funds were being withdrawn from the government bond houses due to tax needs, and, because June 30th is a published balance sheet date for commercial banks, the giant commercial banks did not want to be forced into borrowing from the Federal Reserve to finance the bond houses. This potentially unstable market situation forced a shift in the initiative for repurchase agreements from the

Federal Reserve to the government bond houses.

16. Sales finance corporations do tap corporate cash balances. At present (late 1956) the largest potential source of funds is such corporate balances, and if tight money continues I believe that new type financial institutions will develop which would use these cash balances.

17. For example, the right to rediscount could be withdrawn from the giant commercial banks, and, simultaneously, the government bond houses could be given the right to sale and repurchase agreements. Such a British system would lead to a rate structure compatible with commercial banks paying interest on demand deposits.

18. Actually a fall in the interest rate below $r_1$ will usually not result in the end of the institution whose introduction shifted the velocity relation; so that the effective velocity-interest relation is not infinitely elastic with respect to a fall in interest rates; the movement from $a$ to $b$ is irreversible. Also the interest rate which induces the innovation may be higher than the rate necessary to sustain the institutional change so that the line $a'b'$ may be negatively sloped rather than horizontal. The relations among velocity curves are analogous to the relations among an industry's short-run and long-run supply curves, excepting that the price which will induce investment seems firmer than the price which will induce innovation.

Gurley and Shaw (*op. cit.*) in discussing nonbanking sources of financing state that "Because money becomes a smaller share of total financial assets, velocity becomes a less reliable index of interest rates" (p. 533). They fail to distinguish between the velocity-interest rate relation with constant institutions and the effect of high interest rates in inducing money-market innovations.

19. "In the 1920s nonbank intermediaries gained on banks at an especially rapid rate. The ratio of their assets to assets of banks rose from .77 in 1922 to 1.14 in 1929" (Gurley and Shaw, *op. cit.*, p. 533, footnote 19).

20. The asset (government bonds) and the institution (commercial banks) involved in the two money-market changes taken up in Section II will be stabilized by the central bank. Hence no real financial instability can result from these changes. However other, perhaps still potential, changes (for example, the development of techniques by which "small" cash balances of corportions can be used to finance business or, alternatively, the financing of sales finance companies by corporation funds) are not protected by the Federal Reserve.

21. In this connection note that if the great depression of the 1930s is imputed to the stock market boom of the 1920s which, in turn, is imputed to widespread margin trading, the Federal Reserve today has control over margin trading. On the other hand, if stock market collateral is very important in the financial structure, should not the central bank's responsibility include the maintenance of its value?

22. Gurley and Shaw (*op. cit.*, pp. 536-38) write Financial Control as an alternative (or adjunct) to Monetary Control. Essentially our perspectives are the same except that Gurley and Shaw seem to hold hopes that financial control can aid in achieving stable growth; whereas I maintain that financial instability in boom times is inevitable but that a properly designed and operated central bank can ameliorate its effects. Essentially the difference is one of problems and intuitions.

23. This perspective on central bank abilities is not unlike that of L. W. Mints, *Monetary Policy for a Competitive Society* (New York, 1950) and H. Simons, "Rules Versus Authorities in Monetary Policy," *Journal of Political Economy* XLIV (1936): 1-30.

# 8

## The New Uses
## of Monetary Powers

## Introduction

Over the past several years United States financial markets have experienced their most serious stresses and strains since the great depression of the 1930s. These stresses and strains have been due to both domestic and international developments. As a result market instruments, institutions, and usages have undergone marked changes, and the Federal Reserve System, as well as the other agencies of the peculiarly decentralized central bank of the United States, have responded by adjusting their operations: monetary powers have been used in new ways.

Some of these new uses of monetary powers will be discussed under two headings:[1] the guidance of the evolution of financial markets and the manipulation of uncertainty. As a result of these new uses, the domain of responsibility of the Federal Reserve and the relation between it and other regulatory agencies need to be reexamined.

Central banking has always been a major determinant of what is known with certainty, what is probable, and what is purely conjectural in financial markets. The evolution and development of central banking has not been solely a reaction to an independently-evolving financial structure, but has been also a determinant of this evolution. A sophisticated central bank has always cast a "wider net" than any narrow legislated or contractural responsibil-

Reprinted from the *Nebraska Journal of Economics and Business*, Vol. 8, No. 2, Spring 1969, by arrangement with the publisher.

   This is a revised version of a paper read at the Midwest Economics Association, April 19, 1968.

ities. Thus it can be claimed that these new uses are not really new. The context, however, is new: monetary policy operations are now being undertaken in a world where active monetary and fiscal policy is used to "fine tune" the economy and where there is a wide acceptance of the view that this can be accomplished. As a result monetary policy is being carried out without the constraints upon financial positions and experimentation with new financial market usages that might result from prospects of serious business depressions. That is, fear of the proverbial income and employment "rainy day" is attenuated, and with this attenuation the emphasis on assets to protect against rainy days has decreased.[2]

Whenever central banks undertake to maintain orderly conditions in financial markets or to be the lenders of last resort, they act upon "confidence" and thus uncertainty; they try to diminish this uncertainty by assuring that particular adverse market conditions cannot happen. The new use of central bank powers as they affect uncertainty is a form of financial brinksmanship. The central bank acts so that the range of "possible" market conditions increases: in particular, market conditions which both generate losses and disrupt financial channels are permitted to develop. That is, instead of acting as an insurer (substituting certainty for uncertainty) central banking has taken on some aspects of a casino (substituting uncertainty for certainty).[3]

In this paper reference is made to the credit crunch of 1966.[4] The "crunch" was a miniature financial panic. Effective action by the Federal Reserve and the other financial authorities prevented the escalation of the crunch into a full-fledged money market panic. Nevertheless, the crunch did bring a pause to a runaway investment boom and it did induce some (perhaps transitory) conservatism into portfolios. In retrospect, the crunch was the result of the way in which monetary policy functioned during the expansion of 1960-66. Whether "crunches" should be part of the arsenal of the Federal Reserve, to be induced in appropriate conditions, is a question that needs examination.

## The guidance of the evolution of financial markets

Two aspects of the evolution of the financial system during the continuing expansion of the 1960s will be discussed. First, the role of certificates of deposit in putting pressure on depository savings intermediaries (savings and loan associations and mutual savings banks) and in constraining the Federal Reserve System, especially in the period leading up to the crunch of 1966, will be examined. Then the rapid growth in the volume of commercial paper outstanding since midyear 1966 and the associated changes in bank and bank customer relations will be considered. These developments pose a threat to the "gimmick" used to help ease the pressures on savings intermediaries in 1966 and may require some modifications in Federal Reserve technique.

The major thrust of the argument that follows is that the Federal Reserve should use its monetary powers to guide the evolution of financial markets in directions that are compatible with financial stability in the longer run rather than improvise controls that put out fires but which allow the underlying market situation to remain unchanged.

During the crunch of 1966 interrelations among various elements in the financial system became constraints upon policy. The rise in interest rates on certificates of deposit, combined with the emergence of retail certificates of deposit, posed a threat to the viability of savings and loan associations and mutual savings banks. The mortgage made standard by the reform legislation of the 1930s was an effective constraint upon the use of high interest rates to ration finance for investment.

The financial system is a complex set of linkages. Feedbacks from one market to another are numerous. The market for certificates of deposit, since its emergence in the early 1960s, has always threatened to trigger a run of depositors from savings institutions. The inadequate secondary market and the paucity of price supports for mortgages mean that savings and loan associations and mutual savings banks are always in danger of capital losses when they collectively need to sell out a part of their position. The only meaningful protection for such institutions is to prevent a run-off of their deposit liabilities, i.e., to refinance rather than sell out their position. To do this, however, they must meet market competition day by day; the threat of a run, now called "discrimination," is always present. Thus, one effective constraint upon Federal Reserve policies is the need to maintain interest rates on secure assets available to households in the neighborhood of the rates which savings and loan associations and mutual savings banks can afford to pay.

These savings organizations are heavily invested in long-term mortages which reflect historic interest rates. Even though the expected life of a mortgage is shorter than its contractual life, the assets of savings organizations reflect the relatively distant past of the system to a far greater extent than those of commercial banks. Thus, as long as the fully amortized fixed-interest-rate mortgage is the standard, an effective constraint upon the use of interest rate increases to restrain investment demand is the need to keep current interest rates in touch with historic interest rates.

Of course, we do not revalue the assets (of savings and loan associations, mutual savings banks, and insurance companies) every time interest rates rise and price their mortgages at market rather than at par. Even though savings institutions may be technically insolvent, a fiction of solvency is maintained by valuing assets at par. If the return on assets is less than the cost of doing business, including the cost of retaining deposits, then, even though the organization can be made to look solvent, its net worth will be decreasing as a result of these running losses. Given the thin equity position of savings organizations, such operating losses cannot be long sustained. Thus the Federal Reserve System is constrained by the structure of financial markets and cannot allow too great a rise in interest rates on retail deposits to take place.

A substitution of fully amortized, long-run, variable-interest-rate mortgages for the present fixed-interest-rate mortgages is necessary if rapid and substantial increases in long-term interest rates are to be consistent with the integrity of savings institutions. For the Federal Reserve to be free to adopt policies which lead to sharp increases in long-term rates, it needs to guide the evolution of mortgages in the direction of the adoption of variable interest rates. This could be accomplished by making variable-interest-rate mortgages eligible for discount, by making the paper of dealers in such mortgages eligible for discount, or by extending Federal insurance only to such mortgages. The political difficulties of moving the specialized government agencies to adopt such an alternative convention for mortgages is an argument against the present decentralized central bank structure.[5]

In the mini-crisis of 1966, the various authorities did not face up to the flaw in the financial system due to the standard mortgage. When commercial bank competition for retail-size time deposits threatened the liquidity and solvency of savings institutions, the authorities sought and obtained from the Congress the right to set interest rate ceilings that discriminate by the size of the deposit at all insured deposit institutions. As a result of this "gimmick" a pattern has emerged in which rates on retail time deposits are set at levels that protect the integrity of savings institutions, whereas wholesale time deposit rates are competitive with open market rates (Treasury bills and commercial paper rates). Whenever market rates rise, the authorities must choose between a run on commercial banks or raising the ceiling rate on wholesale certificates of deposit.

Each increase in the rate on wholesale certificates of deposit or market instruments raises the possible gain from arbitrage between the retail and wholesale time money markets. In unit banking states in midyear 1968, wholesale certificates of deposit were profitable investments for neighborhood banks with retail time deposits. New intermediaries and new instruments that skirt the regulations are obvious market reactions to such gaps. There is nothing sacred to the lower limit of $100,000 for a wholesale transaction. This possibility of new intermediaries and new instruments is particularly interesting when the recent rapid growth in the value of commercial paper outstanding is taken into account since commercial paper seems to be an obvious vehicle for such arbitrage.

At the time of the crunch, commercial banks and the Federal Reserve had at best a vague idea of the total amount of outstanding lines of credit, partly because credit lines were often implicit and the most common way in which potential borrowers earned lines of credit, was by keeping deposit balances. A "large" depositor assumed he was buying the availability of credit, and in the near-crisis of 1966 both bankers and depositors found this informal deposit balance convention embarrassing.

The crunch taught many firms that commercial banks were not always reliable sources of financing. Perhaps as a result, the past two years have witnessed an explosive growth of the value of commercial paper outstanding. Its growth rate over the period midyear 1966 to early 1968 was in excess of 40% per year, as the total amount outstanding rose from $10 billion in January 1966, to $19 billion in the spring of 1968.

At present the commercial paper market is a wholesale market —the specialist dealers in commercial paper are among the most substantial of the Wall Street houses—and the typical instrument is so large that the difference between bid and asked is minute. Once again a large gap between open-market rates and rates available to retail time money is an invitation to arbitrage which could lead to a "run" on savings intermediaries. In addition to this danger, however, the growth of the commercial paper market has been associated with the development of a new relationship between banks and some of their large customers.

Over the past two years a rapid increase in contractual lines of credit paid for by an agreed-upon fee (say ¼% or ½% of the line), rather than by a deposit, has taken place. For those firms that combine such contractual lines of credit with short-term financing by way of the commercial paper market, the commercial banking system is now the lender of last resort rather than the initial supplier of credit.

As a result the financial intermediary dealer in commercial paper is of increasing importance in financing business. The problems of how such dealers finance their position, whether a secondary market in commercial paper exists (or should be encouraged), and whether these dealers should have guaranteed refinancing rights are key problems relating to the evolution of the financial system that the Federal Reserve must face. The choice is how to guide market developments: whether to expedite the growth, to do nothing unless circumstances force some action, or to try to prevent any further growth.

The Federal Reserve could expedite the growth of the commercial paper market by making dealers in such paper eligible for accommodation at the discount window. It could create a barrier to these developments by requiring commercial banks to hold reserves against unused portions of contractual lines of credit, thus making it more expensive to use the banking system as a "residual" lender.

Decisions by the authorities whether to support, oppose, or do nothing with respect to the evolution of a financial market need to be based on a view as to how financial markets can best expedite economic efficiency, growth, and stability. It is apparent from the experience of 1966 that policies adopted when a particular stability crisis is at hand may succeed in achieving a short-term resolution of the crisis while leaving market conditions that can breed further difficulties. Whereas segregating markets may have been an effective way of protecting savings intermediaries against an immediate run, savings intermediaries remain vulnerable to rising interest rates as long as the basic mortgage remains unchanged and the availability of interest rate increases, or policies that lead to sharp increases in interest rates, are restricted.

Similarly, the combination of a much larger commercial paper market and contractual loan commitments can lead to a large increase in drawings from lines of credit whenever the Federal Reserve attempts a restrictive monetary policy. Banks, under these conditions, would either hold larger amounts of those short-term assets whose market is protected by the Federal Reserve or would tend to use the discount window more liberally than in recent years. In either case Federal Reserve restrictive policy would not effectively constrain the growth of bank reserves but would change the source and the price of reserves. If this is the way in which the money market is to evolve, then an evolution of all financial institutions and markets so that their stability is consistent with greater fluctuations in interest rates is in order. Once again the nature of the standard mortgage acts as a constraint. It seems that recent changes in money and financial markets are decreasing the availability of monetary policy as a technique for restraining undue expansion.

## The manipulation of uncertainty

The standard textbook model that shows how monetary and fiscal policy can be traded off to generate a desired level of income does not allow for anything as fragile as uncertainty, as the term will be used here. Ideas about uncertainty will be developed within the specific context of the usages and operations of financial institutions and markets.[6]

Financial institutions are organizations which take a position in financial assets by emitting their own financial liabilities. The contracts they own and have emitted state commitments to pay cash on demand, at a particular date, or in the case some state of nature or event occurs. Thus, for each portfolio there is a cash flow to and a cash flow from, over every time horizon, that is explicitly stated in the contracts. The actual cash flows over every time horizon, however, depend on the way in which demand and contingent clauses in the contracts are exercised, and thus on the way in which outside economic and financial market conditions affect the organization. For each contract there is some probability (subjective) that the terms of the contract will not be honored. Thus there is a range of net cash flows with positive and negative values to this organization, with some probability assigned to each net cash flow.

In addition to the cash flows generated by the terms of contracts, cash flows can also be generated by buying and selling contracts in markets, including the sale of newly created contracts. Sales or purchases of assets to acquire or get rid of cash are called "position-making activities" if a short horizon determines the action, or "investment" if a longer horizon guides the activity. For each deficit or excess due to cash flows, some sales or purchases to make position will occur. When the market is functioning normally, the capital exposure from position-making activity is slight. The danger, which can result in significant losses, is that when a unit wants to make position by selling some particular asset, the relevant market is not functioning normally.

Thus, in addition to the frequency distribution of expected short falls and excesses of the cash flows to a unit, there is another type of uncertainty that exists in financial markets. This uncertainty relates to the state of the various money markets at the date a unit wants to make position by operating in those markets.

Note that an unfavorable state of a market does not mean simply that the selling unit has to make large price concessions. Each time a unit sells an asset some other unit takes the asset into position. The purchasing unit is accepting some capital exposure when this is done. If the potential purchasing unit's capital is already encumbered, as happens in a falling market, and if it believes the risk of losses is sufficiently great because of market disorganization, it will not take the position. In periods of rapidly rising interest rates, quoted prices of Treasury bills and other short-term securities always reflect transaction prices, but for longer-term securities quoted prices do not reflect any significant volume of transactions. In addition, the transactions that do take place in longer-term securities often carry conditions with them. The stated price can understate the true cost of making position by operating in these markets.

Rosa, in his fundamental paper on the availability doctrine, discussed the uncertainty introduced into the financial system when the "peg" was withdrawn from interest rates at the end of World War II.[7] This discussion was concentrated on the market for government securities, and largely on the Treasury bill market. Even after the "peg" was withdrawn these markets were protected by the Federal Reserve's commitment to prevent disorderly conditions. Therefore, while reluctance could be induced by small losses, large losses, which could force a reexamination of desired portfolios by all units, were not available as an instrument of policy.

Once Federal funds, certificates of deposits, and even municipal securities replaced government securities as position-making instruments, banks and other money market organizations became dependent upon the behavior of markets whose normal functioning was not guaranteed by the Federal Reserve. Under these circumstances it is possible that markets would not be working smoothly when needed. Thus the uncertainty of the 1960s and that to which Rosa referred are really quite different beasts.

As all units can be thought of as financial units, the cash flows to and the cash flows from income-producing units also can be analyzed by comparing contractual commitments to pay cash with cash flows from operations. The problem is always how much of an expected cash flow to a unit, given expected variability of the cash flow, will be hypothecated or pledged by issuing particular types of liabilities. A protracted period of rising prosperity, during which the economy is functioning ever more successfully, breeds a view in ordinary business corporations and financial institutions which allows them to raise their short-term payment commitments as a ratio, for example, to their expected cash flows from operations. A process of substituting one asset for another or of financing positions with liabilities that require a greater cash flow from the organization relative to the cash flows to the organization takes place. The simultaneous stretching of liquidity positions by corporations and by financial institutions is a characteristic of a boom economy.[8]

If the Federal Reserve is confronted with such portfolio shifts as a major source of the expansion of credit by the financial system, it cannot, by its ordinary quantitative controls, force a quick reduction of credit expansion. Although in the long run, taking the good and the bad, it may be true that owned reserves are a good proximate determinant of the money supply and credit, it is also true that in the short run the relationship is not at all precise.

The weakness of quantitative controls during a period when velocity-increasing portfolio changes are major sources of investment financing is reenforced by the existence of a network of credit lines, explicit and implicit. This makes the loans of any particular date the result of prior and continuing business relations. In an expansion powered by an investment boom the Federal Reserve as well as the major money market banks seem to lose control over the volume of loans.

The liability structure that is acceptable to ordinary corporations and the asset and liability structure that is acceptable to financial institutions reflect both a view about the variability of the cash flows that result from income production, and the belief that, if the necessity arises, position making, by the sale of some assets or the emission of liabilities, will take place without any great sacrifice. Confidence in the normal functioning of financial markets and in the capacity of the system to maintain high-level income leads to an expansion which is not closely articulated to increases in the quantity of money. Increasing willingness to take risks underlies an expansion which is heavily financed by portfolio transformations.

In such circumstances, the Federal Reserve has one way to restrain the expansion. This is to make the desired liability and asset structures more conservative by reintroducing uncertainty. One way to do this is to have fluctuations in income and employment, i.e., by allowing depressions and recessions. Presumably this path is no longer open. Another way to engender uncertainty is to raise doubts that financial markets will function normally when the institution wants to use those markets. Thus disrupting financial markets may be a necessary tool of monetary policy.

The period leading up to the crunch saw the development of a wide spread between position-making rates such as the Federal funds rate and the discount rate. Obviously the barrier to borrowing at the Federal Reserve Banks was a tight administration of the discount window. The doctrine of not borrowing for profits was transformed into a doctrine of not borrowing except with the acquiescence of the managers of the discount window. The traditional central banking doctrine of an infinitely elastic supply of reserves, by discounting eligible paper at a penal rate, was never fully applicable in the United States, because the eligible paper generally carried rates greater than the discount rate. The discount rate, nevertheless, was a penal rate to the extent that it was a more expensive way of making psoition than by using money market instruments. The rates of interest that are relevant to profitability of borrowing at the discount rate are not the rate on the paper pledged in the commercial loan tradition but the rates of interest on Treasury bills, in the Federal funds market, or in other position-making money markets.

In a tightly administered discount market, eligibility to discount becomes a matter of discretion. Such a discretionary discount window does not act as an automatic safety valve when money market tightness is abruptly induced by the Federal Reserve. Thus, when the Federal Reserve finally decreased the rate of increase in reserves during 1966, the rise of open-market rates above the ceiling rate on certificates of deposit resulted in a "run" on commercial banks, as certificates of deposits matured. Due to the growth of collateralized deposits and the decrease in government security holdings in general, banks were not able to make position by dealing in Treasury debt. During July and August they began to make position by decreasing their holdings of municipals, and the fall in municipal prices led to significant losses.

The combination of a tightly administered discount window, a sharp fall in the rate of growth of reserves, a rise in loan demand due to prior commitments to business organizations, and the attempt by commercial banks to make position by selling municipals resulted in disorganized conditions in position-making financial markets. While commercial banks were making price concessions in an effort to acquire liquidity, the Federal Reserve maintained its policy of tightly administering the window. With the breakdown in normal position-making activity, what has been described as near panic conditions appeared on the market. Everyone was certain that the Federal Reserve would do something to save the situation, but the question was when, and after what price had been paid. The Federal Reserve finally stepped in about September 1 and opened the window to banks that had been "good." In particular, the window was opened to the pledging of municipal securities. This had the dual effect of stabilizing a market where prices had fallen precipitously and increasing liquidity by extending eligibility to a new class of paper.

## Conclusion: The domain of the federal reserve system

The events of 1966 can be interpreted as the use of policy instruments to generate a near crisis, the objective being to break an investment boom by making "liquidity" valuable again. Because of the "fortuitous" escalation in Vietnam, no cumulative decline in investment and income took place. Because of the large size of the Federal government relative to the economy, a cumulative decline leading to a great depression is much less likely under any circumstances other than a financial crisis accompanied by a substantial reduction in the size of the Federal sector.

Given the large size of the Federal government and the unavailability of a substantial decline in income as a restraining factor in portfolios, the economy is poised, not on a knife edge but on a volcano. The danger is that an investment explosion financed by portfolio transformation will take place. To constrain such developments the Federal Reserve must operate so as to make liquidity valuable; this it can do by generating crunches, or allowing them to occur from time to time.

The existence of a ceiling rate on certificates of deposit means that the Federal Reserve can always induce a run on commercial banks. It can do this by not increasing certificate of deposit ceiling rates when rates on competing market instruments rise so that certificates of deposit are not attractive. In addition, the existence of other financial institutions and other markets means that the major impact of a rising interest rate pattern may not be at the commercial banks; in 1966 the savings intermediaries bore a great deal of the pressure.

As a result of the events of the 1960s, it is now clearer than ever that the domain of responsibility of the Federal Reserve System extends beyond the set of member banks. Even though the specialized deposit insurance and regulating agencies exist, the Federal Reserve remains the ultimate repository of liquidity and the other organizations require Federal Reserve cooperation if they are to carry out their responsibilities. Ultimately, the Federal Reserve is responsible for the normal functioning of the entire financial system.

This extended domain of responsibility is of greater significance if the generation of crunches is accepted as a method of applying Federal Reserve authority. In our complex interdependent financial system we cannot pinpoint where the rupture of usual financial practices will occur after the sharp application of financial restraint. The crunch technique first imposes losses and fears of great losses throughout the economy and then, by prompt Federal Reserve action, prevents any cumulative deflationary pressures from taking place. For the Federal Reserve to be able to operate in this way it needs to be able to pinpoint its lender-of-last-resort function, presumably by opening the discount window to the appropriate assets. Thus a reorganization of the structure of central banking so that the Federal Reserve is in contact with a wider array of markets and institutions may be in order, perhaps by opening and regularizing the discount window.[9]

The developments in commercial banking and corporate financial techniques which have resulted in closer cash management, growth of the commercial loan market, and greater rise of contractual lines of credit may mean that commercial banks will need ready accommodation at the discount window whenever restraint leads to a slowdown in the amount of commercial paper outstanding. Rationing through an open discount window, however, is rationing by price; thus monetary policy may require more rapid movements, as well as a greater range, for interest rates.

Given segmented markets, the ability of the financial system to function normally if interest rates rise rapidly is limited because of both the threat of arbitrage among markets and the weakness of savings institutions. As a result there are severe limitations upon the use of monetary policy to restrain a rapid expansion. The upward instability of investment, together with the accumulated weaknesses in our financial system, may mean that in the near future greater reliance needs to be placed upon flexible fiscal policy than has been true to date. This is so not because monetary policy is inherently weak but rather because of the peculiar set of institutional arrangements that now exists.

## Notes

1. I do not claim that the developments I discuss represent all, or even the most significant, recent developments; my knowledge is imperfect and from those I know of I have selected elements which seem to have the greatest relevance to the stability properties of the system and the practice of central banking.

2. It may be claimed that the "New Era" of the 1920s was also characterized by confidence in the "new" sophistication of economic policy—in that era the confidence was due to the existence of a "sophisticated" Federal Reserve System.

3. Milton Friedman and L. J. Savage. "The Utility Analysis of Choices In-

volving Risk," *Journal of Political Economy* LVI (1948).

4. I have discussed the crunch and its consequences in two places: "The Crunch and Its Aftermath," *Bankers Magazine*, February-March 1968; and "The Crunch of 1966—Model for New Financial Crises," *Trans-action Magazine*, March 1968.

5. Various alternatives to adoption of a variable interest rate mortgage have been suggested. For the entire issue of the good financial society various writings of Henry Simons are still relevant. See his "A Positive Program for Laissez Faire" and "Rules Versus Authorities in Monetary Policy"; both are reprinted in H. Simons, *Economic Policy for a Free Society* (University of Chicago Press, Chicago, Illinois, 1948).

6. The ideas about uncertainty that will be developed seem to be consistent with those of Keynes in his rebuttal to Viner et al.: J. M. Keynes, "The General Theory of Employment," *Quarterly Journal of Economics* (February 1937).

7. Robert Rosa, "Interest Rates and the Central Bank" in *Money, Trade and Economic Growth* (Essays in Honor of John H. Williams) (New York, 1951), pp. 270-295.

8. The systematic transformation of portfolios over an extended boom as well as the formal cash flow model are examined in Minsky, H. P., "Financial Crisis, Financial Systems and the Performance of the Economy" in Commission on Money and Credit, *Private Capital Markets* (Englewood Cliffs, N. J., 1964).

9. The Board of Governors of the Federal Reserve System, *Reappraisal of the Federal Reserve Discount Mechanism: Report of a System Committee* (July 1968), seems to have adopted a somewhat similar position.

# 9

### The Federal Reserve:
### Between a Rock
### and a Hard Place

The more the Board of Governors fights inflation the worse inflation gets. The new look in Federal Reserve policy that was presented with fanfare last October was designed to enable the Federal Reserve to restrict the growth of "the" money supply, whatever that may be. According to the mainly monetarist theory that guided this action, restricting the growth of "the" money supply would lead, over a number of years, to an end of inflation. The theory is that inflation could be gradually eliminated without undue hardship.

The results of the first six months of the new policy posture are in. The record is dismal. Instead of inflation's diminishing, the rate of increase of prices has accelerated. Furthermore, during the first months of 1980 we have seen a free fall in bond prices take place which, if carried through to the books of financial institutions that hold bonds and mortgages, undoubtedly makes many leading institutions "walking bankrupts"; their net worth at market prices is negative. Overt bankruptcy has been avoided because the marketing of debt instruments at competitive interest rates has enabled walking bankrupts to fulfill maturing obligations. But such institutions are carrying assets that yield yesterday's interest rates with liabilities on which they pay today's much higher rates. Such losses on the carry mean that the walking bankrupts of 1980 are bleeding to death.

The economic record is not all bad, however. As we recite the list of dismal indicators—inflation at more than 16 percent, in-

Reprinted from *Challenge*, May/June 1980, pages 30-36. ©1980 by M. E. Sharpe, Inc.

terest rates above 20 percent, unemployment at 6 percent, slow growth, a dollar under continuing international pressure, and mounting trade deficits——we must recognize one overridingly important virtue of our post-World War II economy: there has not been a deep and long-lasting depression. What is more, in spite of credit crunches, liquidity squeezes, and banking debacles in 1966, 1969-70, and 1974-75, the financial system has not gone through an "interactive" debt deflation such as regularly occurred in the generations before World War II.

There is something about the structure of today's American economy that has made it immune to the financial crises and deep depressions that took place earlier in our history. At the same time there is something about its structure that makes the economy prone to accelerating inflation. The two are linked: immunity to financial crises and deep depressions is one side of a coin; susceptibility to accelerating inflation and exotic diseases like stagflation is the other. To do better in the 1980s than in the 1970s we need to understand this linkage, which means that we have to go beyond the monetarist perceptions of how our economy works.

## Dual role of the Federal Reserve

Monetarist theory holds that the rate of growth of money income is determined by the rate of growth of money, and that the Federal Reserve can control the money supply to achieve noninflationary economic growth. Monetarist theory reduces the operations of a complex evolving economic system that exists in one-directional time to a matter of simple formulas that can be recited by believers and even recent converts.

In monetarist theory, the function of the Federal Reserve is to control the growth of "the" money supply to some rate derived from "the formula" on the basis of assumptions about the growth of productive capacity. In truth the Federal Reserve was not brought into being to control the money supply in an effort to control the rate of growth of money income; it was brought into being in the first decades of this century because the banking and financial system experienced periodic financial crises. It was felt that a lender of last resort was needed to prevent or contain the repercussions of such crises. The Federal Reserve was to stabilize the economy by preventing debt-deflations (such as occurred in 1929-33), not by controlling the monetary supply.

Thus the Federal Reserve is both a lender of last resort, whose mission is to prevent financial instability that leads to a large-scale bankruptcy of financial institutions, and a controller of the economy, whose mission is to help steer the economy on a growth path of full employment and stable prices.

In spite of our current difficulties, the years since the end of World War II are a unique era of success in the history of the American economy in that a debt-deflation, and thus a deep depression, has been avoided. This thirty-five-year history of success falls into two parts. The first, lasting some twenty years, is a regime of rapid economic progress with—on the whole—stable prices. At no time during this period did the Federal Reserve have to intervene as a lender of last resort to maintain the financial system.

Because of the rapid accumulation of private debt and the proliferation of new institutions and instruments in financial markets during these twenty years, tranquil progress was replaced in the middle 1960s by ever-increasing financial and economic turbulence. Since 1966, the Federal Reserve has acted as a lender of last resort three times—in 1966, 1969-70, and 1974-75. Inflation, which had been a modest statistical concept prior to 1966, became a blatant, readily observable phenomenon in the 1970s.

Each time the Federal Reserve acts as a lender of last resort, it prevents some financial institution or some financial market from collapsing. When it does this, it introduces additional Federal Reserve liabilities into the economy and extends a Federal Reserve guarantee over some set of financial practices. Thus in 1966 it protected banks that used certificates of deposits, in 1969-70 it protected the commercial paper market, and in 1974-75 it extended the Federal Reserve guarantee to those who owned the liabilities of offshore branches of American banks. By legitimizing financial market practices through its implicit endorsement, the Federal Reserve in 1966, 1969-70, and 1974-75 set the stage for the financing of a subsequent inflationary burst.

If the Federal Reserve had not protected depositors at the London branch of Franklin National Bank in 1974 or if, after protecting such depositors, it had set prudent and constraining standards for the growth of offshore deposits at American banks, then the various increases in oil prices since 1973 could not have been sustained. Under Arthur Burns' leadership the Federal Reserve either ignored or was ignorant of a fundamental maxim of economics, namely, only that which is financed can occur. If the deposits at the offshore branches of American banks had not been allowed to expand without limit and if such deposits had been assets at risk rather than assets protected by an implicit guarantee of the Federal Reserve, the OPEC price cartel would have been broken soon after the spring of 1974.

## 1929 and 1979

Today's American economy is much different from the economy that collapsed in the Great Depression some fifty years ago. In the accompanying table, the value of and the ratio to the gross national product of various aspects of the economy are exhibited for each end-of-decade year beginning with 1929. About the only "ratio" that has remained relatively unchanged over these years is that of investment to gross national product (15.7 percent in 1929 and 16.0 percent in 1959, 15.6 percent in 1969 and 16.3 percent in 1979). There is a myth that what is wrong with the economy is a "shortfall of investment." In truth, in 1979 we were investing, relative to GNP, at about the same rate as in earlier prosperous years.

The major changes in the composition of demand and output after 1929 are the decline in the ratio of consumption to GNP, the rise in government, however measured, and a quite recent rise in exports. If we compare the 1929 ratios of the various categories to the 1979 ratios, it is evident that the composition of demand has changed radically. There is no reason to expect an economy with small government such as ruled in 1929 (where federal government expenditures were 2.5 percent of GNP) to behave in the same aggregate manner as an economy with big government (where federal government expenditures are 21.4 percent of GNP).

How does the size of government affect the operations of our economy? Our economy is capitalist, which means that production is motivated by profits. Furthermore, in our economy, business uses debts to finance ownership of capital assets. The cash flow of business is approximately the sum of interest payments by business and gross profits after taxes or, in other words, the gross after-tax income of capital. This income is the basic source of funds that are available to meet the payment commitments on debts. For every debt structure of the economy there is a minimum level of gross profits which is consistent with any assigned level of success by business in meeting payment commitments. Below some threshold, which is determined by the size and terms on business debt, any decline in gross profits after taxes will lead to an increase in the number of businesses that fail to fulfill their contractual obligations in debts. New debt financing is always

## Gross National Product and Its Major Components
### Selected Years 1929 Through 1979

| Year | Gross National Produce | Consumption | Investment | Government purchase Total | Government purchase Federal | Government purchase State & local | Transfer payments to persons | Exports | Federal gov. exp. |
|---|---|---|---|---|---|---|---|---|---|
| | | | | Billions of dollars | | | | | |
| 1929 | 103.4 | 77.3 | 16.2 | 8.8 | 1.4 | 7.4 | .9 | 7.0 | 2.6 |
| 1939 | 90.8 | 67.0 | 9.3 | 13.5 | 5.2 | 8.3 | 2.5 | 4.4 | 8.9 |
| 1949 | 258.0 | 178.1 | 35.3 | 38.4 | 20.4 | 18.0 | 11.7 | 15.9 | 41.3 |
| 1959 | 486.5 | 310.8 | 77.6 | 97.6 | 53.9 | 43.7 | 25.2 | 23.7 | 91.0 |
| 1969 | 935.5 | 579.7 | 146.2 | 207.9 | 97.5 | 110.4 | 62.7 | 54.7 | 188.4 |
| 1979 | 2368.5 | 1509.8 | 386.2 | 476.1 | 166.3 | 309.8 | 241.9 | 257.4 | 508.0 |
| | | | | As a Percentage of GNP | | | | | |
| 1929 | 100.0 | 74.8 | 15.7 | 8.5 | 1.2 | 7.2 | .1 | 6.8 | 2.5 |
| 1939 | | 74.2 | 10.3 | 15.0 | 5.8 | 9.2 | 2.8 | 4.8 | 9.8 |
| 1949 | | 69.0 | 13.7 | 14.9 | 7.9 | 7.0 | 4.5 | 6.2 | 16.0 |
| 1959 | | 63.9 | 16.0 | 20.1 | 11.1 | 9.0 | 5.2 | 4.9 | 18.7 |
| 1969 | | 62.0 | 15.6 | 22.2 | 10.4 | 11.8 | 6.7 | 5.8 | 20.1 |
| 1979 | | 63.7 | 16.3 | 20.1 | 7.0 | 13.0 | 10.2 | 10.9 | 21.4 |

*Source:* Economic Report of the President, January 1980, Table B1, page 203, except Government Transfer Payments to Persons, Table B18, page 223, and Foreign Government Expenditures, Table B72, page 288.

needed to sustain or expand income. Any significant increase in the failure of business to meet payment commitments will lead to a decline in the amount of financing available to business. A decline in financing means a decline in investment, which implies a decline in income and employment.

Thus profits, broadly defined, are the pivot around which the normal functioning of an economy with private business debts revolves. It is necessary to understand what determines profits. In the heroically abstract formulations we owe to Kalecki, gross profits equal investment. If government, with its possible deficits, and the rest of the world, as reflected by the balance of trade, are taken into account, then gross profits after taxes equal investment plus the government deficit minus the balance-of-trade deficit.

In 1929 investment amounted to $16.2 billion and federal government expenditures to $2.6 billion. In 1930 investment fell by 36.4 percent to $10.3 billion and the federal government's budget swung from a $1.0 billion surplus to a $0.3 billion deficit. The change in the government deficit could not offset the $5.9 billion decline in investment, so that business gross retained earnings fell from $11.5 billion in 1929 to $8.8 billion in 1930. By this measure the cash available to fulfill payment commitments on debts fell by 23.5 percent; the burden of the debt increased as the country went into recession.

In 1979 investment was $386.2 billion and the total federal government expenditures were $508.0 billion. The effect on profits of a large decline in investment could be offset by a rise in government expenditures and a fall in taxes, which is what happened in the recession of 1975. In 1975 investment was $190.9 billion, some $23.7 billion less than in 1974. The budget deficit was $70.6 billion in 1975, some $59.9 billion greater than in 1974. As a result, business gross retained earnings were $176.2 billion in 1975, some $38.3 billion higher than in 1974. During the most serious recession of the post-war period the cash flow to business after taxes, interest, and dividends had risen by some 28 percent.

The contrast between 1929-30 and 1974-75 is striking. In 1974-75 the deficits that were caused by big government sustained business profits and enabled business to fulfill its payment commitments to banks and other financial institutions. In 1930 business had to pay debts that had been contracted for in 1929 and earlier out of a shrunken cash flow. In fact, the cash flow of business kept on contracting through 1931, '32, and into '33. In 1929-33 the burden of debt inherited from the past increased. In 1975, even as the economy was in its most severe recession of the post-World War II era, the burden of inherited business debt decreased.

In an economy with the 1929 structure a shortfall of profits can take place which makes it difficult or impossible for business to fulfill its obligations on debts. No such shortfall can happen in an economy with the 1979 structure of demands. With the 1979 structure, the impact on profits of a fall in investment will be offset by a rise in the government deficit: the amplitude of the fluctuation in profits will at a minimum be decreased—at a "maximum" it may disappear or even become "contracyclical."

The automatic and discretionary fiscal reactions of 1974-75 were not the only governmental interventions that prevented a deep depression. In May of 1974 a run took place on the money market liabilities of Franklin National Bank. The Federal Reserve Bank of New York opened its discount window to the Franklin National, which allowed it to pay off maturing liabilities. In October 1974 Franklin National Bank was closed. In a period of slightly more than two years, 1973-75, four banks in the billion-dollar class required special assistance from the Federal Reserve and two failed. In addition, in the same period a sizable number of smaller banks failed and there were widespread overt and covert failures by Real Estate Investment Trusts. The spate of failures did not lead to an interactive collapse because the lender-of-last-resort interventions by the Federal Reserve and other government agencies prevented the process by which each failure triggers several other failures.

## Lender of last resort

The Federal Reserve wears two hats. One hat signifies the operator of monetary policy. When the Federal Reserve wears this hat its target is noninflationary growth. The second hat is that of lender of last resort. When the Federal Reserve wears this hat it is actively refinancing and funding the debts of units whose ability to raise finance on commercial terms has been compromised. The lender-of-last-resort actions feed reserves into the banking system and set limits to the default risks carried by holders of liabilities that the Federal Reserve protects. Both the feeding of reserves into the private financial system and the extension of Federal Reserve guarantees increase the ability and willingness of banks and other financial institutions to finance activity. If lender-of-last-resort interactions are not accompanied by regulations and reforms that restrict financial market practices, then the intervention sets the stage for the financing of an inflationary expansion, once the "animal spirits" of business people and bankers have recovered from the transitory shock of the crisis that forced the lender-of-last-resort activities in the first place.

The Federal Reserve therefore is in a dilemma. It is dealing with a very sophisticated and convoluted financial system in which the available financing is responsive to demand. The existence of this complex system means that a great many payments have to be made among the financial institutions and that a set of financial relations exists that depends upon the availability of bank financing as a "fallback" source of funds. The Federal Reserve can bring a halt to an inflationary process only as it forces high enough interest rates so that units which need refinancing are found to be ineligible for financing in the market because of inadequate expected profits or cash flows. The Federal Reserve can break an inflationary process only by first creating "walking bankrupts" and then transforming them into overt, open bankrupts. When walking bankrupts, deprived of bank or other normal financing, try to meet payment obligations by selling assets, a collapse of asset values occurs. When this takes place, an epidemic of bankruptcies is set to erupt. Since the mid-1960s the Federal Reserve has been able to force a contraction only as it has taken the economy to the brink of financial crisis. In 1966 the Federal Reserve forced both a virtual run on bank certificates of deposit, and disorderly conditions in the municipal bond market. In 1969-70 it broke an inflationary expansion by forcing the disruption of the commercial paper market. In 1974-75 it reined in an inflation by allowing money market conditions to develop which led to widespread bank failures (Franklin National was not alone) and the virtual liquidation of the $20-billion Real Estate Investment Trust financial industry.

Disorderly conditions and widespread overt or covert failures in financial markets draw forth lender-of-last-resort intervention. The Federal Reserve intervenes to halt that which it has triggered. Intervention and government deficits set the stage for a subsequent inflationary expansion. The seeds of the Carter inflation of 1979-80 were planted in 1975 and 1976, during the Ford administration, when the government ran a $70-billion deficit and the Federal Reserve did not follow up on its lender-of-last-resort interventions by placing effective constraints on the overseas operations of United States banks.

## The need for structural reforms

Is there an alternative to this dismal cycle in which what is done to halt an inflation triggers a debt-deflation and what is done to abort a debt-deflation and deep depression leads to a subsequent inflation? The argument above makes it evident that controlling money is not sufficient; if we are to bring a halt to the dismal cycle, far-reaching structural reforms are needed.

The instability of the American economy, so evident since the middle of the 1960s, has been accompanied by widespread deterioration as measured by the rate of economic growth, the path of real wages, unemployment rates, the trend in the exchange rate of the dollar, and the status of the dollar as an international currency. Such multidimensional malfunctioning indicates that comprehensive reform is needed; there is no "magic bullet" that can cure what now ails the economy.

Our present economic structure was largely put into place during the first Roosevelt administration. During those creative years, institutional arrangements were established which aimed at preventing any recurrence of the kinds of disastrous wage and price declines that had taken place in 1929-33. Many of the reforms were consciously designed to raise prices. In 1933, an inflation which returned prices at least partway to the 1929 level was much desired; such a "reflation" would lower the inherited debt burden.

The Roosevelt reforms took place in an intellectual vacuum that followed the failure of the then standard economic theory, and thus the inability of the day's leading economists to understand American capitalism and to develop effective programs for controlling and reversing the great contraction. Keynes' *General Theory*, which explained why capitalist economies have great depressions and which offered programs to cure and then prevent such disasters, had not as yet appeared.

Since World War II, a vulgar form of Keynesian demand management policies has been used in an economy whose structure largely reflects devices adopted in pre-Keynesian days to prevent prices and wages from falling. Once experience shows that if government is big enough so that swings in the deficit can compensate for the effects on aggregate demand and profits of swings in investment, then structural devices like those introduced in the 1930s to prevent wage and price declines become counterproductive. These devices lead to the absorption of a large part of demand sustaining and increasing monetary and fiscal actions  by price increases. Stagflation followed by accelerating inflation is the result of demand management policies within a capitalist economy that is characterized by large-scale grants of market power to firms, financial organizations, and labor alongside inefficient transfer payment schemes which push presumed "beneficiaries" out of the labor force.

The analysis above enables us to discern the contours of the reforms that are needed. Big government remains necessary to prevent a shortfall of investment from triggering an interactive debt-deflation process, but it can be considerably smaller than the present government, and it can be different. Reform of the transfer payment system is needed, not as a punitive measure against the poor, the old, and the infirm, but to introduce flexibility and remove barriers to work. Children's allowances should be granted by right, replacing both the income tax deduction for children and the aid to families with dependent children. In this way, adult "beneficiaries" of welfare can be in the labor force. At the same time, the provisions of the Social Security Act that set up barriers to income from work should be eliminated.

Beginning with the National Recovery Act (NRA), the Roosevelt administration followed soft anti-trust ·policies; this softness was interrupted for a brief period in 1937-38. In order to constrain the inflationary absorption of income maintenance measures, the private market power of giant corporations must be "broken." A structure of industry policy which emphasizes the control function of competitive markets is an essential element in any package of reforms designed to eliminate the dismal cycle of the 1970s. Such reforms would not only set limits on the resources controlled by any private center of power, but would also entail changes in the tax laws which eliminate the present corporate income tax and the employer "contribution" to Social Security, both of which induce a substitution of capital for labor.

The crisis in financial markets in the spring of 1980 makes it clear that private business cannot finance capital-intensive industries such as railroads and nuclear power, which have social benefits and costs that are not reflected in market prices and costs. Public ownership and operation of such industries is needed; paradoxically, perhaps, private ownership capitalism does not work well for industries of extreme capital intensity.

The change from the tranquillity and progress of the first two decades after World War II to the turbulence and stagnation of the past fifteen years is clearly related to the emergence of the fragile financial structure that led to crunches, squeezes, and debacles in financial markets. There should be a basic restructuring of the financial system so as to promote smaller and simpler organizations weighted more toward direct financing then they now are.

Of course, the reforms suggested above do not constitute a program to resolve the present crisis of inflation and financial disarray. The economy is on a path that leads to a longer and deeper replication of 1974-75. Before we can do better we must understand our economy. Unfortunately, policymakers and advisors are the slaves of an economic theory that misspecifies the nature of our economy by ignoring its instability. That perhaps is a true measure of our crisis: nobody "up there" understands American capitalism.

# 10

## An Exposition
## of a Keynesian Theory
## of Investment

## 1. Introductory remarks

The standard IS-LM macro-economic model has as one of its building blocks a negatively sloped relation between investment and the interest rate [13]. The validity of this investment function has been questioned by Haavelmo. Derivations have been suggested by Lerner, Clower, and Witte which recognize that unsophisticated references to the properties of a well-behaved production function are not sufficient grounds for deriving this standard investment function. Foley and Sidrauski have recently presented a sophisticated version of the IS-LM apparatus which is less clearly dependent upon an assumption that such a negatively sloped investment function exists. Jorgenson in his various writings derives investment as the result of a time consuming process by which units go from an initial to a desired stock of capital; the desired stock is inversely related to the interest rate.

These various formulations of investment theory are deficient as representations or critiques of Keynesian ideas [17, 18]. They never come to grips with the Keynes' view as to the essential financial and speculative character of private asset holding and investment in a modern capitalist economy. In this view assets are held because they are expected to generate cash flows. These cash flows can take either the form of annuities——dated receipts of cash—— or of payment for title to the asset. The annuities for financial assets are stated in the contract, the annuities for real assets depend upon the results of the asset being used in production.

Reprinted from *Mathematical Methods in Investment and Finance*, Szegö/Shell (eds.) by arrangement with the publisher. 1972 © North-Holland.

The standard production-function-related model of real assets and investment only considers the cash that an asset or an investment will generate as it is used in production. That such an asset might also be sold—or hypothecated—to generate cash is ignored. Whereas bankers may be concerned about the liquidity of their assets, in standard theory an ordinary business firm investing in real capital presumably is not. A sloganeering way of looking at Keynesian theory is to assert that all units are like banks, i.e. a bank has to stand ready to pay cash as deposits are withdrawn; an ordinary firm or household has to be prepared to pay cash due to its liabilities even though its available cash receipts vary due to demand and cost changes.

This banker perspective of Keynesian theory means that it is relevant only to capitalist economies and how relevant it is depends upon the financial sophistication and complexity of the economy. It is unlike neo-classical economics which is the economics of an abstract economy. The characteristics and evolution of institutions are embodied in Keynesian model building.

Whereas the cash flow from operations and the cash flow from contract fulfillment are repetitive phenomena so that ideas about frequency distributions can be derived from observations, for many assets—especially durable real capital—obtaining cash flows by sale or hypothecation is a "rare" and "unusual" phenomenon which usually occurs in special circumstances. Because of this, ideas about the relevant probabilities are vague and imprecise and subject to sharp changes. The speculative demand for money—the speculative impact upon the pricing of real assets—is related to the use of assets for acquiring cash by sale.

When one develops a new theory, as Keynes did, one has some things in mind that are not explained in a satisfactory manner by the existing or standard theory. These poorly explained observations are an anomaly from the perspective of the standard theory, they are what is expected from the alternative theory. The anomaly of the nineteen thirties for standard economic theory was the great depression and its quite obvious financial attributes (Fisher). Keynes constructed an investment theory of the business cycle and a financial theory of investment. The standard presentations of Keynes, following the lead of Hicks, attenuated the financial and the cyclical traits of Keynesian theory (Ackley), although when Hicks turned to business cycle theory he found it necessary to reintroduce, albeit in an artificial manner, financial characteristics [14]. Duesenberry, Turvey, Leijonhufvud and Brainard-Tobin all reflect attempts to resurrect the financial aspects of Keynesian theory.

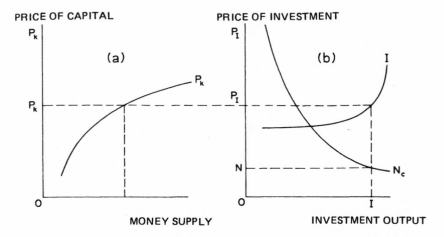

Figure 1

It is important to note that on the whole the econometric fore-casting models abstract from financial considerations. Even in the most "monetary" of the econometric models—the F.R.B.-M.I.T. model—the liability structure and the variable value placed upon liquidity do not appear. One purpose of the research of which this exposition is a part is to develop an enriched macro-economic model which does a better job of integrating the financial and the real aspects of American Capitalism.[1]

The reference to interest rates in Keynes' original presentation in the *General Theory* was an inappropriate way of getting at a more basic phenomenon: What in a particular situation determines the relative prices of real and financial assets and how are these prices related to the flow of investment? In his rebuttal to Viner's famous review Keynes clarified his views of the investment process [17]. This rebuttal is the foundation of the views on investment that follow.[2]

## 2. The basic components

The basic components of a Keynesian model of investment are represented in Figure 1. The Keynesian model postulates that two sets of markets interact in determining investment. The first set consists of those markets in which the prices of the units in the stock of capital goods and financial assets are determined. This is represented in Figure 1a by the $P_k$ function. The second set con-sists of the markets in which the pace of investment is determined by a combination of financing and supply conditions. This is represented by the $I$ and the $N_c$ functions in Figure 1b.

In Figure 1b, the $I$ function gives the supply price of real investment goods as a function of the rate of output. The $N_c$ function gives the internal financing per unit of investment as a function of the pace of investment ($N_c$ is a rectangular-hyperbola if the flow of internal business funds is independent of investment). For any given pace of investment the vertical difference between the two curves $N_c - P_I$ gives the surplus or deficit of internal funds per unit of investment.

The money and capital market determine on what terms such deficits are to be financed and such surpluses are to be utilized. Thus, at a deeper level the Keynesian theory of investment has to include a model of the behavior and evolution of money and capital markets [21]. It is by way of the money and capital markets that the financial flows set up by the current financing of investment feed back to the markets which determine the prices of items in the stock of capital. Whatever changes in financing terms result as investment is financed affect the terms upon which positions in the stock of capital goods and financial assets are financed. This in turn affects the price of units in the stock of capital assets: financial market connections integrate stock and flow prices.

These relations are not necessarily simultaneous and the sequence of reactions as well as the initiating disequilibrium are not always the same.[3] In particular both the evolution and the instability of financial sectors can affect the terms upon which investment can be financed—and thus its pace—as well as the prices of the stocks of capital goods.

The theory as sketched will abstract from the time-consuming nature of the investment process. Presumably the price of capital encompasses the price of a nuclear power plant. The gestation period for a nuclear power plant is at least five years. In the empirical implementations of such a model, the investment flow relates to the investment per period—say per quarter. A decision to pay $P_k$ for a nuclear power plant results in a flow of investment $I_t$ over the next 20 quarters such that (ignoring discounting)

$$\sum_{t=1}^{20} I_t = P_k,$$

where each $I_t$ is determined by the technical conditions of producing nuclear power plants.

In implementing this theory for an econometric model, the investment process might well be divided into capital goods ordering and investment flow phases. With that dichotomy in mind it might very well be that the first part of the theory sketched here is more of a theory of investment ordering than a theory of investment flows. The second part, which emphasizes financing and financial repercussions, reflects what happens as investment flows and financing actually take place——perhaps long after the initial decision to invest was made.

In summarizing research which involved the replication with a consistent body of data of a number of alternative econometric formulations of investment, Bischoff remarked that accelerator based models——whether simple or flexible (the flexibility depending upon relative prices of inputs)——did better than the cash flow or security price alternatives. The cash flow or security price models tested by Bischoff are not adequate representations of what is here viewed as the Keynesian theory of investment. We can take Bischoff's tests as missing the point about Keynesian models.

However, we have to face up to the fact that we do not explicitly consider the accelerator in our formulation. Long ago (see next essay) I examined interrelations between accelerator effects and monetary (financial) behavior. In my formulation the accelerator model gave us ex-ante investment. Ex-post investment resulted from the interaction of monetary (financial) factors and accelerator considerations. That formulation ignored the supply function for investment goods output and the pricing process for stocks of capital goods, which are central to the present exposition.

Investment activity is the result of a combination of productivity and speculative factors. The productivity and scarcity of capital services result in current and expected future cash flows to owners of capital. The accelerator basically is an assertion that if an output greater than current output is to be produced, an increment to the capital stock *of a particular size* can be expected to yield satisfactory or adequate cash flows. In terms of price theory concepts this means that for a given long run average variable cost curve——derived from a "production function"——there exists a minimum average planning total cost curve. This curve defines the sets of product prices and outputs that are expected to result in such adequate cash flows. Thus, the cash flows from operations of real assets as used in the text that follows embody the productivity of investment.

Let us assume that wages are fixed and as a result the minimum supply price of the investment good is $P_I(0)$. If $P_k > P_I(0)$, then investment is taking place at a rate so that $P_I = P_k$ after allowing, as in the text, for financing discounts. Any entrepreneur purchasing an investment good at $P_k = P_I > P_I(0)$ expects to "earn" extraordinary quasi-rents for a long enough time, so that when $P_I = P_I(0)$, the extra costs will have been written off. Thus expectations with respect to future cash flows are imbedded in $P_k$. The higher $P_k$ for a given $P_I(0)$, the larger and the longer the expected duration of premium quasi-rents. Because the capital stock is increasing due to investment, the higher $P_k$ the greater the capital stock that is assumed to be necessary for quasi-rents to be at their normal or adequate level. Thus, the excess of $P_k$ over the minimum normal supply price of investment output is a measure of the difference between the existing and the target capital stock.

Accelerator ideas can thus be read into the pricing of capital assets. However, the strong Keynesian view is that in an economy with cyclical experience and capitalist organization speculative elements dominate productivity consideration in determining the price of investment. By concentrating on how elements other than expected cash flows affect the price of real assets in our uncertain world, the speculative aspects of the investment decision are brought into focus.

To summarize: In market investment relations estimated over periods characterized by rather steady economic growth variables which are interpreted as embodying accelerator conceptions turn out to have a large explanatory weight. In our present formulation productivity concepts are embodied in the cash flows from operations that capital assets earn, especially in the cash flows anticipated as investment decisions are being made. However, the speculative element is introduced into the pricing of assets by way of the contingent cash flows by way of "sale." At times the weight of the two sources of value for assets changes so that speculation dominates. This is so even though for long periods the regularity of investment, output, and cash flows from operations are such that measures which can be interpreted as reflecting accelerator relations seem to dominate in what happens.

In Bischoff's research the cash flow model, which is poorly specified from the perspectives of this paper, does very well in explaining investment over the data period. It does quite poorly in explaining investment in 1969 and 1970. However, as I have emphasized [23] a run of success such as was enjoyed in the 1960s will trigger a euphoric investment boom. During this boom debt financing of investment will expand rapidly, i.e., the investment-gross profit after taxes relation will change. Whereas the 1969-70 period illustrates the weakness of a narrowly constructed cash flow formulation, it is evidence that a financial theory of investment, which allows for liability structures—actual and desired—has a large measure of plausibility.

## 3. The pricing of the capital stock

The left-hand portion of Figure 1, Figure 1a, asserts that for a given capital stock, the price per unit of capital is a function of the money supply. This assertion rests upon an argument about how assets are valued in the face of uncertainty and in the light of the existence of complex financial structures.

Underlying Figure 1a is the view that all assets—real and financial—are equivalent in that they are expected to generate cash flows. These cash flows fall into two classes. The first class of cash flows result as assets do their thing—are used in production processes if they are real assets or as contract conditions are satisfied for financial assets. This first class will be called cash flows from operations for real assets and cash flow from contract fulfillment for financial assets. The second class of cash flows result as assets are sold or pledged.

The non-Keynesian theory of asset valuation concentrates only on the first class of cash flows. In this view the cash flows that a set of real assets collected in a firm will generate are the future cash flow from operations as given by total revenue minus out of pocket costs (the out of pocket costs are the variable costs of "cost curves analysis" with Keynesian user costs excluded from the variable costs). Obviously for a firm these cash flows from operations will be conditional upon the state of the economy, the product and factor markets, and the management of the firm.

The current fashion is to argue that assets with different probability distributions should be valued not in terms of their expected values but in terms of their expected utilities—where the transformation between income and utility reflects the units attitude toward risk (Arrow).

Even though Keynes was skeptical of the validity of the Benthamite calculus when applied to incomes, the expected utility hypothesis is a useful expository device for Keynesian ideas if it is accepted that (1) the probabilities set on various alternatives are subjective and thus subject to sharp changes if appropriate triggering events take place, and (2) the curvature of the transformations between income or cash flows and utility—the aversion or attraction to risk of the various actors—is itself an endogenously determined relation and will undergo both slow and sharp changes depending upon what happens.

The expected utility hypothesis yields for each distribution of expected incomes an expected utility. There also exists an income with certainty that will yield utility equal to the expected utility. We can call this income the certainty equivalent income. The conclusion on asset price formation has been that assets will exchange at the same ratio as their certainty equivalent incomes. Given that a dollar yields a utility with certainty, this certainty equivalent approach to asset valuation yields the absolute price of various assets.

Note that this argument holds for both real and financial assets. For debts the cash flows are given by the face of the contract and the probability judgments have to be made with respect to the likelihood that the contract will not be fulfilled and the cash flow that will take place in this event.

The above valuation theory has to be modified by taking into account the second way in which an asset can generate cash—by being sold or hypothecated. Assets differ greatly in the ease with which they can be marketed or pledged. In conventional money market analysis the marketability of an asset is sometimes treated by alluding to the breadth, depth, and resilience of its market. The same factors apply to real assets—except that the weight normally attained to the circumstances under which they will have to be sold or pledged is slight and typically the sales market is expected to be narrow, shallow, and non-resilient.

The likelihood that cash will have to be raised by selling or pledging assets depends upon the cash position and the cash payment commitments of a unit. These cash payment commitments are embodied in the liability structure of firms. At any date the liability structure of a firm is determined by market conditions which ruled when the firm financed asset acquisitions and refinanced its positions in assets.

Cash payment commitments include both the repayment of principal as well as the payment of interest.[4] If control over assets is financed by liabilities which are of shorter life than the asset, then the cash required by the liability contract over its life may well exceed the cash the assets will generate over these periods. In such circumstances the cash needs due to the liability will have to be met by the issuance of a new liability. Such refinancing of positions by sale of liabilities is a characteristic banker's behavior: commercial banks, bill dealers, and finance companies normally engage in such refinancing. At the time of its failure, the Penn-Central railway had short-term liabilities outstanding which had to be "turned over" for the railway to remain "liquid." When this became impossible, the railway went bankrupt.

In Figure 2 the short run cost conditions of a firm are sketched. The given plant defines the marginal and average variable cost (net of Keynesian user costs) for given wage rates. The other average cost curves reflect the payment commitments as embodied in liabilities; the curves for three alternative balance sheets are sketched. Given an expected price $P$, the differences $P - ACL_1$ and $P - ACL_2$ indicate the fall in output price that would lead to the cash flow from operations falling short of the cash needs as given by the liability structure.

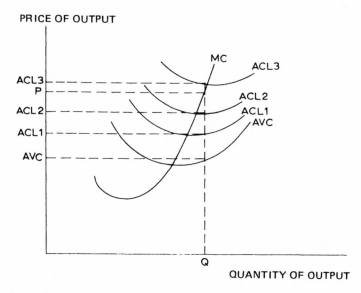

Figure 2

The third average cost curve $ACL_3$ reflects a situation in which the cash flow from operations is insufficient to meet the cash needs of the liabilities. Often, but not always, this situation arises when the principal amount of some liabilities falls due. If the expected cash flows from operations $Q(P - AVC)$ are large enough and if financial market conditions are orderly a rolling over of liabilities will usually be feasible. If expected cash flows are "too small" relative to payment commitments or if market conditions are disorderly, such refinancing might be expensive if not impossible.

If the payment commitments are large relative to the cash flow from operations, the alternative to refinancing is the sale—or the mortgaging—of assets. The various real and financial assets are saleable to the extent that they can be transferred cheaply to easily located buyers and that they are expected to generate desired cash flows for these buyers. If an asset is a special purpose asset embedded in a production process then it has only a limited ability to generate cash by sale.

Thus the valuation of assets in a capitalist economy can be structured as a two stage process. One stage estimates the value of the cash the asset can generate as the owning unit operates it in the current and expected economy; the second stage estimates the value of the cash it can generate by "sale," under pressure, at any date. The market value is some weighted average of these two values.

If assets are equivalent with respect to the cash flows they are expected to generate from use or contract, then assets with a poor secondary market will sell at a discount relative to assets with a good secondary market.

The weight attached to the likelihood that assets will have to be sold to raise cash can change rapidly and thus affect the relative prices of real capital assets with restricted secondary markets to that of readily marketable financial assets. For real and financial assets therefore the market price reflects both productivity and contract concepts as embedded in the expected cash flow from operations and contract fulfillment, and speculative aspects which reflect views as to the likelihood of circumstances arising in which a forced sale of such assets is necessary.

## 4. The role of money

The special Keynesian argument is not that assets are valuable because they will yield cash in the future either in use or by contract fulfillment or as they are sold, but rather that with perhaps a few exceptions the price of real and non-monetary financial assets are non-decreasing functions of the money supply.[5] That is $dPk/DM > 0$; and it is also assumed that $d^2 Pk/dM^2 < 0$.

The special liquidity trap assumption of which much has been made is that circumstances can be such that $\lim_{M \to \infty} P_k < \overset{*}{P}_k$. Once this is associated with the proposition $I = 0$ if $P_I < \overset{*}{P}_I$, Max $P_I = \overset{*}{P}_k$ and $\overset{*}{P}_k < \overset{*}{P}_I$, then increases in the money supply cannot increase investment. If this assumption is combined with the proposition that money affects income only as it affects investment, then monetary changes are not available as a policy instrument.

A number of reasons can be advanced for the view that the price of real capital is a rising function of the quantity of money.

(1) Money is an asset whose value for settling contracted debts is fixed. All money and all real assets—as well as all inherited financial assets—are in some portfolio [17]. An increase in the quantity of money, other assets fixed, will lead to a rise in the money price of other assets inasmuch as the money price of money is fixed.

(2) Moneyness also characterizes those assets whose contractual cash payments are virtually certain and which have good secondary markets; government debt is such an asset. The greater the proportion of such safe assets available for portfolios, the higher the price of the risky assets—as long as the expected cash flow per dollar of the risky assets is greater than that of the certain asset.[6]

(3) Furthermore, the greater the amount of money in a representative portfolio the smaller the chance that a decline in receipts will force the representative unit to sell assets for cash. If the price that can be realized by sale tends to be depressed the greater the rate of sales, the greater the amount of money in portfolios the smaller the likelihood that assets will have to be sold to raise cash and therefore the higher their market price.

(4) Even if the sectors holding real capital and having balance sheet payment commitments are not holding reserves of money, the larger the amount of money in existence the easier it will be for such units to raise money by selling assets or additional liabilities. For example, if the money supply is large because banks own a large amount of treasury debt, loan demand by business, even if it arises due to transitory shortfalls of cash from operations, can be more easily satisfied than if the money supply was smaller. Basically, the larger the money supply, the easier it is to make portfolio adjustments that accommodate needs for cash.

(5) Note that a decrease in the rate of increase in the money supply is an immediate signal to units with debts that at some future date "standby," "covering," or "emergency" financing may be harder to arrange and more costly.

The same reasons indicate that if we ignore the role, if any, of excessive increases in the money supply as guaranteeing future inflation,

$$dP_k/dM > 0 \text{ and } d^2 P_k/dM^2 < 0.$$

If we assume that the $P_k = P_k(M)$ function is a useful construct it is necessary to determine what phenomena shift the function and affect its shape.

Underlying this function are the existing stock of real capital and the existing set of financial institutions. Accumulation will tend to shift the $P_k$ function downward. We can assume that there exists a balanced growth of the money supply, financial layering, cash flows from financial assets and real capital, labor force and output which would leave the price of a representative unit of capital unchanged as accumulation takes place.

Financial layering influences the price of real capital in two ways. With a given stock of money and real capital, the greater the financial layering the greater the flexibility and reliability of financing: financial layering and sophistication create both specialized and generalized money substitutes. Financial intermediaries make available secure assets for the portfolios of both ultimate and intermediate units. This allows a greater degree of tailor-making of portfolios to individual attitudes toward uncertainty and to institutional constraints. In addition, the greater the financial layering the larger the number of alternative sources available to finance ultimate positions in real assets. These reasons indicate that the greater the financial layering the higher the price of assets.

However, the greater the financial layering the greater the number of payments both on principal and income account that have to be made: each layer sets up payments to and from financial institutions. With a fixed amount of money this indicates that money will have to turn over more rapidly (transactions velocity) and that there will be more portfolios that want a "money buffer" the greater the extent of layering. Furthermore, financial intermediaries are organizations that typically make positions in one set of assets by emitting liabilities or selling other assets. The dangers of market disruption in refinancing markets increases as layering increases. This indicates that the greater the financial layering, the greater the "implicit" yield on money——which tends to lower the price of real assets.

More fundamentally, the $P_k = P_k(M)$ function embodies the preference systems and views as to expected cash flows from operations.

If we take the Friedman-Savage view of the preference system, then for some range of incomes a representative unit is a risk averter and for another range of possible incomes he is a risk seeker. Risk seeking reflects the lure of a bonanza. An option which includes a chance of a very large increase in income will sell at a premium over an option which does not include such a chance even if both have the same expected income. In respect to a bonanza, the distinction between "holding period" and asset life is important. Great fortunes are made by capital gains, not by saving out of income as defined by the National Income Accounts.

Asset prices can rise and fall rapidly when a "market" modifies its views about the cash flows assets can be expected to generate. If a "long-shot" innovation begins to yield substantial and apparently secure quasi-rents, the underlying assets as collected in the innovating firm will be revalued upward sharply. If assets have been valued on a consensus that business cycles are "inevitable" and a new era is proclaimed (and the proclamation is believed) then the value of real assets will increase. Symmetrically if business cycles reappear after a formal proclamation of their demise, the value of real assets will decrease.

With invariant preference systems, if "bonanzas" appear in goodly numbers, and views that business cycles are now "obsolete" become dominant, then the price of a representative unit of real capital will rise: the $P_k = P_k(M)$ function shifts upward. To put the above succinctly, successful functioning of an economy tends to raise the price of units in the stock of capital.

Preference systems are creations of society, not genetic characteristics. The representative aversion to or delight in risk of a population is a result of the population's history. If the population is replete with risk seekers who succeeded, if those who played it safe lost out, then even if there is no change in the expected payoffs, the preferences systems will change so that "risk" assets rise in price relative to "safe" assets. A major element affecting the price of real capital, for a given portfolio structure, are the views as to the likelihood of the need arising to use the asset to raise cash and the costs that may be assessed if this contingency is realized. If fears of illiquidity decrease the value of real assets will rise.

Conversely, the experience of financial difficulty and disorderly markets for financial assets—such mild events as the crunch of 1966 and the liquidity squeeze of 1970—may lead to a sharp fall in the value of real assets.

For firms, if we consider the debt structures as generating cash payments and the real assets as generating the cash to meet these payments, financial developments during a boom time tend to increase cash payments relative to cash receipts. Even as success breeds preference systems and views as to the future of the economy which lower the weight to emergencies in which assets will have to be sold or pledged under disadvantageous conditions, the objective conditions change so that the likelihood increases that operations will generate insufficient cash to service debts—that cash needs will have to be met by recourse to asset sale or borrowing.

Thus, the price of capital as a function of the money supply shifts. These shifts are not random: success of the economy raises, failure lowers the function. In particular, success can lead to an investment boom and a financial crisis or stringency can lead to a stagnation of investment and incomes.

If $P_k = P_k(M)$ is interpreted as the liquidity preference function, then a basic proposition of Keynesian investment theory is that the liquidity preference function shifts.

## 5. The stock market

An objection to writing $P_k = P_k(M)$ for real capital is that there is no clear market price for used items of many types of capital. One reason for this is that the transaction costs—the cost of searching for a purchaser and of dismantling, transporting, and setting up such items—can be so great that it is not feasible to market such items individually.

In the current (1971) taut financial environment, firms under financial pressures or with profit problems are in fact divesting themselves of operating divisions and units. These divestitures are a way of selling real capital to raise cash to retire pressing debts. The special property of these transactions is that whereas it is often not feasible to raise cash by selling real assets individually, it often is feasible to do so by selling capital goods collected in operating "bundles."

Often the process by which such divestitures take place involves the sale of the "stock" in a wholly or predominantly owned subsidiary. For our purposes, such organization properties—that operating units are often organized as separate corporations—is not significant.

On a regular basis corporations are valued in the stock market. While in general capital goods may not be traded regularly, common stock (shares) are. From the market value of the stock and the balance sheet of the corporation, a valuation can be placed upon the combination of the firm's real capital and the firm's special market and management traits. The stock market therefore provides an index, with considerable noise, of the value of the capital goods as collected in corporations in the economy: the implicit price of capital is a function of the explicit price of common stock modified by the items mentioned earlier (Turvey).

Stock market valuations do enter into various investment functions primarily as an element in the cost of capital, where cost of capital is defined as financing terms. A high price to common stocks is presumed to lower the cost of capital. This increases, in a production function, the desired amount of capital for any output (wages, etc., unchanged). This is supposed to tend to increase investment. In this formulation, the lower cost of capital by way of stock market valuation may be offset by a higher cost due to other financing terms. Within the models that use stock market valuations as an input in determining the cost of capital, there is no precise way in which the valuation of capital goods can be treated separately from the terms on which debts are available to finance control over the existing stock of capital as well as investment.

Ultimately, the test of whether it is better to use stock market information as a measure of the implicit price being placed upon the economy's stock of real capital or as one element in the determination of financing terms will depend upon how well theories based upon these different formulations do in explaining what happens (Brainard-Tobin, Turvey, Bischoff).

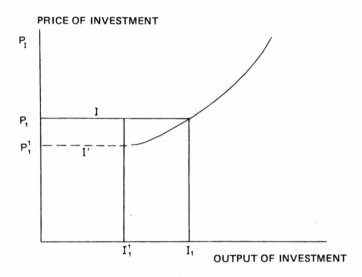

PRICE OF INVESTMENT

Figure 3

## 6. The supply of investment

Investment is a part of output. The amount of investment goods produced is decided by investment goods producers. Given the capital stock specialized to the production of investment goods there is a rate of production of investment goods such that a further increase will result in rising costs per unit. Thus there is a rising portion of the supply curve for investment goods. If we assume the investment goods industries are sufficiently competitive this rising supply curve is a summation of marginal cost curves.

In addition there is a horizontal or virtually horizontal portion to the supply curve for investment goods. This "horizontal" portion is at the minimum point of an average cost curve for each producing unit. This average cost curve contains variable and user costs. Fundamentally Keynesian user costs are the present value of future quasi-rents that will be sacrificed if capital goods are used in current production. Keynesian user costs integrate the costs of utilizing inventories and durable capital equipment. Inventories or durable capital goods will be used only if the present return is at least equal to the present value of foregone expected future returns. The returns to stocks are essentially rents, except that technical conditions can lead to a reservation price.

In Figure 3, the supply curve of investment goods as discussed in the text is illustrated by the curves labeled *I*. The dotted line labeled $I'$ is the supply curve if user costs were ignored. The effect of a decline in wages can be examined with the aid of Figure 3.

Wages are a parameter of shift in both the $I$ and $I'$ curves. A decline in wages that is assumed to be transitory will shift both curves downward by the same amount. User costs will not decline as long as the future expected rents do not change. Under these circumstances the offer price will have a larger markup on labor costs after wages fall than before. The higher price of investment goods relative to wages can be presumed to induce a substitution against capital in the choice of production techniques.

On the other hand, declining wages may also be taken to signal that a return to the former price level is not to be expected—or at best it will take place at some date so far in the future that it can be ignored. Under these circumstances the quasi-rents that determine current user costs are either smaller or in the more distant future. This means that user costs will decline. As a result the supply price of investment may fall by a greater percentage than wages.

Thus depending upon how a decline in money wages is interpreted the supply curve of investment may fall by a smaller, larger, or equal percentage as wages. It follows that as far as substitution effects are concerned falling wages may be unfavorable, favorable, or neutral with respect to inducing investment.

In Figure 3, if investment produced is $I_1$, we assume that current period quasi-rents are sufficiently large so that the reservation effects of user costs are of minor importance. Current quasi-rents are $(P_1 - P'_1)I_1$ and these quasi-rents are presumably sufficient to satisfy the internal funds requirements of a representative firm producing investment goods.

If output is $I'_1$, quasi-rents equal to $(P_1 - P'_1)I'_1$ are being earned. If these cash flows are sufficient to meet the pressing needs for cash or if firms earning such smaller cash flows can still receive adequate financing to sustain the reservation rents then $P_1$ will be maintained. If a large enough number of firms find $(P_1 - P'_1)I_1$ insufficient to meet cash commitments, then firms will violate the user cost constraint in an effort to achieve larger cash flows through volume output. (Note that bankruptcy eases cash commitments due liabilities and thus allows user cost to act as a reservation price. Bankruptcy restores orderly conditions so beloved of oligopolists.)

If the need for cash forces prices to $P'_1$ then the representative firm is not generating positive quasi-rents: sufficient funds are not being generated internally to meet payment commitments embodied in the liability structure. Under these circumstances illiquidity will be prevalent.

User costs explain why excess capacity is associated with positive cash flows to capital owners even in highly competitive industries. They also help explain why the economy can operate at levels in between boom and zero gross profits to firms. Without the reservation pricing of the services of capital goods the unreliability of cash flows from operations would stand as a barrier to debt financing of durable capital.

Of course the argument with respect to user cost is of general validity: the supply curve for consumption goods looks just like that for investment goods.[7]

Thus, there are two parameters of shift for the investment (and consumption) supply function. One parameter is the wage rate. A fall in wages may increase, decrease, or not affect the pace of investment, depending upon what happens to user costs.

The second parameter of shift is user cost. A fall in user cost lowers, an increase raises the supply curve. Note that as user costs are present valuations of future returns a rise in interest rates lowers and a fall in interest rates raises user costs. The situation where present cash needs dominate foregone future rents discussed earlier can be interpreted as the reaction when effective interest rates become very high to the affected unit.

On the whole the supply curve of investment goods can be considered to be more "stable" than the $P_k(M)$ function which sets the price of capital goods. The parameters of shift, wage changes, and the pressing needs for cash which dominate normal user costs are the result of prior system functioning. Shifts in the investment supply function tend to be induced. We can approximate system behavior by assuming that the $P_k(M)$ function of Figure 1a shifts with reference to the stable $I$ function.

Note that if the need for cash results in a fall of the supply curve of investment goods from $I$ to $I'$, the need for cash will also tend to increase the weight attached to the forced sale price in valuing real assets. Such an increase in the importance attached to liquidity will lower the $P_k$ function.

## 7. Ex-ante and ex-post investment: The flow of internal funds

Let us assume that the flow of corporate internal funds, $N_c$——gross profits after taxes of the Flow of Funds accounts is a close approximation to the relevant concept——is invariant with respect to the pace of investment. Then for any period we have that

$$N_c = \hat{N}_c$$

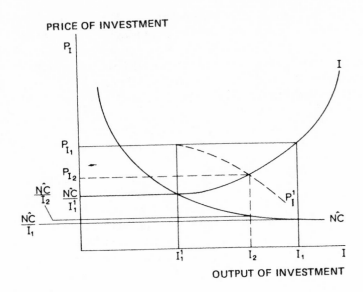

PRICE OF INVESTMENT

OUTPUT OF INVESTMENT

Figure 4

a constant. This means that internal funds will pay for $\hat{N}_c$ out of the total investment bill $P_II$. On a per unit basis the contribution of internal funds to the financing of investment can be designated by the rectangular hyperbola

$$P_II = \hat{N}_c.$$

Let us assume that $P_{I_1}$ in Figure 4 is the ex-ante demand price for investment goods. This means that given the structure of financing by the owners of the stock of capital, the price per unit of real capital is $P_k = P_{I_1}$. If there were no financing of investment constraints this implies that an investment of $I_1$ will take place.

The total investment bill will be $P_{I_1}. I_1$ of which $N_c$ will be internal funds. External financing requirements will be $(P_{I_1} - N_c/ I_1 )I_1$. Let us further assume that if $I'_1$ of investment were financed then with $N_c/I'_1$ of internal funds per unit of investment the various balance sheet relations for financing the flow would be consistent with the way in which the "stock" is financed. Investment in excess of $I_1$ implies a greater dependence upon debt for the increment of investment than is true for the stock of capital. The negatively sloped function $P'_1$ indicates how the demand price for investment goods declines as the financing terms become progressively more constraining.

In Figure 4 the equilibrium is achieved with realized investment of $I_2$, a supply price of investment goods of $P_{+2}$ with $N_c/I_2$ of internal financing per unit of investment put into place. As a result of financing constraints ex-post investment is less than ex-ante investment.

## 8. Interrelations between financing investment and the price of capital assets

The equilibrium of Figure 4 is partial even for the investment model. The external financing terms for investment are the prices at which various liabilities with specified cash flow attributes can be sold by the investing units. These financing terms can be such that increments to real capital assets are valued as the stock of capital assets. This means that $I_1$ of investment in Figure 4 will take place. Alternatively the financing terms may be such that beyond some rate further increments to capital are valued at less than units in the stock. If this is true the demand for investment goods will be nagatively sloped. The $P_I'$ curve of Figure 4 reflects such an effective financing constraint.

At any moment of time the stock of private real capital is owned by some units. These asset positions are financed by liabilities. For equivalent contract terms such as maturity and collateral clauses, the liabilities of a unit which finances its ownership of the stock of capital and those liabilities which finances purchases from the flow of investment output must sell at equivalent prices.[8] Thus a constraining change in financing terms, as illustrated by the curve $P_I'$, will feedback and affect either the price of the stock of capital or the price of the stock of outstanding debts of the firm under examination.

Over time as debts financing ownership of the stock must conform to the terms ruling in the market for financial instruments the effect will be upon the price of capital $P_k$. Initially, however, the losses may accrue mainly to the owners of the inherited stock of private liabilities.

For purposes of our discussion the liability structure of units holding the real stock of capital can be broken into three parts: equity, bank debt, and other debt. For the existing stock of capital the value of equity is the value of the capital goods minus bank and other debt. The stock market valuation is the only way in which the equity investment in a firm can be measured.

The financing techniques for investment are internal funds— gross profits after taxes net of dividends—and external funds. The external funds are divided into bank and other external financing.

The other external financing consists of new equity issues and net other debt financing. By adding new equity financing and internal funds a breakdown of corporate financing of investment into equity, bank debt, and other debt financing is possible.

The class other debt is heterogeneous containing many different types of liabilities. However, the technique of considering all debts as setting up cash flow commitments should enable us to deal with this heterogeneous class.

For every pace of investment there exists at least one way in which the investment can be financed so that no change will occur in the financing conditions for holding the stock of real capital. Presumably if investment flow and stock holdings are financed in the same way then no changes in the financing condition of the stock will be induced by the need to finance the flow. If we assume that the money stock is related to bank financing of positions in the stock of capital, if internal funds are the only way in which equity financing can occur, then we have that

$$\frac{I}{K} = \frac{\Delta M}{M} = \frac{N_c}{E} = \frac{\Delta \text{ other debt}}{\text{other debt}} .$$

That is if $K$, $M$, $E$ and other debt all grow at the same rate, then there will be no changes in the terms upon which positions in the stock of assets will be financed as a result of the investment process.

Note that if $I/K \neq \Delta Y/Y$, then the neutral rate of growth of the money supply with respect to income, $\Delta M/M = \Delta Y/Y$, is not equal to the neutral rate of growth of the money supply with respect to financing investment $\Delta M/M = I/K$.

Furthermore, if there is a third component to balance sheets which consists of outside government debts then financing neutrality will require that $\Delta G/G = \Delta M/M = I/K$, i.e. the government deficit must be such that government debt grows at the same rate as capital.

The concept of monetary neutrality becomes amorphous and vague as the domain of relevant observations is expanded. For example, the evolution of the financial structure involves a substitution of other financial assets for money and for direct liabilities in portfolios. Some concept of evolutionary neutrality is needed once such observations are recognized [21].

Presumably no change will occur in the price of liabilities relative to the price of real capital if the cash flow commitments by the incremental liabilities are to the cash flow expectations from the incremental capital as the cash flow commitments for the stock of liabilities are to the cash flow expectations from the stock of capital. The negatively sloped portion of the demand for investment function reflects a need to pledge increasing portions of the expected cash flows in order to finance the acquisition of capital goods.

If financial growth is not balanced—if for example $\Delta M/M <$ $N_c$/equity $< I/K$—then there will be a feedback from the financing terms for investment to the financing terms for items in the stock of capital. These will in turn imply changes in the price of items in the stock of capital.

If for instance financing terms for investment are such that $P_I <$ $P_K$, then the feedback from investment financing to the price of capital will operate so as to decrease the gap between them; if initially $P_K - P_I > 0$ then the financial feedback will induce $\dot{P}_K < 0$.

Underlying the prices of the items in the stock of capital goods are the evaluations of uncertainty with respect to the cash flows that operations are expected to generate and the terms upon which positions in assets can be sold out or refinanced as well as subjective attitudes toward risk. A run of success by the economy changes both the views as to what is likely to occur and the relative aversion-attraction of risk in preference systems. These phenomena will lead to upward shifts in the $P_K(M)$ function of Figure 1A. Such a shift implies increases in the market valuation of common stock. The increment in the value of capital due to such unrealized capital gains is reflected as an increase in the (implicit) equity financing of positions, i.e. the equity to value of capital ratio increases. It follows that for owners of the underlying stock of capital who are simultaneously investors there exists the possibility of hypothecating the stock to finance investment.

In terms of Figure 4 a rise in $P_K$ implies a rise in $P_I$ and an increase in the ex-ante pace of investment. With the increase in the owner's equity in the existing stock of capital, the ability of the unit to debt-finance investment is improved. Capital gains due to upward shifts in the $P_K(M)$ function tend to make the ability to finance investment elastic at terms equivalent to those at which the stock of capital is held. The negatively sloped portion of the investment demand curve—which was due to financing constraints—tends to evaporate. That is the "increased" protection involved in the larger equity financing of the new revalued stock induces lenders to sustain favorable terms for financing investment.

This latter phenomenon—that supply conforms to the demand for financing during an investment boom—is often the result of evolution and change in the financial system. It is evident that the financial system during a period such as the 1960s in the U.S.A. changed rapidly, tended to facilitate the financing of investment, and invented new or modified old ways in which positions in the stock can be financed. In terms of the LM diagram of conventional theory, the historic liquidity preference function for a given supply of money is a step function with infinitely elastic segments. These segments represent periods in which a financial innovation such as CD's, commercial paper use by non-financial corporations etc. are working their way through the market [21, 22, 23].

In terms of conventional quantity theory language a LM curve such as is illustrated in Figure 5 indicates that velocity conforms to business cycles. But this is the result of increased financial intermediation. The layering process implies that aggregate payment commitments on financial account increase relative to the underlying income related payment receipts. This means that financial organizations which make position by dealing in assets grow relative to the rest of the economy. Although financial innovation and its associated velocity increases are part of the way in which good times are financed, the very growth of financial intermediation increases the likelihood that a financial feedback will occur that lowers the $P_K(M)$ function by increasing the weight attached to the value of real assets as a source of cash by sale or hypothecation.

In a boom the rise in common stock prices implies a decrease in the ratio of debt to the market value of real capital. This implies that a high debt to internal funds ratio for investment will be acceptable to both bankers and investors as it tends to offset the effects of the capital gains. A willingness to debt finance investment during booms is evidenced by increases in dividends, not only absolutely but as a ratio of gross profits after taxes, by firms that are engaged in debt-financed investment programs. This is so because a stock market boom lowers the ratio of debt to the market valua-

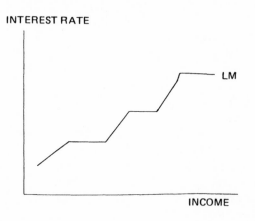

Figure 5

tion of the firm. If firms have views as to acceptable debt ratios, such an improvement means that increments to capital can be more heavily debt financed.[9]

A prolonged or extended period of good times also changes views as to the cash flows that can be expected from operations. A belief that these cash flows are both larger and more stable than hitherto expected will lead to a willingness to hypothecate a larger share of the expected cash flows.

Thus in terms of what investing units are willing to do, what financing units are willing to accept and the layering of financial commitments an extended period of prosperity culminating in an investment boom generates a financial structure in which the "making of position" by the sale of assets or the creation of additional liabilities becomes increasingly prevalent. In this increasingly active financial environment a triggering event which leads to the sale of assets in a thin market can lead to a sharp increase in the view that real assets may have to be used to raise cash by sale or hypothecation.

This change in subjective probabilities leads to a sharp fall in the $P_K(M)$ function. In Figure 6 the effect of a revaluation downward of asset prices is illustrated. With the configuration of the $P_k$ and the $I$ curves no increase in the money supply will increase investment. This configuration illustrates the liquidity trap.

The problem of financial crises—whether of the magnitude of the great debt-deflation process of 1929-33 or of the minor scale of the crunch of 1966 or the liquidity squeeze of 1970—is that they occur. Historically—prior to World War II—financial crises were the identifying phenomena of the great depressions of history. These great depressions were associated with stagnation of

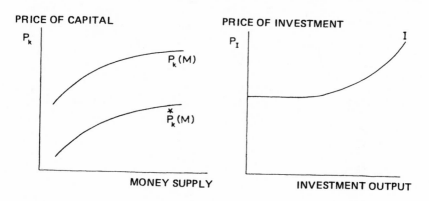

Figure 6

enterprise, of investment. The debt-deflation process once triggered was easy to describe: Irving Fisher did it admirably. But for Fisher and Keynes the initiation of a debt-deflation was basically unexplained.

The model sketched here makes a debt-deflation process up to the triggering event an endogenous phenomena not in any deterministic sense but in the sense of creating an environment in which the likelihood of such an event taking place increases.

With modern Central Banking and large scale central governments the course of events following a triggering event can and does diverge from the cumulative debt-deflation process. Instead of plunging into a great depression the economy retreats from a boom. Nevertheless following the triggering event for many sectors the desired liability structure will include less debt than the actual liability structure. Even in the absence of a cumulative process there exists the possibility that after a protracted boom and a financial trauma the inherited financial structure will act as a prolonged constraint upon investment.

Whereas in the past the business cycle of experience may have been characterized by boom and bust, currently the business cycle may be characterized by boom and high level stagnation.

## 9. Concluding remarks

The model sketched here makes the debt-deflation process through the triggering event an endogenous phenomena. It is the ever-increasing financial layering of a boom that makes the need to raise cash by the sale of assets more likely to occur. Once this takes place the failure of the asset market to be broad, deep, or resilient will lead to a revaluation of asset prices. In this revaluation a much greater weight is placed upon liquidity attributes than hitherto. It is by way of the financial attributes of a decentralized capitalist economy that we can develop a theory of investment that fits into an investment theory of the business cycle.

In the U.S.A. there are two popular competing models—the monetarist and the income-expenditure—which have been vying for the favor of our recent Princes and which have been used as the theoretical basis for forecasting models. These forecasting models have been conspicuously in error in recent years. On the basis of the failure of forecasting efforts, the validity of the underlying theoretical model can be questioned.

The monetarist and the income-expenditure models are similar in they tend to ignore the complex financial interrelations of the economy. The construction of an empirical model of investment consistent with the theoretical formulation advanced here would emphasize liability structures and the demand, dated, and contingent cash flows they entail. A first approximation to a data base for such a model exists in the sectoral balance sheets of the Flow of Funds accounts. An integration of this data with interest rate and term to maturity data in order to generate estimates of cash flow commitments that are more accurate than a mere detailing of liabilities outstanding is required.

The key significance of the contingent need to raise cash by selling assets implies that attention should be paid to the structure of financial assets of the corporate sector. If assets with good, smoothly operating secondary markets become relatively scarce in portfolios, then a need to raise cash will be more likely to entail an attempt to sell or pledge assets with thin markets. Sharp price declines—and even episodes of markets not functioning can result. Thus the ratio of "good" or "protected market" assets to the current cash flow requirements due to debts becomes a key indicator of the likelihood that asset prices will decline. Data on this attribute of the economy are available in the flow of funds accounts.

Thus, measures of the cash flow from operations available to service debt will generate one aspect of the financial picture. Another aspect is generated when internal funds (cash flow from operations after debt services) are related to investment, either anticipated or realized. The technique of financing investment— whether the ratio of investment to internal funds is high or low— is a key indicator of the stability of investment. Fundamentally it is postulated that a high and increasing ratio of debt financing to investment cannot be sustained.

It seems likely that an equal rate of growth of internal funds and investment cannot be permanently sustained. If sustained for awhile, the temptation to experiment with balance sheets increases, leading to greater rate of increase of investment than internal funds.

A strong stock market is a signal for a higher ratio of debt financing to internal funds in investment. However, with the long lag of investment delivery behind the initiating of investment, a stock market boom may result in an investment backlog. As a result a long lag between a stock market decline and a decline in investment may exist. That is if we use stock market data as the proxy for the implicit price of capital there may be long and variable lags—depending upon the gestation periods of the investment involved—between stock market changes and investment changes.

Fundamentally in a Keynesian model of investment speculative elements are as vital as production function attributes in determining the pace of investment. The $P_k = P_k(M)$ function embodies the speculative elements of the investment process. Current neoclassical based aggregate investment theories ignore speculative phenomena. As a result the dominant academic theory of investment has but little relevance to an economy such as the U.S. economy of the 1970s.

REFERENCES

[1] Ackley, G. Macroeconomic Theory. New York: Macmillan, 1961.

[2] Arrow, K. J. Essays in the Theory of Risk-bearing. Ansterdam: North-Holland Publishing Co., 1971.

[3] Bischoff, C. W. "Business Investment in the 1970's: A Comparison of Models." Brookings Papers on Economic Activity I (1971).

[4] Board of Governors, Federal Reserve System. Flow of Funds Accounts.

[5] Brainard, W. C. and Tobin, J. "Pitfalls in Financial Model Building." American Economic Review, May 1968, pp. 99-122.

[6] Clower, R. "An Investigation into the Dynamics of Investment." American Economic Review, March 1954, 64-68.

[7] Duesenberry, J. S. Business Cycles and Economic Growth. New York: McGraw-Hill, 1958.

[8] Ederington, L. Unpublished Ph.D. research, Washington University (St. Louis).

[9] Fisher, I. "The Debt-deflation Theory of Great Depressions," Econometrica, October 1933.

[10] Foley and Sidvauski. "Portfolio Choice Investment and Growth." American Economic Review, March 1970.

[11] Friedman, M. and Savage, L. J. "The Utility Analysis of Choices Involving Risk." Journal of Political Economy, August 1948, 279-304.

[12] Haavelmo, T. A Study in the Theory of Investment. Chicago: University of Chicago Press, 1960.

[13] Hicks, J. R. "Mr. Keynes and the Classics: A Suggested Interpretation." Econometrica, April 1937.

[14] Hicks, J. R. A Contribution to the Theory of the Trade Cycle. London: Oxford University Press, 1950.

[15] Jorgenson, D. W. "Capital Theory and Investment Behavior." American Economic Review, May 1963.

[16] Jorgenson, D. W. "The Theory of Investment Behavior." In: Determinants of Investment Behavior (ed. by R. Ferber). New York: NBER, 1967, pp. 129-155.

[17] Keynes J. M. "The General Theory of Employment." Quarterly Journal of Economics, February 1937.

[18] Keynes, J. M. The General Theory of Employment, Interest and Money. New York: Harcourt, Brace, 1936.

[19] Leijonhufvud, A. *On Keynesian Economics and the Economics of Keynes.* New York: Oxford University Press, 1968.

[20] Lerner, A. P. *The Economics of Control.* New York: MacMillan, 1944.

[21] Minsky, H. P. "Central Banking and Money Market Changes." *Quarterly Journal of Economics*, May 1957.

[22] Minsky, H. P. "Monetary Systems and Acceleration Models." *American Economic Review*, December 1957.

[23] Minsky, H. P. *Financial Instability Revisited.* Washington, D.C.: Board of Governors, Federal Reserve System, 1970.

[24] Robinson, J. *Introduction to the Theory of Employment.* 2nd edition. London: MacMillan and Co., 1960.

[25] Tobin, J. "Comment." *American Economic Review.* May 1963.

[26] Turvey, R. *Interest Rates and Asset Prices.* London: George Allen and Unwin, 1960.

[27] Viner, J. "Mr. Keynes on the Causes of Unemployment." *Quarterly Journal of Economics*, November 1936.

[28] Witte, J. G. "The Microfoundations of the Social Investment Function." *Journal of Political Economy*, October 1963, 441-456.

## Notes

1. There is no precise reference to the F.R.B.-M.I.T. model. However, Bischoff has given a straightforward exposition of the F.R.B.-M.I.T. investment model, which stands as a basically flexible accelerator—the accelerator adjusting to relative prices of factor inputs.

2. Prof. J. Robinson in the Preface to [24] argues that Keynes' analysis ". . . attributed too much importance to the rate of interest as a regulator of the economy" (p. xii). Keynes' restatement of his views in his rebuttal to Viner in 1937 is, I believe, not subject to Prof. Robinson's criticism.

3. In his Ph.D. research [8] L. Ederington has shown that the yield and dealer spreads are system determined variables. The variation in these spreads is the way market pressures from the financing of investment are transmitted by way of the financing of positions in the stock of capital to the perhaps implicit price of capital assets.

4. The standard balance sheet by ignoring longer term rental contracts by business understates payment commitments. A restructuring of financial data in terms of payments and receipts is needed.

5. A chain of substitution among assets is possible so that with a money supply of $M_0$ a financial asset, $L_i$, is used as if it were money, but with a money supply $M_1 > M_0$, $L_i$ is no longer used in this way. For such an "inferior" money substitute it is possible that $P_{L_i}(M_1) < P_{L_i}(M_0)$.

6. It is necessary to distinguish between the "stock" and the "flow" impact of government debt—where "government debt" includes not only the statutory debt but also all interest bearing debt which is effectively guaranteed against default by government endorsement—implicit or explicit.

For given stocks of money, private debt, and real capital and a given set of expectations about the behavior of the economy the greater the stock of government debt the higher the price of the stock of real capital and private debt. On the other hand, with given stocks of money, government debt, private debt, and real capital, a given (exogenously determined) rate of growth of the money supply, and a given income level, the greater the rate of increase of the government debt the lower the price (the higher the conventionally measured interest rate) on new issues of private debt and on new investment output. That is as a stock government debt is a complement to real capital and private debt, as a flow they are substitutes. This ambiguity in the relationship causes a considerable amount of confusion in the analysis of financial markets.

7. Keynesian user cost is not a planning cost of capital concept—the planned-for quasi-rents are larger than the reservation price which enters user cost. For example, if by producing *now* a firm sacrifices a quasi-rent of 100 sometime in the future, the current user cost is the discounted value of the future expected quasi-rent and this can be smaller than the "planning" rate used in determining factor proportions. This view differs from that of Jorgenson and is somewhat like that of Tobin.

8. Because of the yield spread, new issues are sold at a discount as compared to outstanding issues, however, if they are priced correctly, there is an immediate rise in the price of the new issue. Observed market yields on seasoned issues are not the cost of funds to units selling new issues and the difference between the two (market yield and cost to borrowers) is not constant over time (Ederington).

9. If existing management is unwilling to increase debt financing of investment, then mergers, take-over-bids, etc.—which are debt financed—will take place so as to "redeploy" financial assets.

# 11

## Monetary Systems
## and Accelerator Models

A significant part of recent literature on both growth and business-cycle theory has been based upon some form of an interaction between a consumption (saving) relation and an induced investment relation. The authors who have constructed these accelerator-multiplier models have paid little, if any, attention to the monetary prerequisites and effects of the assumed processes.[1] Obviously the accelerator-multiplier process takes place in the context of some monetary system. In this article the manner in which the time series generated depends upon the interaction of an accelerator-multiplier process and the monetary system will be investigated: the main emphasis will be on the upper turning point and the possibility of generating steady growth. In this article the lower turning point is unexplained aside from noticing how the various monetary systems can act as a brake on disinvestment and also, by changing liquidity, set the stage for a recovery.

The procedure will be to examine the result of combining a linear accelerator-multiplier model with a number of alternative monetary systems. The terms (interest rate) and the manner (type of liability) of financing investment are affected by the behavior of the monetary system. In turn, both money-market conditions and the balance-sheet structure of firms affect the response of firms to a change in income. This can be interpreted as making the accelerator coefficient an endogenous variable related to the monetary system. Hence the material in this article could be formalized as a series of nonlinear accelerator-multiplier models.[2]

The author wishes to acknowledge his debt to Julius Margolis, Roger Miller, and Merton P. Stoltz for their helpful comments and suggestions.
Reprinted from *The American Economic Review*, Vol. XlVII, No. 6, December 1957, by arrangement with the publisher.

This article is divided into three sections. The first is a brief review of the attributes of both linear and nonlinear accelerator-multiplier models. It is followed in the second section by an analysis of the behavior of the accelerator model with the quantity of money constant. The third and last section is an investigation of how the system would behave with the quantity of money varying in a number of different ways.

## I. Formal attributes of accelerator-multiplier models

The essential linear accelerator-multiplier model can be written:[3]

(1) $$Y_t = C_t + I_t$$

(2) $$C_t = aY_{t-1}$$

(3) $$I_t = \beta(Y_{t-1} - Y_{t-2})$$

where $Y$ = income, $C$ = consumption, $I$ = investment, $a$ = marginal (= average) propensity to consume, $\beta$ = accelerator coefficient and $t$ is the number of the "day." By substitution, equations (1)-(3) yield:

(4) $$Y_t = (a + \beta)Y_{t-1} - \beta Y_{t-2}$$

Equation (4) is a second-order difference equation; its solution in general is of the form:

(5) $$Y_t = A_1 \mu_1^t + A_2 \mu_2^t$$

where $A_1$ and $A_2$ depend upon the initial conditions and $\mu_1$ and $\mu_2$ are determined by the values of $a$ and $\beta$.

Aside from the effects of the initial conditions, the time series generated by a second-order difference equation can be any one of the following: (1) monotonic equilibrating; (2) cyclical equilibrating; (3) cyclical with constant amplitude; (4) cyclical explosive; (5) monotonic explosive.[4] By itself, no one of these five types of time series is satisfactory for business-cycle analysis. Types 1 and 5 are not cyclical. If they are to be used, either floors or ceilings to income or pushes (systematic or random) from outside have to be posited. A time series of type 2 would in time result in the cycle dying away, so that some systematic or random push is required to maintain the cycle. A time series of type 4 would in time generate fluctuations greater than any preassigned value. Hence floors and ceilings have to be posited to constrain the fluctuations. A type-3 time series is a self-sustaining cycle, but its existence depends upon a particular value of $\beta$ and, in addition, the time series it generates is "too" regular.

A way out of this difficulty is to have the $a$ and $\beta$ coefficients vary over the cycle, thus generating a time series which is a combination of the different types of time series. Hicks and Goodwin do this by assuming that the value of $\beta$ is so great that, unless constrained, an explosive time series is generated, but that constraints, in the form of a maximum depreciation rate and full employment (or the capacity of the capital-goods-producing industries), exist. These constraints force realized investment to be different from induced investment, and, formally, they can be interpreted as changing the value of $\beta$. As the value of $\beta$ is assumed to fall (rise) when income is very high (low) or increasing (decreasing) very rapidly, an acceptably irregular cyclical time series is generated. Obviously by linking explosive, cyclical, and damped movements together, any type of time series which is desired can be generated.

A set of formal nonlinear models similar to those of Hicks and Goodwin can be generated by positing that the value of $\beta$, the accelerator coefficient, depends upon money-market conditions and the balance sheets of firms. These factors in turn depend upon the relation between the level and rate of change of income and the behavior of the monetary system. In this paper however the mathematical model of the accelerator process will be a simple linear form. It is hoped that what is lost in mathematical neatness may be offset by what is gained in the identifiability of the economics.

So far we have not taken up the effects of the initial conditions. The initial conditions are particularly important in determining the income generated by a type-5 (monotonic explosive) time series for small values of $t$. To generate a type-5 series, $\mu_1$ and $\mu_2$ are both greater than 1 in the relation $Y_t = A_1 \mu_1^t + A_2 \mu_2^t$. To set off the recursive process two levels of income $Y_0$ and $Y_1$ (the initial conditions) are needed, which determine the values of $A_1$ and $A_2$. If $Y_1$ is greater than $Y_0$ and the ratio of $Y_1$ to $Y_0$ is less than $\mu_2$, the smaller root, then $A_1$, the coefficient of $\mu_1$, the larger root (also called the dominant root), will be negative. As the larger root will in time dominate, a negative $A_1$ will in time result in a negative $Y_t$. Hence if the rate of increase of income given by the initial conditions is less than the smaller root, there will be a turning point in the time series even though the values of $a$ and $\beta$ are such as to generate a monotonic-explosive time series.[5]

This leads to an alternative way of interpreting the Goodwin-Hicks type of nonlinear accelerator models. When the floors and ceilings become effective, a new set of initial conditions is, in effect, imposed on the time series. If these new "initial conditions" result in the sign of the coefficient of the dominant root changing, then in time the direction of the movement of income will be changed. The effects of monetary constraint can also be interpreted in this manner.

Following Goodwin and Hicks we will assume that the value of $\beta$ is so large that, unless it is constrained, the accelerator-multiplier process will generate an explosive time series. The solution of the accelerator-multiplier model will be $Y_t = A_1 \mu_1^t + A_2 \mu_2^t$ where $\mu_1 > \mu_2 > 1$ and the initial conditions are such $(Y_1 / Y_0 > \mu_2)$ that $A_1$ and $A_2$ are both positive. For the range of magnitudes of $Y_1 / Y_0$ which it seems sensible to posit, $A_2$ will be much larger than $A_1$. This means that at the early dates ($t$ small) of the development the weight of $\mu_2$ is high while at the later dates $\mu_1$ dominates. The rate of growth of income generated by the explosive process being considered increases in time, approaching $\mu_1$ as a limit.[6]

The increasing rate of increase of income that such an explosive accelerator process generates will in time be greater than the accepted possible rate of growth of productive capacity. In order to be able to maintain the continuity of the accelerator process, we assume that all the relations are in money terms and that the accelerator process may generate changes in the price level. We will, at a number of points, call attention to some specific effects of price level changes.

## II. The accelerator model with the quantity of money constant

In this and the following section we will derive several time series that result from the interaction of an accelerator-multiplier process and various types of monetary systems. The monetary systems to be considered are classified in terms of the monetary changes which can take place. Monetary changes are changes in either the velocity of circulation or the quantity of money. Therefore we will consider the following alternative monetary systems: (A) neither velocity nor quantity changes; (B) only velocity changes; (C) only quantity changes; (D) both velocity and quantity change.[7] The first two monetary systems will be considered in this section, the last two in the next section.

Except in the first monetary system, we assume that there exists a fractional reserve banking system. The money supply is changed by either the creation of deposits in exchange for business firms' debts or the destruction of deposits by business firms' repayment of bank debt. That is, the banking system is a commercial banking system rather than one that deals in government and other securities.[8] In all that follows the central bank's relations with the commercial banks are integrated into the "monetary system." For example, an infinitely elastic money supply can be achieved by a central bank lending to commercial banks, or by a central bank purchasing open market paper. Also in a monetary system we include the specialized financial intermediaries.

The income velocity of money and the liquidity preference relation can be characterized as mirror images of each other.[9] When income velocity rises, the liquidity of the economy falls and vice versa. A useful construction is to assume that for each level of money income $Y$, there exists a minimum quantity of money $M_T$ which is necessary to sustain the volume of payments associated with $Y$. If $M_T$ is the total quantity of money in existence then there is no money available for portfolio use; we have a maximum income velocity of money $V_m$ for each $Y$, so that $M_T \cdot V_m = Y$. If $M$ is greater than $M_T$ then the actual velocity, $V$, is less than $V_m$. The difference between $M$ and $M_T$ is $M_L$, the amount of money which is held as a liquid asset. If the quantity of money is constant, portfolio money $M_L$ must fall when $V$ rises.

If $V < V_m$ then $M_L > 0$. Abstracting from changes in the quantity of money, with $M_L > 0$, the interest rate is determined by the demand curve for investment, *ex ante* saving, and the terms upon which holders of liquidity are willing to substitute earning assets for money. Similarly, if $M_L = 0$, then the interest rate is determined by the demand for investment, the supply of saving, and the terms upon which individuals are willing to hold cash as an asset. With a given money supply in excess of $M_T$ there exists a rate of interest at which housholds and business firms as a whole are not willing either to increase or to decrease their holdings of money. Any other market interest rate involves either an increase in cash balances so that savings are utilized to increase liquidity, or a decrease in cash balances so that investment is financed from the reservoir of purchasing power. It is assumed that changes in the market rate of interest will affect the amount of investment induced by a given change in income.

Assume that all investment is made by business firms. On a consolidated balance sheet of all firms, investment is represented by an increase in plant, equipment, or work in progress, and it will be offset by an increase in liabilities (equity or debt) or a decrease in other assets (cash or liquid assets). Business investment can be equity-financed as a result of either *ex ante* saving by households and firms or a decrease in the cash balances of households. Business investment can be debt-financed as a result of *ex ante* saving by households, a decrease in households' cash balances or by an increase in bank debt of business firms. The financing of investment by a decrease in the cash (liquid assets) balances of firms does not affect either the debt or the equity liabilities of firms: it only makes firms less liquid.

Whereas *ex ante* saving and decreases in the liquidity of households can be used for either debt or equity financing of investment, increases in the quantity of money can be used only for the debt financing of investment. Households, business firms, and banks are sensitive to the composition of the balance sheets of firms; in particular an increase in the ratio of debt to equity or a decrease in the ratio of cash to other assets in firms' balance sheets will make business firms less willing to borrow and households and banks less willing to lend. Hence if investment is financed in such a way as either to increase the ratio of debt to total liabilities or to decrease the liquidity of business firms, the amount of investment induced by a given change in income will fall. The value of the accelerator coefficient therefore depends upon two variables, the market rate of interest and the structure of the balance sheets of firms. Changes in these variables can dampen what otherwise would be an explosive movement of income.

## A. Neither velocity nor quantity changes

Using the Swedish concepts,[10] we define $Y_{t-1} - C_t = (1-a)Y_{t-1}$ as *ex ante* saving. Assuming, as pure accelerator-multiplier models do, that all of investment is induced, then $I_t = \beta(Y_{t-1} - Y_{t-2})$ is identified as *ex ante* investment. From equations (1)-(3), it follows that for $Y_t \geqslant Y_{t-1}$ it is necessary that $I_t = \beta(Y_{t-1} - Y_{t-2}) \geqslant (1-a)Y_{t-1}$, for $Y_t < Y_{t-1}$ it is necessary that $I_t = \beta(Y_{t-1} - Y_{t-2}) < (1-a)Y_{t-1}$.

With a monetary system in which neither the velocity of circulation nor the quantity of money changes, if *ex ante* investment is greater than *ex ante* saving, the *ex ante* saving has to be rationed among investors, and the market in which this rationing takes place is the money market. The excess of demand over supply results in a rise in interest rates, which will continue until realized investment is equal to *ex ante* saving. In Figure 1, *ex ante* investment is based upon the rate $R_1$ so that $\beta(Y_{t-1} - Y_{t-2}) = I_t'$. The inability to finance more than $I_t$ ($=S_t$) of investment results in a rise in the interest rate to $R_2$. Such a monetary system leaves no room for an accelerator-multiplier cycle. A necessary condition for the functioning of an accelerator process during an expansion is that a source of financing of investment in addition to *ex ante* saving should exist.[11]

Symmetrically, if *ex ante* saving is greater than *ex ante* investment then an increase in investment is forced so that all of the

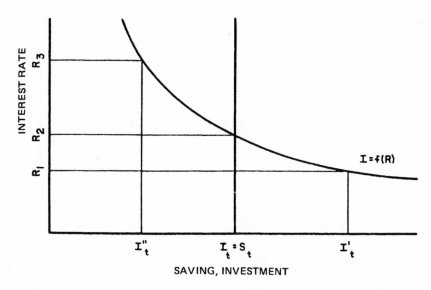

Figure 1

Reconciliation of ex ante saving and investment

available financing is absorbed by real investment. If there exists no way in which savings can be utilized other than in investment, then the terms upon which firms can finance investment must change so that realized investment is greater than *ex ante* investment. This equality of *ex ante* saving and realized investment stabilizes income, thereby halting the "inducement to disinvest."

### B. Only velocity changes

With a constant money supply, realized investment can differ from *ex ante* saving only if the velocity of circulation of money changes. We will first take up the purely mechanical implications of the existence of a floor and a ceiling to velocity. We will then consider the effects on the value of the accelerator coefficient of changes in velocity when no excess liquidity exists and when excess liquidity exists (the Keynesian liquidity trap). To the extent that a fixed money supply and a ceiling to velocity set an upper limit to the money value of income, secular growth requires a falling price level, and this has implications for the accelerator process.

We have assumed that the interest rate and the balance-sheet structure of firms (liquidity and the debt-equity ratio) affect the value of the accelerator coefficient. The financing of investment by absorbing idle cash balances does not necessarily change the debt-equity ratio of business firms, for we can assume that the debt-equity preferences of households are not strikingly different when *ex ante* saving and when idle cash balances are used to finance investment.[12] Therefore the balance sheets of investing firms do not deteriorate during an expansion financed by increasing velocity. Of course the liquidity of households and firms is reduced but, unless the liquidity trap is operative, this is reflected in the interest rate. Therefore in this section only the interest rate and, in the liquidity-trap situation, the changes in liquidity at a constant interest rate can affect the accelerator coefficient.

Assume that a cumulative rise in income is set off. This increases the quantity of money needed for transaction purposes and, therefore, as the process continues there are progressively smaller asset holdings of money which can be used to finance investment in excess of *ex ante* saving. The highest attainable level of money income is that level at which all of the available money supply is required for transactions (see Table 1). At that income realized investment cannot exceed *ex ante* saving. Realized investment equal to *ex ante* saving results in a constant income which, given the accelerator assumption, induces zero investment. Ignoring any effects that the interest-rate and balance-sheet changes accompanying velocity increases have upon the accelerator coefficient, a monetary system with a constant quantity of money may impose a ceiling to money income. This ceiling is not determined by full employment or by the capacity of the investment goods industries; it is determined by the limited ability of changes in velocity to finance investment.

Symmetrically if a minimum velocity exists, a floor to money income exists. However the floor is not entirely symmetrical with the ceiling, and in this article the lower turning point is essentially unexplained.

Let us examine what would be happening in the money market during a process such as is detailed in Table 1. Ignoring the liquidity trap, a rise in transaction money as income rises means that with a constant money supply portfolio money becomes scarcer. The interest rate at which cash can be withdrawn from portfolios into the income stream rises as asset money is used to finance investment in excess of saving. With a fixed quantity of money and a rise in income, the balance sheets of households and firms show a smaller ratio of asset cash to total assets, liquidity decreases. The decrease in liquidity and the rise in the interest rate both tend to decrease the accelerator coefficient.

Alternatively, on the downswing *ex ante* investment is smaller than *ex ante* saving. With a constant money supply, this excess

Table 1

## Only Velocity Changes
## (Constant Money Supply—No Interest-Rate Effects)

| | | | Accelerator process $a=.8, \beta=4.0$ $Y_0=100, Y_1=110$ | | | Monetary system Money supply = 100 Maximum velocity = 2 | |
|---|---|---|---|---|---|---|---|
| Time | Y | C | Savings ex ante | Investment Ex ante | Realized | Investment financed by $\Delta V$a | Realized velocity |
| 0 | 100 | – | – | – | – | – | 1.00 |
| 1 | 110 | 80 | 20 | – | 30 | 10 | 1.10 |
| 2 | 128 | 88 | 22 | 40 | 40 | 18 | 1.28 |
| 3 | 174 | 102 | 26 | 72 | 72 | 46 | 1.74 |
| 4 | 200 | 139 | 35 | 184 | 61 | 26 | 2.00 |
| 5 | 200 | 160 | 40 | 104 | 40 | 0 | 2.00 |
| 6 | 160 | 160 | 40 | 0 | 0 | –40 | 1.60 |

[a]Investment in excess of *ex ante* saving. Obviously negative investment financed by $\Delta V$ means that *ex ante* saving is greater than investment.

saving is absorbed by a reduction in velocity. Money available for asset purposes increases as it is withdrawn from the income stream. The interest rate falls and the liquidity of the community rises so that the amount of disinvestment induced by the given downward shift in demand decreases. Both on the upswing and the downswing, the monetary system which is based solely upon changes in velocity acts as a stabilizer of realized induced investment unless the fall in income is so great that the money released from transaction purposes lowers the interest rate to the floor interest rate of the liquidity trap. At this interest rate the stabilizing effect upon aggregate disinvestment of the fall in financing terms will cease, although increasing liquidity can continue to act as a stabilizer.[13]

Figure 2 illustrates the use of cash balances to finance investment and to offset *ex ante* saving. At the interest rate $R_1$, and income $Y_0$, the velocity of circulation of money remains constant. This is illustrated by the $L_1$ curve intersecting the zero change in cash balances line at $R_1$. At higher interest rates cash assets would be freed to finance investment; at lower interest rates saving would be absorbed by cash balances. The amount of investment which can be financed at any interest rate is equal to the sum of *ex ante* saving and the change in cash balances. Assume that income rises so that at the interest rate $R_1$, $I_2'$ of investment is induced. The $I_2$

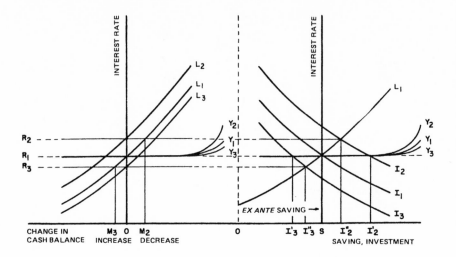

Figure 2

Saving, investment, and cash balances

curve illustrates how the value of the accelerator would be changed by a change in interest rates. The excess of demand over the supply of finance results in a rise of the interest rate to $R_2$. As $I_{2\ ''}$ is greater than *ex ante* saving, income will rise and the transaction demand for cash will increase. This will raise the schedule relating the change in cash balances to the interest rate to $L_2$, so that the interest rate at which investment will be financed by a fall in liquidity will be higher.

If a fall in income shifts the investment demand curve to $I_3$, *ex ante* investment is $I_3'$- With a constant money supply the excess of *ex ante* saving over induced investment will depress the interest rate, and realized investment will be $I_3'' > I_3'$, $OM_3$ being added to cash balances. As $S > I_3''$ income will fall, and this will shift the liquidity curve downward so that cash balances can be used to finance investment at an interest rate lower than $R_1$.

If the cash balance-interest rate relation is as the $Y_3$, $Y_2$, and $Y_1$ set of curves indicate, then excess liquidity exists; this is the Keynesian liquidity-trap situation. With an investment curve $I_2$, $I_2' - S$ of investment will be financed by a decrease in cash balances; and if the investment curve is $I_3$, $S - I_3'$ will be added to cash balances. In both cases no change in interest rates will occur. In the Keynesian liquidity-trap situation the money market damps down neither the "boom" nor the "bust." On the boom side, the liquidity trap will exist until the need of cash for transactions absorbs a sufficiently large portion of the money supply so that the Keynesian liquidity trap comes to an end. There is no endogenous limiting factor to the liquidity trap on the downswing aside from the effect that improved liquidity has upon firms' balance sheets. Therefore the Keynesian liquidity-trap situation allows full scope to an explosive accelerator coefficient. And in the upswing, an explosive accelerator process will generate greater increases in money demand than the increases in productive capacity, so that a strong accelerator in combination with excess liquidity will generate large price increases.

Either the ceiling to velocity or the effect of rising interest rates and decline in liquidity upon the accelerator coefficient will break the cumulative expansion. A fall in money income will occur. The quantity of money needed for transactions falls, and *ex ante* saving which is not realized in investment will result in the addition of money to portfolios. If the price level does not fall during a depression the ceiling real income remains fixed, while if the price level falls, even though the ceiling money income remains fixed, the ceiling real income rises.

Net investment implies an increase in productive capacity. With a constant money supply and in effect a ceiling to velocity, larger real incomes can be realized only if the price level falls. To the extent that the accelerator inducement to invest is large only when income is approximately equal to productive capacity, strong expansions can only occur if the price level falls secularly.

The effect of the expectation that in the long run the price level will fall is to increase the expected pay-off period of an investment. This is equivalent, in its effect upon investment by firms, to a rise in interest rates with a constant price level, so that a falling price level will tend to lower the value of the accelerator coefficient. Therefore the business cycle will be characterized by weaker booms than would occur with a permissive monetary system. Such a monetary system will be associated with a tendency toward relatively stable income for, unless liquidity is greatly increased during a downswing, long periods in which realized investment exceeds *ex ante* saving cannot occur.

### III. The accelerator model with quantity of money variable

In this section we will consider two monetary systems, those in which only the quantity of money can change and those in which both the quantity of money and its velocity can change.

We assume that commercial banks create money by lending to business firms. The maximum realized increase in the money supply is equal to the difference between *ex ante* investment and *ex ante* saving:

$$\Delta M = ex\ ante\ I - ex\ ante\ S = \Delta Y$$

Assume that $V = \dfrac{Y}{M} = \dfrac{\Delta Y}{\Delta M} = 1$. The increase in the money supply

in the hands of households is the asset which makes the change in net worth equal to *ex ante* investment.[14] As income velocity is 1, there will be no net change in the quantity of money that individuals hold as assets. This is equivalent to assuming that the interest rate at which banks lend to business is the interest rate at which money and earning assets are substituted in household portfolios.[15] The only relevant monetary change in these models is in the quantity of money.

When the money supply increases at an independently given rate, the autonomous increase in the money supply is not necessarily equal to the difference between *ex ante* investment and *ex ante* saving. If the increase in the money supply is greater than the difference between *ex ante* investment and *ex ante* saving we assume that this difference accumulates in the banking system (as excess reserves) and can be used to finance future investment. If the increase in the money supply is less than the difference between *ex ante* investment and *ex ante* saving, realized investment will be less than *ex ante* investment and the increase in income will be equal to the increase in the money supply.

For each monetary system we will first investigate the mechanical properties of these relations, assuming that the accelerator coefficient does not change, and then investigate the possible effects of the associated money market and financing developments upon the value of the accelerator coefficient.

### A. Quantity changes but not velocity

Two monetary systems in which only the quantity of money can change will be taken up. In the first, the money supply will be assumed to be infinitely elastic, and in the second the money supply will be assumed to increase at a fixed arithmetic or geometric rate.

1. *Infinitely elastic money supply.* If the quantity of money can increase without limit then no matter what the difference between *ex ante* investment and *ex ante* saving, the difference can be financed. Also we can assume that the terms upon which the banking system lends do not change. Such a monetary system is consistent with the existence of an explosive accelerator process since it permits a cumulative rise in money income. Is there anything inherent in the operations of such a monetary system which will lead to a dampening of the accelerator process? (We will ignore the

political repercussions of the cumulative rise in prices which is implicit in a full-employment situation in which the rate of growth of money income is greater than that of productive capacity.)

During an expansion, the increase in money supply occurs as investing firms add bank debt to their liabilities (see Table 2). Assuming that the percentage distribution of *ex ante* saving between debt and equities of business firms is constant, a cumulative explosive expansion on the basis of the creation of money will (*ceteris paribus*) result in a fall in the ratio of equity to debt in the balance sheet of firms.[16] Even if the terms upon which firms can borrow are unchanged by the deterioration of their balance sheets, borrowers' risk will rise.[17] This will lower the amount of investment induced by a given rise in income. Hence, even with a monetary system that permits all of *ex ante* investment to be realized, the financing of investment by bank debt can result in lowering the accelerator coefficient which in turn lowers the rate of increase of income. This continues until the accelerator coefficient falls sufficiently to replace the explosive by a cyclical time series, in which there eventually occurs a fall in income. With a fall in income, the excess of *ex ante* saving over induced investment will be utilized to reduce bank debt. Also, the failure of some firms which have relied heavily upon debt financing will result in the substitution of equity for debt in balance sheets. Both changes during the downswing raise the ratio of equity to debt in firms' balance sheets[18] which acts as a stabilizer. The endogenous limits to an explosive accelerator process, in the absence of restrictions on the money

---

Table 2

Infinitely Elastic Money Supply
(Constant Velocity—No Interest-Rate Effects)

| Time | Y | C | Savings Ex ante | $\beta(Y_{t-1} - Y_{t-2})$ Ex ante | Realized | $\Delta$ Money supply | $\dfrac{\Delta \text{Equity financing}}{\Delta \text{Total investment}}$ |
|------|------|------|------|------|------|------|------|
| 0 | 100. | – | – | – | – | – | – |
| 1 | 110. | 80. | 20. | – | 30. | 10. | .67 |
| 2 | 128. | 88. | 22. | 40. | 40. | 18. | .55 |
| 3 | 174. | 102. | 26. | 72. | 72. | 46. | .36 |
| 4 | 323. | 139. | 35. | 184. | 184. | 149. | .19 |

Accelerator process
$a = .8$   $\beta = 4$   $Y_0 = 100$

Monetary system
All *ex ante S* used for equity financing.
All increases in money used for debt financing.

Investment

supply, are the deterioration of firms' balance sheets due to debt-financing of investment on the upswing; and the reverse circumstances during the liquidation process on the downswing.

Two possible offsetting factors to the increasing debt-equity ratio in the financing of investment during an explosive expansion are an increase in the ratio of *ex ante* saving flowing to equities and the capital gains that accompany an increase in the price level of capital goods. As *ex ante* saving finances a decreasing proportion of total investment during an explosive expansion, a possible increase in the proportion of *ex ante* saving flowing to equities cannot for long prevent a deterioration of the balance sheets of firms. If, however, cumulative price-level inflation is politically permissible a deterioration of firms' balance sheets need not occur. Business firms are borrowers and the real burden of a debt decreases with a rise in the price level. If the assets of business firms are valued at their current replacement costs, then the rising price level raises the equity account. Such capital gains improve the balance sheets of firms and they occur generally in an inflation. The price-level rise plus the flow of *ex ante* saving to equity investment may be sufficient to keep the debt-equity ratio constant, thereby preventing any deterioration in the balance sheets of firms. However, this requires an increasing rate of change in the price level of capital goods.[19] Nevertheless, if an explosive inflation is politically tolerable, there is no endogenous reason why an accelerator process with an infinitely elastic money supply need come to a halt.

Therefore, at least two monetary situations allow full scope to an explosive accelerator process: the Keynesian liquidity trap and an infinitely elastic money supply. It is perhaps no accident that the emphasis upon "real" floors and ceilings as causes of the nonlinearity of the accelerator coefficient occurred at a time when the high volume of government bonds outstanding and their support by central banks made the money supply in fact infinitely elastic. An era of tight money on the other hand naturally leads to an examination of the monetary prerequisites for the operation of the accelerator phenomena.

2. *Money supply increases at a fixed rate.* A monetary system in which the rate of growth of the money supply is exogenously given, for example a fractional reserve banking system based upon a gold standard, is equivalent to an infinitely elastic money supply if the difference between *ex ante* investment and *ex ante* saving does not exceed the per-period growth of the money supply. The only endogenous limitation to expansion in this case comes from the deteriorating balance sheets and liquidity of business firms, as is true with an infinitely elastic money supply. The interesting alternative

exists when the difference between induced investment and *ex ante* saving is greater than the rate of growth of the lending ability of banks.

Throughout this section we will assume that at the initial period the banking system does not possess excess liquidity. Hence the available financing is equal to *ex ante* saving plus the possible increase in the money supply. If induced investment is equal to or greater than this, realized investment will be constrained to the available financing. In this case income will grow at the same rate as the money supply.[20]

(a) *Arithmetic rate of increase in the money supply.* If the money supply increases by a fixed amount per period (constant arithmetic rate of increase), income will grow at this rate until *ex ante* saving increases sufficiently so that induced investment per period becomes less than the available financing. When this happens, the per-period increase in income will fall below what it had been, and therefore induced investment will decrease. The downturn occurs when *ex ante* saving catches up with the expansion process so that all of the investment induced by the constant arithmetic rate of growth of income can be realized without using all of the newly available credit.[21] (This case is illustrated in Table 3.)

During the expansion, the demand for financing is always greater than the available supply; the money market constrains investment. When the arithmetic increase in income becomes less than the increase in the money supply financing conditions ease. The resulting decline in the rate of interest may act to increase the inducement to invest (decrease the inducement to disinvest); this possibility is ignored in Table 3. Since the banking system finances a decreasing proportion of realized investment during the expansion, the deterioration of the balance sheets of investing firms will be limited during such an expansion.

When income declines, the autonomous increases in the money supply result in an accumulation of excess reserves in the banking system, and *ex ante* saving in excess of induced investment results in a repayment of bank debt by firms. These changes should brake the decline in income.

The accumulation of excess reserves by banks and the improved balance sheets of firms during the downswing imply that if an expansion begins it will not at once be constrained by the money-market and balance-sheet effects. If the arithmetic rate of growth of the money supply is small compared to the accumulation of financing ability during the decline in income, a sharp fall in investment will occur at the date that the accumulated financing ability

Table 3

## Arithmetically Increasing Money Supply
## (Constant Velocity—No Interest-Rate Effects)

| Time | $Y$ | $C$ | Accelerator process $a=.8$ $\beta=4$ Savings Ex ante | Investment Induced $\beta(Y_{t\text{-}1} - Y_{t\text{-}2})$ | Realized | Monetary system +10 per time period Investment financed by increased money supply |
|------|------|-------|------|------|------|------|
| 0 | 100.0 | — | — | — | — | — |
| 1 | 110.0 | 80.0 | 20.0 | — | 30. | +10.0 |
| 2 | 120.0 | 88.0 | 22.0 | 40 | 32. | +10.0 |
| 3 | 130.0 | 96.0 | 24.0 | 40 | 34. | +10.0 |
| 4 | 140.0 | 104.0 | 26.0 | 40 | 36. | +10.0 |
| 5 | 150.0 | 112.0 | 28.0 | 40 | 38. | +10.0 |
| 6 | 160.0 | 120.0 | 30.0 | 40 | 40. | +10.0 |
| 7 | 168.0 | 128.0 | 32.0 | 40 | 40. | + 8.0 |
| 8 | 166.4 | 134.4 | 33.6 | 32 | 32. | − 1.6[a] |

[a]In time period 7, *ex ante S* + $\Delta M$ > *ex ante I*; therefore $Y_7 - Y_6 < \Delta M$. As a result, in time period 8 the accelerator expansion is broken.

is absorbed, thereby decreasing the per-period increase in income. The smaller increase in income will lead to a fall in induced investment, and a sharp fall in income may occur. A constant arithmetic rate of increase of the money supply in conjunction with an explosive accelerator process will tend to generate a cyclical time series.

(b) *Geometric rate of increase in the money supply.* Consider a money supply that increases at a constant geometric rate, $\mu_3$. As was noted earlier the solution of an explosive accelerator process can be written as $Y_t = A_1 \mu_1^t + A_2 \mu_2^t$ with $\mu_1 > \mu_2 > 1$ with $A_1$ and $A_2$ depending upon the initial conditions. That is, the rate of growth of income is a weighted average of the two rates of growth $\mu_1$ and $\mu_2$. If $\mu_3$, the rate of growth of the money supply, is greater than (or equal to) $\mu_1$, the greatest rate of growth that income can achieve, the system behaves as if the money supply were infinitely elastic. Hence the cases that have to be examined are when $\mu_1 > \mu_2 > \mu_3 > 1$ and when $\mu_1 > \mu_3 > \mu_2 > 1$.

Take the first case in which $\mu_1 > \mu_2 > \mu_3 > 1$. With no excess liquidity, the maximum attainable rate of growth of income is the rate of growth of the money supply. To sustain this rate of growth, it is necessary that induced investment be equal to or greater than the available financing. When the rate of growth of the money supply, and therefore the rate of growth of income, is less than $\mu_2$ induced investment will not be large enough to absorb the available financing.[22] The rate of growth of income will be smaller than the rate of growth of the money supply, and this new smaller rate of growth of income also will not be sustained. These progressively smaller rates of growth of income will in time result in insufficient induced investment to offset *ex ante* saving and at this date income will fall. Therefore, if the rate of growth of the money supply is smaller than the smallest rate of growth that the accelerator process, if unconstrained, would generate, an upper turning point in income will be produced.[23]

The argument as to what happens once income turns down for a geometric rate of increase in the money supply is essentially the same as for an arithmetic increase in the money supply. Excess reserves accumulate in the banking system and firms' balance sheets improve during the downward movement. Once a sufficient upward movement again begins, an unconstrained expansion can take place until the excess liquidity is absorbed, at which time the rate of growth of the money supply will again constrain the rate of growth of income. A money supply growing at "too small" a rate will lead to a cyclical rather than a steady-growth time series.

If the rate of growth of the money supply is equal to the smaller root of the accelerator process (i.e., $\mu_3 = \mu_2$), both income and the money supply will grow at this rate. Throughout this process the ratio of *ex ante* saving to bank financing of investment will be constant. If this ratio is consistent with the balance-sheet goals, there is nothing in this process which would lead to a downturn in income. Also this rate of growth of income may be consistent with a fairly stable price level. Steady growth may result from combining an explosive accelerator process and an appropriately increasing money supply.[24]

Consider now the second case, in which $\mu_1 > \mu_3 > \mu_2 > 1$. In this case the rate of growth of income during any time period will depend upon the weight of the two roots. If the weight of $\mu_2$ is high, then the accelerator process will generate a rate of growth of income less than the rate of growth of the money supply. However, since $\mu_1 > \mu_2$, in time $\mu_1$ will dominate the rate of growth of income so that income will be increasing faster than the money supply. The money supply does not constrain the growth of income until the total growth of income equals the total growth of the money supply. Whether this case results in steady growth or in a downturn of income depends upon what happens to the accelerator coefficient once the monetary constraint becomes effective.

At the beginning of such an explosive expansion the rate of growth of income is less than the rate of growth of the money supply. At the date when the total growth of income becomes equal to the total growth of the money supply the rate of growth of income will be greater than the rate of growth of the money supply. Therefore at some intermediate date, the rate of growth of income will be the same as the rate of growth of the money supply. This rate of growth of income will induce sufficient investment, at the financing terms and balance sheets ruling, for the rate of growth of income to increase. Therefore if the rate of growth of income is constrained to the rate of growth of the money supply, and the accelerator coefficient does not change, a sufficient amount of investment will be induced to generate a rate of growth of income greater than the rate of growth of the money supply.

However until the increase in income and in the money supply become equal, this system operates with excess liquidity. At the date that the excess liquidity is absorbed, the rate of growth of income will be greater than the rate of growth of the money supply so that when the monetary constraint becomes effective two things will occur: the rate of growth of income will fall and financing terms will rise. When financing terms were relatively easy because of excess liquidity a rate of growth of income equal to the rate of growth of the money supply induced sufficient investment to increase the rate of growth of income. However in a suddenly tight money market financing terms may so change that the accelerator coefficient will fall, and this can lead to a fall in income.

Nevertheless, if the money supply is growing at a geometric rate greater than the smaller root of the accelerator process, a constant rate of growth of income may be generated. In this case money income will grow at a faster rate than if the money supply grew at the rate given by the smaller root. Hence such a steady rate of growth of income can be associated with a substantial rate of increase in the price level. In addition, the ratio of bank financing to ex ante saving increases as the rate of growth of the money supply increases.

If the accelerator falls as a result of the tightening of the money market, income can turn down. The behavior of the economy with this monetary system on the downturn and on subsequent expansions would be essentially the same as in the previous case where the rate of growth of the money supply was smaller than the smaller root of the accelerator process.

## B. Both velocity and quantity change

The earlier consideration of the interaction of an otherwise explosive accelerator-multiplier process with monetary systems in which only changes in velocity and changes in the quantity of money can occur enables us to consider monetary systems in which both quantity and velocity of money can change. We first assume that the quantity of money is changing but that velocity is greater than 1; we then consider the effects of changing velocity. Finally we take up changes in liquidity preference.

1. In the cases where investment in excess of *ex ante* saving is financed by an increase in the quantity of money, we assumed that the income velocity of money was 1. We can now drop this assumption. If income velocity is greater than 1, and if an excess of *ex ante* investment over *ex ante* saving is financed by an increase in the quantity of money, then excess liquidity results. This excess liquidity can be utilized to finance investment.

Assume that the excess liquidity resulting from an investment initially financed by the banks is used to substitute business debt or equities to the public for business debt to banks. If $\Delta M = Y_t - Y_{t-1}$ and $V > 1$, then new transaction cash is

$$\frac{\Delta M}{V} \text{ , and asset cash is } \Delta M - \frac{\Delta M}{V} = \left(1 - \frac{1}{V}\right) \Delta M.$$

After the public purchases business debts or equities, the net increase in debt to banks is

$$\frac{1}{V} \left(Y_t - Y_{t-1}\right)$$

and investment is $Y_t - aY_{t-1}$, therefore:

$$\frac{\Delta \text{Bank Debt}}{\Delta \text{Total Assets}} = \frac{\dfrac{Y_t - Y_{t-1}}{V}}{Y_t - aY_{t-1}} = \frac{1}{V} \frac{Y_t - Y_{t-1}}{Y_t - aY_{t-1}}$$

As an explosive accelerator process takes hold, the ratio $\dfrac{Y_t - Y_{t-1}}{Y_t - aY_{t-1}}$

rises and the ratio of the change in bank debt to the change in total assets approaches $\dfrac{1}{V}$. If the public's distribution of *ex ante* saving and excess liquidity between debt and equity assets is constant during an expansion, the balance sheets of business firms deteriorate. As the weight of bank financing is smaller than in the case of unit velocity, the deterioriation will not be so rapid as in the case in which bank creation of money is the sole technique by which investment in excess of *ex ante* saving can be financed. Therefore, the possibility that the deterioration of firms' balance sheets will lower the accelerator coefficient is smaller.

2. Note that in $\dfrac{1}{V} \dfrac{Y_t - Y_{t-1}}{Y_t - aY_{t-1}}$ a rise in velocity decreases the ratio

of bank financing to the total change in assets and that a rise in the propensity to consume increases the dependence upon bank financing of investment. Therefore, autonomous or cyclically induced changes in these parameters can change the ratio of debt to equity financing, which can change the accelerator coefficient. In particular a rise in velocity tends to counteract the deterioration of firms' balance sheets in a business-cycle expansion financed by bank creation of money.

3. Autonomous or cyclically induced changes in the liquidity preference relation can change the dependence of an expansion upon changes in the money supply and therefore affect the ratio of bank debt to total assets of firms. If liquidity preference decreases, the excess of investment over *ex ante* saving can be financed by withdrawals from cash balances at lower interest rates than were previously ruling. Such an "autonomous" decrease in liquidity preference can, both by improving financing terms and by decreasing the dependence of business firms upon bank financing, raise the accelerator coefficient. A great stock-market boom, such as in the late 1920s, may be interpreted as reflecting a lowering of liquidity preferences; as a result business expansion could be financed with less reliance upon the banking system than otherwise.

Alternatively, an autonomous rise in liquidity preference may lead to the result that business borrowing from banks will increase the liquidity of households rather than finance investment. That is, a portion of business borrowing from banks ends up as "liquid hoards" of households. Such borrowing by business firms in excess of the difference between *ex ante* saving and realized investment will increase the rapidity with which firms' balance sheets deteriorate. An explosive accelerator process may be broken by such changes in liquidity preference.

Such changes in liquidity preference have been labeled autonomous. There exist plausible mechanisms by which the upward movement of an explosive accelerator process would lead to a fall in liquidity preference. However, there do not exist equally plausible mechanisms by which a rise in liquidity preference can be considered as endogenous during an expansion. During a downswing there exists a plausible mechanism which can raise the liquidity preference of households. This can force a deterioration of firms' balance sheets, and thereby, through its effect upon the accelerator coefficient, a further fall in investment. There does not seem to be any endogenous factor which would lead to a fall in liquidity preference on a downswing. Changes in liquidity preference seem to be destabilizing.

## IV. Policy implications

Let us assume that the policy goal is steady growth at a stable price level. The policy measures to be used are monetary policy, which in the language of this article means to choose a monetary system, and fiscal policy. It has been shown that steady growth requires a money supply that increases at a geometric rate: but that a too rapidly growing money supply results in rapid price inflation and that a too slowly growing money supply results in a downturn of income.

The smallest self-sustaining rate of growth of income is equal to the smaller root of the accelerator process, $\mu_2$. If productive capacity can also grow at this rate, then the policy goal of growth without inflation is attainable. If the rate of growth of income is greater than the maximum possible rate of growth of productive capacity, the policy goal is not attainable. In the latter case, we assume that steady growth accompanied by secular inflation will be chosen in preference to a constant price level and intermittent growth. The policy goal therefore becomes steady growth with a minimum rate of secular inflation.

If the policy-makers prize steady growth and abhor falling income, and if secular inflation is accepted as the price that has to be paid for growth, then the policymakers would be able to "play it safe" by allowing the actual rate of growth of the money supply to be greater than the minimum self-sustainable rate of growth of income. That is, the policymakers would accept some unnecessary inflation in order to be on the safe side in maintaining full employment.

For a given consumption coefficient, the greater the rate of growth of the money supply, the greater the ratio of bank debt to debt and equities to households in the balance sheets of firms. Therefore the greater the rate of increase in the money supply, the greater the chance that induced investment will decrease because of the unsatisfactory nature of firms' balance sheets. Two policy measures which can counteract this effect are: (1) an interest rate policy designed to keep velocity greater than one; (2) a fiscal policy designed to increase the money supply without increasing business debt to banks.

It was shown that if income velocity is greater than one and if the money supply is being increased by business borrowing from banks, the net increase in business borrowing from banks will be smaller than the difference between realized investment and *ex ante* saving. In order to achieve this result bank financing of business must be at a high enough interest rate to keep income velocity greater than one. But the accelerator coefficient also depends upon the interest rate. Thus if the monetary policy designed to keep income velocity greater than one is carried too far the accelerator coefficient will fall and the self-sustained growth will be interrupted.

To keep interest rates at a given level, the central bank must be willing to supply reserves to commercial banks, in response to commercial banks' demands, without limit at a fixed rediscount rate. Therefore the rediscount rate seems the appropriate tool of central bank policy.

Nevertheless if the money supply can increase only by business borrowing from banks, a ratio of debt to equities in business balance sheets can result which will lead to a decline in induced investment. Government deficits financed by borrowing from banks result in an increase in the money supply without any corresponding increase in business debt. If interest rates are such that velocity is greater than one, debts and equities to households will be substituted for debts to banks in the business firms' balance sheets. This is more conducive to steady growth than the situation in which all of the increase in the money supply required for steady growth is created in exchange for business debt. Therefore government deficit financing, even during a period of sustained growth and secularly rising prices, may be desirable in order to maintain the conditions for further growth.

## Notes

1. J. R. Hicks, *A Contribution to the Theory of the Trade Cycle* (Oxford, 1950) and S. C. Tsiang, "Accelerator, Theory of the Firm, and the Business Cycle," *Quarterly Journal of Economics*, August 1951, LXV, 325-41, briefly consider monetary factors.
2. Obviously the interest rate and consumer debt affect consumption expenditures also; therefore the consumption coefficient also depends upon the behavior of the monetary system. The "Pigou effect" can be interpreted as a particular relation between the consumption coefficient and the monetary system. Such effects are ignored in this article.
3. This stripped model exhibits the characteristics of a linear accelerator-multiplier model which are important for the problems discussed in this

article. The incomes should be interpreted as deviations from a "zero" level of income given by $Y_0 = \lambda/1 - a$ where $\lambda$ could be identified with autonomous investment or "zero income" consumption.

W. J. Baumol, *Economic Dynamics, An Introduction* (New York, 1951), Chapter 10, 11, gives a very simple discussion of the solution to second-order difference equations.

4. The type of time series generated is determined by the values of $\mu_1$ and $\mu_2$, which in turn depend upon the values of $a$ and $\beta$. For a type-1 series, $\mu_1$ and $\mu_2$ are both less than 1, for a type-2, 3, or 4 series $\mu_1$ and $\mu_2$ are conjugate complex numbers, and for a type-5 series $\mu_1$ and $\mu_2$ are both greater than 1.

5. If the two roots are equal, then the solution to the difference equation is $Y_t = A_1 \mu_1{}^t + A_2 \mu_1{}^t$ (see Baumol, *op. cit.*, Chapter 10, 11). If $Y_1/Y_0 = \mu_1$, then $A_2 = 0$ and a constant-rate-of-growth series is generated. If $Y_1/Y_0 < \mu_1$, then $A_2 < 0$ and in time $Y_t < Y_{t-1}$; if $Y_1/Y_0 > \mu_1$, then $A_2 > 0$ and, at least in the early days, the rate of increase of income is significantly greater than $\mu_1$. In terms of a second-order difference equation, a steady rate of growth of income can be characterized as a knife edge: it requires not only that $a$ and $\beta$ be such that $\mu_1 = \mu_2 > 1$ but also that $Y_1/Y_0 = \mu_1$ (see S. S. Alexander, "The Accelerator as a Generator of Steady Growth," *Quarterly Journal of Economics*, May 1949, LXIII, 174-97).

6. In Sections II and III a number of tables will be exhibited to illustrate the results of combining an explosive accelerator-multiplier process with a number of different monetary systems. In each case it is assumed that $a = .8$, $\beta = 4$, $Y_0 = 100$, and $Y_1 = 110$. For these values $\mu_1 = 3.73$, $\mu_2 = 1.07$, $A_1 = 1.1$, and $A_2 = 98.9$ so that $Y_t = 1.1(3.73)^t + 98.9(1.07)^t$. In time $Y_{t+1}/Y_t$ will approach 3.73.

7. Cases A and B, where the quantity of money is constant, may be thought of as worlds of 100 percent money. If at the "initial point" excess liquidity exists, so that velocity can increase, it is Case B, otherwise it is Case A. Case C(1), where the money supply is infinitely elastic, is a world of a paper-money authority which ignores price-level considerations (perhaps a world in which the central bank follows a "needs of business" rule). Case C(2), where the quantity of money has an exogenously determined rate of growth, is a gold-standard world where gold production is autonomous and determines the rate of growth of the money supply. Case D of course is similar to the existing monetary system.

8. Some of the differences between the classical quantity theory of money and the Keynesian liquidity preference theory of money can be imputed to the way in which the banking system is assumed to operate. The quantity theory approach is consistent with bank lending to business (commercial banking) whereas the liquidity preference theory follows from banks purchasing securities on the open market. In commercial banking an increase in the quantity of money enables a business firm to effect a decision to purchase goods and services. On the other hand, open-market operations substitute money for another asset in the portfolios of the public, and whether or not purchases of goods and services result depends upon the reaction of the public to this change in liquidity.

9. A. C. Pigou, *Keynes's General Theory* (London, 1951); H. S. Ellis, "Some Fundamentals in the Theory of Velocity," *Quarterly Journal of Economics*, May 1938, LII, 431-72.

10. B. Ohlin, "Some Notes on the Stockholm Theory of Savings and Investment," *Economic Journal*, March and June 1937, XLVII, 53-69 and 221-

40. Reprinted in American Economic Association, *Readings in Business Cycle Theory* (Philadelphia, 1951), pp. 87-130.

11. A fall in the price level of investment goods may result in $S_t$ of monetary savings being sufficient to finance $I_t$ of real investment. Conversely a rise in the price level of investment goods will lower the amount of real investment that a given amount of money savings can finance. In Figure 1 the savings curve can be read as a supply curve and the investment curve as the demand curve (with respect to price) for investment goods at a fixed interest rate. Then reading $R_2$ and $R_1$ as price levels, the accelerator phenomenon determines the price level of investment goods. This interpretation of Figure 1 must be what a writer who uses a ceiling to investment-goods production in his models has in mind (for example, Goodwin, *op. cit.*). In the original interpretation of Figure 1, even if $I_t'$ of investment is financed, the supply conditions of investment goods (with respect to price) may be such that spending $I_t'$ on investment goods results in a rise in the price of investment goods; as indicated earlier the accelerator process can lead to a rising price level.

12. J. G. Gurley and E. S. Shaw, "Financial Aspects of Economic Development," *American Economic Review*, September 1955, XLV, 515-38, discuss the effect of available assets on saving behavior. It may be true that the asset preferences of households when using cash balances are different from their preferences when using *ex ante* saving to finance firms. In this connection, the legal and traditional limitations on the portfolios of financial intermediaries no doubt tend to affect business investment.

13. Increasing liquidity raising the consumption coefficient is of course the "Pigou effect."

14. Assume that *ex ante I* > *ex ante S*, realized *I* = *ex ante I*; also that (*ex ante I* − *ex ante S*) is financed by an increase in bank debt. The changes in the consolidated balance sheets of households, business firms, and banks will be:

#### Households

| Debt and Equity of | | Net Worth | +*(ex ante I)* |
|---|---|---|---|
| Firms | +*(ex ante S)* | | |
| Demand Deposits | +*(ex ante I − ex ante S)* | | |

#### Firms

| Productive Assets | +*(ex ante I)* | Debt and Equity to | |
|---|---|---|---|
| | | Households +*(ex ante S)* | |
| Demand Deposits | (no change) | Debts to | |
| | | Banks | +*(ex ante I − ex ante S)* |

#### Banks

| Debts of | | Demand | |
|---|---|---|---|
| Firms | +*(ex ante I − ex ante S)* | Deposits | +*(ex ante I − ex ante S)* |

15. Alternatively if the liquidity-trap rate of interest rules, even if $V > 1$, the rise in the quantity of money in excess of transaction needs can all be absorbed by households' portfolios without lowering the interest rate. However, in this case any rise (virtual) in the interest rate would imply a substitution of earning assets for money in the portfolios of households. This then becomes a case of financing investment from cash balances. If $V > 1$ the money supply

and firms' debts to banks do not increase as rapidly as income.

16. Total induced investment is $\beta(Y_t - Y_{t-1})$. *Ex ante* saving is equal to $(1-a)Y_t$. Assuming that a constant proportion of *ex ante* saving is used for equity financing, the latter is $\lambda(1-a)Y_t$. The ratio of the change in equity to total investment, therefore is:

$$\frac{\lambda(1-a)Y_t}{\beta(Y_t - Y_{t-1})} = \frac{\lambda(1-a)}{\beta\left(1 - \dfrac{Y_{t-1}}{Y_t}\right)}$$

The general solution to the second-order explosive accelerator process is of the form $Y_t = A_1\mu_1{}^t + A_2\mu_2{}^t$ where $\mu_1 > \mu_2 > 1$. Therefore, we can write:

$$\frac{Y_{t-1}}{Y_t} = \frac{A_1\mu_1{}^{t-1} + A_2\mu_2{}^{t-1}}{A_1\mu_1{}^t + A_2\mu_2{}^t} = \frac{1 + \dfrac{A_2}{A_1}\left(\dfrac{\mu_2}{\mu_1}\right)^{t-1}}{\mu_1 + \left(\dfrac{A_2}{A_1}\right)\left(\dfrac{\mu_2}{\mu_1}\right)^{t-1}\mu_2}$$

The limit of $\left(\dfrac{\mu_2}{\mu_1}\right)^t_{t\to\infty} = 0$, therefore the limit of $\left(\dfrac{Y_{t-1}}{Y_t}\right)_{t\to\infty}$ is $\dfrac{1}{\mu_1}$.

Hence $\dfrac{\lambda(1-a)Y_t}{\beta(Y_t - Y_{t-1})}$ approaches as a limit $\dfrac{\lambda(1-a)}{\beta\left(1 - \dfrac{1}{\mu_1}\right)}$ .

In the early stages of an explosive accelerator process the ratio of $\dfrac{Y_{t-1}}{Y_t} > \dfrac{1}{\mu_1}$.

Therefore, the ratio of equity financing to total investment decreases as the accelerator process continues.

17. M. Kalecki, "The Principle of Increasing Risk," *Economica*, N.S., November 1937, IV, 440-47.

18. On the downswing (*ex ante S* > *ex ante I*), the balance sheets of the three sectors change as follows:

Banks

| Business Debt | | Demand Deposits | |
|---|---|---|---|
| | $-$(*ex ante S* $-$*ex ante I*) $= -\Delta M$ | | $-$(*ex ante S* $-$*ex ante I*) $= -\Delta M$ |

Firms

| Capital Equipment | $+$*ex ante I* | Debt and Equities to Households | $+$*ex ante S* |
|---|---|---|---|
| | | Debt to Banks | $-$(*ex ante S* $-$*ex ante I*) $= -\Delta M$ |

Households

| Demand | | | |
|---|---|---|---|
| Deposits | $-(ex\ ante\ S$ | Net Worth | $+ex\ ante\ I$ |
| | $-ex\ ante\ I) = -\Delta M$ | | |
| Business | | | |
| Assets | $+ex\ ante\ S$ | | |

If failures occur in the account of households labeled Business Assets, equities will be substituted for debt and in the account of business firms labeled Debt and Equities to Households, equity will be substituted for debt. Also as business firms fail banks acquire titles and debts which are considered unsuitable for bank portfolios. The sale of such assets to the public results in the substitution of business assets for demand deposits in the public portfolios, and in a net reduction of demand deposits. These changes obviously do not affect the net worth of households and the capital equipment accounts. However, as the value of productive capacity may be reduced during a downturn, the value of the capital equipment account of firms and the net worth account of households may be reduced; the equity liabilities of firms and equity assets of households lose a part or all of their value. This in turn can affect the "subjective" preferences of households and firms so that liquidity preference rises.

19. In the arithmetic example of Table 2, in time-period 3, only .36 of the total new investment was financed by savings. If, in period 3, the price level of capital goods rose so that the value of existing capital goods rose by 2.0, then the ratio of the increase in equity to the increase in assets would be .5. In period 4 only .19 of a larger total investment was financed by savings. For the ratio of the increase in equity to the increase in the value of the assets to be .5, the value of existing capital must rise by 11.4. As total assets in period 4 are presumably only slightly larger than in period 3, this implies that the rate of increase in the price level of capital goods must rise if a constant ratio of equity to total assets is to be maintained. For example:

| Period | 3 | 4 |
|---|---|---|
| Saving, *ex ante* | 26.0 | 35.0 |
| $I$ realized | 72.0 | 184.0 |
| $\Delta$ money | 46.0 | 149.0 |
| Required $\Delta$ value of existing capital | 20.0 | 114.0 |
| $\Delta$ equity $= S + \Delta$ value | 46.0 | 149.0 |
| $\Delta$ assets $= I$ realized $+ \Delta$ value | 92.0 | 298.0 |
| Ratio of $\Delta$ equity to $\Delta$ assets | .5 | .5 |

20. $\beta(Y_t - Y_{t-1}) > (1 - a)Y_t + \Delta M$ and $Y_t = M_t$; so that $Y_{t+1} = aY_t + (1 - a)Y_t + \Delta M$; $Y_{t+1} = Y_t + \Delta M$.

21. In an accelerator-multiplier model a necessary condition for $Y_t > Y_{t-1}$ is that $\beta(Y_{t-1} - Y_{t-2}) > (1 - a)Y_{t-1}$. We posit an arithmetical increase in the money supply per period of $\Delta M$ so that the available financing is $(1 - a)Y_{t-1} + \Delta M$: hence if $\beta(Y_{t-1} - Y_{t-2}) > (1 - a)Y_{t-1} + \Delta M$ then realized investment is $(1 - a)Y_{t-1} + \Delta M$. Hence $Y_t = Y_{t-1} + \Delta M$ so that $c(Y_t - Y_{t+1}) = \beta\Delta M$ which we once again assume $> (1 - a)(Y_{t-1} + \Delta M)$ so that $Y_{t+1} = Y_{t-1} + 2\Delta M$. Eventually $\beta(Y_{t+n} - Y_{t+n-1}) = \beta\Delta M < (1 - a)(Y_{t-1} + n\Delta M) + \Delta M$;

so that $Y_{t+n+1} < Y_{t+n} + \Delta M$; therefore $\beta(Y_{t+n+1} - Y_{t+n}) < \beta(Y_{t+n} - Y_{t+n-1})$ and the accelerator process turns down.

22. Assume $M_{t-1} = Y_{t-1}$ and $M_t = Y_t = \mu_3 M_{t-1} = \mu_3 Y_{t-1}$.

$$\beta(\mu_3 - 1)Y_{t-1} - [(1-a)\mu_3 Y_{t-1} + (\mu_3 - 1)\mu_3 M_{t-1}] \overset{>}{=} 0$$

is necessary for $Y_{t+1} = \mu_3 Y_t$. Therefore $\beta(\mu_3 - 1) - (1-a)\mu_3 - (\mu_3 - 1)\mu_3 - \epsilon = 0$, so that $\mu_3{}^2 - (a+\beta)\mu_3 + \beta + \epsilon = 0$. It follows that

$$\mu_3 = \frac{a + \beta \pm \sqrt{(a+\beta)^2 - 4(\beta+\epsilon)}}{2}.$$

The relevant root is

$$\mu_3 = \frac{a + \beta - \sqrt{(a+\beta)^2 - 4(\beta+\epsilon)}}{2}$$

and if $\epsilon = 0$ (induced investment is equal to *ex ante* saving plus the increase in the money supply), $\mu_3 = \mu_2$; if $\epsilon > 0$ (induced investment greater than *ex ante* saving plus the increase in the money supply) $\mu_3 > \mu_2$. Therefore a rate of growth of the money supply equal to or greater than the smaller root of the accelerator process is a necessary condition for self-sustained growth.

23. This can be demonstrated by noting that $Y_0 = A_1 + A_2$ and $Y_1 = A_1\mu_1 + A_2\mu_2$ and given that $\mu_1 > \mu_2 > \mu_3 > 0$ and $Y_1 = \mu_3 Y_0$ then $A_1 = Y_0 - A_2$; $\mu_3 Y_0 = (Y_0 - A_2)\mu_1 + A_2\mu_2$ so that

$$\frac{Y_0(\mu_3 - \mu_1)}{\mu_2 - \mu_1} = A_2.$$

As $Y_0 > 0$, $\mu_3 - \mu_1 < 0$ and $\mu_2 - \mu_1 < 0$, $A_2 > 0$.

Also $A_2 = Y_0 - A_1$, $\mu_3 Y_0 = A_1\mu_1 + (Y_0 - A_1)\mu_2$ so that

$$\frac{Y_0(\mu_3 - \mu_2)}{\mu_1 - \mu_2} = A_1.$$

As $Y_0 > 0$, $\mu_3 - \mu_2 < 0$ and $\mu_1 - \mu_2 > 0$, $A_1 < 0$.

$A_1$ the coefficient of the dominant root $\mu_1$ is negative. As $A_1\mu_1 + A_2\mu_2 > A_1 + A_2$ and $\mu_1 > \mu_2$ it follows that $|A_2| > |A_1|$. However in time $A_1\mu_1{}^t + A_2\mu_2 t$ will be $< 0$, so income must turn down.

24. That is, the Harrod-Domar case of steady growth can be the result of appropriate monetary conditions.

## 12

The Integration
of Simple Growth
and Cycle Models

## Introduction

Various ceiling models of cycles or cyclical growth have appeared.[1] In all except one, Kurihara's model, the rate of growth of the ceiling is exogenous. However, the saving and investing that takes place as income is at or below the ceiling implies that the ceiling grows. This paper investigates the conditions under which the rate of growth of ceiling income, as generated by the demand-determined division of income between investment and consumption, is sufficiently large that self-sustained growth can take place.

Existing econometric income models can be divided into two broad classes: short-run forecasting and long-run growth. The short-run forecasting models are basically extensions of the simple Keynesian aggregate demand-determining models. The long-run growth models assume that sufficient aggregate demand always exists and investigate the implications of various patterns of input changes for the growth of capacity.

In many ways, the most interesting analytical and forecasting range is neither the very short run nor the very long run. An intermediate horizon, of ten to fifteen years, is of great practical interest for economic policy, for this is the time span that encompasses the possibility of major or deep depression cycles. Although it is legitimate in constructing short-run forecasting models to ignore the impact of investment upon productive capacity and of finance upon the stock of financial instruments outstanding, over a

Reprinted from Michael J. Brennan, ed., *Patterns of Market Behavior, Essays in Honor of Philip Taft*, by permission of University Press of New England. © 1965 by Brown University.

ten- or fifteen-year period these small changes will cumulate and be of decisive importance in determining system behavior. On the other hand, the standard strategy in constructing long-run models is to assume that the impact of financial variables can wash out. Thus, both practical and theoretical possibilities open up when an intermediate horizon is adopted.

Recent work in the long waves in economic growth rates[2] and on mild and deep depression cycles[3] also indicate that a complete model of the income-determining process that can be iterated to generate a ten- to fifteen-year time series is of interest.

Both the short-run and the long-run models are one-sided, in that they are concerned with either aggregate demand or aggregate supply, and incomplete, in that they do not include, in any deep sense, monetary and financial phenomena. Friedman and Schwartz[4] have imputed the observed pattern of cycles to the behavior of quite narrowly defined money; Tobin,[5] implicitly, and Minsky,[6] explicitly, have examined the implications of financial factors for the longer waves. Aside from the previously mentioned paper by Kurihara, scant attention has been paid to how the productive capacity ceiling is generated, or to the interaction of the production ceiling with demand determination. In this short paper we shall undertake only a part of the total analytical work, and we shall essentially ignore the monetary-financial feedbacks in the growth process. What will be undertaken is to integrate aggregate demand and supply determination in an income model.

Special attention will be paid to those conditions which must be satisfied if self-sustained growth is to take place. Our results show that self-sustained growth is not likely, except as an intermittent phenomenon, unless inflation succeeds in curtailing consumption, or technological progress, whether embodied or disembodied, raises the rate of growth of ceiling income. With a sufficiently rapid rate of growth of ceiling income, the ceiling constraints will not necessarily trigger a downturn. Thus, once again, we have to turn to the characteristics of the aggregate demand-determining relation to generate a downturn. In the conclusion it is suggested that if the coefficient of induced investment decreases as a result of financial changes, a downturn can take place because the rate of growth of ceiling income needed to maintain growth increases. That is, as a self-sustained growth process matures, it becomes necessary to run faster in order to stay in the same place.

## The ingredients

A simple income model that allows for both the behavior of aggregate demand and supply can be built out of well-known ingredients. To be precise, the model that will be discussed here consists of:

(1) a demand generating relation which is the familiar Hansen-Samuelson[7] accelerator-multiplier model,

(2) a maximum supply (or productive capacity or ceiling income) generating relation derived from the Harrod-Domar[8] growth models,

(3) a minimum supply (or floor income) generating relation which is based on the assumption that there exists (a) a part of consumption (and perhaps investment) demand which is independent of current income, although not necessarily of past incomes or of the value of the capital stock, and (b) a maximum to the disinvestment that can take place per period, which is related to the size of the capital stock and hence to the maximum supply.

(4) a reconciliation relation which states that actual income equals aggregate demand unless aggregate demand exceeds the maximum aggregate supply or falls below the minimum aggregate supply, in which case actual income will equal the appropriate aggregate supply.

Due to our present interest in self-sustained growth, the implications of assumption (3) will be ignored. This will enable us to simplify our demand-determining functions and write these as homogeneous relations. In another paper,[9] I have examined how the nonhomogeneous portions of these equations affect both the interval of time for which self-sustained growth can take place, if the ceiling is not growing rapidly enough to sustain growth permanently, and the depth of the depression.

Self-sustained growth takes place when actual income and maximum supply income grow without the existence of any exogenous growth stimulating factor, i.e., an internally sustained state of steady growth. Within the framework of the Hansen-Samuelson plus Harrod-Domar integrated model under discussion, this means that the maximum aggregate supply is growing at a sufficiently high rate so that, with actual income equal to this maximum supply income, the demand induced by the achieved level and rate of change of income is sufficient to utilize fully the increasing productive capacity.

Standing by itself, the Hansen-Samuelson model states that income is determined by aggregate demand. In periods when demand is not constrained by aggregate supply, this Keynesian assumption is valid, especially if the nonhomogeneous part of the consumption function depends upon wealth which, of course, is a reflection of the economy's capital stock. With this interpretation of the Hansen-Samuelson model, the consumption function of this part of the integrated model is said to determine *ex ante* consumption, and the accelerator based investment function is interpreted as determining *ex ante* investment.

The second-order difference equation of the Hansen-Samuelson model provides a simple framework, one that yields the variety of time series necessary for cyclical analysis and also the possibility of a *one-shot* turning point based upon initial conditions, which is vital for our analysis.

We assume that at any date the maximum available supply depends upon the existing capital stock. This capital stock changes by the amount of net investment. The rate of change of aggregate supply depends upon the net investment that occurs, and its productive efficiency. This obviously means that the saving coefficient of the Harrod-Domar part of the integrated model is an *ex post* saving coefficient.

The productive efficiency of investment put into place relates the change in aggregate supply to the change in capital stock. As such it is an incremental output/capital coefficient. The way in which the Harrod-Domar growth model is typically written focuses attention on the reciprocal of the output/capital coefficient, the capital-output ratio. This way of writing the productive efficiency of investment makes it easy to assume that the productive efficiency of investment in the aggregate supply-determining relation is the reciprocal of the coefficient of induced investment in the demand-determining relation.

The coefficients of induced investment and of the productive efficiency of investment are two quite different things. The coefficient of induced investment—the accelerator coefficient in the relation that determines *ex ante* investment—is in part based upon the productive efficiency of investment, but it is also related to the willingness of investors to take risks and the terms upon which investors can finance their endeavors. In spite of this recognition of the difference between the coefficients of induced investment and the productive efficiency of investment, we will initially assume that they are equal. This enables us to focus on the extent to which adjustments in consumption make it possible for self-sustained growth to occur.

The reconciliation relation, as used here, is a purely formal assertion that supply is, if necessary, an effective constraint. The really deep economics in any ceiling model focus on how supply is rationed. Whether consumption or investment demand, or both in varying degrees, are cut back is a result of market processes.

The model as set out here is not sufficiently complete to cover these phenomena. The function of financial markets is to ration investment funds. The available nominal supply of investment funds depends upon the functioning of the financial system. The ability of the financial system to constrain consumption depends upon the existing and desired portfolios of households. An integration of financial phenomena with the real demand- and supply-generating relations would be necessary to enable us to deal more precisely with the reconciliation relations.

We can look at the rationing process a bit more closely even without constructing a formal model of the financial system. In the diagram below, Log $Y_c$ is the ceiling income and at each date $t$, aggregate demand is greater than the ceiling, i.e., the ceiling is an effective determinant of income. Given that the demand for consumption goods is determined by income of the $t$-1st period, consumers have the "cash in hand" to finance, at existing prices, the purchase of the consumption component of $Y_d$. However, investors, independent of the separation between saving and investing units, have to finance investment in excess of planned saving.

This presumably requires changes that increase velocity or the money supply. To the extent that investment can be cut back to the difference between productive capacity and planned consumption without any rise in interest rates, the income-generating process need not be affected. However, if the rationing phenomenon results in a rise in interest rates (or its equivalent, a rise in the price of investment goods as against consumption goods), then the income-generating process will be affected. If we make the Keynesian assumption that consumption demand is independent of interest rates, but assume that investment demand, and hence the $\beta$ coefficient, depends upon interest rates, then a rising set of interest rates will lower the $\beta$ coefficient. A fall in $\beta$ raises the minimum rate of growth of capacity that leads to demand's rising faster than capacity, when income is at the ceiling. Thus the reconciliation process can affect the effect of the ceiling by raising the rate of growth required to sustain growth.

The assumption that changes in the size of the capital stock are

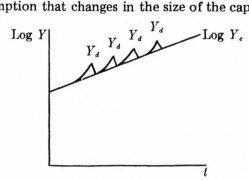

the sole determinants of the rate of growth of productive capacity is, of course, heroic. The alternative is to adopt a production function which allows for factor substitution and relate ceiling output growth to the growth of the labor force as well as capital equipment. However, once we assume that technological change occurs, the growth of capacity will not be dependent solely upon the growth of capital stock. As is usual, the technological change coefficient becomes a catchall that allows not only for technical progress, but also for differential growth rates of the labor force and capital and the improvement of the labor force due to education, public health, etc.

As a result, within a Harrod-Domar framework for the growth of capacity, we allow for both embodied and disembodied technical change. Embodied technical change works by way of the capital put into place and, in our formulation, will result in a rise in the productive efficiency of investment. Disembodied technical change results in a rise in productive capacity that is independent of the amount of investment put into place. Such "progress" is as inevitable and well-nigh as universal as the passage of time; and, like time, it covers a multitude of sins.

## The formal model

The formal model can be written as:

(1) $$Y_n^s = Y_{n-1}^s + \frac{I_{n-1}^a}{\bar{\bar{\beta}}}$$

(2) $$C_n^d = a Y_{n-1}^a$$

(3) $$C_n^s = \bar{a} Y_n^s$$

(4) $$C_n^a = \lambda_1 C_n^d + \lambda_2 C_n^s$$

(5) $$I_n^d = \beta(Y_{n-1}^a - Y_{n-2}^a)$$

(6) $$I_n^s = (1 - \bar{a}) Y_n^s$$

(7) $$I_n^a = \lambda_1 I_n^d + \lambda_2 I_n^s$$

(8) $$Y_n^a = C_n^a + I_n^a$$

(9) $$\lambda_1 = 1 \quad \text{if} \quad Y_n^d = C_n^d + I_n^d \leqslant Y_n^s$$
$$= 0 \quad \text{otherwise}$$

(10) $$\lambda_1 + \lambda_2 = 1.$$

$C$, $I$, and $Y$ have their usual meanings, the superscript $a$ means actual, $d$ means demand and $s$ = supply, $a$ = *ex ante* marginal (= average in these models) propensity to consume, $\beta$ = *ex ante* coefficient of induced investment, $\bar{a}$ is the *ex post* marginal (= average in these models) propensity to consume, and $1/\bar{\beta}$ = *ex post* productive efficiency of investment (i.e., the marginal output per unit of investment coefficient). The switching coefficients $\lambda_1$ and $\lambda_2$ have no interpretation aside from their definition in equations (9) and (10). The subscripts $n'n_{-1}$ on $Y$, $C$, and $I$ refer to the dates.

## Behavior of aggregate supply

Equation (1) states that the change in aggregate supply depends upon the investment put into place. Equation (1) plus equation (6) yields us the familiar Harrod-Domar growth model where the rate of growth depends upon the saving and the investment coefficients. For we have

$$Y^s_n = Y^s_{n-1} + \frac{(1-\bar{a})}{\bar{\beta}} Y^s_{n-1}$$

(11)
$$\bar{\nu} = Y^s_n / Y^s_{n-1} = 1 + \frac{1-\bar{a}}{\bar{\beta}}$$

and

$$Y^s_n / Y^s_{n-2} = Y^s_n / Y^s_{n-1} \cdot Y^s_{n-1} / Y^s_{n-2} = \left(\left(1 + \frac{1-\bar{a}}{\bar{\beta}}\right)\left(1 + \frac{1-\bar{a}}{\bar{\beta}}\right)\right) = \bar{\nu}^2 ,$$

so that

(12)
$$Y^s_n = Y_0 \bar{\nu}^n$$

where $\bar{\nu}$ is the rate of growth of aggregate supply when income actually equals supply income. The above is the familiar result: that the rate of growth of income is a constant, given that the *ex post* saving coefficient and the *ex post* marginal output-capital ratio are constants. This result, of course, holds within our model when $\lambda_2 = 1$. If $\lambda_1 = 1$, then

$$Y^s_n = Y^s_{n-1} + \frac{\beta(Y^a_{n-2} - Y^a_{n-3})}{\bar{\beta}} ,$$

$$\nu^s_{n-1} = Y^s_n / Y^s_{n-1} = 1 + \frac{\beta}{\bar{\beta}} \frac{Y^a_{n-1}}{Y^s_{n-1}} \left(\frac{Y^a_{n-2} - Y^a_{n-3}}{Y^a_{n-1}}\right) ,$$

$$(13) \qquad \nu^s_{n-1} = 1 + \frac{\beta}{\bar{\beta}} \frac{Y^a_{n-1}}{Y^s_{n-1}} \frac{\nu^a_{n-3} - 1}{\nu^a_{n-3} \nu^a_{n-2}}$$

The rate of growth of the maximum available supply depends upon:

(1) the ratio of the coefficient of induced investment to the capital-output ratio,

(2) the ratio of actual income to the maximum aggregate supply, and

(3) the rate of change of actual income in the previous two periods.

As (2) and (3) are variables, the rate of growth of maximum supply income is also a variable. Of course $\nu^a_{n-3}$ can be less than 1, which means that the maximum supply income can decrease.

Note that as long as

$$\beta(Y^a_{n-2} - Y^a_{n-3}) < (1 - \bar{a})Y^s_{n-1} \ , \quad \nu^s_{n-1} < \bar{\nu},$$

there is no way that lost growth in productive capacity can be made up unless $\nu^s_{n-1} < \bar{\nu}$ implies that subsequent $1/\beta$'s will be larger than they otherwise would have been.

## Behavior of aggregate demand

Equation (2) plus equation (5), together with a definition of income as $C^d + I^d$, yields the Hansen-Samuelson accelerator-multiplier model. As is well known, the characteristics of the time series which this model will generate depend upon the values of $a$ and $\beta$. We assume that normally a certain minimum buoyancy of entrepreneurs and investors exists so that the coefficient of induced investment is sufficiently greater than 1 so that in the solution equation

$$(14) \qquad Y_n = A_1 \mu_1^n + A_2 \mu_2^n,$$

we have that $\mu_1 > \mu_2 > 1$. The values of $\mu_1$ and $\mu_2$ are

$$(15) \qquad \begin{aligned} \mu_1 &= \frac{a + \beta + \sqrt{(a + \beta)^2 - 4\beta}}{2} \ , \\ \mu_2 &= \frac{a + \beta - \sqrt{(a + \beta)^2 - 4\beta}}{2} \ . \end{aligned}$$

The values of $A_1$ and $A_2$ are determined by the initial conditions.

Assuming that the two initial conditions are $Y_0, Y_1 > 0$ and that $Y_1 = \tau Y_0, \tau > 1$. We then have

$$Y_0 = A_1 + A_2$$

$$\tau Y_0 = A_1 \mu_1 + A_2 \mu_2$$

so that

(16)
$$\begin{cases} A_1 = \dfrac{\tau - \mu_2}{\mu_1 - \mu_2}\ Y_0 \\[3mm] A_2 = \dfrac{\mu_1 - \tau}{\mu_1 - \mu_2}\ Y_0 \end{cases}$$

if $\mu_1 > \tau \geqslant \mu_2$, $A_1 \geqslant 0$, $A_2 > 0$; however, if $\mu_1 > \mu_2 > \tau$, then $A_1 < 0$. As $A_1$ is the coefficient of the larger root, $A_1 < 0$ implies that in time $A_1 \mu_1^n + A_2 \mu_2^n < 0$, so that the "explosion" of income will be in the direction opposite from the initial displacement. Even if the roots of the solution equation are real and greater than 1, the time series generated by the solution equation can generate one turning point. The cause of this turning point lies in the initial conditions. If the initial conditions do not supply a sufficient push to income, a turning point will result. The minimum push that will yield a monotonic explosive series is given by $\mu_2$, the smaller root of the solution equation.

*Behavior of the integrated model*

We can now sketch how the integrated model operates. The essential question is what happens when demand income exceeds supply income. As the pattern of behavior of the model is independent of where we begin, we can in all generality assume that the two initial incomes, $Y_0$ and $Y_1$, are both less than the maximum supply income and that

$$Y_1 / Y_0 = \tau > \mu_2$$

so that a particular solution of the income-generating function $Y_n^d = A_1 \mu_1^n + A_2 \mu_2^n$ with $A_1$, $A_2 > 0$ and $\mu_1 > \mu_2 > 1$ will be set in motion to generate future demands. As long as $Y_n^d < Y_n^s$, actual income will be determined by this particular income-generating relation. However, as $A_1 > 0$, the rate of change of actual income will in time approach $\mu_1$, the larger of the two roots. But values of $a$, $\beta$ which lead to a $\mu_2$ in the neighborhood of achieved rates of growth, generate a $\mu_1$ that is far larger than observed rates of growth. Hence in time

$$Y_n^d = A_1 \mu_1^n + A_2 \mu_2^n > Y_n^s$$

will result. This means that actual income will be $Y_n^s$ and all of demand will not be realized.

Before examining how the reconciliation process is carried out when $Y_n^d > Y_n^s$, and noting the implications of some reconciliations for the generation of self-sustained growth, it is best if we interpret the switch that occurs when $Y_n^d > Y_n^s$. $Y_n^d$ is the result of a self-sustaining demand-generating process based upon the structural characteristics of the economy and some initial conditions. Such an income-generating process once set in motion will not generate actual incomes for all times in the future. The path of actual income will be affected by exogenous events and constraints as well as the structural elements and history embodied in the ruling demand-generating relation. These exogeneous events and constraints are interpreted as determining new initial conditions for a particular demand-determining relation that will determine aggregate demand as long as no external event or constraint prevents this demand income from being realized. Hence whenever $Y_n^a \neq Y_n^d$, $Y_n^a$ and $Y_{n-1}^a$ are new initial conditions for a demand-determining relation. Within our framework this new demand-determining relation will determine actual incomes until the incomes so determined are inconsistent with the supply constraints, for we are ignoring external shocks in this paper.

When $Y^d$ is inconsistent with $Y^s$, then actual values of $C$ and/or $I$ will differ from their demand or *ex ante* values. The problem now becomes to what extent the cutback $Y^d$ to $Y^s$ takes the form of a reduction of consumption or of a reduction of investment. Equations (3) and (6), which tell us how income, when it is equal to aggregate supply, is divided between consumption and investment, do not describe how the reconciliation process affects consumption and investment.

When $Y_n^d > Y_n^s$, then $Y_n^a = Y_n^s$. This means that new initial conditions, $Y_n^s$ and $Y_{n-1}^a$, determine $A_1$ and $A_2$ in a specific demand-generating relation. If $Y_n^s / Y_{n-1}^a < \mu_2$, then $A_1 < 0$ and a single turning point will be generated, whereas if $Y_n^s / Y_{n-1}^a \geqslant \mu_2$, then $A_1 \geqslant 0$ and $Y_{n+1}^d / Y_n^s > Y_{n+1}^s / Y_n^s$ will be generated so that $Y_{n+1}^s$ becomes the $n + 1^{st}$ period's actual income. In this case we know that $Y_{n+1}^s / Y_n^s = \bar{\nu}$ and steady growth will take place if $\bar{\nu} \geqslant \mu_2$ and a single turning point will be generated if $\mu_2 > \bar{\nu}$. Steady growth is the result of setting off new demand-generating processes each period which in the next period generate demand that is equal or greater than supply, whereas the turning point with the accompanying fall of income below supply occurs if the demand-generating process leads to a smaller increase in demand than in supply.

Hence, whether steady growth or a cyclical downturn occurs when the available supply becomes a determinant of actual income depends upon the rate of growth of aggregate supply; this model is a ceiling model of cycles and growth. However, as aggregate supply is growing, it is the rate of growth of aggregate supply rather than the existence of some fixed ceiling to productive capacity that is the critical factor. As there is no doubt that the rate of growth of supply that can be sustained when the economy is at or close to full employment is lower than the rate of growth of income that does take place when the economy is recovering from a depression, a decrease in the rate of growth of actual income occurs when income approaches aggregate supply income. This decrease in the rate of growth of actual income is the critical constraint in this model.[10]

### The possibility of self-sustained growth

The rate of growth of aggregate supply is given by

$$\bar{\nu} = 1 + \frac{1 - \bar{a}}{\bar{\beta}}$$

and the lower root of the solution equation is given by

$$\mu_2 = \frac{a + \beta - \sqrt{(a + \beta)^2 - \beta}}{2}.$$

From these equations we get:

(17)     $$\beta = \frac{\mu_2 (\mu_2 - a)}{\mu_2 - 1},$$

(18)     $$\bar{\beta} = \frac{1 - \bar{a}}{\bar{\nu} - 1},$$

which are straight lines in $a, \beta$ and $\bar{a}, \bar{\beta}$. (Given that $\mu_2 > 1$, the domain of $a$ and $\beta$ is restricted.) If we assume $a = \bar{a}, \beta = \bar{\beta}, 0 < a < 1$, and $\beta > 0$, then for any $a, \beta$ pair $\mu_2 > \bar{\nu}$; that is, the rate of growth of productive capacity will be below the minimum rate of growth of income that must take place if self-sustained growth is to occur. This is illustrated in Figure 1. For example, at point $A$, $a \approx .92$ and $\beta \approx 2.825$ yield $\mu_2 = 1.05$ and $\bar{\nu} = 1.03$. Hence, if $Y_n^d = Y_n^s$, $Y_{n-1}^d = Y_{n-1}^s$ the demand-generating relation set into motion with $Y_n^s, Y_{n-1}^s$ as initial conditions will have $A_1 < 0$ which implies that growth will not be self-sustained.

For self-sustained growth to occur, it is necessary for $a$ and $\beta$ to be "greater" than $\bar{a}$ and $\bar{\beta}$. For example, if $a$ and $\beta$ are such that they lie along the line $\mu_2 = 1.04$, then $\bar{a}$ and $\bar{\beta}$ must be such that they lie on or below the line $\bar{\nu} = 1.04$ if self-sustained growth is to occur. In Figure 1, self-sustained growth would be attainable if the

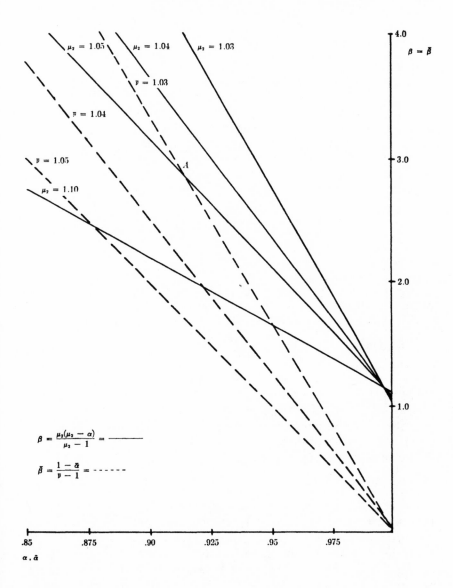

Figure 1

set of lines $\bar{\nu} = 1.03$, etc. could be shifted upward so that for every $\bar{\nu} = \mu_2$ the line for $\bar{\nu}$ would lie above the line for $\mu_2$. For this to occur, some combination of factors that tend to yield $\bar{a} < a$ and $\bar{\beta} < \beta$ must be operative.

### Ex-ante and ex-post consumptions

The assumption that $a = \bar{a}$, given that $C_n^s = \bar{a} Y_n^s$ and $C_n^a = a Y_{n-1}^s$ and that $Y_n^s = \bar{\nu} Y_{n-1}^s$, implies that $C_n^s = C_n^a > C_n^d$. The rise in income between the $n^{th}$ and the $n - 1^{st}$ period result in *ex post* consumption being larger than *ex ante* consumption. As supply income effectively determines income because $Y_n^d > Y_n^s$ and $C_n^a > C_n^d$, the entire burden of adjustment is upon investment.

Rather than assume that *ex post* consumption exceeds *ex ante* consumption, we can assume that *ex post* consumption equals *ex ante* consumption. If this occurs,

$$Y_n^s = Y_{n-1}^s + \frac{Y_{n-1}^s - a Y_{n-2}^s}{\bar{\beta}},$$

$$\nu_n = 1 + \frac{1 - a/\bar{\nu}}{\bar{\beta}}.$$

From this we get

(19)
$$\bar{\beta} = \frac{\bar{\nu} - a}{\bar{\nu}(\bar{\nu} - 1)}.$$

As is illustrated in Figure 2, the lines for equation (19) also lie below the lines for equation (17), so that for any given $a$, $\beta = \bar{\beta}$ pair $\mu_2 > \bar{\nu}$. Even if *ex post* consumption is restricted to *ex ante* consumption, the adjustment process still results in *ex post* investment being lower than *ex ante* investment. The rate of growth of supply that results is too low to maintain self-sustained growth.

### The impact of inflation

In order to have $\bar{\nu} \geqslant \mu_2$ it is necessary that when $Y^d > Y^s$ (recall that we are assuming that $\beta = \bar{\beta}$), *ex post* consumption be less than *ex ante* consumption. One way in which consumers can be *forced* to lower their consumption below the *ex ante* level is for consumer prices to rise; this is, of course, particularly true if a large portion of consumers use all their income for consumption and have no means by which they can spend more than their income. Writing $p^*$ for $p_n/p_{n-1}$, we have

$$\bar{\nu} = 1 + \frac{Y_{n-1}^s - \dfrac{a Y_{n-2}^s}{p^*}}{Y_{n-1}^s \bar{\beta}}$$

$$= 1 + \frac{1 - a/\bar{\nu}p^*}{\bar{\beta}}$$

so that

(20)
$$\bar{\beta} = \frac{\bar{\nu}p^* - a}{\bar{\nu}p^*(\bar{\nu} - 1)} .$$

Assuming $p^* > 1$, there exist values of $a$ and $\beta$ which generate rates of growth of aggregate supply that are larger than the lower root of the demand-generating relation. This means that if inflation that decreases consumption below *ex ante* consumption occurs, self-sustained growth can take place. Even though consumption is lowered below *ex ante* consumption by inflation, with a constant rate of increase in consumers' prices, real consumption will still be growing:

$$\left( \frac{aY^s_{n-2}}{p^*} \middle/ \frac{aY^s_{n-3}}{p^*} = \bar{\nu} > 1 \right).$$

In Figure 3, point $A$ shows that if $a \approx .875, \beta \approx 3.675$ then $\mu_2 = 1.05$ and $\bar{\nu} = 1.05$ with $p^* = 1.02$. That is, if *ex post* consumption is approximately 98 percent of *ex ante* consumption so that $Y^s_{n-1} - .98aY^s_{n-2}$ can be invested, real supply will grow at 5 percent. Points $B$ and $C$ have similar interpretations.

It is doubtful that in the United States, as now organized, inflation is an efficient or an effective way of depressing consumption in order that investment be sufficient to generate a growth rate of income large enough to satisfy the conditions for self-sustained growth.

*The effect of technological change*

We can distinguish two types of technical change. Disembodied technical change, where productive capacity increases independently of investment, and embodied technical change, where investment is the carrier of technical change.

*Disembodied technical change.* To take technical change into account, we write

(1')
$$Y^s_n = \tau Y^s_{n-1} + \frac{I^a_{n-1}}{\bar{\beta}} , \qquad \tau > 1.$$

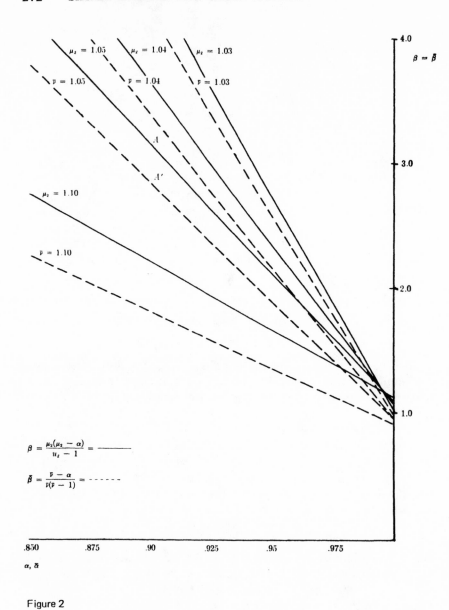

$$\beta = \frac{\mu_2(\mu_2 - \alpha)}{u_2 - 1} = \text{————}$$

$$\bar{\beta} = \frac{\bar{\nu} - \alpha}{\bar{\nu}(\bar{\nu} - 1)} = \text{-----}$$

Figure 2

*Ex post C = Ex ante C*

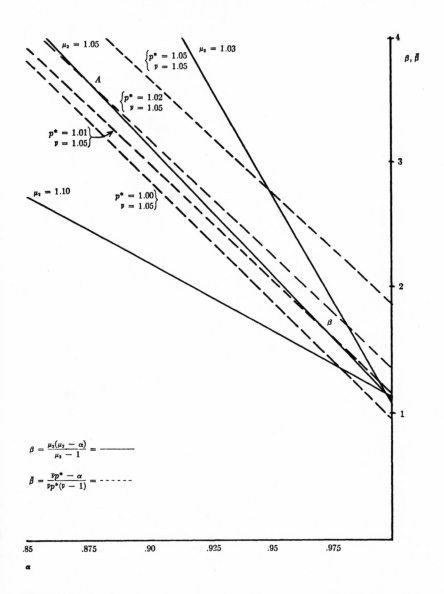

Figure 3

Effects of Inflation

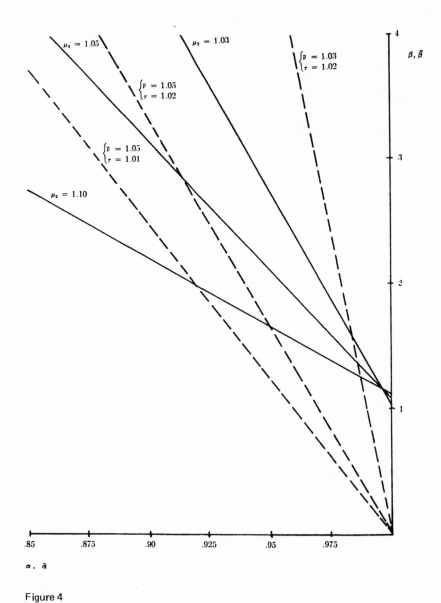

Figure 4

Disembodied Technological Change

This results, when income is at the ceiling, in

$$\frac{Y^s_n}{Y^s_{n-1}} = \tau + \frac{1 - \bar{a}}{\bar{\beta}}$$

and, with less than capacity income, in

$$\frac{Y^s_n}{Y^s_{n-1}} = \tau + \frac{\beta}{\bar{\beta}} \frac{Y^a_{n-2} - Y^a_{n-3}}{Y^s_{n-1}} \ .$$

The rate of growth of ceiling income, when income is at the ceiling, is

$$\bar{\nu}_1 = \tau + \frac{1 - \bar{a}}{\bar{\beta}}$$

which yields

$$\bar{\beta} = \frac{1 - \bar{a}}{\bar{\nu} - \tau} \ .$$

As is shown in Figure 4, with a 2 percent per year growth in productive capacity due to disembodied technical change, it is possible with $a = \bar{a}$, $\beta = \bar{\beta}$ for the rate of growth of ceiling income $\bar{\nu}$ to be greater than the critical value $\mu_2$ derived from the demand-generating relation.

*Embodied technical change.* We will assume that embodied technical change results in $\bar{\beta} < \beta$; i.e., the productive efficiency of investment is higher than "expected" because of technological progress.

In Figure 2, note that if $a = .9$ and *ex post* consumption equals *ex ante* consumption, $\beta = 3.15$ and $\bar{\beta} = 2.85$ will yield $\mu_2 = \bar{\nu} = 1.05$, i.e., it takes but a small decline in $\bar{\beta}$ below $\beta$ to satisfy the conditions for self-sustained growth.

## Conclusions

Given that technological change, whether embodied or disembodied, takes place, and that the effect of technological change is to increase the rate of growth of ceiling income beyond that which would result just from accumulations, it has been shown that the ceiling income can grow fast enough so that self-sustained growth is possible. Therefore, in a technically dynamic world, we have to look beyond productive capacity constraints to explain the observed pattern of cyclical growth.

The coefficient of induced investment $\beta$ is not a technical production function characteristic as is $\bar{\beta}$, but rather reflects investors' and entrepreneurs' attitudes toward risk. Thus, $\beta$ would be a variable that depends, at least in part, on the menu of financial instruments available to asset owners and the liability structure of investing units.

In the demand-generating relation, the smaller root of the solution equation was the critical value for sustaining growth. However, the derivative of this coefficient, $\mu_2$, with respect to $\beta$, the coefficient of induced investment is negative.[11] Anything that tends to lower $\beta$ will raise $\mu_2$ and thus increase the minimum rate of growth of ceiling income that will sustain growth.

Cumulative unbalanced changes in the menu of available financial instruments take place during a period of self-sustained growth. The unbalanced nature of financial developments should affect the relative interest rates at which the public and financial institutions are willing to hold their available stock of primary liabilities; this, together with the fact of increasing risk as the independence of the expected performance of financial assets decreases,[12] will feed back upon the willingness to invest. Thus the rate of growth of ceiling income (including the effect of technical change) that is sufficient to sustain growth with one set of portfolios can become inadequate with another. A cyclical growth pattern can emerge due to cumulative changes that affect demand rather than from any necessary insufficiency of the rate of growth capacity.

It seems evident that the integration of ceiling models of growth with the financial flows that accompany growth is a fruitful research path in any attempt to develop econometric models that have the interesting intermediate time horizon.

## Notes

1. R. M. Goodwin, "The Non-Linear Accelerator and the Persistence of Business Cycles," *Econometrica*, January 1951; J. R. Hicks, *A Contribution to the Theory of the Trade Cycle* (New York: Oxford University Press, 1949); K. Kurihara, "An Endogenous Model of Cyclical Growth," *Oxford Economic Papers*, October 1960; R. C. L. Mathews, "A Note on Crawling Along the Ceiling," *Review of Economic Studies* XXVII (1) No. 72 (October 1959); H. P. Minsky, "A Linear Model of Cyclical Growth," *Review of Economics and Statistics*, XLI (May 1959), reprinted in R. A. Gordon and L. R. Klein, *Readings in Business Cycles* (Homewood, Ill.: Richard D. Irwin, 1965).

2. M. Abromowitz, United States Congress, 86th Congress, Joint Economic Committee, *Employment, Growth and Price Levels, Hearings Part 2, Historical and Comperative Rate of Production, Productivity and Prices.*

3. M. Friedman and S. J. Schwartz, "Money and Business Cycles," *Review of Economics and Statistics*, Supplement (February 1963), p. 55.

4. *Ibid.*

5. J. Tobin, "An Essay on Principles of Debt Management," in *Fiscal and*

*Debt Management Policies*, Commission on Money and Credit (Englewood Cliffs, N.J.: Prentice-Hall, Inc., 1964).

6. H. P. Minsky, "Financial Crisis, Financial Systems and the Performance of the Economy," *Private Capital Markets*, Commission on Money and Credit (Englewood Cliffs, N.J.: Prentice-Hall, Inc., 1964).

7. P. A. Samuelson, "Interactions Between the Multiplier Analysis and the Principle of Acceleration," *Review of Economics and Statistics* XXI (May 1939). Reprinted in *Readings in Business Cycles* (Philadelphia: Blakiston and Co., 1944).

8. R. F. Harrod, *Toward a Dynamic Economics* (London: Macmillan, 1948); E. D. Domar, *Essays in the Theory of Economic Growth* (New York: Oxford University Press, 1957).

9. Minsky, "A Linear Model of Cyclical Growth."

10. The formal apparatus is set out in Minsky, *ibid.*

11. Minsky, *ibid.*, p. 137, footnote 12.

12. Tobin, *op. cit.*

## 13

*Private Sector*
*Assets Management and*
*the Effectiveness of*
*Monetary Policy:*
*Theory and Practice*

## I. Introduction

The controversy about how money affects the economy is deeper and more fundamental than is evident in the current literature. From the current literature it seems as if the dispute is over either the definition of money and the specifications of the variables in a demand function for money or whether stable monetary growth is a) capable of being defined, b) obtainable, and c) superior, as a stabilization technique, to active discretionary monetary and fiscal policies.[1] In truth the above are peripheral or secondary issues. The fundamental issue in monetary theory is whether a capitalist economy is inherently stable or whether, due to its very nature, it is unavoidably unstable; that is whether unsustainable booms and deep depressions are due to essential characteristics of capitalism.

Financial crises, domestic and international, have been associated with capitalism throughout its history. This does not prove that they are inherent in capitalism——the crises of history may have been due to a combination of ignorance, human error, and avoidable attributes of the financial system.

One polar view in the stability of capitalism is represented by the Chicago School. An article of faith, nowhere better stated than in Henry Simons' famous article "Rules Versus Authorities. . ." [22], is that serious depressions are due to man-made imperfections in the financial system. Friedman and Schwartz argue that

Abridged by the author for this volume. From *The Journal of Finance*, Vol. XXIV, No. 2, May 1969, by arrangement with the publisher.

I want to thank Maurice Townsend, Lawrence Ritter, and R. C. D. Rowan for helpful comments and constructive suggestions.

"The monetary collapse [of the 1930s] was not the inescapable consequence of other forces, but rather a largely independent factor which exerted a powerful influence of the course of events. The failure of the Federal Reserve System to prevent the collapse reflected not the impotence of monetary policy but rather the particular policies followed by the monetary authorities and, in smaller degree, the particular monetary arrangements in existence" [10, p. 4].

In this "Chicago" view there exists a financial system, different from that which ruled at the time of crisis but nonetheless consistent with capitalism, which would make serious financial disturbances impossible. It is the task of monetary analysis to design such a financial system, and of monetary policy to execute the design. In Simons' view this depression-proof good financial society required a radical restructuring of the financial system. In Friedman's view the establishment of the good financial society requires only the adoption of a stable money growth rule by the Federal Reserve System, given that the reform represented by the introduction of deposit insurance has already taken place.[2]

The alternative polar view, which I call unreconstructed Keynesian, is that capitalism is inherently flawed, being prone to booms, crises, and depressions. This instability, in my view, is due to characteristics the financial system must possess if it is to be consistent with full-blown capitalism. Such a financial system will be capable of both generating signals that induce an accelerating desire to invest and of financing that accelerating investment.[3]

An accelerating pace of investment is associated with high animal spirits of both entrepreneurs and financiers. In the absence of an infinitely elastic supply of finance from the monetary system, the accelerating investment is financed by velocity-increasing, liquidity-decreasing portfolio transformations. In addition, positions in the stock of existing real and financial assets are refinanced by similar portfolio transformations, so that over time, liability structures emerge which can be serviced only if the euphoric expectations are fulfilled. In order to finance the increasing pace of investment and the more complicated liability structures, rising interest rates are required to induce the successive portfolio adjustments.

These "better terms" on new issues, put out for investment purposes or for refinancing positions in the stock of assets, feed back upon and lower the market value of outstanding long-term debts. The emergence of a taut liability structure means that a not unusual short-fall of cash receipts can lead to a need to make position by selling assets.[4] Rising interest rates mean that the assets available for sale may have market values less than face values. The combination of the transformation of paper losses into realized losses and the downward pressure upon asset prices due to the attempt to make position by selling assets can trigger a financial crisis. This breaks the euphoric expectations and a deep depression will follow unless the central bank effectively acts as lender of last resort and stabilizes asset prices, and fiscal measures offset the initial fall in investment so that a cumulative decline in aggregate demand does not occur.[5]

It is my view that Keynes emphasized the primary importance of financial factors in determining how a capitalist economy functions. I believe this financial interpretation of Keynes is especially evident in Keynes' statement of what the "General Theory" is all about in his rebuttal to Viner's review [Viner, 26, Keynes, 14]. In this rebuttal he emphasized the importance of uncertainty in determining decisions relating to wealth and for the short-run determination of the prices for investment output.[6]

My interpretations of Keynes is not the conventional view which is mainly derived from Hicks' "Mr. Keynes and the Classics," an article which I believe misses Keynes' point completely.[7] However, intellectual history is not our topic; our task is to help formulate a useful framework for analyzing the current behavior of American capitalism and for evaluating the performance of the Federal Reserve System. It is my view that this requires a model which starts with a theory of asset management by private sectors and allows for the development of financial stringency or crisis, as well as for the impact of such a crisis upon system behavior. After the crunch of 1966, the spectre of a great depression once again haunts policymakers.

## II. The portfolio view of asset management

Capitalism requires that financial institutions and instruments exist which permit flexibility in financing. Before the impact and efficacy of money can be traced it is necessary to specify the financial institutions; monetary economics cannot escape being institutional economics. Once the problem of monetary theory is identified as revolving around the financing of positions in the stock of assets and the financing of additions to the stock, then a portfolio or asset-management view of the monetary process is natural. In this view the liability structures of units impose cash flow commitments and these in turn become constraints upon behavior [Tobin, 23; Turvey, 24; Minsky, 17; Duesenberry, 6].

In a portfolio view the impact of an initial monetary disturbance, say following an open-market operation, is the result of changing relative prices among a wide array of financial and real assets. As well-nigh perfect substitutes for items in the existing stock of real assets can be produced, these changing relative prices stimulate or depress production. "At first (following an open market addition to the money supply) the additional money is excessive relative to the other forms of wealth held; the attempt by money holders to exchange their excess balances for other assets raises asset prices and lowers rates of return across the board. The decline in rates thus spreads to all financial and physical assets, so that an increase in the money stock may eventually stimulate new investment in many directions" [Cagen, 4, p. 171].

The transmission process involves production relations in finance, preference systems, and expectations. These are typically assumed to be given and exogenous—or at least to be stable in the short-run. However, if they are at times in fact variable and quickly changeable, they provide for the slippage which makes control of the monetary base or even the money supply an inadequate instrument of economic policy. If they are determined by economic variables, with perhaps discontinuous reactions, then our work, to be useful and interesting, must encompass such relations.

A financial innovation is equivalent to the introduction of a new production technique or a new product. Even though the new may be advantageous, there will be an absorption period in which units experiment with and assimilate the new institution or instrument. The reintroduction of trading in Federal Funds in the 1950s did not see all banks shift immediately to active reserve management; it took six years for the value of wholesale C.D.'s to grow to $20 billion. The ultimate impact upon household cash positions of bank credit cards and redi-credit schemes can only be conjectured at this date.

As a result of the existence of financial innovations and learning, the relation between money—or the monetary base—and economic activity changes. The evidence indicates that differences among countries in income velocity can be explained by the sophistication of the financial system, so that the greater the sophistication the greater the velocity. Thus, during a period in which the financial system is rapidly becoming more sophisticated —financial innovation and the diffusion of innovation is proceeding apace—the rate of increase of economic activity compatible with any rate of increase in the money supply will rise.[8]

The diffusion of innovations is in part a pure learning process. Thus the use of a new instrument may increase at constant or even deteriorating relative prices. However profit opportunities and the threats of losses do affect the willingness to experiment. Both in-novation and the speed of diffusion can be expected to respond to profit opportunities. "Euphoric" investment demand, combined with rising costs in conventional financial channels, will lead, via feedbacks on the potential payoffs to financial innovations, to an expansion in the effective ability to finance activity. This will take place even though some monetary variables will not be affected; monetary policy may be attempting to constrain the economy even though interest rates are constant, and a modest rate of in-crease in the reserve base, or in the money supply, can be associ-ated with a rapid rate of increase in the financing of activity.

Thus a rising interest rate structure may affect the relation be-tween money and income by inducing the economizing of cash holdings within a fixed set of institutions and instruments, by stimulating institutional innovation, and by increasing the rate at which recent innovations are diffused.

It is difficult to disentangle preferences and expectations. They cannot be measured objectively, they relate to the impact of un-certainty upon decisions, and they react in parallel fashion to events.

A portfolio reflects a choice of assets and liabilities made under uncertainty. Uncertainty affects portfolios in two ways: the first is that the expected cash receipts from assets and cash payments due to liabilities are uncertain; the second is that each decision unit has a preference system which embodies its taste for uncer-tainty.[9]

Views as to the future of the world are based upon evaluations of the past. It is easy to accept that expectations of payoffs from assets and payments on account of liabilities are based upon the observed performance of the economy and the particular sector or unit on which the investor, so to say, is betting. In addition tastes for taking chances are affected by observed payoffs to those who have taken chances. Animal spirits are the result of observed bonanzas—even though the typical payoff from chance-taking may be small. The observed rise in loan-deposit and the decline in government securities-deposit ratios of commercial banks can be interpreted as the result of changes in bankers' preference.

Expectations and tastes for uncertainty are affected by success and failure of the economy. Successful functioning results in de-creasing the weight of unfavorable events thus increasing the ex-pected value and decreasing the variance of the payoffs from a contingency. In addition preference systems change; as a result of success, the aversion to risk "decreases." Symmetrically poor performance will decrease expected payoffs and "increase" the aversion to risk.

The curvature of a utility-income preference system is not a genetic trait of persons. It is a product of the behavior of the economy. With no change in the weight attached to possible outcomes the expected utility of an uncertain proposition will vary with a change in the taste for uncertainty.

Although the effect of the past upon expectations may be considered to be continuous, it is possible to interpret history as showing that dramatic changes in the taste for uncertainty have occurred. Dramatic events, in particular financial crises, can be viewed as having quick and marked effects upon tastes for uncertainty. A possible asymmetry in the evolution of preference systems with respect to uncertainty exists. A great crash—such as that of 1929-33 —will lead to a sharp rise in the aversion to risk, and it may take the better part of a generation for this aversion to decrease.[10] However, once the extreme risk aversion is abandoned, the "new view" accepting uncertainty may take place at an accelerating rate, giving rise to booms.

Both the possibility of financial innovations and of rapid changes in preference systems and expectations reflecting events in the economy means that the stimulus for portfolio adjustments may come from the functioning of the economy, not the operations of the authorities. Since the world is not born *de nova* each day, inherited financial and real assets must enter into some unit's position as long as they exist. A rapid increase in the aversion to risk —brought on for example by the experience of a credit crunch— can shift desired portfolios away from layered financial assets toward cash. But the amounts of cash and non-cash (financial and real) assets are virtually fixed in the market period. A rise in the demand for money can only be affected by offering non-cash assets for money. Given fixed supplies of money and other assets, such a shift in the demand for money may lead to a sharp fall in the price of non-cash real and financial assets, so that the market price for secondhand reproducible assets may fall below their current production cost [Keynes, 14].

Thus with a portfolio view of the monetary process it is possible to accept that a state in which causation runs from money to activity rules most of the time and nevertheless to hold that the most interesting economics centers around those perhaps transitory states in which the causation runs from innovations, expectations, and preference systems to activity.

We all are familiar with the Chicago slogan "money matters."

May I suggest an alternative: "Money matters most of the time, at some rare but important times it is all that matters, and sometimes money hardly matters at all." The tasks of monetary theory are to make precise the conditions defining each of these three states, the process of transition from one state to another and to indicate how transitions can be avoided or induced.

### III. An unreconstructed Keynesian model

The fundamental instability of capitalism is upward. After functioning well for a time a capitalist economy develops a tendency to explode, to become "euphoric." This is so because an initial condition is a world with uncertainty, and in such a world success feeds back upon expectations and preference systems so as to increase 1) the desired stock of capital, 2) the desired debt-equity ratios for owners of real capital, 3) the willingness to substitute earning assets for money, and 4) the rate of investment. That is, instead of starting from ". . . an Elysian state of moving equilibrium. . ." [Friedman and Schwartz, 9, p. 59], we start from an economy that is now doing well, better than in the past.

In a world with uncertainty, a distinction between inside and outside assets is meaningful. Inside units are those whose behavior is determined by the performance of the economy—households, business firms, and financial intermediaries. Outside units are those whose behavior is independent of the performance of the economy (except to the extent that a theory of economic policy guides their behavior)—governments, central banks, etc. The nominal (dollar) cash flow that an outside asset will generate is independent of the performance of the economy and no inside unit is committed to make payments because this asset is its liability. The nominal cash flow that an inside asset will generate depends upon the performance of the economy and for financial assets some inside unit is committed to make payments because this asset is its liability. Government debt, gold, and fiat money are all examples of outside assets; real capital, corporate bonds, and installment debt are all examples of inside assets. In addition there are mixed assets: an F.H.A. insured mortgage is an inside asset except that once the insurance becomes effective the asset becomes an outside asset to its owner; similarly, to a depositor fully covered by deposit insurance, deposits are outside assets although the bank may own inside assets [Tobin, 23; Gurley and Shaw, 11; Minsky, 17].

The price of a representative unit of the fixed stock of real and financial inside assets is determined, for a given uncertain stream of cash receipts, by the relative weight of outside and inside assets

in the economy. That is, the mixture of uncertainty-free and un-
certainty-bearing assets determines the price of the uncertainty-
bearing assets, given that the price of government or gold dollars is
fixed at $1. Abstracting from the financial layering process, the
fundamental inside asset is the capital stock and the fundamental
outside asset is the government debt money supply. Thus the price
per unit of a fixed capital stock is a rising function of the amount
of outside money, other things constant: the money supply determines the price level of the stock of capital goods[11] [Turvey,
24; Tobin, 23; Brainard and Tobin, 2].

The other things constant include the amount of fixed assets.
An increase in financial intermediation and of government endorsements will tend to raise the price per unit of capital as a function
of the outside money supply.[12] Preferences and expectations will
also position the price of capital function and as these can be sensitive to the performance of the economy, these subjective elements can induce sizable shifts in the function. That is, the price
of capital-money supply function, which is the analogue to the
liquidity preference function, is under particular circumstances unstable. An upward and perhaps accelerating migration of the function will take place after a period of sustained prosperity without
deep depressions. A sharp downward shift will take place after a
financial crisis. The crisis is not an exogenous or accidental event.
The way in which investment and positions in the stock of assets
are financed during the upward migration of the price of capital
function sets the stage for the crisis.

## IV. The effectiveness of monetary policy in the recent past

Before the aptness or effectiveness of monetary policy can be
judged, it is necessary to determine the constraints upon the monetary authorities. The United States "Central Bank" is a peculiarly
decentralized institution. Specialized organizations such as the
Federal Deposit Insurance Corporation and the Home Loan Bank
Board as well as the Federal Housing Authority are, along with the
Federal Reserve System, part of this "Central Bank." The Federal
Reserve may be the leading member of this syndicate, but it is
constrained by the need to make sure that the specialized institutions can carry out their mandates.

The need to maintain "institutional integrity" is a constraint
upon the Central Bank. That is, whereas the Federal Reserve is
willing to see particular, isolated, moderately sized banks and nonbank financial institutions fail, it cannot stand by without trying
to prevent the failure of entire classes of institutions. This is so be-

cause the authorities believe, rightly or wrongly, that disrupting institutions will have dire consequences for the economy and because it is the will of Congress that particular sets of institutions survive and prosper. Thus the need to prevent any escalation of the obvious difficulties of savings banks and the closely related housing industry into a general collapse of the system and industry was, and remains, an effective constraint upon monetary policy.

With present usages Mutual Savings Banks and Savings and Loan Associations are poorly equipped to cope with rapidly rising interest rates. These institutions hold long-term fully amortized mortgages which carry interest rates that were current at their date of issue. These savings intermediaries finance their position by emitting short-term or call liabilities. That is, their liabilities must meet the market on a well-nigh day-to-day basis while their assets lag, often by many years, behind current market terms.

There are two roads to ruin (negative net worth) for these savings institutions. One via a revaluation of assets, the second via the accumulation of operating losses.

By convention, mortgages not in arrears are carried on the books of savings institutions at face value. As a result, no mortgage intermediary will be declared insolvent by the authorities as a result of falling market prices of its mortgages. On the other hand, if an institution needs to make position by selling such assets at the market such "paper" losses are realized; the net worth of the organization must be adjusted to reflect this loss. Thus central bankers must prevent any large scale encashment of depreciated mortgages or they must provide some way for mortgage holders to obtain the face value of these depreciated assets if encashment is forced.

In addition, even though the fiction of face value is maintained, the cash flow these mortgages generate reflect the lower, past interest rates. On the other hand, the cost of money for deposit institutions is determined by current interest rates. A rise in deposit interest rates can transform a hitherto profitable institution into one suffering losses. Given the thin equity position of savings institutions, they cannot endure losses on the carry for very long. However, as the assets are long-lived, the turning over of the portfolio so that it yields returns consistent with the higher cost of money takes time. As a result, with any given initial set of assets there exists a maximum to the cost of money which can be established and sustained, for each assumed course of total deposits and initial net worth, that will permit the survival of the institution. Thus the authorities must try to constrain deposit rates to levels consistent with the existing portfolios.

Thus there are two ways to bankruptcy: a quick execution, by revaluing assets at market or realizing losses in an effort to make position, and a slow bleeding to death, as losses accumulate on income account. The authorities need to prevent both paths from operating in periods when interest rates have risen. In 1966 at the time of the crunch the authorities obtained and used the power to discriminate by size of deposit in setting ceiling rates on time deposits. This successfully aborted a switch of savings deposits from savings to commercial banks, which would have forced a large scale encashment of mortgages. In addition this discrimination has succeeded in lowering the effective cost of money to savings banks below what it would have been, thus decreasing the losses on income account.

Since the crunch of 1966, a constant threat of disintermediation has existed due to the large gap that has developed between long-term market rates and deposit rates. The unanswered question is how large a gap is consistent with the maintenance of deposits in savings institutions. That the retailing of corporate bonds does not seem to have increased significantly is an important indication of the value of deposit insurance and the strength of memories of the 1930s. Nevertheless, with the threat of disintermediation ever present, it is not surprising that the Federal Reserve is seeking ways of making discount facilities available to mortgage holders, thus providing means for "encashment" at face or close to face value.[13]

It is easy for an academician to characterize these constraints upon the exercise of monetary powers as being based upon groundless fears. But the preference function of the authorities must contain some trade-off between the rate of increase of the price level and the subjectively determined likelihood of a run (disintermediation) on the savings institutions. An attempt to moderate the rise in interest rates by increasing the rate at which the reserve base increases is an appropriate use of monetary policy, even at the considerable risk of added price pressures.

REFERENCES

[1] Board of Governors of the Federal Reserve System. *Reappraisal of the Federal Reserve Discount Mechanism: Report of a System Committee.* July 1968.

[2] William C. Brainard and James Tobin. "Pitfalls in Financial Model Building." *American Economic Review*, May 1968.

[3] Karl Brunner. "The Role of Money and Monetary Policy." *Federal Reserve Bank of St. Louis, Review*, July 1968.

[4] P. Cagan. "A Commentary on Some Current Issues in the Theory of Monetary Policy." In Brennan, M. J. (ed.) *Patterns of Market Behavior; Essays in Honor of Philip Taft.* Providence, 1965.

[5] R. Clower. "The Keynesian Counterrevolution: A Theoretical Appraisal." In Hahn, F. H. and Brechling, F. P. R. (eds.) *The Theory of Interest Rates.* New York, 1965.

[6] J. Duesenberry. "The Portfolio Approach to the Demand for Money and Other Assets." *The Review of Economics and Statistics,* February 1963.

[7] I. Fisher. "The Debt Deflation Theory of Business Cycles." *Econometrica,* October 1933.

[8] M. Friedman. "The Monetary Theory and Policy of Henry Simons." *The Journal of Law and Economics,* October 1967.

[9] M. Friedman and A. Schwarz. "Money and Business Cycles." *Review of Economics and Statistics,* Supplement, February 1963.

[10] _____. *The Great Contraction.* Princeton, 1965.

[11] J. Gurley and E. Shaw. *Money in a Theory of Finance.* Washington, 1960.

[12] J. R. Hicks. "Mr. Keynes and the 'Classics': A Suggested Interpretation." *Econometrica,* April 1937.

[13] J. J. Kaufman and C. M. Lotta. "The Demand for Money: Preliminary Evidence from Industrial Countries." *Journal of Financial and Quantitative Analysis,* September 1966.

[14] J. M. Keynes. "The General Theory of Employment." *Quarterly Journal of Economics.* February 1937.

[15] _____. *The General Theory of Employment, Interest and Money.* New York, 1936.

[16] Axel Leijonhufvud. "Keynes and the Keynesians: A Suggested Interpretation." *American Economic Review,* May 1966.

[17] H. P. Minsky. "Financial Intermediation in the Money and Capital Market." In Guilio Pontecervo, Robert P. Shay, and Albert G. Hart, *Issues in Banking and Monetary Analysis.* New York, 1967.

[18] _____. "Financial Crisis, Financial Systems and the Performance of the Economy." In Commission on Money and Credit *Private Capital Markets.* Englewood Cliffs, N.J., 1964.

[19] _____. "The Crunch and Its Aftermath." *Bankers' Magazine,* February, March 1968.

[20] R. V. Roosa. *Federal Reserve Operational in the Money and Government Securities Market.* Federal Reserve Bank of New York, 1956.

[21] G. L. S. Shackle. "Recent Theories Concerning the Nature and Role of Interest." In American Economic Association, Royal Economic Society, Surveys of Economic Theory, *Vol. 1.*

[22] H. C. Simons. "Rules versus Authorities in Monetary Policy." *Journal of Political Economy,* 1936; reprinted in Simons, H. C., *Economic Policy for a Free Society.* Chicago, 1948.

[23] James Tobin. "An Essay on Principles of Debt-Management." In Commission on Money and Credit, *Fiscal and Debt Management Policies.* Englewood Cliffs, N. J., 1963.

[24] R. Turvey. *Interest Rates and Asset Prices.* London, 1960.

[25] _____. "Does the Rate of Interest Rule the Roost?" In Hahn, F. H. and Brechling, F. P. R. (eds.), *The Theory of Interest Rates*. New York, 1965.

[26] J. Viner. "Mr. Keynes on the Causes of Unemployment." *Quarterly Journal of Economics*, November 1936.

[27] J. G. Witte, Jr. "The Micro Foundation of the Social Investment Function." *Journal of Political Economy*, October 1963.

## Notes

1. For an example of the current "controversy" literature see Brunner [3]. A fairly complete bibliography can be derived from Brunner's citations.

2. Friedman in his Henry Simons lecture [8] recognizes that Simons proposed thoroughgoing reform of the financial system whereas his own view is that all that was really wrong is the way in which the central bank exercises its control of the money supply. Simons, being a skeptic, even questioned the adequacy of thoroughgoing reform: "Banking is a pervasive phenomenon, not something to be dealt with merely by legislation directed at what we call banks. The experience with the control of note issue is likely to be repeated in the future; many expedients for controlling similar practices may prove ineffective and disappointing because of the reappearance of prohibited practices in new and unprohibited forms" [22, p. 172 in *Economic Policy in a Free Society*]. Note that Simons had a financial system rather than a narrow monetary view of the "Banking" problem.

3. There is a minimum set of financial characteristics which an economy must possess for it to be capitalist. I don't believe this question has ever been properly faced. The obvious characteristics of private ownership of the means of production and decentralized decisions implies, in a complex society, that financial instruments exist which permit both indirect and layered ownership. In addition, the existence of a wide array of permissible liability structures and a large menu of financial assets is necessary; as well as institutions which facilitate the changing of portfolios and the adjustment of liability structures [Keynes, 15, Chapter XII]. Thus markets in financial assets must exist and these markets for, so to speak, the financing of positions in secondhand assets must also be available for financing the creation of new tangible—and intangible—assets.

In addition, as a corollary to the encouragement of innovation in production, innovation in financial usages must be permissible [Minsky, 17].

4. The concept of "making position" is central to an understanding of how banks and other money market institutions operate in a sophisticated financial system. The "position" is a set of assets (loans and investments for banks, government debt for bond dealers, etc.) title to which needs financing. The need to finance position may take the form of a need to acquire reserve money—either to pay for an acquisition or to meet a clearing drain, etc. The acquisition of a deposit via a certificate of deposit, the borrowing of reserves via the Federal Funds market, the sale of Treasury bills are ways in which positions can be made.

Position-making thus takes the form of liability management or transactions in money market assets. During the post-war period substantial changes in the instruments and markets used by money market banks in position making have occurred.

Failure to make position can lead to a forced sale of other assets and thus substantial losses.

5. Awareness of the possibility of a financial crisis and a recognition of the Board of Governors' responsibility in that eventuality is evident in the recent Board of Governors' review of the operations of the discount apparatus [1].

6. Shackle [21] emphasizes the importance of Keynes' rebuttal to Viner, referring to it as the 4th of Keynes' great contributions. This restatement by Keynes of his views has been ignored by the dominant contemporary "Keynesian" economists.

7. "This standard model [that derived from Hicks' "Mr. Keynes and the Classics"] appears to me a singularly inadequate vehicle for the interpretation of Keynes' ideas" [Leijonhufvud, 16, p. 401].

Clower refers to ". . . The Keynesian Counterrevolution launched by Hicks in 1937 and now being carried forward with such vigor by Patinkin and other general equilibrium theorists" [5, p. 103]. Most "Keynesian" economists are devoted agents of the counterrevolution.

8. "The evidence presented indicates that income is an important component of the demand for money in all leading industrial countries. In addition income elasticities were found to be inversely related to the state of development of the money markets in the respective countries, being highest in Italy and Japan——countries with the least developed markets, and lowest in the United Kingdom and the United States——the countries with the most advanced financial centers. Thus slower accretions to money may be expected in response to a given percentage increase in income in countries with advanced money markets and ready availability of a large variety of high quality, interest yielding money substitutes than in less financially developed countries" [Kaufman and Lotta, 13, p. 83].

9. The economic significance of uncertainty was nowhere better summarized than by Keynes in [14].

10. Keynes [15, Chapter XII] discusses this asymmetry——that crises may come suddenly but that a rebuilding of confidence may be time-consuming: "A collapse in the price of equities——may have been due to the weakening either of speculative confidence or the state of credit. But whereas the weakening of either is enough to cause a collapse, recovery requires the revival of both" (p. 158).

11. I am avoiding the terms "interest rates," or "interest rate" in this section. If the price of an asset, financial or real, is known, and the stream of cash it will yield is known, then an interest rate can be computed; the interest rate is an arithmetic result useful in comparing different time series of cash receipts. Certainly for financial contracts, new and outstanding, the important variable is the payment commitments and rights under varying circumstances; for a collection of real assets in a plant or firm, the corresponding cash flow is gross profit after taxes corrected for debt servicing. (I have tried to deal with this phenomena in [18].) Turvey [25], argues that the interest rate is not really needed in the analysis of investment.

12. Differential government endorsements may also affect relative prices ——thus government endorsements available for the financing of new housing may have affected the relative prices of new and old houses.

13. ". . . In addition, the redesigned window recognizes, and provides for, the necessity that——in its role as lender of last resort to other sectors of the economy——the Federal Reserve stands ready, under extreme conditions, to provide circumscribed credit assistance to a broader spectrum of financial institutions than member banks" [1, p. 2].

# Index